What They <u>Didn't</u> Teach You About the 60s

Other Books by Mike Wright

What They <u>Didn't</u> Teach You About the Civil War

What They <u>Didn't</u> Teach You About World War II

What They <u>Didn't</u> Teach You About the American Revolution

What They <u>Didn't</u> Teach You About the Wild West

What They <u>Didn't</u> Teach You About the 60s

Mike Wright

PRESIDIO

Published by Presidio Press, Inc.
505 B San Marin Drive, Suite 160
Novato, CA 94945-1340

Library of Congress Cataloging-in-Publication Data

Wright, Mike, 1938–
    What they didn't teach you about the sixties / by Mike Wright.
    p. cm.
    Includes bibliographical references and index.
    ISBN 0-89141-724-9
    1. United States—History—1961–1969. 2. United States—
Social conditions—1960–1980.
    I. Title.
    E841 .W75 2001
    973.923—dc21

                                2001036749

Printed in the United States of America

This is dedicated to the one I love.
To Lin

This is my generation.

—Peter Townsend, 1965

I'm not nostalgic about the sixties. I never left them.

—"Little Stevie" Van Zandt, guitarist, E Street Band

Contents

Acknowledgments

It would probably take a note the size of this book itself to thank those individuals and institutions who have assisted and encouraged this project. I will, however, keep the list down to the barest minimum: The staff of the John F. Kennedy Library in Boston, especially the photographic staff. Susan Bates Cook for sharing her time and memories with me. McArthur Davis of the International Civil Rights Center and Museum in Greensboro, North Carolina. The staff of the Kennedy Space Center in Florida and faculty and staff members at Kent State University. The Boeing Company and Dan Kays. Willie Turner and the staff of the Hiller Air Museum in Seattle, Washington. AP and UPI photo libraries. The National Archives still picture staff and the photographic staff at the Library of Congress. To the small staff of one of my favorite small bookstores for pointing out items that have aided me in this as well as other books in this series.

To members of the classes of 1955 and 1956 at Woodrow Wilson High School in Portsmouth, Virginia, who shared their memories of life in our prime time. To Jim Tilmon. To the staff of the Chicago Historical Society. The staves of public and private libraries I visited and telephoned; if they didn't have the answer to my questions, they told me where I might find it. To everyone at Presidio Press for encouraging me and letting me continue this series and for sometimes letting me not talk about books but about the Chicago Cubs (who constantly break my heart) and the San Francisco Giants (who occasionally break theirs). To my Alaskan Malamute, The Denali Doll of Marchris, known informally throughout the neighborhood as Dolly, who usually forgives me when I get bogged down and neglect her afternoon walks. And especially to my wife Lin—over and over and over again. You listen, you read, you help me.

To all of you and many more: Thank you.

Chronology

1960

February 1: When a waitress at a "Whites Only" lunch counter at Woolworth's in Greensboro, North Carolina, refuses to serve African Americans, four students begin a sit-in. The movement quickly spreads to other states.

May 1: USSR shoots down U.S. U-2 spy plane, captures pilot Francis Gary Powers.

May 9: FDA approves the use of Enovid, the first birth-control pill.

July 13: Democrats nominate John Fitzgerald Kennedy for president, Lyndon Baines Johnson for vice president.

July 28: Republicans nominate Vice President Richard M. Nixon for president, Henry Cabot Lodge for vice president.

September 24: The children's TV show, *Howdy Doody* ends its thirteen-year run.

September 26: First televised debate between Kennedy and Nixon.

November 8: Kennedy-Johnson ticket edges out Nixon-Lodge in election.

December 20: Ho Chi Minh organizes South Vietnamese communists into the National Liberation Front (NLF).

1961

January 3: U.S breaks off diplomatic relations with Cuba.

January 20: JFK inaugurated president.

April 12: Soviet cosmonaut Yuri Gagarin becomes first man to orbit earth.

April 15: CIA-trained anti-Castro Cubans invade Bay of Pigs.

May 4: Freedom Riders test desegregation in South.

May 5: Astronaut Alan Shepard becomes first American to fly in suborbital flight.

May 14: White mobs in Alabama attack Freedom Riders.

August 13: East Germany begins Berlin Wall, closing the East-West border at Berlin.

December 11: JFK sends 400 American military personnel to South Vietnam.

1962

February 1: Ken Kesey's *One Flew Over the Cuckoo's Nest* published.

February 20: Astronaut John Glenn becomes first American to orbit the earth.

June 11: Students for a Democratic Society (SDS) hold first national convention.

July 10: Telstar satellite broadcasts first live intercontinental television transmission.

September 20: James Meredith tries to enroll at Old Miss.

September 26: TV sitcom *The Beverly Hillbillies* debuts.

October 22: Cuban missile crisis.

December 31: More than 11,000 U.S. military personnel are now in South Vietnam.

1963

February 19: Betty Friedan's *Feminine Mystique* published.

April 2: Dr. Martin Luther King Jr. leads Birmingham, Alabama, campaign against segregation; Sheriff Bull Connor sets police dogs on demonstrators.

April 10: Atomic submarine *Thresher* sinks; 129 crew members die.

May 18: U.S. Supreme Court rules that state courts must supply free counsel to all indigents facing serious criminal charges.

June 11: Buddhist monk immolates himself in South Vietnam.

June 12: Civil rights worker Medgar Evers murdered in Jackson, Mississippi.

June 26: Almost a quarter of Berlin's population turns out to greet JFK.

August 10: Pope John XXIII dies in Vatican City at age eighty-one.

Chronology

August 28: Martin Luther King delivers "I have a dream" speech.
August 28: "Hot line" opens between U.S. and USSR.
September 15: Bomb kills four African American girls in a Birmingham church.
November 2: President Nhgo Dinh Diem of South Vietnam murdered in coup.
November 22: JFK murdered in Dallas; Lyndon Johnson assumes office.
November 24: Lee Harvey Oswald murdered in Dallas.

1964

January 8: LBJ declares "unconditional war on poverty in America."
February 9: The Beatles make U.S. television debut.
February 17: U.S. Supreme Court issues "one man, one vote" ruling.
April 5: General of the Army Douglas MacArthur dies.
June 21: Three Mississippi civil rights workers disappear; their bodies are discovered forty-four days later.
July 2: LBJ signs Civil Rights Act of 1964.
July 15: Republicans nominate U.S. senator Barry Goldwater for president.
August 4: LBJ announces air strikes against North Vietnamese Gulf of Tonkin gunboat bases.
September 24: Warren Commission says Lee Harvey Oswald was sole killer of JFK.
November 3: LBJ elected president in landslide.
December 10: MLK awarded Nobel Peace Prize.

1965

January 24: Winston Churchill dies.
February 7: LBJ orders bombing raids on North Vietnam.
February 21: Malcolm X assassinated.
March 7: Two hundred police attack civil rights marchers outside Selma, Alabama.

March 8: First American combat troops land in South Vietnam.

June 30: LBJ launches Head Start Program.

July 30: LBJ signs Medicare law.

August 11: Thirty-four people die during rioting in Watts section of Los Angeles.

October 15: Upwards of 100,000 demonstrators nationwide protest American involvement in Vietnam War.

November 9: Massive power failure blacks out seven American states and two Canadian provinces.

December 20: American field commanders in Vietnam allowed to pursue enemy troops into Cambodia.

1966

January 24: LBJ submits nation's first $100 billion budget.

March 24: U.S. Selective Service says college deferments will be based on scholastic performance.

May 16: SNCC elects Stokely Carmichael as chairman, shifting emphasis from civil rights to black power.

October 15: Black Panther Party formed.

1967

January 2: Fred Rogers begins his television series *Mister Rogers' Neighborhood.*

January 14: Some 25,000 hippies jam San Francisco's Golden Gate Park for "Be-In."

January 16: In Tuskegee, Alabama, Lucius Amerson is sworn in as the first black Southern sheriff of the 20th century.

January 27: Fire in the Apollo I spacecraft kills three astronauts.

May 1: Elvis Presley marries Priscilla Beaulieu.

July 23: Rioting breaks out in Detroit.

October 21: More than 100,000 anti–Vietnam War protestors rally at Washington's Lincoln Memorial, then march to the Pentagon where they're met by a cordon of military police.

December 20: The last movie theater newsreel, *Universal Newsreel,* released.

Chronology

1968

January 1–June 15: National Student Association estimates that 221 major demonstrations at 101 colleges involve some 39,000 students.

January 23: USS *Pueblo* seized by North Korean gunboat crews.

January 31: North Vietnamese and Viet Cong troops use the Tet truce to launch a massive offensive in South Vietnam.

February 8: South Carolina state police kill three students when blacks try to desegregate South Carolina State College in Orangeburg.

March 12: Peace candidate Eugene McCarthy wins 41.4 percent of the vote in the New Hampshire Democratic presidential primary; President Johnson wins 49.6 percent.

March 16: U.S. troops massacre villagers in My Lai, Vietnam.

March 31: LBJ announces halt of U.S. air and naval bombardment of North Vietnam, then says he will not seek another term in office.

April 4: MLK assassinated in Memphis, Tennessee.

May 17: Antiwar protestors break into the draft board office in Catonsville, Maryland.

June 5: Robert Kennedy assassinated.

June 18: The U.S. Supreme Court bans racial discrimination in the sale and rental of public and private property.

July 29: Pope Paul VI upholds the Catholic Church's prohibition against artificial contraception.

August 8: Republicans nominate Richard M. Nixon for president.

August 28: Democrats in Chicago nominate Hubert Humphrey for president while thousands demonstrate outside in "police riot."

November 6: Richard Nixon elected president.

1969

March 10: James Earl Ray pleads guilty to the murder of Dr. Martin Luther King Jr.

March 28: Former President Dwight David Eisenhower dies of heart failure.

July 20: U.S. astronauts land on Moon.

August 15: Woodstock Music and Art Fair begins in pasture outside Bethel, N.Y.

September 3: In North Vietnam, Ho Chi Minh dies at age seventy-nine.

November 15: Some 250,000 anti–Vietnam War demonstrators rally in Washington.

December 1: Selective Service uses lottery to determine draft eligibility.

December 4: Chicago police kill Black Panther Party leader Fred Hampton.

1970

May 4: Ohio National Guardsmen kill four Kent State University students protesting President Nixon's announced plan to launch a major offensive into Cambodia.

A Sixties Prelude:
The Fifties

Just as I thought. No one is in charge.
>Senator Eugene McCarthy, seeing police and
>antiwar dissidents battle in Chicago, 1968

People that are really very weird can get into sensitive positions and have a tremendous impact on history.
>Vice President J. Danforth "Dan" Quayle

The thing about the swinging sixties is that they came after the sedate fifties—"feel-good innocence," was how some critics referred to the decade's lack of public emotion. PDA wasn't our thing in any sense, no Public Display of Affection. In other words, no kissing or fondling in public. We could barely hold hands in public, which of course was not the case in movie theater balconies or while watching submarine races in the backseats of cars.

The sixties were a decade of profound social change, but in the fifties we tried to coast along. We'd just survived the largest, most deadly war in the world's history, and now we wanted to sit back and relax, if only the rest of the world would let us get back to *I Love Lucy* and *Father Knows Best.* After two years of Harry Truman, perhaps our feistiest president, we elected Dwight Eisenhower, one of our most laid-back White House residents, although we didn't use the phrase *laid-back* until the sixties.

When we write about "what happened in the 1960s," we set arbitrary parameters that exist only on the calendar. After all, God invented time; man only came up with a way to record it. Obviously, some "sixties" events began earlier and concluded later.

Take the Vietnam War. Our part in that conflict began in the forties. On the same day that representatives of Japan surrendered to

Allied forces in a ceremony aboard the battleship *Missouri*, in a celebration in Hanoi's Ba Dinh Square, Ho Chi Minh proclaimed Vietnam's independence from French colonial rule. He also announced the founding of the Democratic Republic of Vietnam (DRV), which despite the name was neither democratic nor republican but was Communist backed and controlled from the start.

Ho opened the ceremonies with words that most Americans would recognize: "We hold these truths to be self-evident, that all men are created equal"—Thomas Jefferson's Declaration of Independence from another revolution one hundred sixty-nine years earlier and thousands of miles away. A group of U.S. Army officers shared the reviewing stand with Ho and former history professor turned army general Vo Nguyen Giap. The Vietnamese band played "The Star-Spangled Banner" and a formation of American planes flew overhead. Giap even spoke of the "particularly intimate relations" between Vietnam and the United States, something, he noted, "which it is a pleasant duty to dwell upon."

It may have been the beginning of a new government, but it was also the start of the Indochina War. Nine years later, in May 1954, nine national delegations, including the United States, met in the old League of Nations building in Geneva, Switzerland, to talk about ending that war. The Vietnamese delegation wanted France, which had held Vietnam as a colony since 1847, to leave immediately. French Premier Joseph Daniel rejected the demand, and the conference quickly neared an impasse. They finally reached an agreement that temporarily split Vietnam into two sections separated by a three-mile demilitarized zone at the seventeenth parallel. A plebiscite would be scheduled in 1956 to determine which group— Ho's Communists or French- and American-backed Emperor Bao Dai—would rule the combined nation. For the next two years, people from either side could, if they chose, move to the other. The plebiscite never happened. In fact, American president Dwight Eisenhower was one who opposed it, believing the Ho Chi Minh's faction would easily win and take over both North and South.

In the meantime, the Indochina War raged on until November 1953 when the French found themselves wedged into the small, hard-to-resupply town of Dien Bien Phu.

It looked as if the French might lose the battle (and the war), and U.S. secretary of state John Foster Dulles assembled a group of eight congressional leaders in Washington, D.C.

Dulles wanted America to jump into the war in Indochina. "The president," Dulles said, "has asked me to call this meeting," thereby putting the blame on Ike, who likely was out at Washington's Burning Tree Country Club playing eighteen holes of golf.

The French situation had become critical, Dulles claimed, adding that Eisenhower wanted a joint congressional resolution allowing him to use air and naval forces to save America's World War II ally. Admiral Arthur Radford, chairman of the Joint Chiefs of Staff, stepped forward and pointed to a map on the wall: Dien Bien Phu was under siege and might fall at any moment. If America didn't act fast, the West would be pushed out of Asia. He proposed "Operation Vulture," a neat but massive U.S. air attack against the Vietminh. Maybe even use nuclear weapons.* His plan had carrier-based planes assisted by land-based craft from the Philippines. Dien Bien Phu could be rescued, the admiral claimed.

Did that mean war? the congressmen asked. Well, yes, Radford admitted, using dozens of planes, with thousands of tons of bombs— let's not mention The Bomb—meant we'd be at war with the Vietminh. Well, someone asked, what if "Operation Vulture" didn't work? In that case, America would have to find some other way to save Dien Bien Phu. You mean ground troops?

Admiral Radford couldn't answer that one.

With that, a congressmen asked him, Does this plan have the approval of the Joint Chiefs of Staff?

No.

Okay. How many of the chiefs agree with you?

None. Actually, the Joint Chiefs believed that Vietnam was "devoid of decisive military objectives." But Radford believed that he'd spent

---

* It was John Foster Dulles, who pushed for nuclear strikes on the Vietminh during the battle of Dien Bien Phu. According to French foreign minister Georges Bidault, when Dulles presented the idea to Ike, the president told him, "You must be crazy. We can't use those awful things against Asians for the second time in less than ten years." Ten years later, U.S. senator Barry Goldwater proposed on nationwide television that "low-yield atomic weapons" be used in South Vietnam.

more time in the Far East than the others, so he understood the situation better than they did.

Among the congressmen present at this meeting was none other than Lyndon B. Johnson, senator from Texas. He asked Secretary Dulles if other nations—say, some of our World War II allies—supported the plan.

I haven't asked them.

The room exploded! The Joint Chiefs don't agree with you, and you haven't even *asked* for outside support? And you expect us to go along with your idea? LBJ made it clear, and the other seven congressional leaders loudly agreed: No allies, no war! Actually, members of the National Security Council had already voiced Johnson's objections. Dulles could, and often did, ignore the NSC, but he couldn't ignore LBJ; the senator from Texas was just too powerful and too vocal.

John Foster Dulles spent the next two weeks looking for allies to save Dien Bien Phu. He couldn't find any—not Britain, not the United Nations, not anybody. By then, Dulles was "exhausted and disheartened by his unsuccessful attempts to promote allied unity," Richard Nixon later wrote. Dulles went to Canada to relax, and Ike went to Augusta, Georgia, to play a round or two of golf.

On May 7, 1954, the French surrendered at Dien Bien Phu, which basically ended the Indochina War and began the Vietnam War.

In 1948, John F. Kennedy fell desperately ill while visiting his ancestral home in Ireland. In London, a doctor diagnosed his condition as Addison's disease, an insufficiency in adrenal production. It leaves its victims fatally vulnerable to infection. Dr. Daniel Davis, who was also newspaper owner Lord Beaverbrook's physician, told Winston's daughter Pamela Churchill, "That young American friend of yours, he hasn't got a year to live." He was so ill that when he arrived home aboard the liner *Queen Elizabeth* a priest gave him the last rites of the church.

John F. Kennedy was dying of Addison's disease: "The doctors say I've got a sort of slow-motion leukemia, but they tell me I'll probably last until I'm forty-five." Which, if true, meant that he would die around 1965, unless something more drastic should befall him before then. During Kennedy's race for the White House in 1960, someone raised the question of his health. The Democratic Party and Kennedy's family and aides all denied that he was ill. He had a bad back left over from World War II, but Addison's disease? No way.

In 1951, as a thirty-four-year-old bushy-haired U.S. congressman from Boston's Eleventh District, Kennedy went on a Far East tour and visited Vietnam. When he arrived in Saigon he was greeted by what seemed to him to be "half the French army." Considering how much money the United States was supplying the French military effort worldwide, the Paris government thought turning out the troops to greet Congressman John F. Kennedy was the proper thing to do.

With the congressman were his brother and sister, Robert and Patricia. "Papa Joe" Kennedy had ordered Pat and Bobby to go along to make certain Jack took his medicine,* which he was inclined to forget.

The Kennedy group visited combat zones where French Foreign Legionnaires were fighting Ho Chi Minh's troops. Jack said that he admired the courage of the French fighting men but believed the French and American policies in Vietnam were disastrous. "We have allied ourselves to the desperate effort of a French regime to hang on to the remnants of an empire," he wrote in a report on his trip. "There is no broad, general support of the native Vietnam government [by] the people of that area.

Bobby Kennedy agreed, writing in his private journal that America was "pouring money & arms down a bottomless hole" in Vietnam. "We have only the status quo to offer these people," he added, but the "Commies can offer a change."

During the fifties, the Central Intelligence Agency (CIA) went looking for a mind-controlling drug, hoping to drop it into an en-

---

* Daily injections of dexacortizone. Later, JFK took twenty-five milligrams of cortisone orally along with shots of pain-killing novocaine directly into his back.

emy's water supply in order to disable towns.* So the CIA, meaning the federal government and all of us, "funded and supported and encouraged hundreds of young psychiatrists to experiment with this drug," which happened to be lysergic acid diethylamide, or LSD.** One of those eager psychologists was Dr. Timothy Leary. "The fall-out," he said, "was that young psychologists began taking it themselves, discovering it was an intelligence-enhancing consciousness-raising experience." Again, Tim Leary was an eager participant. "I give the CIA total credit," the guru of LSD said, "for sponsoring and initiating the entire consciousness movement counterculture events of the 1960s."

Fidel Castro was the son of an immigrant laborer who owned a twenty-three-thousand-acre sugar plantation in Oriente province. Obviously, Fidel wasn't your average poor and landless peasant.

In 1952, as Fidel was running for a seat in parliament, General Fulgencio Batista overthrew President Carlos Prío Socarrás's government and canceled the election. Castro went to court and charged Batista with violating Cuba's constitution. The court rejected Fidel's petition, so Castro gathered together about 165 men for an armed attack on the Moncada Barracks in Oriente province. That attack, on July 26, 1953, failed miserably, with half the attackers killed and Fidel and his brother Raúl taken prisoner and put on trial. In a speech during his trial, Fidel condemned Cuban dictator Batista and cried out: "*La historia me absolverá*," history will absolve me.

Castro got out of prison in 1955, and went on a fund-raising tour in Mexico and the United States, hoping to raise money to continue his rebellion against Batista. It was in Mexico that he met Argentine

---

* During the 1968 demonstrations at the Democratic National Convention in Chicago, rumors spread that Yippie's planned to dope the city's water supply with LSD. The governor called out the National Guard, but nothing was done to the water.

** In 1966, the Sandoz Pharmaceutical Company of Switzerland, the sole distributor of LSD for medical research, recalled the product and discontinued its production. However, a company spokesman claimed that "I should not be surprised if at any one of a number of [college] campuses there is more LSD than we have ever made."

revolutionary Ernesto "Che" Guevara. Together, they organized a group of Cuban exiles into another fighting force they called the "26th of July Revolutionary Movement," in honor of Fidel's failed attack back in 1953.

American mobster Meyer Lansky controlled the Havana casinos, and every Monday at noon, one of his underlings slipped into the presidential palace with a sackful of money. Batista's personal "cut" of the Mafia gambling operations amounted to more than $1.28 million a month. From this, Batista dribbled down money to his top officers and the secret police.

Meanwhile, the officers themselves were raking in money of their own from gambling houses outside Havana, and they had to kick some of the money back to Batista. A regimental commander, for instance, had to pay Batista fifteen thousand dollars a month. This alone amounted to an additional one million dollars a year for Fulgencio Batista.

By 1957, Fidel Castro was raising hell in the Sierra Maestra, and Batista was raising money all over the island. In November 1958, Fidel moved his men down from the mountains. He realized that Batista's regime was nearing collapse, but he wasn't sure what America might do—send in troops to aid Batista, or join Castro in ousting the dictator. In the end, America did nothing of consequence.

On January 1, 1959, realizing his days in the Cuban sun were over, Fulgencio Batista and a small group of his closest aides drove to Camp Columbia outside Havana. They toasted each other in champagne, then Batista boarded a government plane and flew off into history. Fidel Castro had won. He was only thirty-one years old. Six days later the United States recognized Fidel Castro's government. A month later, Castro assumed the position of premier. His first order of business was to set up a nationwide system of education and housing and to begin handing out land to peasants, property previously held by some of Cuba's richest ranchers.

Castro's battle to control the island paradise came in the fifties, but conflict between his regime and America became major episodes of the sixties.

The 1960s would see major civil rights battles in America, but they, too, began much earlier. In 1954, the U.S. Supreme Court issued its landmark *Brown v. Topeka, Kansas, Board of Education** decision, overturning earlier the *Plessy v. Ferguson* doctrine, which had allowed so-called "separate but equal" schools. Most Southern school systems didn't even come close to "equal" facilities and education for blacks. On average, for every four dollars spent on white students only one dollar was spent on Negro students.

The justices set no date for compliance but instructed the seventeen states (plus the District of Columbia) that had compulsory segregation laws and four others that had permissive segregation statutes to comply "with all deliberate speed." Many Southerners refused to accept the decision. Southern governors at a November conference promised to use "every prerogative" to uphold state control of school policy. The White House wasn't much help. "I am convinced," President Dwight Eisenhower said,

> . . .that the Supreme Court decision set back progress in the South at least fifteen years. . . . It's all very well to talk about school integration—if you remember that you may also be talking about social disintegration. Feelings are deep on this, especially where children are involved.

On December 1, 1955, Montgomery, Alabama, police jailed a forty-two-year-old African American department-store tailor's assistant named Rosa Parks, because she refused to give up her bus seat to a white man. She'd sat in the rear area—the "colored" section—of the bus, near the dividing line between the white and black seats. While the first ten rows were always for whites, the last twenty-six seats in the Negro section could shrink.

With all of the white seats filled, a white man boarded the bus, and driver J. F. Blake ordered African Americans in the first row of the "colored" section to "let him have those . . . seats." Three did, but Rosa Parks refused. When she wouldn't give up her seat, Blake got off the bus, phoned police, and when officers arrived they arrested Parks.

---

* When Oliver Brown tried to register his daughter in a nearby all-white school, she was refused because she was black.

Her refusal and her arrest began a year-long boycott of Birmingham buses by local Negroes, led by a young, pretty much unknown, preacher named Martin Luther King Jr. The boycott continued until November 1956, when the U.S. Supreme Court struck down Alabama's law requiring segregated buses.

The Montgomery bus boycott was so successful—bus revenues dropped by sixty-five percent—that, in 1957, African Americans formed the Southern Christian Leadership Conference (SCLC) to continue a "direct action" assault on segregation. One of SCLC's founders was that same Martin Luther King.

Rosa Parks's refusal to give up her bus seat nudged the American Civil Rights movement from newspapers' back pages to a spot where it competed with Vietnam for our attention. It was a ten-year campaign to overturn Jim Crow laws, and it, too, would come in the sixties.

The fifties have been called the Golden Age of Television, and maybe they were. They certainly offered a variety of programs, many of which themselves were golden.

On September 3, 1950, Edie Adams was chosen as Miss Television USA. Her crowning was carried by the DuMont Television Network, America's first television network. It was DuMont, along with ABC, that in 1954 carried live the Army-McCarthy hearings—mainly because neither network had much in the way of daytime programming, and the hearings were cheap, which is to say except for manpower, broadcasting them didn't cost anything.

DuMont had begun on April 13, 1946, with a cable connection between New York City and Washington, D.C. By the following year, ABC, CBS, and NBC had joined in using AT & T's coaxial cable to form networks, mainly along the East Coast. For TV stations in cities outside AT & T's cable area, DuMont offered kinescopes, grainy pictures made by filming live television pictures. The original pictures themselves weren't the greatest, and with the kinescope camera simply aimed at a TV set, you can imagine the poor quality of the picture. In 1958, with only five stations left in its stable, the DuMont network folded. Its final telecast was of the *Monday Night Fights.*

The ninety-minute *Your Show of Shows* was one of the brightest of the Golden Age. It starred Sid Caesar and Imogene Coca, backed up by supporting players Carl Reiner and Howard Morris. It was wacky and sharply funny. Several writers who worked for the show went on to fame of their own: Mel Brooks *(The Producers)*, Larry Gelbart *(M*A*S*H)*, Neil Simon, and Woody Allen.

At the same time as *Your Show of Shows*, we had what may have been television's funniest game show ever, emceed by—no, he was the star, virtually the whole show—Groucho Marx. Look carefully enough (and late enough), and you can still catch reruns of *You Bet Your Life* complete with a toy duck (it looked strangely like Marx himself) that displayed "the Secret Word." Groucho, announcer George Fenneman (he also kept score), and the duck continued their run until 1961, when the secret word apparently was: *canceled.*

On Saturday nights we stayed home to watch *Your Hit Parade*, a list of the week's top-selling records, with the songs played, sung, and danced by the show's regulars.

As part of the anthology series *Climax*, CBS brought to television British author Ian Fleming's James Bond in "Casino Royale." Barry Nelson became the first actor to play the super spy, unless you count Fleming himself, who'd been a World War II agent.

Not spies, but space, was the subject of a couple of long-running TV shows in the fifties, aimed mainly at the younger set. *Space Patrol* ran on ABC for five years and was set in the thirtieth century. The second, *Tom Corbett, Space Cadet,* not only ran on all four networks during its five-year history, but at one point ran on two networks at the same time.

For fifteen months beginning in May 1950, we had *Broadway Open House*, the first regularly scheduled late-night program. On alternating nights it starred two veteran comedians, Jerry Lester and Morey Amsterdam. More a variety than a talk show, it featured singer Andy Roberts, accordionist/band leader Milton DeLugg,* and a buxom blonde named Jennie Lewis, or as she was known on the show, "Dagmar."

---

* Delugg's son later became the audio and sound-effects specialist on *Late Night With David Letterman.*

A Sixties Prelude

Broadway Open House was the brainchild of Sylvester "Pat" Weaver, who year after year in the fifties came up with some of television's best shows.* Four years after *Broadway Open House* closed, Weaver conceived another NBC late-night program: *The Tonight Show*, then called simply *Tonight!* Steve Allen was the original host, before Jack Paar, Johnny Carson, and Jay Leno.

Two years before *Tonight!* NBC launched network television's first early-morning program, *Today*. Its first host was Dave Garroway, who traditionally ended the show with his hand, palm forward, in front of him as he intoned, "Peace!" to the accompaniment of Lionel Hampton's version of "Sentimental Journey."

One of *Today*'s gimmicks right from the start was that it came from a studio on the ground floor of the RCA (then owners of NBC) Exhibition Hall on West Forty-ninth Street in New York City. It had large plate-class windows that let an outside audience watch the show and allowed the cameras periodically to pan the audience. Once, the show's producers talked President Harry Truman, who was in town and out for his usual morning walk, into being shown standing outside.

Another gimmick came in its second year, when *Today* introduced a chimpanzee named J. Fred Muggs. He was so famous and so well liked by the audience** that he made several personal appearance tours.

Kukla, Fran and Ollie were the hand-puppet children of creator Burr Tillstrom (who never referred to them as puppets) and of Fran Allison. Kukla means "doll" in Russian, and Ollie is short for Oliver J. Dragon; he had only one tooth, by the way. Tillstrom did most of the voices. They had several friends: Fletcher Rabbit, Buelah the Witch, Madame Ooglepuss, and Colonel Crackie. All ad-libbed without a script, it did have several semi-scripted shows, including a puppet version of *The Mikado*.

---

* His daughter, Sigourney Weaver, didn't do too badly herself out in Hollywood in the eighties and nineties.
** Not by the show's staff, however, because as J. Fred grew up he also grew cantankerous.

In the fall of 1955, actor Bob Keeshan, wearing a extra large fake mustache and a coat with huge pockets, began television's longest-running network children's series: *Captain Kangaroo*—those out-sized coat pockets in which he carried toys and things.

The Mickey Mouse Club began its four-year ABC network run the same day as the captain. While *Captain Kangaroo* had Mr. Green Jeans and Bunny Rabbit for companions, *The Mickey Mouse Club* had Annette and Tommy, Darlene and Cubby, Sharon, Bobby, Lonnie, Dennis, and Doreen—the Mouseketeers.

And what would a Tuesday night be without "Mr. Television"?—*The Milton Berle Show*. "Uncle Miltie" had a commercial-singing chorus of "Texaco Men" dressed as attendants at Texaco service stations: "You can trust your car to the man who wears the star. . . ." And if you have to ask what a gas station attendant was, then you weren't around in the fifties.

Before anyone asked whether we wanted to be a millionaire, we had Michael Anthony (actor Marvin Miller), who acted on behalf of his employer, John Beresford Tipton, to give away that amount, which was a lot more money than it is today.

One thing that may have made fifties TV golden was that a lot of it was done live. That gave spontaneity to the programs, and let performers, who for the most part had come over from live stage and vaudeville, do what they did best: entertain an audience. Only late in the decade did videotape come into widespread use, and when it did television changed from being a performance to being a product.

When the hot war known as World War II ended, the Cold War of the fifties and sixties began. It was "colder" sometimes than it was at others, but one of the "hottest" times came in 1948: the Berlin Blockade. The Soviets tried to strangle an already divided city, cutting off all road and rail access. But they forgot the air routes. The Allies countered with a massive airlift that provided much of the goods that the desperate West Berliners needed. Food, clothing, you name it, they flew it in. These supplies amounted to 2 million tons, which had a total cost of more than $200 million. The blockade continued for eleven months, a total 277,264 flights, and each day it seemed that World War III might start.

A Sixties Prelude

• • •

On April 10, 1951, nine months after the Korean War began, President Truman fired General MacArthur, because, Truman said, "he wouldn't respect the authority of the President." The war continued for another year and a half with both sides losing a lot of men but neither side gaining much territory. On January 20, 1953, Dwight Eisenhower took the oath of office as America's thirty-fourth president. The former general had campaigned under the promise to go to Korea if he were elected. He did, but it was the death of Josef Stalin on March 5, not Eisenhower's visit, that stopped the war.

In 1953, Julius and Ethel Rosenberg were electrocuted for their part in World War II spying, supplying Moscow with secrets that allowed the Russians to build an atomic bomb. Having the bomb had given the Soviets confidence to support the North Korean war effort.

In 1957, the Soviet Union launched the world's first man-made satellite. Sputnik—it means "companion" in Russian—was a 184-pound sphere that reached eighteen thousand miles per hour in an elliptical orbit above Earth.

So now they had a rocket powerful enough to reach America and nuclear weapons that could obliterate American cities. The Cold War heated up again.

After numerous failures, the United States finally succeeded in launching an ICBM of its own, the Atlas. With the race on, NASA, the National Aeronautics and Space Administration, began culling the country for candidates to take the American flag into space. They had to be under forty years old, under five feet eleven inches tall,* in excellent physical condition, hold a bachelor's degree or equivalent, be a qualified jet and test pilot, and have a minimum overall flying time of fifteen hundred hours. In April 1959, NASA named its first seven astronauts, the Mercury Seven. All bright and chipper young men. And white. No nonwhite or nonmale astronaut was in

---

* Soviet cosmonauts were even smaller: maximum height five feet seven inches and weight no more than 154 pounds.

the first group. The first black astronaut would be air force captain Edward J. Dwight Jr., in 1962. The previous year, President Kennedy had written to Captain Dwight, asking him to enroll as the first black in the astronaut program. "If I do this," he said to his white commanding officer, "I have a chance to go on the cover of *Ebony* magazine."

"What's *Ebony* magazine?" the commanding officer asked.

Captain Dwight enrolled as an astronaut, but following John Kennedy's death, he was abruptly transferred out of the program. *Ebony* put his picture on a cover, because Dwight apparently had been forced out by racism.

It wouldn't be until 1983 that an African American man was sent into space, Guion S. Bluford Jr. Two months before Bluford went up on the eighth shuttle mission, the first American woman* went into space, Sally Ride.

The fifties may have been a dull, sad time, a time of high unemployment, ticky-tacky tract houses, and garish automobiles. A time of black knit neckties and pink shirts for men, of poodle cuts and poodle skirts for women. The time of the Korean War. But it also was a time of Lucille Ball and the first sighting of a bikini on an American beach. A time for Bobby Thomson's ninth-inning home run for the New York Giants—a new "shot heard round the world"—that won the pennant race against the Brooklyn Dodgers. It was a time for Miss Frances and TV's *Ding Dong School.* And a time for Tupperware, the flexible containers—they burped!—that became the excuse for many housewives' parties.

So what did the sixties have to offer that could top that? The answer, of course, is: plenty.

---

* Soviet cosmonaut Valentina Tereshkova blasted into space twenty years earlier, in Russia's sixth successful launch.

CHAPTER ONE

TV or Not TV:
That Is the Message

Unless we get off our fat surpluses and recognize that television in the main is being used to distract, delude, amuse, and insulate us, then television and those who finance it, those who look at it and those who work at it, may see a totally different picture too late.

Edward R. Murrow, Speech at the Radio and Television
News Directors Convention, Chicago, October 15, 1958

And that's the way it is.

Walter Cronkite, sign-off sentence, *CBS Evening News*

During the 1960 presidential campaign, some of Republican Richard Nixon's critics labeled him "Tricky Dick," but when he and Democrat John Kennedy met in the first of four debates, Kennedy may have outtricked Dick. It was on September 26, 1960, in a television studio on Chicago's Fairbanks Court.

A month or so earlier, while campaigning in Greensboro, North Carolina, Nixon had banged his knee getting into a car. Twelve days later the pain had become so bad that he checked into Walter Reed Army Hospital in Washington, D.C. Nixon's knee was badly infected, and doctors shot him full of penicillin and other antibiotics. For two weeks, he lay there in the hospital, itching to get back on the campaign trail and scratching at his infected leg. Finally, doctors gave him the go-ahead, and Richard Nixon began a two-week, fifteen thousand mile push across twenty-five states, hoping to make up lost time in his promise to campaign in all fifty American states.

But the antibiotics hadn't totally worked, and the infection drove Nixon's temperature to over 103 degrees. Due to that infection and his hospital stay, due also to his campaign schedule, Richard Nixon was physically worn out and had dropped ten pounds by the time of the debate. His clothes hung on him—for some reason, rather than

1

buy a new shirt, that Saturday night Nixon wore one that was a full size too big.

That wasn't all. At the suggestion of the Kennedy camp, the two candidates stood throughout the hour-long session. For an hour, Richard Nixon was in pain.

In spite of his own pain due to a World War II back injury, John Kennedy looked fit, tanned, and rested; he seemed poised and experienced, despite GOP claims that he wasn't. Kennedy was young, handsome, and capable, and he'd accepted the services of a television makeup artist. Nixon looked tired and ill at ease, and he'd refused makeup, allowing only a small amount of "beard stick" to cover his perpetual five o'clock shadow.

At the request of the Kennedy staff, the temperature in the normally cold TV studio was raised. It didn't bother JFK, but Nixon began to sweat. Meanwhile, a Kennedy aide in the control room pressured the television director to use frequent closeup shots of Nixon mopping his brow.

So we have a candidate with a painful knee infection, and he had to stand throughout the debate. We had a candidate who'd recently lost weight, and he looked gaunt and uncomfortable in a shirt too large for him. We had a candidate who sweated and whose appearance begged the question: "Would you buy a used car from this man?"

Both radio and television carried the debates, and who won depended on whether you watched or listened. The TV audience of eighty million perceived Kennedy as the winner. The radio audience, of course, didn't get to see Nixon sweat under the hot studio lights, and many perceived *him* as the winner.

Nixon later took to wearing makeup whenever he might be on television. Once, when Richard Nixon reputedly accused John Kennedy of telling a "barefaced lie," Kennedy replied: "Having seen [him] four times close up—and made up—I would not accuse Mr. Nixon of being barefaced, but the American people can determine who is telling the truth."

JFK undoubtedly was the darling of the media, and they gave him greater leeway than they did the often testy and petulant Nixon. Late in the 1960 campaign, for instance, Kennedy appeared in an informal postmidnight news conference in the hallway of a midwest hotel. Microphones and cameras pointed at him, Kennedy stood in shirt and tie, shoes, socks, and voluminous white boxer shorts. Yet not one television or print cameraman showed the candidate's full-length picture.

It wasn't the only "underwear" incident of JFK's campaign. In the final days of his run for the White House, Kennedy found himself in New York City—which he knew he'd win handily—instead of in California, which it turned out he'd lose. Not only was he in the wrong state, preaching, as it were, to the choir, his motorcade got lost. Just moments before a planned major address at the Biltmore Hotel, Kennedy stomped out of his suite into a reception of the party's bigwigs and faithful. "Who the hell was leading that motorcade?" he demanded from his aides, adding that "I'd like to find the son of a bitch who was driving." Told he was probably outside, JFK stormed out of the room, into a gathering of stunned guests, and headed straight for the man he assumed was the errant individual. "Are you the driver?" he demanded. Yes, sir, the man answered. "Well, next time get a road map." And JFK walked back into his suite, oblivious to those standing around, oblivious that about all he was wearing were those voluminous boxer shorts.

To those born after World War II, television was always there, just the way radio had been there for their parents. It was their medium, and young Americans responded to its often inane outpourings. Yet these same young Americans also saw television pictures of fire hoses being turned on children in Alabama, of snarling dogs being sicced on young people their same age. Such incidents, CBS reporter Eric Sevareid said, were recorded in the permanent photoelectric file of every human brain.

As television grew, radio died. The same year of the Kennedy-Nixon debates, after twenty-eight seasons and 7,222 episodes, the radio soap opera *The Romance of Helen Trent* ended its long run. *Ma Perkins,* which had begun only five months after Helen Trent hit the airwaves in 1933, was also canceled.

When radio made a comeback, it wasn't your uncle's kind of radio anymore. Many stations had gone over to a Top-40 record format, and radio no longer was the political force it had been. But then, too, in the sixties, it seemed as if life itself would change.

Television was a child of the twenties that took tentative steps in the thirties, and became an orphan in the forties. Not long after TV was invented, we found ourselves in the middle of the Great Depression. Nearly everybody was hurting for money. We weren't likely to spend the going price of a couple of thousand dollars on something like a television set, not when we could get into a movie for about a dime. When World War II came along the television technology (not to mention the industry needed to build it) went into military hardware, radar and such.

When victory in Europe and the Pacific seemed likely, we renewed our interest in television. In 1948, about 172,000 families owned TV sets, and by 1960 the figure was over fifty million sets, a lot of people for the time. By 1960, some ninety percent of American homes had at least one TV set, and that's when television began to flex its cultural muscles.

Television in the sixties featured a fantastic array of anthropomorphized products. We had dancing packs of Old Gold cigarettes and a blond Muriel cigar. We had Ajax cleanser's "Bathroom Pixies" and a cute and jubilant "Speedy" Alka-Seltzer.

The sixties may not have been the Golden Age of Television, but we had Dick Van Dyke and Mary Tyler Moore, David Janssen, Bill Bixby, and Ray Walston. We had E. G. Marshall in *The Defenders*, Melvyn Douglas in *Inherit the Wind*, and Dame Judith Anderson in *Elizabeth the Queen*. Situation comedies—sitcoms—were big in the sixties: We lost *Leave It to Beaver* ("With Jerry Mathers as the Beaver") in 1963 after a six-year run. But we gained (?) *Mister Ed, McHale's Navy, That Girl* (which proved that Marlo Thomas was much prettier if not as funny as her father, Danny Thomas), and *The Monkees* (a Beatles takeoff that proved that if you're frantic enough and have at least one member of the group who girls squeal over, you can be a success, even if none of you can sing).

Monsters were big in mid-sixties television sitcoms, at least *The Munsters* and *The Addams Family*. Herman Munster (Fred Gwynne) and Grandpa (Al Lewis) starred in *The Munsters*, all about a decidedly freakish family plunked down in the real world at 1313 Mockingbird Lane. When *The Munsters* made its debut in 1964, brunette-in-blond-wig Beverly Owen played niece Marilyn, the only "normal" member of the family. At the end of the first season Owen left the show to get married, and the producers brought in a real (?) blonde (at least she didn't wear a wig), Pat Priest.

The entertainment industry newspaper *Variety* clearly preferred *The Munsters* over *The Addams Family*, saying that the edge must go to *The Munsters* for, as "'unnatural' shows go, this one is more natural." Herman Munster and company hit the air six days after *The Addams Family* and ended six days after Gomez, Morticia, Thing, Cousin Itt, and Lurch (with his signature phrase "You rang?") folded their Charles Addams–inspired tent and went into reruns.

Addams Family costar Carolyn Jones and The *Munsters* Pat Priest shared something other than macabre families. Before becoming Morticia in *Addams*, Jones had starred with Elvis Presley in *King Creole*, and Priest turned up as Elvis's leading lady in *Easy Come, Easy Go* after her TV series. For a while, Pat Priest even owned Elvis's 1967 Cadillac, but she traded it in on a Pontiac. Go figure.

In 1966, both *Addams Family* and *The Munsters* fell to that cartoon of cartoons, *Batman*, with Adam West as the caped crusader and Burt Ward as his sidekick, Robin. The series was so popular that for the first year of its two-year run, ABC showed it in two-part episodes that ran on consecutive Wednesday and Thursday nights. Suzanne Pleshette was originally scheduled to wear the vinyl suit of Catwoman on the show, but contract talks broke down and five-feet eleven-inch, 135-pound Julie Newman took over. When Newman left the show to make a big-screen movie, she was replaced by sultry-voiced Eartha Kitt. When *Batman* itself became a movie, yet a third Catwoman showed up, former Miss America Lee Ann Meriwether.

We had burlesque queen Gypsy Rose Lee doing a talk show, and her sister competed with her on *The June Havoc Show*.

For a short while, about nineteen months over a three-year period, we had Patrick McGoohan's stylish *Secret Agent*. McGoohan's character was a comparatively moral intelligence agent—he had his own theme song, "Secret Agent Man," sung by Johnny Rivers—and may have been the precursor to the equally enigmatic and stylish *The Prisoner*.

A lot of us dreamed of Jeannie and Barbara Eden, as we did for *Bewitched*'s Elizabeth Montgomery. For comedy's sake we tuned in

Don Adams's James Bond spoof *Get Smart*, but we stuck around to see Barbara Feldon's Agent 99. Another James Bond sendup, *The Man From U.N.C.L.E.*, somehow or other managed to be a four-year success without any female stars. *Mission Impossible, I Spy*, and *Julia*. If this wasn't another Golden Age, it was a pretty fair Silver. From 1964 to '66.

For every *Adam 12, Hawaii Five-O*, or *Wild Wild West* in the sixties, it seemed we also had an *F Troop, Green Acres, The Flying Nun*, and *The Dating Game*. When *Peyton Place* came along in 1964, it proved that America was ready for nighttime soap operas. Okay, so maybe it was more the Bronze Age of television.

On January 7, 1961, Honor Blackman made her English TV debut on the British-produced series *The Avengers* as Mrs. Catherine "Cathy" Gale, the stylish and agile anthropologist with a penchant for firearms and karate and leather, partner to Patrick Macnee in his guise as debonair, bowler-hatted, umbrella-toting John Steed. Together they were a death-defying, crime-solving team.

Most Americans didn't get to see or know Honor Blackman until several years later when Bond, James Bond, came along and Honor gave up her ongoing, small screen, black and white role for glorious color and the glamour of *Goldfinger*. Even then, she didn't get the attention she perhaps deserved. Shirley Eaton—shown stretched out, the gilded victim of Goldfinger's Midas touch—got much of the attention in *Goldfinger*.

When Honor Blackman shed her *Avengers'* leather to make movies with Connery, Sean Connery, in stepped thirty-one-year-old, Shakespeare-trained Diana Rigg. Five years after it debuted in England, *The Avengers* finally hit American TV sets in 1966, and television hasn't been the same since then. Mrs. Emma Peel, Rigg's character, was a saucy, sexy, charming more-or-less liberated woman. Certainly liberated for the times. The *Mrs.* referred to Emma's husband, Peter Peel, who had mysteriously flown off to South America or somewhere, only to return just as mysteriously in 1967 and recapture Emma. Or Diana.

Like Blackman's Cathy Gale, Diana Rigg's on-screen persona leaned toward leather jumpsuits, drove a sports car, chopped a mean judo, picked locks, and could discuss nuclear physics with the best of 'em. And she did it all in spiked-heel boots. Mrs. Peel, Rigg says,

> was definitely a different type of character for television. For the first time a woman in a TV series was intelligent, independent, and capable of looking after herself. That is why the show became such a success—it reflected what was happening to women throughout the world in the sixties.

In 1999, *TV Guide* magazine listed Diana Rigg as Number 8 in their list of "TV's 50 Greatest Characters Ever." The only other woman on the list was No. 3, Lucille Ball. That same year *Playboy* made Rigg Number 75 on its list of "100 Sexiest Stars of the Century." (Julie Newmar, incidentally, was Number 88.)

Diana Rigg had something other than *The Avengers* in common with Honor Blackman. In 1969, she stepped away from television to become—you guessed it!—a James Bond girl. Unlike Honor, however, Diana didn't get to share a martini, shaken or otherwise, with Sean Connery. By the time *On Her Majesty's Secret Service* came along, Connery was gone and in his place, for one shot only, came the highly forgettable Australian model George Lazenby.

Television in the 1960s had the American version of morality plays: westerns. We had *The Tall Man* with Clu Gulager and Barry Sullivan and *Bonanza* with all the Cartwrights. *Wagon Train* and *Maverick* were joined by *Rawhide* with Eric Fleming and—what's his name? Clint Eastwood. And of course we still had *Gunsmoke*, left over from radio and the fifties.* Be careful out there, Matt.

Every week thousands of American men strapped on their six-shooters to face James Arness's Marshal Dillon at the beginning of the show as he strode down Dodge's Main Street. Several of these less than brilliant would-be gunslingers blasted holes in their TV sets while facing down the marshal, and at least one man shot himself in the foot.

---

* *Gunsmoke* began in September 1955 and ran until September 1975, becoming television's longest-running prime-time series with continuing characters, and TV's longest-running western, as well.

Sixties television replayed World War II in the series *Combat,* which lasted longer (1962–67) than America's role in the real war did, as did *Hogan's Heroes* (1965–71), TV's comic version of Broadway's and Hollywood's *Stalag 17* ("I know nothing, nothing"). *American Bandstand* lasted longer than *two* world wars, daily telecasts from 1957 to 1963, and even then Dick Clark didn't completely turn off the cameras, just changed it from a daily show to once a week on Saturday afternoons. During an early-sixties *Bandstand* Clark played a record by a new group (they weren't yet important enough to have on in-person). Then he showed photographs of the singers. Dick's audience rated the record as only so-so and the general impression was Yuck! when shown a picture of John, Paul, George, and Ringo— the Beatles.

Beginning on September 9, 1966, and for a three-year period, NBC carried the original *Star Trek* program. It truly became the show that wouldn't die. A few years after the network canceled *Star Trek* over the objections of thousands of its viewers, the producers turned it into several big-screen movies, then into animated shows, and then into several "after *Star Trek*" series. Not to mention sending cast members around to conventions of fans called Trekkies, later called Trekkers. For *Star Trek* there seemed to be no "final frontier."

Nineteen sixty-seven was the year Dr. Richard Kimble stopped running. Based loosely on the story of Cleveland doctor Sam Shepard, who'd been convicted of murdering his wife, *The Fugitive* began in 1963 and ended in 1967. Television's Dr. Kimble found his wife's true killer in the last episode of the show. The real-life Dr. Shepard, however, had his conviction overturned, without benefit of a "one-armed man."

For five years *Rowan and Martin's Laugh-In* gave audiences sight gags, one-liners, cameo appearances (even President Nixon showed up to say "Sock it to me!"), trapdoors, and an offbeat look at the news. "Verrrry interesting!"

Sixties television wasn't just debates and westerns, sitcoms and cartoons. We also had news. As the decade wore on, television became the only way many Americans got news. Whatever "news" was. Some old-line TV journalists claim that "news" is what's happening right now, at this very moment. Or, as one reporter commented, "News is what is new in the world since our last broadcast."

Twenty-first-century television newscasts are so much more sophisticated technically than they were in the 1960s, it's not even funny. Well, actually, some sixties newscasts were pretty funny, come to think of it. And yesterday's news sets were downright plain: The sole anchor (always a male) sat behind a bare wooden desk (the anchor often as wooden as the desk) shuffling papers while speaking into a large microphone. An American flag stood behind him.

In the early sixties, TV news used 16mm film; black and white at first, then color. The black and white, incidentally, early on was negative film—just like the negatives you used to get from the corner drug store—that had been electronically made positive. The picture wasn't too good and it was hard as hell to edit, because you saw nothing but, in effect, shadows.

At both local stations and the networks, a news department's day would begin with producers and assignment editors, sometimes with reporters and correspondents offering input, sitting around a table discussing what events they'd cover that day. Which means "what preplanned events" they'd cover. Very simply, with a "newshole" of as little as eleven and a half minutes in a half-hour program, you had to be prepared. A complete "package" of reporter, event footage, and one or more "experts" seldom ran longer than a minute fifteen seconds.

To a greater or lesser extent, if there were more news (or more ads) one day, newspapers could expand or contract (adding or cutting at least two, usually four, pages), but television news was pretty much bound by the thirty-minute rule. For local stations and networks to expand a newscast, there had to be a major breaking event; they simply didn't cut back on their scheduled time.

That's when preproduced packages came in, filling in the newshole left after two or three breaking news stories. Reuven Frank, executive producer of the *NBC Evening News*, once wrote a memo declaring:

> Except for those rare days when other material (e.g., breaking stories) becomes available, the gap [between breaking sto-

ries] will be filled by planned or prepared stories, and we are assuming the availability of two each night.

Until the Tet Offensive in 1968, with a few exceptions the mass media mainly parroted reports picked up in Saigon at the Mission Press Center, the infamous "five o'clock follies." A bored air force major read a boring report to a dozen or so bored correspondents: so many air strikes, so many enemy killed, so few Americans killed. If it was boring enough, the "follies" feeling was, no one back in America would pay any attention to the increasing number of body bags being shipped home. Television reporters seldom "saw" the "war" or the "enemy." Some sounded as if they were on the scene when fighting took place, but in reality many relied on either in-person sources or official reports.

Television news seldom questioned how we were to win the war or even if we *should* win it. Television news almost never showed footage of the dead or dying. For television news, the "queasy quotient" was a big factor: how much blood and gore could TV show before the audience felt queasy and tuned out?

Following the Tet Offensive, some reporters and producers began questioning the government's long-accepted promise of victory in Vietnam. CBS's Walter Cronkite was one:

> The only rational way out . . . will be to negotiate, not as victors, but as honorable people who lived up to their pledge to defend democracy and did the best they could.

For television, Vietnam in the mid-sixties was not a fast-breaking event. Due to technological constraints TV couldn't bring us a live picture from Vietnam. Pictures and reports about the war were at best hours, usually days, away. To get around this time lag, TV news relied on those prepackaged events, and making them exciting became both a problem and the be-all, end-all.

A "talking head"—a witness or an expert—explaining the whys and wherefores of the war might make sense out of what was going on, but TV executives believed their audiences wanted action—combat footage. They gave it to us, but it wasn't a necessarily accurate picture about what was going on.

Partially because of the difficulty in getting news stories back from Vietnam, beginning in the late sixties the networks even changed what kind of stories they covered. With the administration in Washington claiming that the war was coming to a close, the networks decided that they should change their coverage. In 1969, Av Westin, the executive producer of the *ABC Evening News*, wrote to his correspondents:

I have asked our Vietnam staff to alter the focus of their coverage from combat pieces to interpretive ones, pegged to the eventual pullout of American forces. This point should be stressed to all hands.

In a telex to ABC's Saigon bureau, Westin told the staff:

I think the time has come to shift some of our focus from the battlefield, or more specifically American military involvement with the enemy, to themes and stories under the general heading: We Are On Our Way Out of Vietnam.

Beginning in 1968, when President Johnson announced a complete halt in the bombing of North Vietnam, NBC News informed its staff that the "story" was now the peace talks, not the fighting. Cameramen continued to shoot combat footage and correspondents and producers continued sending them back to New York, but the "focus" had changed. Newscasts showed stories about preparations to leave Vietnam, little about the continued fighting and continued death.

While students were getting their heads banged in the streets of Saigon, American television news carried stories on the "new stability" in South Vietnam. But how stable was it? The answer is: not very. One regime toppled another, which was itself toppled, taken over, or undercut, often with America's blessings. Leaders were executed or went into exile. During much of this time, Buddhists marched in the streets of South Vietnam. American ambassadors claimed, and American TV reported, that the Saigon government was stable.

Initially, many television reporters and editors and producers went to Vietnam with a limited knowledge of conditions in Southeast Asia.

As the war went on, and our television coverage of it continued, TV personnel learned the lay of the land and gained knowledge and experience. They began questioning "official" sources. The more they questioned these sources, the more it became apparent that the "officials" were deliberately misleading them and, therefore, misleading the American people about what really was happening. That's when the "five o'clock follies" were recognized for what they were: fiction, not fact.

The change in reporters' attitude didn't go unnoticed back in Washington. Often, when they spoke out against the official grain, politicians and administration supporters accused reporters of being "an effete corps of impudent snobs," as Spiro Agnew had it.

"Snobs," of course, were the very people who brought us *The Beverly Hillbillies*, the number one show on television in its first two seasons, 1962–63 and 1963–64. Jed Clampett and his family were "poor mountaineers" who discovered oil on their Appalachian property and became immensely rich. At the urging of their "kinfolk" they moved to the hills—Beverly Hills, that is. Of course they were met by the real snobs and, of course, they beat them at every turn.

On October 3, 1960, former stand-up comic and former schoolteacher Andy Griffith began a new TV sitcom with Don Knotts, Frances Bavier, and Ronny Howard: *The Andy Griffith Show*, about the fictitious small town of Mayberry, North Carolina. It was one of the few shows on television that didn't show a Mom-Pop-two-kids-and-a-dog traditional family. Apparently, the lead character's wife had died (no way in the sixties would television show a divorced individual), leaving Andy Taylor with this cute, freckle-faced boy named Opie (some referred to him as Dopie) to be cared for by Andy's mother's sister, the loving Aunt Bee. And, of course, Opie had a dog, Gulliver. They were all happily ensconced at 322 Maple Street. Mayberry had so few telephones that the Taylor's home number had only three digits, 426.

We remember such 1960s programs as *The Andy Griffith Show* as describing the typical American family. But not so, according to sociologist Stephanie Coontz. As she puts it, TV's picture of life was *The Way We Never Were*. Life that simple and kind just didn't exist, except on television.

• • •

One thing that Andy—Sheriff Andy Taylor, that is—had was the thing that every other TV sitcom hero possessed, a not-too-bright sidekick: Don Knotts in the form of deputy Barney Fife. Knotts (and Barney) left after the series's third year, but we always associate him with Andy and Opie and Aunt Bee.

Your average movie or television script in the sixties ran about a minute per page; a sixty-page script equaled about sixty minutes of show. Not so on *The Andy Griffith Show*. That one took about a third fewer pages of script than your average sitcom, because the characters spoke more slowly in a modified Southern drawl.

No drawl from Airman Adrian Cronauer—he came from Pittsburgh—but he was one of the most unusual American troops to serve in the Vietnam War. He was also one of the most popular. Among the troops, that is; not necessarily so among the brass.

Beginning after World War II, just about wherever American troops were sent—Germany, Korea, or Vietnam—an Armed Forces Radio (AFR) station went with them, broadcasting in English, often spouting the "truth" of the day as perceived by those who didn't actually get their feet wet and their boots muddy, and playing music à la American disk jockeys back home. In the late 1960s, Armed Forces Radio even had its own television stations.

It was as a disk jockey that Airman Cronauer came into the story. In May 1965 the powers-that-be sent Adrian to Vietnam and put him to work as a radio announcer, where he began each broadcast day shouting, "Good morning, Vietnam!" It was a combination made in Stateside heaven or Vietnam-side hell. Using imagination, enthusiasm, and innovation, Cronauer tried to make Armed Forces Radio "sound like a Stateside radio station," he said.

In 1962, Adrian was a student at American University in Washington, D.C.—just eleven credit hours short of a degree in broadcasting—when the draft board pushed him to volunteer. He joined the air force, hoping for a better choice of assignments than he might get if drafted into the army. The air force sent him to Greece. Then with a year left in his enlistment, they packed him off to Vietnam.

Hollywood later made a movie about Adrian Cronauer and his cry of "Good morning, Vietnam!" Things weren't as bad for the real Cronauer as for the reel version, actor Robin Williams.

The brass didn't push the airman around as much as Hollywood had it but, yes, there was some music censorship that he had to fight. As the film showed, Adrian went out into the countryside to interview the crunchies, and he also taught English to some locals during his off-duty hours. Hollywood had him almost getting blown up when he was out in the field and his vehicle ran over a land mine; didn't happen, though. But he *was* at a diner shortly before the Viet Cong blew it up; Hollywood got that right. Cronauer said that if he'd acted in real life the way Robin Williams portrayed him on film, he'd still be serving time in the military prison at Fort Leavenworth, Kansas.

Some of the most popular songs Airman Cronauer and other AF disk jockeys played were the same ones they'd have been playing if they hadn't been several thousand miles away from their local drive-in restaurant or wherever back in the States. Peter, Paul and Mary's "Leaving on a Jet Plane" was popular for obvious reasons; it gave the troops hope that they could do just what the song said and go home. The Animals' "We Gotta Get Out of This Place" for the same reason. "Proud Mary" by Creedence Clearwater Revival was big, as was "Bad Moon Rising." Other songs popular for obvious reasons were Bobby Vinton's "Coming Home Soldier," the Lovin' Spoonful's "Darling Be Home Soon." "Reach Out, I'll Be There" by the Four Tops, and "Ruby, Don't Take Your Love to Town," Kenny Rogers and the First Edition's hit about a paraplegic veteran trying to talk his wife into not leaving him for the sake of sex.

Some sentimental songs also made the "must-play" list in Vietnam: Tammy Wynette's "Stand By Your Man," which is exactly what the guys hoped their girls back home were doing. "Walk Like a Man" by the Four Seasons, and Percy Sledge and "When a Man Loves a Woman." Of course there was the Animals' "House of the Rising Sun," and Sgt. Barry Sadler's "The Ballad of the Green Berets." But one of the most popular of all songs played by Airman Adrian Cronauer and his fellow AF disk jockeys was Tony Bennett's 1962

TV or Not TV

Grammy-award-winning "I Left My Heart in San Francisco." It was San Francisco, after all, where many troops said good-bye to America and good morning to Vietnam.

As for Adrian Cronauer, after his one-year tour of duty in Vietnam, he joined the ranks of civilians. Thanks to profits he made from selling rights to his story, Cronauer studied at the University of Pennsylvania Law School. Good morning, Judge!

Not to be outdone by Adrian Cronauer and his radio show, beginning in 1967, Bobbi Keith of Winthrop, Massachusetts, did a television show in Vietnam. She was hired as a secretary in Saigon for USAID, Aid to International Development, and got into Armed Forces Television, she later admitted, "by a fluke." AF-TV was looking for someone to do the weather show and asked her to audition. She did and got the job. She was only nineteen when she did her first weathercast, and if you were a twenty-two-year-old soldier or Marine, that was about right.

Over time, Bobbi's weathercasts in Vietnam weren't much like weathercasts in the United States, unless you could imagine Willard Scott doing the *Today Show* weather in a bikini, which boggles the mind. For other gimmicks, she recalls,

> I flew around the studio on a broomstick for Halloween. . . . I arrived on a motorcycle one time. I was put in a box one time, like the Houdini type style, and elevated up. They threw a lot of buckets of water on me when I announced rain. People thought that was funny. I wore different costumes. One time they painted the temperatures on my body in a bikini.

Eat your heart out, Willard Scott.

We had many things on our minds in the sixties: We elected a new president from a new generation. We saw increasing numbers of civil rights advocates challenge bigotry in our laws and mores. We saw many of these advocates beaten and bloodied and murdered. We saw a president, a would-be president, and a people's leader murdered. We even saw one killer murdered. We sent men into space. We built bigger and more powerful cars. We adopted a small, underpowered car. We grew our hair long, longer, longest and changed our style of clothing. Some of us changed our style of living. We changed our music. Our rock 'n' roll became simply "rock" and took on a harder edge. We momentarily revived folk music. We saw a new record set in major league baseball home runs. And we saw a new football league become part of an older one; together, they joined for an annual "super" game that, in its third year, saw a brash young man with long shaggy hair guarantee to tear the field apart, and make good on the pledge.

The peaceful glory of the fifties may be a myth. And the sixties certainly weren't as wild as we may remember them. Still, the times were both frivolous and sensual. We were politically active and socially serious. It was a time when civil rights, free speech, and a back-to-the-land movement came of age.

Oh, what a time it was.

CHAPTER TWO

Culture Shock:
The Times They Are A-Changin'*

We are at a crisis point in the history of American education and probably in that of the Western world.
Richard Hofstadter, professor, Columbia University, 1968

When I hear the word culture ... I reach for my pistol.
Hanns Johst, Schlageter, 1933

In the 1960s, San Francisco State University graduate design student Charles Prior Hall changed the world in a modest, albeit culturally meaningful, way. But in the manner of most culturally meaningful changes, his first effort didn't work out quite right. He tried to build the most comfortable chair in the world. Hall based his design on the then-popular bean-bag chair, just a big plastic bag filled with—you guessed it!—beans. Go to any semimodern home in the early 1960s and you'd likely see young children climbing, sitting, and sleeping on bean- bag chairs in front of the family's black-and-white television set.

For what he called the "Incredible Creeping Chair," Charlie Hall filled a large vinyl bag with about three hundred pounds of cornstarch. Well, creep it might, but it wasn't very comfortable; sit on it and you felt as if you'd been swallowed by the chair. So Hall tried again, this time using Jell-O. That didn't work either; Jell-O may be fun to eat but not to sit on; it turned lumpy and uncomfortable. With that, Charlie Hall gave up trying for the world's most comfortable chair and turned his attention elsewhere.

* Copyright 1963, Bob Dylan (Robert Zimmerman).

17

He designed a device that used a water-filled plastic bladder, a wood frame, and a waterproof liner just in case the bladder sprang a leak. He got an A in design class, got a patent for his invention, and got rich on the product. Charlie Hall invented the waterbed.

As long as you squeezed out all of the air bubbles (if you didn't, every time you moved you'd create rather disconcerting wavelike sloshing sounds), as long as you had a floor that would withstand the bed's weight (all that water was pretty heavy, and some apartment building owners refused to let tenants use the beds), and as long as you remembered to put bleach in with the water (if you didn't, algae would grow in a most disgusting manner), waterbeds were fairly comfortable. Later, a couple of changes were made in the original design: a heater kept it from being excessively cold, and instead of a single mattress-size bladder, manufacturers developed waterbeds with several compartments, claiming this eliminated some users' complaints that they got seasick at the most inopportune times.

Waterbeds ready, we're set for the swinging sixties.

The sixties were Highway 80, between Selma and Montgomery. Sit-ins at Berkeley and Columbia. Fighting in Da Nang and the Mekong Delta. They were the burning cities of Newark and Detroit and Los Angeles.

In the 1960s, we would "Shout! Shout!" and knock ourselves out. The Beatles sang "All You Need Is Love," but we needed much more. We tried to make both love and war. We went "Downtown" and told "Mrs. Brown" that she had a lovely daughter. We had "Good Vibrations" and listened for "The Sounds of Silence." We were "Poetry in Motion" and learned just who was a "Natural Woman" and who was a "Soul Man." We could do our own thing while the windmills of our minds lifted us to "Folsom Prison" and/or "Galveston." We had Elvis and the Beatles; Simon and Garfunkel; Led Zeppelin; Creedence Clearwater Revival; and Blood, Sweat and Tears. Meanwhile, out in the middle of a dance floor, fully clothed nineteen-year-old Ernest Evans used an invisible towel to dry his backside, then moved his hands in opposite directions. For a guy who used to work—literally!—as a chicken plucker, he did all right. Bobbie Clark, *American Bandstand* host Dick Clark's wife, gave Ernest his new name, "Chubby Checker," and his backside-drying movement became "The Twist," spawning a whole series of other twistlike songs and movies. One of them, *Don't Knock the Twist* in 1962, featured Chubby waving his hands in the air and singing about another new dance: "The Fly." That one didn't catch on.

We started the decade with Dwight David Eisenhower still in the White House for a few weeks more. The office passed to a more eloquent president but all too soon shots rang out and stilled his words forever. The president's brother was also killed and a people's leader was murdered and American cities burned.

In response to the hundred-plus riots that burned American cities over a two-year period, former Illinois governor Otto Kerner headed a commission investigating the causes of the tumult. His answer wasn't easy to swallow: Blacks and whites were growing farther apart every year. Growing crowds demanded, not just the right to sit in the front of the bus if they wanted to, but to vote, and—far more than that—the right simply to be.

The 1960s were prime time for the Cold War, and it just plain scared us. We watched as bombs grew larger and fear accelerated; we dug bomb shelters or thought about digging them or wondered what we'd do if, in the event of a nuclear war, someone tried to get into our shelter. That, and the belief that once we emerged from our shelters into a post-nuclear-war world, nothing would be left of life, caused many of us not to build shelters. Other people did, however, and some of those shelters are still around today.

The sixties were a time of momentous social movements, sweeping legislation, remarkable space achievements, silly clothing, weird hair, new music, riots, assassinations, and a war that nearly tore America apart. No wonder it's our favorite decade.

In the 1960s we challenged the nation's social and political idealism. We harvested good and evil from previous decades and planted the seeds of discontent for times that followed. It was a wild and woolly ride. Before the decade of the sixties ended, all hell broke loose.

We developed "attitudes" and took "ego trips." We would "freak out" or be "with it." We took in "sit-ins" and became "Freedom Riders"—new words for the sixties, as were "anchorman," "compact car," and "wild-card rule."

We learned about "splashdowns," "kooks," "skateboards," and "op art"; we learned how to "do our own thing" and discovered who "groupies" were. A wife or girlfriend might be our "old lady"; a husband or boyfriend might be our "old man." Hopefully, we gave off good "vibes." Life in general could be so "mind blowing" that we'd "lose our cool." We might frequent a "head shop," but we'd better lay off the "uppers" and "downers" if a "narc" was on the scene.

Almost overnight, a wall separated West from East.

In the 1960s, the Vietnam War shifted into high gear, and American troops began firing shots, not just advising others on the ways of war; the sixties were the prime years of the longest war in American history.

We tried to stop the fall of communist dominoes in Southeast Asia and sacrificed our best and brightest in the attempt. Draft resisters left the country to live in Canada, and resisters of progress left reality to form communes.

The 1960s were an age of youth, with seventy million children from the postwar baby boom becoming teenagers and young adults.

The 1960s were a time of change, of conflict and argument, the Bay of Pigs and the Cuban Missile Crisis: Did John Kennedy save the world by refusing to back down, or did Nikita Khrushchev salvage us because he *did*?

Drugs were good. Drugs were bad.

The Bomb was the great deterrent. The Bomb was the great monster.

Men (and a very few women) rocketed into space.

The 1960s were not a "me" generation but a generation of "We Shall Overcome."

Unemployment was up. Unemployment was down.

We grew unbelievably prosperous—the sixties saw the nation's greatest economic boom ever until the nineties boomed even higher, but we maundered along in a stupor of fat.

We dropped out, did our own thing, turned on, tuned out, made great gains, and took little steps toward racial equality.

As the 1960s began, nearly two and a third times more of us lived in cities than in rural areas. We paid $.58 for a dozen eggs, $.26 for a quart of milk, and $.75 for a pound of coffee. A GE electric spray iron cost us $21.95 and a Philco portable TV cost $139.95. A box of Quaker Oats cost $.47 and a Lilt home permanent was $1.42.

The sixties saw an end to many fifties styles. Women who had primly worn white gloves (but who'd also gladly shared backseat groping), took to heart Betty Friedan's *Feminine Mystique.* In 1963, the Presidential Commission on the Status of Women presented some disturbing facts about women's place in American society. For the first time, we heard the term *glass ceiling* used to describe the problems and frustration women felt when they weren't allowed to advance in corporate America. The newly founded National Organization for Women questioned the unequal treatment of women and fostered the birth of Women's Liberation.

As the sixties began, men who had worn crew cuts and flattops, began sporting greased-down, carefully parted, longer hair. It would get worse and longer.

In the sixties, some young girls fought so desperately to avoid bouffant hairstyles—known to some simply as "big hair"—that they ironed their hair, laying it out on an ironing board while a trusted friend flattened their long tresses. Depending on the length of one's hair (and the care of one's ironer) the process could take upwards of an hour. Leave the iron on your hair too long and you'd scorch it and leave burn marks. Or you'd make it too dry or brittle. Hair ironing seems to have been a predominantly northeastern style. Southern belles held on to the big-hair look. It finally died out in the early seventies . . . well, maybe. Don't tell the Texas women that big hair no longer is in fashion.

Singer Bob Dylan said the decade of the sixties ultimately was "about clothes," dressing up or dressing down.

Gone were men's charcoal-gray suits with buckles—called "hiney binders" by some—on the back of our pants. Gone were pink shirts and skinny black neckties. In the early 1960s, American men wore stodgy three-buttoned, "Ivy League"–style suits with white, beige, or tan shirts and thin, thin, thinnest neckties; no "casual Fridays." In business, we didn't dare wear a sport coat. Check out old newsreels—baseball, football, even basketball, it doesn't matter—or kinescopes of old in-studio television shows: the men are all wearing suits and ties.

In the early 1960s, guys still wore pants that were so tight at the ankle that they sometimes had to have zippers put in. Luckily, that fad didn't last long.

In the early sixties, girls wore skirts and blouses, even in the winter. About the only time they wore pants—called "slacks" for a long time—was on weekends, and then there were girl-style jeans that zipped up on the side (Don't ask why, it's a sexual thing), purchased extra long and rolled up at the bottom. And a man's dress shirt— usually Daddy's but sometimes a boyfriend's, seldom a brother's— with sleeves rolled up and the shirttails tied together in front, underneath their breasts.

And hats. As the decade began, women wore hats, indoors or out. When Jackie Kennedy and the president got off the plane at Dallas that fateful day in 1963, she wore a pink pillbox hat. After that, women's hats in general faded off the fashion scene. We can credit Jack Kennedy with doing to the hat industry what Clark Gable had done to the undershirt industry back in the thirties: seeing Gable walk around sans athletic undershirt in *It Happened One Night* told every man and boy that it was all right not to wear the garments. And we didn't. Jack Kennedy apparently disliked hats, and he very seldom wore one. That meant the rest of us no longer had to wear hats. Baseball caps, however, are still accepted by both sexes, even though men and women wear them differently. Check it out.

At his inauguration, Jack Kennedy wore a top hat—Ike hated the idea and wanted to wear the Homburg he'd made Harry Truman wear in 1953. But tradition has it that the incoming president sets the fashion tone on inauguration day, so Ike grinned and bore Kennedy's top hat.

Up until John Kennedy, whenever a political candidate went looking for votes, he'd end up being presented with some kind of hat and be expected to put it on—even an Indian headdress now and then. Not for Kennedy. He'd accept a hat and hold it firmly in his hands, despite efforts by the local chamber of commerce or whoever to get him to put it on, just once, for a photograph during what we now refer to as a "photo-op."

The 1960s were *not* a time of "designer" labels; we didn't wear the manufacturer or designer's name plastered all over our clothing. Oh, we sported those leather Levi's and Lee labels on the back of our jeans, but that was it. At school, chances are we weren't even allowed to wear blue jeans, except on some special day. Say we were going to build the homecoming float or decorate the high school gym for the prom. It was okay then to wear jeans to class.

No Nike. No Adidas. We wore—simply—sneakers or tennis shoes, probably PF Flyers or Keds.

Don't even think of tattoos or guys wearing earrings. They'd be laughed at by their classmates and tossed out of school by the principal.

About the only jewelry a guy wore in the early sixties was a wristwatch. Oh, in junior high there was a short time when ID bracelets were popular, but that didn't last long. We certainly didn't wear chains and necklaces. Occasionally, left over from the forties' zoot suits, men and boys might wear key chains that went from a belt loop—sometimes from a watch pocket—and carried just what the name implies. Zoot-suit wearers sported long key chains. By the sixties, when they were worn at all, they were relatively short, just long enough to have a slight loop to them.

Until about mid-decade, the only time we wore boots was in the winter. If it rained hard, guys might be told by Mom to Wear your rubbers! Which of course weren't the same "rubbers" we're told to wear now. Today's rubbers are protection, but protection from sexually transmitted diseases, not rainy streets. In the sixties we wore the other kind of rubbers over our dress shoes, which probably were penny loafers. Each shoe had a small, rounded notch on the front over the arch and we'd jam a penny into each one. Maybe a dime or a quarter once in a while, but they were (and still are) called penny loafers, never dime or quarter loafers.

And then, somewhere in the middle of the sixties, things began to change. Men's stodgy black and gray suits evolved into brightly colored, double-breasted sport jackets, polyester pants, and Nehru jackets* with turtlenecks; don't forget your gold pen-

---

* Nehru shirts and jackets got their name from Indian leader Pandit Jawaharial Nehru, which may be the only time an Indian leader has set a fashion style. They had a thin collar up around the neck and dropped straight to the bottom of your butt.

dant necklace. By the end of the decade, when men *did* wear neckties, they were brightly patterned or striped and up to five inches wide at the bottom, matched by nearly shoulder-to-shoulder polyester coat lapels.

Toward the end of the decade both men and women took to wearing bell-bottomed jeans (much like World War II navy dungarees), love beads (not like *anything* in the navy), tie-dyed T-shirts (not like anything anywhere else), and clunky high-heeled shoes. Members of the counterculture often wore clothing bought at military surplus stores, apparently to "prove" that clothing was less a statement of fashion than of necessity.

One of the worst things about the mid-sixties fashions is that they were made with a high proportion of polyester, were sometimes all polyester, and that stuff never wears out. Polyester became the most famous, or infamous, of the synthetic fibers.

It actually came along in 1953, and at the time we thought it was the wonder fabric. It was cheap. It was strong. It resisted stretching and shrinking. It was wrinkle and mildew and abrasion resistant. Got a polyester shirt from the sixties? You might not be able to get into it now, but chances are it's still in one gaudy, uncomfortable piece. A joke told was that "a lot of polyesters gave their lives for your coat."

On February 5, 1966, singer Nancy Sinatra's song "These Boots Were Made for Walking" hit the *Billboard* chart of top records. It became Number 1 and went on to sell almost four million copies. Because of that record, and the picture of blond and shapely Nancy wearing them, leather or vinyl "go-go boots" became all the rage. Parisian André Courrèges introduced white midcalf boots (he called them "kid boots"), and they were so popular that his collection outshone those of other, more seasoned, high-fashion designers. With go-go boots, women began to wear hot pants or short, shorter, and shortest skirts—the miniskirt introduced in 1965 by Britain's Mary Quant (or France's Courrèges). Despite some predictions, the miniskirt did not lead to a breakdown in law and order or to rioting in the streets. We had lots of that, but it had nothing to do with short, sexy miniskirts.

Toward the end of the sixties, the mini lost out somewhat to the maxi, long skirts that some people (erroneously) claimed to be equally sexy because of what they did not reveal. Women began wearing peasant skirts, peasant blouses, and granny dresses.

At the start of the decade, men wore heavy black or dark-brown, tortoiseshell frames for their eyeglasses—the military must have bought a helluva lot of them, because well into the 1990s they continued issuing them. Women wore clear or lightly tinted plastic frames, sometimes pointed at the edge of the eyes, and if they were really classy, the frames might have a little heart attached where the front and the earpieces met.

And then that changed. Both sexes began wearing wire-framed or frameless "granny glasses." Actually, granny glasses became a token, not of senior citizenship, but of vibrant if unconventional youth. Also known as "Ben Franklin" glasses after the eighteenth-century Founding Father, granny glasses were worn by such famous people as John Lennon and members of the rock group the Byrds. These small, half-framed glasses became a staple of "mod" fashion.

In 2000, a statue of John Lennon, complete with granny glasses, was erected in downtown Havana, Cuba. Dictator Fidel Castro himself dedicated the statue. However, within a few months the statue no longer was "complete with granny glasses." Somebody stole them, either as a joke or as a souvenir. The statue's granny glasses, of course, had no lenses.

In the summer of 1965, another eyewear fad began (as so many other fads do) on the West Coast but luckily didn't travel far: wearing glasses *without* lenses, making fun of the intellectual "Clark Kent look" that became popular among some adults of the day. Groovy, as the saying of the sixties had it.

Contact lenses had been available for several years, but not many people wore them in the 1960s. For one thing they were expensive, three hundred dollars and up at a time when three hundred dollars was a lot of money. And they were hard—no gas permeable, soft, or disposable contacts then. Hard lenses were, well, hard to get accustomed to. So difficult, and so painful when you first put them in, frequently you'd have to explain to your eye-care specialist just *why* you wanted them. Of course, if you lost a lens, you and everybody around you wound up crawling on the floor searching for it.

And hair. When the Beatles invaded America, they came complete with long hair, or at least hair long for the time. Later, locks grew longer and longer and cartoons frequently showed couples from the rear, both long-haired individuals, making you wonder which was male and which was female.

Nineteen sixty-one saw a new invention change women's fashion: pantyhose, or, as some mail-order catalogs spelled it, "pantihose." Whatever the spelling, this nylon one-piece combination of stockings and brief appealed to women who, except for those who clung to the more elaborate (and some say, sexier) garter belts, rushed to stores looking for them. Sometimes, however, would-be buyers had trouble finding them. Pantyhose frequently baffled clothing-store operators, who stocked them with leotards rather than regular hosiery. Initial price, by the way, was $1.99.

In the 1960s, college campuses became centers of debate and scenes of protests as the country became more involved in the Vietnam War. Some items, however, reflected military enthusiasm: in 1963 "GI Joe" made his debut at your favorite toy store. "Barbie" had been around since 1959, but she was, after all, a doll and meant for girls. GI Joe, on the other hand was an "action figure" and meant for boys. Go figure the difference. Actually, one difference befitted Joe's more masculine self: he was twelve inches tall, towering over Barbie's eleven and a half inches.

For slightly more adult individuals of both sexes, there was another doll, the long-haired troll known as the "Dammit Doll." It was named not for emotions it might provoke but for its inventor, Joseph Dam.

In 1962, the U.S. Supreme Court ruled that prayer in public schools was unconstitutional, this at a time when Transcendental Meditation and Zen Buddhism began to draw interest. Hippies* took over San Francisco's Haight-Ashbury district and New York City's East Village. Others lived in communes.**

We learned about the "big-bang theory" of Earth's birth and were wary of "glitches" with our "chips." "Beatlemania" hit the under-

---

* The word apparently was coined in 1967 by members of the forties and fifties "hip" generation who felt youngsters were just young, therefore "hippies."
** See the chapter, "High Ole Times" following.

twenty-five set. In fact, *Time* magazine in 1966 chose the under twenty-five set at its collective "Man of the Year." Notice that it was not yet "Person of the Year."

In 1960, workmen demolished Ebbets Field, the former home of da Bums, the Brooklyn Dodgers; the team had moved to Los Angeles. The stadium had been built in Brooklyn's Flatbush section back in 1913 at a cost of $750,000, cheap perhaps because the area had been the site of the Pigtown garbage dump. Legend has it that the team got its nickname, the Dodgers, because to get to the stadium fans had to dodge the streetcars running right in front of the park's entrance. It was at Ebbets Field on April 15, 1947, that Jackie Robinson became the first black man in the twentieth century to play in major league baseball. But on February 23, 1960, the wreckers went to work. An apartment complex now occupies the space where Ebbets Field had stood for forty-seven years.

Four years after da Bums' old home bowed to the future, on April 10, 1964, the same wrecking ball workmen had used to demolish Ebbets Field swung back into action, this time destroying New York's Polo Grounds, home for many years to the New York Giants. (They'd gone to San Francisco.)

Sixties men were different from their fifties counterparts. Fifties men were hardworking, responsible, fairly well disciplined. A man did what a man had to do, and that was: to like football, be aggressive, never cry, always provide for his family, and stick up for the ol' US of A. During the 1960s, however, another sort of man showed up, one who began looking at women's concerns. In fact, some sociologists say that men began seeing "their own feminine side." In the sixties men became more thoughtful and gentle. The 1960s man was a nice guy who now pleased not only his mother but also the young woman with whom he was living. Notice the *with whom he was living*. In the sixties many unmarried men and women openly lived together without, as they used to say, the benefit of clergy. Of course, unmarried couples' living together wasn't new, but in the sixties it became more widespread and open.

Probably the biggest social change in America wasn't *what* we bought but *where* we bought it. Suburbs began enticing people to sleep there, even if they worked downtown, and shopping centers began replacing downtowns. In the early 1960s, many downtown business districts died, seemingly almost overnight. No longer relying on public transportation, shoppers needed a place to park their big, bigger, biggest cars, and many cities lacked downtown space to accommodate the growing number of automobiles. Out in the suburbs, roadside shops were joined with others into shopping centers and then into enclosed malls. Some even incorporated churches and community buildings. The first enclosed mall opened in Edina, Minnesota, in 1956. Minnesota seems to have led the way in building enclosed shopping malls, possibly because of the state's harsh winters. In Minneapolis, for instance, some downtown parking lots provided electrical outlets into which motorists could plug car-engine heaters.

Some cities fought suburban flight by converting their downtown areas into malls with no cars (or, certainly, few cars) allowed. The effort backfired, and Chicago is a typical example of what happened. The city whose State Street was "that great street" of musical fame closed a roughly four-block-long area to all vehicles except buses, fire trucks, and police cars. But Chicago, like many other large cities, didn't have enough downtown parking spaces. How could anyone drive downtown, park the car, and then go shopping? State Street decayed. It wasn't until the 1990s that city fathers finally admitted that State Street no longer was such a great street. They opened it to auto traffic, spruced up the sidewalks, installed new, old-style streetlamps, built parking garages (even though they might cost you a fortune to park in them), and businesses (and customers) returned in droves.

It used to be that nearly everyone used public transportation—buses, trolleys, and trains. But with the end of World War II, members of America's growing middle class wanted to own their own automobiles. Forget handcrafted cars, praise Henry Fords's mass-produced gas guzzlers. Who cared about the price of gas? It was cheap! The sixties were the time of tail-finned behemoths, and we loved them. General Motors, the company that began the "battle of the tail fins," raised it to new heights with the 1969 Cadillac: tail fins forty-two inches off the ground.

• • •

Perhaps an indication of America's love of cars was the toy slot car, small toys that ran in grooves on a track. You had a hand control to change the speed and race another slot car around the track. Slot cars had arrived from England in 1959 and, for the first time, passed toy electric train sales in America in 1963. By 1965, 3.5 million Americans a year were buying slot cars at prices ranging from three dollars to eight dollars per car. You could even race your slot car in what you might think of as "slot-car emporiums." You'd pay so much per half hour to race your car around a storefront tract. Not just kids either. Adults got in on the act. By 1967, however, the craze had died down, slot-car emporiums closed up, and toy sets began appearing at swap meets and antique stores.

But while the bloom may have been off the toy car fad, interest grew in the real thing. Car buyers during much of the sixties wanted something that would make them feel good, and as a *Collier's* magazine article put it, styling was "practically everything." This feeling lasted until Chevrolet came out with the, perhaps, misdesigned Corvair, the car that ultimately shattered America's confidence in Detroit's products.

In 1965, Department-of-Labor bureaucrat-turned-consumer-advocate Ralph Nader wrote *Unsafe at Any Speed*, primarily indicting the Corvair but claiming that the auto industry as a whole was guilty of sacrificing safety for style. Nader made the Corvair what it is today—extinct. General Motors responded by hiring private detectives to investigate Nader, a fact that GM president James Roche reluctantly admitted during a Senate Commerce Subcommittee hearing in 1966. Nader sued and Roche apologized publicly, settling out of court in 1970. Nader used the settlement money to set up the Center for the Study of Responsive Law. Students and lawyers, nicknamed "Nader's Raiders," compiled critical reports on industries and bureaucracies. On May 12, 1969, after ten years, Chevrolet discontinued the Corvair line.

While GM had trouble with Nader and the Corvair, Ford had one of the biggest successes in automotive history: the Mustang. During

World War II, Detroit automakers built tanks and planes. Immediately after the war they began producing big cars with space and safety for the tykes of the baby boom, but let's face it, those big cars looked and handled like tanks. By 1964, American families were ready for a second car, something a little more sporty than Ford's ill-fated, ill-designed Edsel, if you please. In what was officially called the model year 1964-½, the Mustang was an instant success when it was introduced on April 17, 1964.

About three weeks earlier, on April 1, Plymouth had introduced its own sporty car, the Barracuda. But all the excitement, both industry and public, went to the Mustang, brainchild of Ford executive and future Chrysler Motors headman Lee Iacocca.

An advertising campaign showed a mild-mannered Milquetoast named Henry Foster turn into a freewheeling playboy when he got behind the wheel of a Mustang. In its first twelve months Ford sold a record one million of these cars. In 1967, when GM finally brought out the Chevrolet Camaro as competition for the Mustang, it didn't come even close. The Camaro sold fewer than half as many cars as the Mustang.

Built by definition for those with a "need for speed," muscle cars came into being in 1964. Sure, there had been many high-performance cars before: think of the Stutz Bearcat and the triumvirate of Auburn-Cord-Duesenberg—"Gee, it's a Doosy" became a saying for "Gee, it's great."

Until 1964, *high performance* virtually meant "high priced" and production was limited, but then came Pontiac's ground-breaking (almost sound barrier-breaking) GTO. As *Car and Driver*'s David E. Davis put it, the GTO "appeared on the scene like a Methodist minister leaving a massage parlor." It wasn't just horsepower; it was the way that horsepower was packaged. GTO=Gran Turismo. Over the sixties, almost every American automaker used the letters GTO or GT and the GTO image to promote its big-block cars.

It was no mistake that, in 1964, rock singers Jan and Dean, clones of the Beach Boys, spun out "Drag City," then "Dead Man's Curve," and "Little Old Lady from Pasadena"—driving her bitchin' shiny red superstock Dodge all the way to No. 3 on the record charts. Singers and record producers publicized muscle cars to hot-blooded young car buyers.

Picking up on Pontiac's lead, Oldsmobile transformed its more sedate F-85 into the "four-barrel, four-on-the-floor, dual exhaust" 4-4-1. Mercury's Cyclone might have had more machismo than muscle at first, but it caught up. Today's sedate Buicks are unrecognizable to those who grew up on the Gran Sport (like Olds's 4-4-2, it had an earlier, more prim name: Skylark).

Chevrolet shoehorned its big-block MK IV V-8 into the Chevelle and created the SS 396. In 1966, Chrysler introduced its 426 "street hemi," a power option for the Dodge Charger. Even American Motors—it referred to itself as No. 4 after GM, Ford, and Chrysler's "Big Three"—got into the muscle-car act in 1968 with the two-seat AMX.

Almost as soon as Detroit kicked its muscle cars into gear, efforts were made to stop them. In 1965, the Clean Air Act was amended, forcing the advent of the PCV (positive crankcase valve). Instead of venting crankcase vapors directly into the atmosphere through a road draft tube, the PCV valve rerouted those gases back into the intake to be reburned. While helping to solve air pollution problems, the valve played hell with muscle cars.

Then came the mandated use of lower-octane unleaded fuels, and Ralph Nader began asking questions about automotive safety. In his State of the Union Address in 1966, President Lyndon Johnson claimed that our dangerous roadways represented America's largest problem, topped only by the Vietnam War. The auto insurance industry got in on the act, and by 1967 an unmarried, under-twenty-five male could expect to pay as much as seven hundred dollars a year on his GTO. If, that is, he had a halfway-clean driving record.

Still, muscle cars remained relatively popular. In 1969, when 8.2 million American cars were sold, ten percent of them were muscle cars. It had its tight little niche—not for everyone, not your uncle's kind of car—and it hung in there.

Then along came the counterculture and hippies. And flower power replaced horsepower.

For much of that you can thank a man whose name today is synonymous with style and power: Ferdinand Porsche. In the 1920s, he began tinkering with the idea of a small car that, like Henry Ford's Models T and A, would be for every man, the "people's car." He didn't have much luck pushing his idea till the thirties, when German dictator Adolf Hitler agreed to finance Porsche's experiments.* Hitler, who couldn't drive himself, loved to be chauffeured around in his big Mercedes, but he pushed the idea of a small car for everyone in the new Reich.

It would be called the KdF-Wagen, for *Kraft durch Freude*, "Strength through joy." It was Porsche, however, not Hitler, who designed the people's car. But the chancellor-dictator wanted the car to boost Germany's industry,** and he specified several things about it: A 26-horsepower engine that could get approximately 40 miles per gallon while achieving 100 kilometers (62.2 miles) per hour and maintaining that speed. Air cooled, because there were few private garages in Germany and an air-cooled engine wouldn't fail in cold weather. A four-seater, because it was, after all, to be a family car and cheap: base price, 990 German marks.

The price changed, but the basic KdF-Wagen as it was wasn't much different from the Beetle of the sixties in America or even from the Beetle that ended its American run in 1977. Well, Porsche did add rear windows to his KdF-Wagen in 1938; the prototype didn't have any, which of course made looking out the back kinda hard to do. Ferdinand Porsche also changed the way the car's doors opened. He'd originally had them opening front-to-rear (they're now referred to as "suicide doors") but changed them to the prevailing rear-to-front after visiting the United States and seeing how the automotive wind was blowing.

The KdF-Wagen was built by the German Labor Front, which Hitler had established to maintain industrial peace and to indoctrinate the workers. During World War II, production on the people's car pretty much stopped. Instead, the company built a strange-looking car named the Kübelwagen, or "bucket car," an open, almost square car, with the familiar VW slanting front, on which the spare tire was mounted. It was used by the German military and, with its air-cooled engine, was impervious to both African heat and Russian

---

* Volkswagen of America insists that "Volkswagen" became the official name only after the war, thus disassociating it from Hitler.
** Hitler wanted people to spend money on hard goods, not just on food or such.

cold. There was even a watertight version with snorkel and propeller called the Schwimmkübel.

In 1945, the American military took over the KdF plant near Fallersleben in Lower Saxony, five miles west of the Russian-occupied zone. At the end of the war, the town had been called Strength-through-joy but that had become unfashionable, and the city hadn't yet been named Wolfsburg. The Americans didn't know what to do with the bombed-out autoworks, and it passed into the hands of the British, who were delighted. America may have looked forward to big cars again, but the Brits wanted as many of the small, fuel-efficient vehicles as possible. The British people, however, weren't as accepting of a German car as had been the British military. Londoners said it was too ugly, bizarre, noisy, and flimsy, a mere toy not to be taken seriously. Which precisely described the little car's attributes and which were, in the 1960s, exactly what America's counterculture took to.

Following World War II, Britain controlled the auto plant. (American automaker Henry Ford looked at the little car but didn't want any part of it.) Four years later the plant was returned to German control. In that same year, 1949, America first imported the KdF-Wagen, now known as the Volkswagen "Beetle." Exactly two Beetles were sold here in '49.

By the sixties, they'd become the vehicle of choice for hippies—Beetles and the Volkswagen "microbus." Even today, you mention sixties and hippies, and the picture many people have is of a VW microbus, painted in psychedelic colors, driven by long-haired, pot-smoking hippies. The microbus, of course, led to vans (carlike bodies on top of full-size pickup frames), which led to minivans (carlike bodies on top of small pickup frames), which led to sports utility vehicles (SUVs), which led to Yuppies gobbling them up as soon as they hit the dealers, and that led to nearly every available parking space and parking lot being full.

In 1960, VW* pushed its size with the classic "Small Wonder" and

---

* In 1937, engine designer Franz Xavier Reimspiess produced the famous "VW" emblem, with the letters one above the other, enclosed in a circle. For his work, Reimspiess received a hundred-mark bonus on the next payday.

"Think Small" ad campaigns. At the end of the decade, the year NASA landed a man on the moon, Volkswagen used the practical-but-homely lunar lander in its ads: "It's ugly, but it gets you there." Along with: "While in Europe, pick up an ugly European."

Many Americans, even those not of the counterculture, thought the Bug's "ugliness" was one of its big selling points. They believed Porsche's people's car went beyond ugly to cute, which caused some company officials to wonder, "What happens when the Americans stop being amused by the Beetle?"

In 1962, Americans bought 192,570 of the little rear-engined cars, and despite an on-again, off-again "Buy American" campaign, the Beetle changed the way we drove and especially the way U.S. automakers built cars. The last of the German-made Type 1 Beetle sedans rolled off the assembly line in 1974. The U.S. plant continued production for three more years. The last of the American-made Beetle convertibles was produced in 1979, and the last German one in 1980. Meanwhile, the company's plant in Puebla, Mexico, continued building the Beetles. And then, in the 1990s, the "new" Beetle came along.

Maybe those hippies of the 1960s knew something.

Prior to World War II, poverty was a predominantly rural problem, but by the sixties, more than half of the nation's poor (fifty-five percent) lived in cities. Another thirty percent lived in small towns. Mechanized farming had driven many poor farm laborers* off the land and into urban centers. The advent of the mechanical cotton picker, for instance, displaced some 2.3 million farm workers, most of them African Americans. Through the mid-sixties, few rural blacks had much formal education beyond simple reading and writing; segregated school systems in the South either didn't allow poor blacks to move up the education ladder or the ladder simply didn't

---

* During the nineteenth-century young men working as migrant farm laborers would go from state to state, hired to hoe out crops. They were known as "hoe-boys," with the name shortened to "hoboes" and given to men (and women) of all ages who rode the rails from town to town during the Great Depression.

exist. When they moved to the cities, these "internal migrants" had few useful vocational skills.

In the early sixties, more whites than blacks were poor and were getting public assistance. These poor whites made up a small percentage of all whites and, for the most part, were either the elderly or were tucked away in rural areas. Because most African American poor now lived in cities, they were more visible than their rural white counterparts. They also were much younger.

Just as they would in the prosperous 1990s, during the prosperous 1960s, those who held the wealth looked upon those who didn't as a diminishing, but bothersome, group. Many of the wealthy believed that America's abundance was so great that something had to be wrong with anyone who was poor, or else he just didn't give a damn and wanted to stay on the public dole.

For those who shared the nation's prosperity, it was a wonderful life. As author John Updike put it: You'd drive your supercar along the superhighway to the supermarket where you bought Super Suds.

In 1960, federal courts ruled that D. H. Lawrence's novel *Lady Chatterley's Lover*, written thirty-two years earlier and sold openly in Europe since then, was not obscene. The U.S. postmaster general's office had struggled to keep Americans from reading the book about a young English noblewoman and her gamekeeper lover. Until the Supreme Court's favorable ruling, the publisher was barred from sending the books through the mail, and in effect that kept it out of bookstores. The high court ruled that *Lady Chatterley's Lover*, or any work, was acceptable if it didn't violate "prevailing community standards," whatever that meant. Very quickly, books such as Henry Miller's long-suppressed *Tropic of Cancer*, the eighteenth-century *Fanny Hill: Memoirs of a Woman of Pleasure*, and Frank Harris's autobiography, *My Life and Loves*, were allowed on the shelves, and a bookshop in one Ivy League college town began grouping such salacious works on a shelf labeled "Dirty Books."

With the publication of *Fanny Hill* and such, literary pornography, which had been around since the seventeenth century, virtually disappeared as a legal concept. Which is not to say the controversy ended in 1960. It continues today.

Take Terry Southern and Mason Hoffenberg's *Candy*—and a lot of people did—took the novel and, in the novel, took the character Candy Christian. Since its original publication in 1958, *Candy* has become a cult hit and went through several editions in the sixties. The paperback version was even a Book of the Month Club selection in 1994. As the blonde and beautiful nymphet herself might say, "Good grief!"

In the 1960s, Americans didn't read only "pornography"; they took to political works as well, such as John Le Carré's novel *The Spy Who Came In from the Cold*, Nevil Shute's antinuclear story *On the Beach*, Burdick and Wheeler's *Fail Safe*, depicting an accidental nuclear bombing, and Fletcher Knebel's *Seven Days in May*, something of a fantasy about a military coup in Washington. All four books became movies and depicted the threat and aftermath of nuclear war. Perhaps the best of all such antiwar books-into-movies, however, was *Dr. Strangelove, or How I Learned to Stop Worrying and Love the Bomb*. The screenplay, written by Stanley Kubrick, Peter George, and Terry Southern, was based on George's novel *Red Alert*. It had fictional air force general Jack D. Ripper sending his nuclear-laden bomber wing to strike the Soviet Union, whom Ripper believed had been poisoning the world's supply of water so as to contaminate man's "precious bodily essences." *Dr. Strangelove* came at a time when some extremists claimed that putting fluoride in America's water wasn't a plan to prevent millions of dental cavities but rather was an international Communist conspiracy to poison us. These books and movies, along with such films as *Easy Rider* and *Alice's Restaurant*, became part of the antiestablishment, antiwar, pro-youth movement.

Alice's Restaurant starred folk singer Arlo Guthrie, the son of perhaps the nation's greatest folk singer, Woodie Guthrie. The movie took its title from a real incident during which Arlo Guthrie was arrested for illegally dumping trash on a Thanksgiving Day, which "crime" later caused his rejection by the military draft. Being a litterbug, it seems, kept Arlo out of the Vietnam War. He turned the incident into a folk song—actually, about twenty minutes of hilariously droll story-telling—and turned the song into a movie and a career.

Just about everybody involved in the incident, it seems, profited from it. In the movie, the police officer who, in real life, had arrested Guthrie out of hatred of all hippies, played himself. Alice, who owned the restaurant, a bohemian bistro of sorts, wrote a cookbook and licensed a chain of "Alice's Restaurants." Arlo Guthrie, of course, not only made money on the movie and the song he wrote and sang, he later bought, renovated, and moved into the church where it all was said to have begun.

After a while, Arlo Guthrie retired "Alice's Restaurant" from the songs he sings in his frequent concerts. But thirty years after the original incident, it changed from being a sixties anti–Vietnam War protest song into something of a Thanksgiving ballad. Come Thanksgiving, Guthrie says, "we really work hard."

Maybe, Arlo Guthrie believes, the song "was never about the war. I think maybe it's about how to maintain a sense of humor in the face of adversity."

CHAPTER THREE

Burn, Baby, Burn:
The Riots of Summer

The mad truth: the boundary between sanity and insanity is a false one....The proper posture is to listen and learn from lunatics as in former times.
Norman O. Brown, Love's Body

The policeman isn't there to create disorder. The policeman is there to preserve disorder.
Chicago Mayor Richard J. Daley, during 1968
Democratic convention riot

In 1964, President Lyndon Johnson announced the opening of his War on Poverty, and in 1965, he signed into law the Voting Rights Act. It mandated the U.S. Justice Department intervene to provide federal examiners anywhere voter registration discrimination occurred. Thirty-seven Southern House members and six Southern Senators voted in favor of the bill, which surprised a lot of their constituents.

In 1965, Los Angeles's black ghetto of Watts erupted in flames, figuratively and literally. It began with a DWI, a charge of driving while intoxicated.

On August 11, a hot and muggy evening, police stopped a motorist named Marquette Fry on suspicion of drunken driving in Los Angeles's Watts area. Fry was, in twenty-first-century-speak, an African American; in 1960s language he was "black." In any case, the arresting officers were white, and as they questioned Fry, a crowd gathered around to watch and listen. Fry was argumentative and uncooperative, and frustrated police officers began beating him. Fry's mother and brother who were witnessing the scene, charged the cops with brutality, and police arrested them also. Soon the crowd of around two hundred was screaming insults and throwing rocks at the officers. It got worse and police headquarters sent in twenty-five car-loads of officers to hold the lid on the steaming crowd. It didn't work. The first major riot of the decade was under way. There would be hundreds more riots in the sixties, most of them between 1965 and '68, many of them beginning with a police incident.

At the time of the Los Angeles riot, 200 of the 205 police in the ninety-eight-percent African American area of Watts were white. In Los Angeles, as in many other American cities, many white police-men were admitted racists.

On the first night of the Watts riot, local black leaders organized a mass meeting at Athens Park to protest the police action. Civil Rights activist and comedian Dick Gregory used a police loud-speaker to speak to the crowd. He appealed to the mob to go home. The crowd not only ignored Gregory, but shot him, a bullet grazing his leg. Quickly, a crowd of more than a thousand gathered in the open park, and they took their protest beyond words. They spilled out into the streets of Watts, where they smashed store windows and looted everything in sight.

Watts erupted and violence quickly spread into other sections of the City of Angels. On Friday August 13, rioters began setting fires—from 4th Street to 108th Street; soon, southeast Los Angeles was cov-ered in thick black smoke. Rioters stoned city buses, looted shops and stores, and whole gangs fired shots at police, whom they accused of brutality. As a white motorist drove through the area, a crowd of angry blacks stopped the car, threw a Molotov cocktail into it, pulled the driver out, and beat the hell out of him. California governor Pat Brown called out the National Guard, and around 9:45 that night, two thousand guardsmen arrived. Meanwhile, a phrase begun by a local disk jockey became the cry of the mob: "Burn, baby, burn!" On Friday officials declared Los Angeles a disaster area and imposed an 8:00 P.M. curfew. From the *Los Angeles Times:**

---

* At this point, the *Los Angeles Times* had no black reporters or editors. In fact, during a twenty-year period, the *Times* ran only one or two major stories on the black community.

There are no words to express the shock, the sick horror. The first grim order of business is to put down what amounts to civil insurrection, using every method available.

Nine thousand armed police cordoned off a twenty-block area trying to contain the rioting. Finally, five days and thirty-four deaths after it began, things simmered down. Forty-one hundred people had been arrested, two hundred buildings destroyed, and another six hundred damaged. Property damage totaled $45 million.

Even before the riot, it was obvious that Watts hadn't benefited from President Johnson's War on Poverty. Everywhere were slums, slums, and more slums. Public facilities in the area were far below standard. For instance, none of the thirteen elementary schools in Watts had cafeterias, but that's all right; most pupils couldn't have afforded to eat there anyway. Some children weren't enrolled in school because they didn't have any shoes.

After the Watts riot, Los Angeles police chief William H. Parker defended his staff. They were, he claimed, "the most downtrodden, oppressed, dislocated minority in America."

A year later, in 1966, violence erupted on Chicago's west side after authorities shut off a fire hydrant black children were using to cool down in the ninety-eight-degree temperature. Later, in a Chicago park, whites attacked civil rights marchers demonstrating against unfair real estate practices. Riots occurred in several other U.S. cities in 1966: San Francisco; Cleveland; Atlanta; Omaha; Brooklyn; Lansing, Michigan; and Jacksonville, Florida. In Baltimore, white teenagers overran a black district after a National States' Rights Party convention was held in the city; and in Grenada, Mississippi, a mob of whites armed with ax handles and pipes attacked blacks trying to integrate schools. Then came 1967, and four thousand people were injured and at least ninety died in more than 120 riots.

In Detroit, it started with a blind pig. A blind pig?

A bit of background: In the sixties, the word *pig* became a derogatory term for police, but both *pig* and *blind pig* may have come from Civil War–era Richmond, Virginia. Police there were called the Public Guard, and guardsmen wore on their hats an insignia that read: "PG." That is: P (no I) G.

Now, a pig without an eye is blind, which in this case meant that the public guards were "blind pigs." Police officers who do not see (or choose not to see) illegal drinking establishments are blind pigs, and by extension, illegal clubs themselves are blind pigs.*

Early on Sunday, July 23, 1967, Detroit police raided a blind pig on the city's west side, at K Street and Linville. Detroit was suffering through a heat wave, and Saturday the twenty-second was the hottest day of a long, hot summer. Few innercity Detroit homes had air conditioning; residents opened windows, slept on fire escapes and rooftops, wherever they might get a slightly cool breeze. Both adults and children stayed out late at night, sitting on porch steps, joking, playing, and hoping things would cool down enough to get some sleep. Another way to cool off was to grab a quick beer at a local bar or, if it was past the bar's legal closing time, from a blind pig. In the early morning hours of Sunday, this particular blind pig was doing a good, if neither legal, unusual, nor unexpected, business. Neither unusual nor unexpected, because the small club had operated for several years with, if not their blessing, the acceptance of local police at the precinct right around the corner. Why police chose this particular blind pig at 3:45 in the morning isn't known, but they did and local residents didn't seem to mind too much. In fact—probably more as a sign that they were having a good time than that they approved the raid—locals stood on either side of the door and cheered as police brought illegal imbibers out in handcuffs. At first.

Cheers, however, changed to jeers. Maybe somebody—police or citizen—bumped into someone else; in the heat of the night someone said to back off; and someone else pushed or hit back. Soon, the raid on the blind pig had turned into a riot, with charges of police brutality and countercharges of attacks on officers. The riot grew and overwhelmed city police. Rioters smashed windows and looted stores, not just white-owned stores, but any store or business they came across. "Perhaps," as historian Arthur Marwick wrote, "it was a

---

* In Chinese communities, illegal gatherings in which a game called "tiger" is played are called "blind tigers."

perverse tribute to the more integrated nature of [the] city." Arson fires began licking at buildings. Even middle-class blacks joined in the burning and looting; children joined in "the fun."

About then the riot claimed its first victim: Krikor Messerlian, an immigrant shoemaker, was clubbed to death by looters while others looked on. Soon, another victim was killed: a forty-five-year-old white man shot by a white store owner allegedly for looting.

Within hours, two hundred people had been arrested, and Detroit's popular Democratic mayor, Jerome "Jerry" Cavanagh, was faced with a problem. He likely would run for his party's presidential nomination next year, but how could he expect to govern a nation if he couldn't control one city?

By 8:00 A.M., the crowd around the blind pig was estimated at more than three thousand. Finally, Cavanagh had no other choice, and he asked Michigan governor George Romney to declare a state of emergency and call out the National Guard. Romney, a Republican, was also expected to make a run for the presidency. It would be to Romney's political advantage to make his potential Democratic opponent sweat a little in the July heat of a riot. Republican Romney let Democrat Cavanagh stew. Finally, Romney called out the guard, but they were too few, too late, and too undertrained. Just as had the Detroit police, the seven thousand mostly white* guardsmen were overwhelmed by the growing, mostly black, crowds.

The tactic was to send armed guardsmen in with unloaded weapons. Sure. Many guardsmen disobeyed the order. Within hours, they'd locked and loaded their weapons, and it wasn't deer hunting season. This led to sometimes fatal situations. In one instance, a guardsman killed a twenty-three-year-old white man. In another, the victim was much younger. Herbert J. Locke, the administrative assistant to the Detroit police commissioner, told the story of young Tanya Blanding:

> Sporadic sniper fire had been reported in the immediate area earlier in the evening and on the previous night. Guards-

---

* Blacks made up only 1.5 percent of the National Guard in 1967.

.

men reported one of their units coming under fire . . . and believed they had pinpointed it as coming from the apartment in which Tanya and her family lived. Precisely what happened next is unclear; apparently as a Guard tank was being moved into position directly in front of the building, one of the occupants of the . . . apartment lit a cigarette. Guardsmen opened fire with rifles and the tank's .50-caliber machine gun. At 1:20 A.M. Tanya . . . was dead.

She was just four years old. A later investigation showed that there had been no civilian gunfire, no civilian snipers when Tanya Blanding was killed. Inexperienced national guardsmen had shot at themselves and the local police.

Plainly, it was time for Michigan authorities to call for outside help, regular troops, something Governor Romney didn't want to do. Just as Democrat Cavanagh had hesitated, so did Republican Romney. Finally, on July 25, the governor called the president to ask for regular army troops. The last time an American city had called on Washington to send in federal troops, it had also been Detroit. That had been in 1943 when Franklin Roosevelt was president.

In 1967, the president was Lyndon Johnson, who hadn't yet decided not to run for reelection the following year, and so he hesitated, making his possible Republican opponent wait. Another thirteen people died before Johnson called in his troops, forty-seven hundred paratroopers. When they arrived, they were fully armed—no "unloaded" weapons for them—complete with tanks, machine guns, and helicopters. Detroit residents (and thanks to television, the nation) were treated to the sight of tanks rumbling down American streets, stopping, aiming, firing, and blasting the hell out of American houses. It looked as if the war in Vietnam had come home.

Black rioters shot or threw stones at police and destroyed businesses owned by both blacks and absentee-landlord whites. However, they spared nearly all public facilities such as libraries and schools.

James Ingram was a Detroit auto worker but later became a newspaper reporter. Police arrested him for trying to buy gasoline on the third day of the riot, after gasoline sales had been halted. "We were taken to the Seventh Precinct," he said in an interview for an oral history of the civil rights movement.

> The [patrol wagon] doors were flung open and somebody started yelling, "Run, niggers, run." And an officer started slinging us out of the van. I couldn't see that clearly what was going on in front of me, but I was the last one out of the van and I saw my brother in front of me being swung at. There were national guardsmen on the right and police on the left, and they were swinging rifles and swinging these brightly painted red pickax handles and I was trying to dodge some of the swings. I don't know how I got through there with only being hit one time with a rifle barrel. That's what broke my right arm.

They were placed in a holding cell, which, Ingram recalled, "was rather large but still very crowded because there were so many people in there." Over the next several days city and state police, national guardsmen, and regular army troops arrested 7,231 people. Most of them were black, but at least 700 of those arrested were white. According to Detroit judge James H. Lincoln, blacks and whites "looted together in the feast of camaraderie. In one police precinct, the white and Negro snipers had one of the best relationships."

That didn't always happen. While James Ingram was in the holding cell, police brought in a young white man. Everybody else was black or Hispanic.

> And this young white kid came in, and some of the younger black guys, as soon as he got inside that door and the door was slammed shut, just charged him. He apparently was fairly alert, because he knew right away he was going to be dead meat. He literally climbed the steel bars of the door and climbed almost all the way up to the ceiling. . . . At that point, [I said], "Leave the kid alone. He's not bothering anybody."

Ingram was taken to be fingerprinted, "a young guardsman holding a rifle to my head." A police officer grabbed his hand and squeezed it real hard and said, "Relax, nigger." The auto worker complained "I can't relax. . . . Why don't you have him take his gun from my temple? What am I, John Dillinger, going to escape? I'm totally surrounded by you guys. I'm cooperating." As an answer, Ingram said, the officer put a cigarette out "right on my hand."

When he was finally released from jail, Ingram left "with a burning, raging fury inside of me." He and seven others formed "something that we called the Order of the Burning Spear, and that was our primary mission—to kill white people, beginning with the police and guardsmen."

At one point, there were more than seventeen thousand law-enforcement officers in Detroit. Within a few hours of the start of the riot, six people were dead and hundreds more were injured. Within a week, frightened guardsmen, who'd been ordered not to load their weapons, had fired 150,000 rounds of ammunition. In Washington, Federal Bureau of Investigation (FBI) director J. Edgar Hoover reported, "They have lost all control in Detroit." He believed that "Harlem will break loose within thirty minutes." Apparently certain that there was some kind of conspiracy, Hoover added that blacks in Harlem "plan to tear [New York City] to pieces."

Forty-three people died in the Detroit riot, and another two thousand were injured. As many as thirteen hundred buildings were damaged or destroyed, and twenty-seven hundred businesses were looted in a hundred block area. Damage was estimated at more than $36 million, and more than five thousand individuals were left homeless. It was the worst riot in American history. Even today much of Detroit is a burned-out hulk because of a riot more than thirty years ago.

In Newark, New Jersey, five days of rioting took twenty-three lives and injured thirteen hundred others. Yet another thirteen hundred individuals—most of them black—were arrested. They singled out white-owned businesses for looting but didn't burn them down, mainly because in many cases rooms above the white-owned stores were occupied by black families.

As they had in Detroit, national guardsmen in Newark proved to be trigger happy. When a guardsman shot at a black man standing in an apartment window, a hundred other guardsmen opened fire. With that, guardsmen began firing at will. They killed a grandmother and her daughter and her four-year-old granddaughter. They shot a young woman as she pulled her two-year-old daughter away from a window. Of the twenty-three dead in the Newark riot, six were women, two were children, and one was a seventy-three-year-old man. It wasn't until the national guardsmen were pulled out of Newark that the rioting ended.

It was obvious that the situation between blacks and whites was volatile, so President Johnson appointed a Special Advisory Commission on Civil Disorders to investigate the riots. In his report to the president, commission chairman Otto Kerner wrote: "Our nation is moving toward two societies, one black, one white—separate and unequal." Racism, the former Illinois governor declared, wasn't just a Southern problem. In what became known as the Kerner Report, he said that every major riot was precipitated by the

> arrests of Negroes by white police for minor offenses. . . . Thus, to many Negroes police have come to symbolize white power, white racism, and white repression. And the fact is that many police do reflect and express these white standards. . . . What white Americans have never understood, but what the Negro can never forget—is that white society is deeply implicated in the ghetto. White institutions created it, white institutions maintain it, and white society condones it.

Newsweek magazine declared 1967 our "Summer of Discontent." Postriot reaction saw suburban whites demand law and order and urban blacks demand an end to police brutality. As for the results of the Detroit riot—other than large burned-over sections of the city— what happened? As in many other cities, whites began abandoning the downtown area; you worked downtown during the daylight hours, but before the sun set, you'd head out the Lodge Freeway to Ferndale, Royal Oak, or Birmingham. Urbanologists debated whether whites left the city because it was unsafe or if it was unsafe because they left it. Never mind; it amounted to the same thing either way.

An ad hoc citizens' committee named New Detroit set out to learn what could be done to correct the problems that many felt had brought on the riot and, importantly, what could be done to prevent a recurrence. After a long study, they recommended everything from brighter streetlights to higher educational requirements for police. And of course they also recommended another study that allowed those who'd thought up the whole thing to perpetuate their employment.

The New Detroit proposal was a grandiose scheme that carried a high price tag. When asked just how much it would cost, city officials claimed it wouldn't cost a thing. How could it *not* cost? they were asked, but the reply was only a smile. Really, the answer was simple: The plan wouldn't cost anything to implement if you didn't implement it.

One thing *did* come out of the Detroit riot: a new style of architecture developed for the lower floors of downtown buildings. It used rifle-slit-like windows reminiscent of the Wild West—you could shoot out the slits, but it was more difficult to shoot in—making the buildings look like concrete forts that would be hard to vandalize. It was the postriot school of architecture.

Even as riots burned on in many cities around the country, Lyndon Johnson's Great Society tried to aid America's poorest citizens. However, it spent only about fifty dollars per person to ameliorate a worsening situation, and that wasn't nearly enough. The government's Great Society handed out a relative pittance to its own people but spent a fortune trying to stop Communism in Vietnam. For each Viet Cong killed, the American taxpayer spent over three hundred thousand dollars, and as one comedian remarked, for that kind of money they could have paid the VC not to fight.

CHAPTER FOUR

Battles Won:
Civil Rights

I forgot about praying, and I just turned and ran.
Sheyann Webb, civil rights marcher at Selma,
Alabama, March 21, 1965

I want every American to stand up for his rights, even if he has to sit down for them.
President John F. Kennedy

On September 20, 1958, in a department store in Harlem, New York, a middle-aged black woman pushed through a crowd of autograph seekers and stood in front of the man who was signing his newest book, *Strike Toward Freedom: The Montgomery Story*. The woman asked the author, "Are you Mr. King?" The Rev. Dr. Martin Luther King Jr. nodded his head and the woman stabbed him with a seven-inch letter opener, then began beating him with her fists.

An ambulance rushed King to a hospital and police rushed Mrs. Izola Ware Curry to jail. King was still sitting in the chair where he'd been signing books and still had the letter opener stuck in his chest, near the aorta, the main heart vessel. Doctors rushed him into surgery and saved his life. It's not certain why Mrs. Curry attacked him, but apparently she meant business. In addition to the letter opener, she had a loaded pistol in her purse.

In 1959 a young Detroit man borrowed eight hundred dollars from his parents' savings club and set up shop as a record producer in a small house on Detroit's northwest side. He called the company Tamla Records, and its first national release was "Money (That's What I Want)." In April 1960, the company changed its name. Founder Berry Gordy Jr. wanted something that would reflect the city of Detroit, the Motor City, so he called it Motown.

Gordy went scouting Detroit high schools, looking for talent, and he ran across an all-girl quintet that called themselves the Cansinyets. Their name pretty much said it all: it was a contraction of "can't sing yet." Gordy wasn't particularly impressed with the Cansinyets but told them to come up with some new material and come see him. They did. Their song was called "Please, Mr. Postman," and Gordy signed the Cansinyets to a contract. Gordy changed their name to the Marvelettes and recorded the song with young Marvin Gaye on drums.

After fifteen weeks of slowly rising on the music charts, the record finally made it to the top. That was the longest it had ever taken a number one hit to reach the top. No matter; it and Motown Records were there.

After the Marvelettes came groups such as the Supremes and the Temptations, known earlier as the Elgins. The Motown Sound took its place in American entertainment, grown from a family-owned business to an international enterprise. Motown was black owned, and the coming of "Please, Mr. Postman" marked the end of all-white control of the record business.

By the end of the twentieth century, some African Americans had come to view integration as a negative force. "Integration" had given way to "black power," then to "nationalism," "Afrocentricity," and "multiculturalism." At the start of the twenty-first century, integration can scarcely be said to be anyone's stated ambition. In the sixties, however, it was a moral lodestar for many, black and white; integration was to the 1960s what emancipation had been in the 1860s.

After the American Civil War, after the Emancipation Proclamation, and with the advent of the Thirteenth Amendment, slavery no longer existed legally. Financial and emotional slavery, however, are different beasts, and the economic gap between blacks and whites continued over the years.

On January 31, 1960, a white waitress at the "Whites Only" lunch counter at the F. W. Woolworth five-and-dime store on Elm Street in Greensboro, North Carolina, refused to serve an African American freshman student from nearby North Carolina Agricultural and Technical College. The student returned the following day with three friends, and again waitresses refused service. Store manager Frank "Curly" Harris had told his employees to ignore the group. With that, the four—Ezell A. Blair Jr., Franklin E. McCain, Joseph A. McNeil, and David L. Richmond—began a sit-in that quickly spread to other states. They argued that the 1954 U.S. Supreme Court ruling in *Brown v. Board of Education of Topeka* said that legally enforced segregation was unconstitutional. The media soon referred to the group as the "Greensboro Four," or in some cases, the "Four Freshmen," after the singing group.

A Woolworth's regional manager denied that the Greensboro store discriminated. "We haven't refused anybody," he told the press. "Our girls have been busy and they couldn't get around to everybody."

Quickly, the sit-in attracted national interest. When a reporter asked them, "How long have you been planning this?" one of the students answered, "All our lives."

Within a few weeks thousands of other African Americans and a few white supporters began hundreds of sit-ins at restaurants across the South. Up North, students staged sympathy sit-ins at local Woolworth's counters. By the end of the year, seventy thousand people in more than 150 cities in five states had participated in sit-ins, and more than three thousand of the protestors had been arrested.

A month after the Greensboro action, San Antonio, Texas, became the first major Southern city to desegregate five-and-dime store lunch counters. Restaurants in Tennessee, North Carolina, and Virginia followed suit, but soon, to avoid integration, variety stores began closing down their lunch counters. Today, part of the original Greensboro, North Carolina, Woolworth's counter is on exhibit in Washington's Smithsonian Institution. The store itself is closed—the last Woolworth's closed in 1997—but may one day become a civil rights museum.

Jim Crow was white—a white stage actor named Thomas Dartmouth Rice, who performed in blackface. He wrote a song-and-dance minstrel tune that became a hit in the 1830s:

Weel a-bout and turn a-bout,
    And do just so.

Every time I weel about
    I jump Jim Crow.

In just a few years *Jim Crow* became a synonym for *Negro*. The image was of a stupid, jumping, and slouching rag doll of a man.

Soon, Jim Crow laws crept onto the books. The first probably dealt with railroad cars. In 1896, the U.S. Supreme Court ruled in *Plessy v. Ferguson* that "separate but equal" facilities were just fine, thank you. African American Homer Plessy had appealed against his conviction for refusing to leave a railroad car reserved for whites. The high court's ruling said the judgment against him did not infringe on his Fourteenth Amendment rights. In dissent, Justice John M. Harlan warned that the ruling was "inconsistent with civil freedom" and would support prejudice. He was right and it did. Following *Plessy v. Ferguson,* localities began operating "separate but equal" schools, restaurants, water fountains, railroad waiting rooms, and just about anything else you can think of. *Plessy* opened the door to racial segregation.

Jim Crow laws went so far as to say that white nurses, for example, could not tend black patients or black nurses tend white patients. For a while, black barbers couldn't cut "white" hair. In Alabama, blacks and whites couldn't shoot pool together. Black and white juvenile delinquents in Florida could be housed "no nearer than one fourth mile to one another." In Georgia, "in no case shall Negroes and white [mental patients] be together. In Louisiana, if whites and blacks attended the same circus, then there had to be separate ticket offices "not less than twenty-five (25) feet apart." You could be fined five hundred dollars and spend six months in jail in Mississippi if you were caught "printing, publishing, or circulating printed, typewritten, or written matter urging or presenting for public acceptance or general information, arguments or suggestions in favor of social equality."

In at least one incidence, the owners of a drive-in theater erected a wire fence right down the middle of the parking area to prevent integration: white-operated cars relegated to one side and black-operated vehicles to the other. Jim Crow at its most ridiculous.

In the post–Civil War Reconstruction Era, African Americans

picketed, boycotted, and marched in protest. And in one of the most horrific chapters in American history, many blacks were lynched. Over the years, integration remained not much more than a dream in black communities. As the 1960s began, resistance to integration remained strong among many whites, but in fact most whites probably never gave the issue much thought. The views of some of those who did think about it were reflected in a sign in a Texas restaurant: "We Do Not Serve Mexicans, Niggers, or Dogs."

By no means was racial segregation and conflict confined to the South. For example, on October 3, 1967, Chicago's sixty-three-year-old Riverview amusement park closed. The official explanation was that the land had been sold for more than $6 million to a group of developers. But that wasn't the real reason. The park and its midway, complete with freaks and geeks and Kewpie dolls, attracted both blacks and whites, and in those racially tense times, that just wouldn't do. As the *Chicago Daily Tribune*'s Herb Lyon reported in his "Tower Ticker" column:

> Midst all the dripping nostalgia over the demise of Riverview, one sorry fact stands out. It was sold to industrial interests primarily because of the unprecedented leap in juvenile delinpunksy this past season. In fact, it was a tinderbox nightly, with violence lurking behind the roller-coaster fun—and is one more casualty of the way things are.

In other words, the still-profitable park located on Chicago's North Side closed due to racial conflict. Rather than cope with the lurking black-white tension, and the possibility of what even a mini–racial riot could cost them, Riverview's owners shut down the park.

Powerful energies were let loose in the 1960s. Americans began to redeem themselves at lunch counters and bus terminals. We developed superhighways and supercomputers, and perhaps more so in the sixties than in any other decade, we began to develop a conscience. But it took a long time, and one of the big sticking points between whites and blacks was housing. Take the Long Island, New

York, community built by former Navy Seabee Bill Levitt. Using Henry Ford's mass-production techniques, in the spring of 1946, Levitt threw up two thousand identical Cape Cod houses and set the price at under seven thousand dollars. With no down payment required, hundreds of desperate veterans with their new wives and even newer children lined up at the sales office. On October 1, 1947, the first family moved into the first completed Levittown home. Eventually, the project expanded to 17,447 homes on Long Island alone; they went on to mushroom just as fast in Pennsylvania.

In 1960, Levittown, New York, consisted of 17,400 houses with 82,000 more-or-less happy residents. Because of the number of young families, and the growing number of children in those families, some folks called Levittown "Fertility Valley" and "The Rabbit Hutch." Others denounced Levittown as a "social cancer," but Bill Levitt offered working people a chance to own a home—white working people that is.

Of the 82,000 who lived in Levittown, none was African American. The developers told black families outright not to bother trying to buy a home in Levittown. They were not welcome.

As described earlier in "A Sixties Prelude," in the early 1950s, Oliver Brown tried to enroll his daughter Linda in a school near where they lived in Topeka, Kansas. But the Browns were black, so the school refused to admit her. Brown sued the school board, and the case went all the way to the U.S. Supreme Court, which, on May 17, 1954, struck down the so-called "separate but equal" doctrine in public education.

Prince Edward County, Virginia, had been part of the original *Brown v. Board of Education* suit and was one of the areas that bused its black students out of the area rather than provide "equal" facilities. After the high court decision, the county shut down *all* public schools and channeled state and local funds to "private" schools. On May 25, 1964, the U.S. Supreme Court unanimously barred the county's actions. Justice Hugo Black wrote that "the time for mere 'deliberate speed' has run out. . . . There has been entirely too much deliberation and not enough speed in enforcing the constitutional rights which we held had been denied." Prince Edward County finally obeyed the order, but white students switched to private schools rather than go to class with African Americans. It would be years before schools were fully integrated in some sections of the country.

On May 4, 1961, the Congress of Racial Equality (CORE) sent two busloads of black and white "Freedom Riders" from Washington to New Orleans. CORE officials envisioned it as a more or less leisurely tour with brief stops along the way to challenge segregated bus waiting rooms and lunch counters. It was the first interracial demonstration in the Deep South, and came while the Kennedy administration was pushing Supreme Court rulings on segregation of public facilities, particularly bus stations.

The high court had earlier outlawed segregated seating in interstate travel on trains and buses, and CORE had tested the ruling's enforcement. Several CORE members were arrested at the Asheville, North Carolina, Trailways station, convicted, and sentenced to thirty days on a chain gang. In 1960, the Supreme Court expanded its earlier decision to include attendant facilities serving interstate travelers, that is, waiting rooms and bus-station lunch counters.

By custom in the sixties South, train and bus stations had separate (but not necessarily equal) facilities: One rest room and lunch counter for blacks and one for whites. Such segregated bus stations cost about fifty percent more in construction than nonsegregated ones but were considered a necessity. At some Deep South bus stations, signs were posted saying, WHITE INTRASTATE PASSENGERS, an attempt to retain segregated facilities for in-state passengers. In effect, this kept all bus stations in the Deep South segregated, no matter where the buses and their passengers were headed.

So, two groups of Freedom Riders—six whites and seven blacks, including CORE president James Farmer—left Washington in two buses, one Greyhound and one Trailways, and headed south. They hoped to reach New Orleans by May 17 in time to celebrate the seventh anniversary of the Supreme Court's *Brown v. Board of Education* decision.

The Freedom Riders got their first serious opposition in Anniston, Alabama, where a group of angry whites attacked the Greyhound bus with chains, sticks, iron rods, and incendiary bombs. They dented the bus, broke out windows, slashed the bus's tires, and tried to board the bus; finally, a group of local police blocked the attackers, and the bus moved on. About two miles out of town, however, on Route 202, the bus's slashed tires gave out. The mob had been following the bus, and with the cops gone off, they resumed the attack in a frenzy of wild cries. Someone in the crowd shouted, "Let's roast the niggers!" and the mob tossed smoke bombs into the bus. Gasping for air, passengers staggered off the bus and sprawled on the roadside grass; many of them were beaten before highway patrolmen returned to clear the area. Twelve passengers were hospitalized and the burned-out skeleton of the Greyhound bus had to be abandoned. Hearing about the attack, Alabama governor John Patterson said, "When you go somewhere looking for trouble, you usually find it."

The Trailways bus driver heard police sirens in the distance and stopped briefly in Anniston. He didn't see what was happening, so he continued on to Birmingham, where another mob awaited and there were no police in sight. As the Trailways passengers exited the bus, the mob attacked. One passenger, James Peck, required fifty-three stitches to close wounds to his head from a beating with an iron pipe; another suffered permanent brain damage. "In Birmingham today," television reporter Howard K. Smith said, "crowds of angry citizens gathered to protest against the so-called 'Freedom Riders' from up North."

> Thirty to forty toughs had been waiting. They grabbed the passengers and pushed them into alleys and corridors, beating them with pipes, with key rings and fists. . . .

Birmingham police responded slowly to the attack, arriving more than ten minutes after it began, because, according to the chief, so many officers were off celebrating Mother's Day. The police chief? Theophilus Eugene "Bull" Connor. He was a combination of police chief, police commissioner, and the city's director of public safety. Connor had vowed to "keep the niggers in their place." After Montgomery's bus boycott in the fifties, many people believed he had been waiting for something to happen, something to make his name known around the country. His wish was about to come true.

Birmingham was forty percent black, and that forty percent was almost one hundred percent poor and destitute. It was a polarized city, the all-black Sixteenth Street Baptist Church representing one pole and Bull Connor the other, church against law. By 1953, black police officers were employed in eighty Southern cities, including Nashville, Tennessee, and Atlanta, Georgia. There were none in Birmingham.

"Some of the attackers got into waiting cars and moved down the street," Smith reported. "I watched some of them talking about what they had just done. The discussion took place under Police Commissioner Connor's window."

Later, two groups of students left Nashville, Tennessee, for Birmingham by car. They showed up at the Greyhound station intent on completing the Freedom Ride to New Orleans, but there were no bus drivers around. Seeing the Tennessee group standing around the bus station, Bull Connor's police took them into custody, and just before dawn, officers drove them the 120 miles back to the Tennessee state line, where they forced the students out of the cars and left them standing by the side of the road.

By nightfall, however, the students were back in Birmingham, where they staged an all-night vigil at the Greyhound station. Frantic telephone calls raced between Kennedy Administration officials in Washington, D.C., and Alabama governor John Patterson at the capital in Montgomery. Finally all sides agreed, a bus driver was found who would drive them, and the Nashville group left Birmingham under state protection, headed for Montgomery. When the bus reached the Montgomery city limits, however, the escort—sixteen highway patrol cars and an airplane—melted away. By the time the bus reached the Greyhound station, the streets were quiet. Too quiet, as all the horror movies say. Waiting at the bus station was another mob of angry whites. They savagely beat the Freedom Riders as well as several bystanders.

U.S. attorney general Robert Kennedy tried to contact Alabama governor Patterson, but this time the governor didn't answer his phone. Kennedy sent in some five hundred federal marshals to restore order, and the next day the marshals broke up a crowd gathered outside the First Baptist Church where Martin Luther King Jr. was preaching to a packed audience of more than fifteen hundred people. The lawmen used tear gas to protect King, who told his audience, "Fear not. We've come too far to turn back."

Four days later the Trailways bus was back on the road, headed for Jackson, Mississippi. It rolled past rows of U.S. marshals and Alabama national guardsmen with fixed bayonets, but when the bus reached the Mississippi line, there was a changing of the guard. The federal marshals withdrew. Bobby Kennedy, it seems, had agreed not to enforce integration law if Mississippi prevented further violence.

Mississippi troopers took over and the bus continued on to Jackson. There was no violence, but at the bus station police immediately arrested some black students for crossing over into the white section of the waiting room. Altogether, more than twenty-seven people, including CORE director Farmer, were arrested for attempting to use white facilities. They were the first of more than three hundred people to be arrested in the Jackson area that summer for testing the Supreme Court ruling. Most Freedom Riders refused bail and refused to pay fines. James Farmer told CORE members, "Fill up the jails, as Gandhi did in India. Fill them to bursting if we have to."

All told, there were twelve Freedom Riders, and despite the violence and arrests—perhaps, because of them—the campaign succeeded in uniting the various groups, succeeded in pulling young blacks into the movement, and succeeded in focusing national attention on the cause of civil rights. On September 22, the Kennedy Administration petitioned the Interstate Commerce Commission (ICC) to forbid common carriers—planes, trains, and buses—to use segregated terminals.

In the end it was blacks and whites working together who made changes in the sixties. As writer James Baldwin said in *The Fire Next Time:*

> The price of liberation of the white people is the liberation of the blacks—the total liberation, in the cities, in the towns, before the law, and in the mind.

In 1961, a twenty-eight-year-old U.S. Air Force veteran named James Howard Meredith applied for admittance at the University of Mississippi. "Ole Miss," as it's still known, was all white; Meredith was African American and the school denied him admission. Meredith sued. In the trial, Ole Miss registrar Robert Ellis testified that he was "shocked, surprised, and disappointed" that James Meredith would think he'd been rejected solely because of his "race and color." Are there any black students at Ole Miss? he was asked. "I have seen students with varying degrees of darkness of skin," Ellis claimed, "but I can't tell you whether any of them were of the Negro race or not." In 2001, well-known African American actor Morgan Freeman (whose last name should tell you something right there) did promotion commercials for Ole Miss. Apparently, the times have changed.

On September 10, 1962, the U.S. Supreme Court ruled that Meredith should be admitted to the school without further delay, and the university's board of trustees reluctantly announced that they would comply. However, Mississippi governor Ross Barnett stepped in to block Meredith's enrollment, claiming it was an issue of state's rights against the federal government. On the twentieth, surrounded by U.S. marshals, Meredith tried to enroll; backed up by his state police, Barnett denied them entrance to the school. Four times Meredith tried to enroll, and four times Ross Barnett stood in his way. At least three Mississippi judges had ordered Meredith arrested instead of admitted to Ole Miss, but on September 28, the U.S. Fifth Circuit Court of Appeals found Governor Barnett guilty of civil contempt and ordered him to admit Meredith to Ole Miss by October 2 or face arrest and fines. On the thirtieth, President Kennedy federalized the Mississippi National Guard, sent in 170 deputy U.S. marshals, and went on nationwide television to explain his actions. Still, rioting broke out, pitting the marshals against more than a thousand white students and hundreds of other segregationists who threw gasoline bombs, bricks, stones, and metal pipes, and then set fire to cars and buildings.

During the riot, Mississippi officials withdrew state police officers, leaving the federal marshals to face the crowds by themselves. Before federal troops could arrive to restore order, 165 people, including 28 federal marshals, were injured.* three bystanders, including French journalist Paul Guilhard, who covered the event, were shot and

---

* One source gives the casualties as 2 killed and 375 injured, including 166 U.S. marshals.

killed. As usual in such disturbances, Ole Miss officials declared that almost all of the rioters were "outside agitators." A Mississippi newspaper headlined: "On Your Guard—Commies Using Negro as Tool" and "Thousands Said Ready to Fight for Mississippi."

Finally, on October 1, 1962, James Meredith registered and began attending classes under federal guard. Twenty-three thousand soldiers guarded him at a time when nearly every other person connected with the military was preparing for war with the Soviet Union if the Cuban Missile Crisis had turned into a shooting match.

Meredith's enrollment didn't settle the issue, however. The Mississippi legislature passed a bill—basically, it was a bill of attainder*— making Meredith a criminal and thus ineligible for classes. As *New York Times* writer Thomas Buckley reported:

> Virtually all 4,638 white students at the University of Mississippi exist in an isolation more profound than that which they impose on the one Negro Student, James H. Meredith. . . . Faculty members and other observers believe that Mr. Meredith's presence on the campus is forcing the white students to think seriously for the first time about the racial issue and their attitudes toward it. . . .
>
> [G]iven the intensity of feeling about Mr. Meredith, the first student to shake his hand or join him for coffee in the cafeteria will be courageous. There are many reports that even a smile or a nod in his direction has resulted in a student's being punched or cursed.

Despite continued objections, continued harassment, and under constant federal guard, James Meredith graduated from Ole Miss, the first African American in the formerly all-white school's history.

---

* A bill of attainder is a legislative act that applies "either to named individuals or to easily ascertainable members of a group in such a way as to inflict punishment on them without a judicial trial." Article I of the United States Constitution prohibits bills of attainder, which doesn't mean they're never enacted. For example, in 1943, the Urgency Deficiency Appropriations Act forbade the paying of salaries to certain named government employees because Congress objected to their views.

Four years after he'd finally been admitted to the University of Mississippi, Meredith began a solo Memphis-to-Jackson march to encourage voter registration. A white agitator, hiding in ambush, shot Meredith in the back with a shotgun. Taken to Memphis Memorial Hospital, James Meredith met with Martin Luther King Jr. of the Southern Christian Leadership Conference, Student nonviolent Coordinating Committee (SNCC) leader Stokely Carmichael, and Floyd McKissick of CORE.

Carmichael wanted to turn the freedom march into an all-black protest. However, King refused and said that if that happened, he'd withdraw his support. Whitney Young of the Urban League and Roy Wilkins of the National Association for the Advancement of Colored People (NAACP) *did* withdraw their support when Carmichael insisted on drawing up a manifesto critical of American society in general and the federal government in particular.

The shooting of James Meredith drew hundreds of civil rights advocates—black and white—to finish the march he'd begun. But throughout, the police continued harassing them, attacking them, and beating marchers along the way. The march ended on June 26 with a rally of fifteen thousand people in front of the Mississippi state capitol in Jackson. Martin Luther King and Stokely Carmichael addressed the crowd, but it was obvious that a schism had developed in the civil rights movement. King told the crowd of his dream, that one day in Mississippi "justice will become reality for all of God's children." But those more closely aligned with Carmichael argued that blacks had to "build a power base so strong in this country that we'll bring [whites] to their knees every time they mess with us."

The march that James Meredith began led to the registration of four thousand black voters; however, it was the last time King's Southern Christian Leadership Conference and Carmichael's Student Nonviolent Coordinating Committee ever marched together. Their differences had become too pronounced.

As for James Meredith, after the shooting, a sheriff on the scene watched as the attacker got away. No one was ever convicted in the attack. Meredith, however, survived his wounds. In September 1963, he wrote Attorney General Bobby Kennedy:

I am a graduate of the University of Mississippi. For this I am proud of my Country—the United States of America. . . . I believe that I echo the feeling of most Americans when I say that "no price is too high to pay for freedom of person, equality of opportunity, and human dignity."

During the 1962–1963 school year, ninety-two of every one hundred black students in the South attended segregated schools. However, change seemed to be on the horizon. On July 18, 1963, the Gallup Poll reported that three out of four Southern voters questioned believed that widespread integration would come within ten years. They were right, but it would take a lot of work and come at the expense of several lives, both black and white.

In June 1964, the civil rights movement planned a "Freedom Summer" to focus national attention on state segregation laws. The movement got attention but not in quite the way desired.

Some one thousand university students, teachers, lawyers, and ministers from around the country went south to work with local chapters of the Student Nonviolent Coordinating Committee (SNCC) to register black voters and to set up forty-one alternative "Freedom Schools." Mississippi newspapers called it "an invasion."

The "invaders" held nightly meetings, explaining to blacks the goals of the newly formed Freedom Democratic Party, and they signed up thousands of members. But the more people who signed up, the stronger the resistance grew. Segregationists burned down fifteen black churches and beat up eighty freedom workers. Police were no help. Instead of protecting the workers, local and state authorities arrested hundreds of them on various, usually unsupported, charges.

Then, on June 21, 1964, the cops fired a shot that was heard almost literally around the world. Three civil rights workers left Meridian, Mississippi, that day to drive out to the nearby Mount Zion Church. Freedom Movement leaders had asked the church's congregation to allow the old hand-built structure to be used as a Freedom School. The congregation had agreed to do so, but before the school could begin, someone—presumably members of the Ku Klux

Klan—torched the church with gasoline. So the three young men went out to see what they could do for the people who'd tried to support the cause. They never reached the burned-out church and they never returned to their office in Meridian.

Earlier in the year, one of the three, Andrew Goodman, a student at Queens College in New York, had written a term paper on the startling racial controversies emerging from the Nation of Islam:

> While it is somewhat of a fantasy to believe that all white men are devils, it is true that the white man (and by this I mean Christian civilization in general) has proved himself to be the most depraved devil imaginable in his attitudes towards the Negro race. . . . The historical contempt that the white race held for the Negroes has created a group of rootless degraded people.

Goodman had followed up on his college paper by volunteering to work in the South for Negro civil rights. With him that June day were project leader Michael "Mickey" Schwerner, a social worker two years out of Cornell University, and James Chaney, a CORE staff worker. On the day they were last seen by fellow Freedom workers, a student volunteer from Bryn Mawr College sat in the movement headquarters and wrote home, explaining why "we're all sitting here in the office being quietly nervous as hell." Nineteen-year-old Edna Perkins wrote:

> This morning Mickey, who's the project director, and Chaney, a local staff member, and Andy [Goodman], who's a volunteer, all went out to one of the rougher rural counties to see about a church that was burned down a few days ago. . . . No word of them of any kind. We've had people out looking for them and they haven't found anything. . . . They said that Meridian was an easy town.

The day after the three disappeared, U.S. attorney general Robert Kennedy ordered a full-scale investigation. As investigators later put the story together, Goodman, Chaney, and Schwerner left the Meridian office only to be picked up by Neshoba County sheriff Lawrence Rainey and his deputy, Cecil Price, and hauled to the local jail for questioning. Rainey and Price held them for six hours—after all, Chaney was black and he was riding around with two white boys known to be outside agitators. Finally, the officers released the three young men, and that's when they "disappeared."

When asked about the disappearances, Sheriff Rainey questioned whether they really were missing. The three "just hid somewhere trying to get a lot of publicity out of it, I figure," Rainey claimed.

Rainey knew it wasn't a publicity stunt, because Deputy Price had followed the three young civil rights workers when they left the jail. Following them also was a Ku Klux Klan death squad. Together, they forced the trio's station wagon deep into the piney woods. Then, the Klansmen stopped the car, pulled Mickey Schwerner out, and shot him in the heart. They grabbed Andrew Goodman and shot him in the heart also. It all happened fast. A Klansman cried, "Hey, save one for me," and he yanked James Chaney out of the car. They beat Chaney with chains until virtually every bone in his body was broken. Then they shot him three times.*

Attorney General Kennedy had not only sicced the FBI onto the missing men, he'd approached President Lyndon Johnson. Kennedy hoped LBJ would make a statement of personal sympathy for the families. "I think," Bobby told Johnson, "it's the human equation that's damn important for everything." Later that day, Johnson got in touch with aides Nicholas Katzenbach and Burke Marshall. "How old are these kids?" LBJ wanted to know, as if their age mattered.

Told they were twenty, twenty-two, and twenty-four (and advised not to see the families, who were in Washington, D.C., at the time) LBJ went for the idea of discreetly putting pressure on Mississippi. Katzenbach and Marshall believed that any matter broached publicly

---

* Just ten days before he was murdered, James Chaney had become a father. The child, Angela McCoy Lewis—Chaney and Angela's mother weren't married—later said that it felt "real strange" to sit in a Meridian, Mississippi, history class, which by then was integrated, and hear her father talked about as just another chapter in the civil rights struggle. Angela is a mother herself now, and her son carries his grandfather's name, James.

in a civil rights case would make cooperation politically ruinous for state officials. So Johnson called longtime friend Senator James East-land of Mississippi. As chairman of the Senate Judiciary Committee, Eastland had killed all but one of the 121 civil rights measures that had gone into his committee over the past decade. Obviously, his wasn't a sympathetic ear to civil rights causes.

"Jim," Texas rancher Lyndon Johnson said to Mississippi Delta landowner Eastland, "we got three kids missing down there."

Eastland replied, "What can I do about it?" Besides, he added, "I don't think there's a damn thing to it." Neshoba County was right next to fellow senator John Stennis's home county, and everyone knew, Senator Eastland said, "There's no organized white man in that area," no Klan klavern, no Citizens' Council. Eastland told the president that "I think it's a publicity stunt."

With two hundred sailors searching the countryside and a tip from a KKK informant, FBI agents found the Freedom Workers' CORE-owned burned-out car. Well, actually, a couple of local Indians had found the still-smoldering Ford Fairlane station wagon. It was in a thicket about eight feet off the highway, near the bridge over Bogue Chitto Creek. They reported the car and admitted stealing the car's hubcaps, but "we didn't set it on fire," they claimed.

Just six minutes after President Johnson talked with Senator East-land, FBI director J. Edgar Hoover called LBJ and said, "I wanted you to know that we have found the car [but] we can't tell whether any-body's in there in view of the intense heat." Soon, photographs of the charred station wagon circled the globe, but the car was empty. The bodies were still missing.

On Tuesday, August 4, 1964, President Johnson announced on na-tionwide television that North Vietnamese PT boats had attacked U.S. destroyers in the international waters of the Gulf of Tonkin, and that he had ordered air strikes against the North. The Vietnam War was heating up.

That same day, in the Mississippi swampland, in 106-degree heat, workers dug into the Olen Burrage earthen dam. Once again, FBI agents had been tipped off. This time, they were told where the bod-ies of Goodman, Chaney, and Schwerner could be found buried.

Taking turns, FBI agents and sailors swatted swarms of blowflies and dug a fourteen-foot-deep pit. Soon, the reason for the many blowflies became obvious: Something dead was buried in the dam. The smell of decay got to the diggers and many of them started puffing away on strong cigars to mask the odor.

Two hours later, they unearthed the body of a shirtless man, face-down in the hole, his arms outstretched. FBI agents bagged the man's hands and someone pulled a billfold out of his back pocket. It contained Mickey Schwerner's draft card. Using a prearranged code designed to thwart eavesdropping Mississippi authorities, an FBI inspector at the scene notified headquarters of the discovery: "We've uncapped an oil well."

Next, another body—Andrew Goodman—was exhumed, partially hidden under Schwerner. Then, in almost a parody of black workers' complaints, James Chaney—the last murdered and the first buried—was uncovered.

Not until December 1964 did the FBI arrest anyone in the murders. Of twenty-one people (including Sheriff Lawrence Rainey and deputy Cecil Price) who originally were charged, a grand jury indicted eighteen. Only seven were convicted and sentenced to jail terms ranging from three to ten years. Rainey and Price weren't among those acquitted. Or found guilty. In fact, they never even went to trial.

The number convicted could have been fewer than it was. The trial judge earlier had become locally famous by comparing blacks to chimpanzees. As it was, the local courts dismissed the confessions of two Klansmen, saying their admissions were hearsay. No state charges were ever brought in the three murders.

Relatives of Chaney and Schwerner wanted them buried side by side. Officials denied the request under a Mississippi law that required segregated cemeteries.

If the killers of Schwerner, Chaney, and Goodman had meant to scare Freedom Workers off, they didn't succeed. The number of blacks registered to vote that summer continued to build and, in the end, totaled more than eighty thousand.

• • •

The murders of the three young civil rights workers were bad enough, but Hollywood made things worse when it told the story in a 1989 film, *Mississippi Burning*. The movie had bright-eyed and bushy-tailed FBI agents storming into Mississippi, miraculously discovering the three bodies and just as miraculously solving the question of who killed them.

In truth, FBI director J. Edgar Hoover only reluctantly sent agents into Mississippi to check out the killings. Certainly there wasn't a black agent along on the hunt, as the movie had it. At the time, the only African Americans employed by Hoover's FBI were chauffeurs.

According to Hollywood, a Rambo-style FBI agent overcame the white-trash racism of the locals and rounded up the killers. Well, maybe. Actually, the FBI made no progress at all in solving the crime until KKK informers were offered a thirty-thousand-dollar bribe. Honor among thieves and murderers, it seems.

Another problem with *Mississippi Burning*, historian William H. Chafe wrote, was that it portrayed the deaths as a war among whites. No black protagonists, not much black participation in the Freedom Summer, and certainly little black outrage. About the only anger expressed came near the end of the movie when a black minister declared at the funeral of a black lynching victim that he was "sick and tired of going to the funerals of black men who have been murdered by white men."

Actress Jennifer Grey played Mickey Schwerner's wife, Rita, in the TV movie, *Murder in Mississippi* and she admitted that shooting the film down South sometimes worried her. "It was a little disturbing," she remembered, "when we did the Klan scene and some of the extras asked if they could bring their own robes."

J. Edgar Hoover may have been more interested in trying to pin charges of communism and sexual misconduct on Martin Luther King Jr. than he was on protecting civil rights workers. Hoover never did like King and he once sent the civil rights leader a note suggesting that King commit suicide.

In 1965, a young U.S. Army pilot named Jim Tilmon tried to become a commercial airline pilot. American Airlines was ready to hire him, but Tilmon couldn't get the army to release him. For whatever reason, everyone from his commanding officer on up the line refused to grant Tilmon an early release. Perhaps because he was African American and, in 1965, the army didn't have many black pilots.

An aide to Vice President Hubert Humphrey heard about Tilmon and he told his boss. And Humphrey told the chairman of the Joint Chiefs of Staff. And the chairman told the secretary of the army. Who told the commanding officer. Who said something to the effect of Happy to oblige, sir. And with that Jim Tilmon got his release and became only the third African American to become a commercial airline pilot. Moving from the back of the bus to the front of an airliner wasn't easy.

In 1963, the centennial of the Emancipation Proclamation, Southern Christian Leadership Conference founder Martin Luther King chose to make a symbolic stand in Birmingham, Alabama, "the most thoroughly segregated big city in the U.S.," he said. It was a time and place where blacks couldn't eat in white restaurants, a time when "white" and "colored" rest rooms were commonplace, and a place where "white" water coolers might stand in the front of buildings while "colored" water spigots were out back. The SCLC wanted to change all that, to desegregate such facilities.

Awaiting King in Birmingham was Bull Connor, a man who prided himself on "keeping the niggers in their place." He'd predicted that "blood would run in the streets of Birmingham before it would be integrated." When protestors in their Sunday best gathered, Bull Connor beat and arrested them—wherever they were gathered, at lunch counters, in the streets, anyplace he found them.

The SCLC's plan was to have Martin Luther King subject himself to arrest on Good Friday, but that was April 12, four days away. King said that he was willing to go to jail and stay there. For the first time, he would be defying a court injunction against protests.

Almost as soon as King walked out into the streets of Birmingham, Bull Connor arrested him, King's hand-picked successor Ralph Abernathy, and about fifty others. It was eight days, not until April 20, before they were released. During King's time in jail, he wrote to a group of unsympathetic white clergymen what came to be known as the "Letter from a Birmingham Jail":

The Negro's great stumbling block . . . is not the White Citizen's Counciler or the Ku Klux Klaner but the white moderate who is more devoted to "order" than to justice . . . who paternalistically believes he can set the timetable for another man's freedom.

For years now I have heard the word wait. It rings in the ear of every Negro with piercing familiarity. This wait has almost always meant never. We must come to see . . . that justice too long delayed is justice denied. . . .

The letter had tremendous impact on the movement across the nation, but it apparently had no effect on Bull Connor. Day after day, the number of demonstrators grew, and day after day Connor arrested them.

Finally, on May 2, more than twenty-five hundred Negroes poured out of churches and tried to push their way downtown. Connor and his cops met the protestors with clubs and fire hoses carrying seven hundred pounds of pressure. An armored car bulldozed its way through the crowd, but that didn't stop the demonstrators. Even as they were being beaten back by the clubs and hoses, Negroes united in anger, and still their numbers grew.

Hoping to negotiate an end to the protests and arrests, U.S. assistant attorney general Burke Marshall flew to Birmingham, but even as he arrived another racial fire blazed up.

Alabama governor George Wallace announced that he would not allow two black applicants to be admitted to the University of Alabama. "I'm gonna make race the basis of politics in this state," he had told legislators the day he was sworn into office, "and I'm gonna make race the basis of politics in this country."

On April 25, Bobby Kennedy joined Burke Marshall and together they flew to Montgomery to meet Wallace face to face in the state capitol. Some six hundred state troopers encircled the building, and when Kennedy tried to go inside, a trooper jabbed him in the stomach with a billy club. "The point," Kennedy later said, "was to try to show that my life was in danger in coming to Alabama because people hated me so much."

Inside, before they began speaking, Governor Wallace turned on a tape recorder. He wanted to make a record of what went on. He tried to get Kennedy to agree not to send any more federal troops into the state, but Bobby reminded the governor that "I have a responsibility that goes beyond integration or segregation to enforce the law of the land and to insure that court orders are obeyed."

With that, George Wallace began a long lecture, preaching to Kennedy and Marshall about states' rights, the Negro "situation," and what he intended doing about those "problems." After an hour of this, with neither side giving in, the meeting ended.

Several weeks later, during a helicopter ride with Wallace to Muscle Shoals, Alabama, where they were to dedicate a Tennessee Valley Authority project, President Kennedy himself tried to win Wallace over. JFK offered to fund several federal projects in Alabama if George would let the two students enroll in Huntsville. It didn't work.

Meanwhile, rumors spread that the KKK planned to attack Martin Luther King in the Birmingham jail. King's wife, Coretta, called the White House to ask for the president's aid in protecting Martin, but JFK wasn't there—Papa Joe was ill, so Jack was with him—and Bobby talked with her. He listened and promised to check into the situation. The next day President Kennedy called Mrs. King to say that her husband was safe and that Martin would soon call her himself. A few minutes after the conversation, Dr. King *was* out of jail and on the phone to Coretta.

The battle for Birmingham, however, continued. When 6,000 African American school students marched and sang through the streets, Bull Connor again turned fire hoses on them, sending children flying into parked cars and curbs and trees. Bull and his boys then arrested 959 children.

The following day 2,000 more protestors marched through Birmingham, and Bull Connor unleashed a pack of snarling attack dogs on them. This time, also, photographers were on hand as the dogs tore into the children's arms and legs. "What really sticks in my mind," remembered one witness, "is seeing a K-9 dog being sicced on a six-year-old girl." Andrew Marrisett used to drive the Sixteenth Street Baptist Church bus and he knew many of the children.

I went in front of the girl and grabbed her, and the dog jumped on me and I was arrested. That really was the spark . . . a big, burly two hundred and eighty-five pound cop siccing a trained police dog on that little black girl. And then I got really involved in the Movement.

Soon, pictures of the attack were in newspapers and on television newscasts all over the world. The effect was devastating, and it once more sent Burke Marshall to Birmingham to try to negotiate a peace settlement with members of the white business community.

Finally, he and his assistant Joe Dolan brokered a deal. It would give Martin Luther King a measure of desegregation in restaurants as well as a promise that white merchants would increase black employment. The question was whether the deal would hold. The answer was no.

The day after the deal was worked out, the KKK held a rally. They burned crosses and threatened to attack any white who agreed to the brokered deal. Within hours, bombs exploded in the black community, one at the home of Martin's brother, Reverend A. D. King. The other hit the SCLC headquarters at the Gaston Motel. In neither place was anyone injured, but blacks were furious and took to the streets. This time they were not nonviolent.

George Wallace sent in state troopers, and they attacked the protestors with rifle butts and clubs. The riot raged on into the night, as blacks set fire to six white-owned businesses and an apartment complex.

President Kennedy chose not to send in federal troops, believing that was just what George Wallace wanted. Instead, he ordered Gen. Earl G. Wheeler to airlift troops to Fort McClellan and to keep them on standby for possible deployment the following day. With three thousand federal troops nearby, police finally restored order in Birmingham, and the nation's attention turned elsewhere.

In Jackson, Mississippi, NAACP field secretary Medgar Evers was just stepping out of his car and was walking into his house with an armful of "Jim Crow Must Go" T-shirts. Someone shot him in the back, killing him almost instantly.

In an abandoned lot across the street from Evers's home, police found a deer rifle that they identified as the murder weapon. It was owned by a former fertilizer salesman named Byron de la Beckwith and even had his fingerprint on it. When he was captured, Beckwith insisted that he had been ninety miles away in Greenwood when Evers was killed. Twice in 1964 Beckwith was tried for Evers's murder and twice the juries deadlocked.

Years later, Evers's widow, Myrlie Evers Williams, convinced Hinds County, Mississippi, district attorney Bobby DeLaughter to reopen the case, and in 1994, at the age of seventy-four, Beckwith once again stood in front of a Mississippi jury. The self-proclaimed white supremacist wore a Confederate flag pin in his lapel, which may not have been his smartest move. The third time around, eight of the twelve jurors were black, and after two weeks of jury selection, testimony, and deliberation, they found Beckwith guilty of murdering Medgar Evers thirty-one years earlier.

On a Saturday morning in 1965, as Martin Luther King and Ralph Abernathy drove from Atlanta, Georgia, to Selma, Alabama, they talked about the line of succession in the SCLC. President Johnson, King knew, worried what might have happened if two years earlier, following Kennedy's death, Johnson himself had died before Hubert Humphrey was sworn in as vice president.

This was before the Twenty-fifth Amendment to the Constitution went into effect, setting out how, in the event both the president and vice-president die, the line of succession will form. At the time, the empty presidency would have fallen to aging House Speaker John McCormack or to the equally frail Senate president pro tem, Carl Hayden.

If Lyndon Johnson had "sense enough" to find a remedy, King said, then "I should have sense enough to do it." Death, Dr. King realized, was never far from where he walked. And now he was about to march from Selma to Montgomery to protest voter discrimination. Both King and Abernathy knew that anything could happen during the march, including their deaths.

During another voter registration drive, Ralph Abernathy went with several people as they tried to register. They failed to pass the four-page literacy test and Reverend Abernathy believed it was because they'd failed to fill in all the blanks, even where the questions were irrelevant. So, when it came his turn to register, he made certain he left no spaces empty, sometimes writing, "This does not apply to me."

The voting inspector thumbed through his test, expecting to say, "You didn't fill in all the blanks." But as she flipped through the pages, she realized that Abernathy had answered all the questions. At least he'd written something in. "Her eyes glazed over," Rev. Abernathy said, "and it was in that moment that I understood what was going on. She didn't know the answers to the questions herself!"

The inspector couldn't fail him on the written test, so she added a new obstacle, an oral question: "Recite the Thirteenth Amendment," she ordered. Abernathy, however, didn't know the amendment word for word—ratified in 1865, it abolished slavery—but he didn't think the inspector did either. So, he recited the Pledge of Allegiance instead. Abernathy was right; the voting inspector had no idea what the Thirteenth Amendment said, and he got to vote.

Selma civil rights leaders hadn't talked much lately about voting rights, hadn't talked much about anything, not since Judge James A. Hare had issued an injunction forbidding discussion of racial issues at any gathering of "three or more persons." His injunction eventually would be declared unconstitutional by the federal courts, but meanwhile those same courts were taking their time with the issue.

King and Abernathy were about to test Judge Hare's opinion (and power) at an address in the imposing, double-towered Brown Chapel AME. It was to be a joint mass meeting: the Brown Chapel congregation along with those of the Tabernacle Baptist and the First Baptist churches. It would help that Dallas County sheriff Jim Clark would be out of town.

He was attending the University of Alabama Crimson Tide–Texas Longhorn football game in Miami's Orange Bowl. The tide lost 21–17, despite the heroics of Alabama's quarterback, a long-haired Yankee named Joe Namath.

When Martin Luther King Jr. was just a child, he was riding with his father when the senior King was stopped by a policeman. In the way of the pre-sixties South, the officer said, "Boy, show me your license."

"Do you see this child here?" Martin Luther King Sr. said, pointing to his young son. "He's a boy. I'm a man." It didn't faze the policeman. He gave Daddy King the ticket anyway.

Back in November 1962, Dr. Martin Luther King Jr. addressed a group of supporters in Rocky Mount, North Carolina, about 130 miles due east of where four young college students had begun a lunch-counter sit-in back in February 1960. That night, King test-drove, if you will, a phrase he'd use later on. Before a crowd of about two thousand, King said:

> My friends of Rocky Mount, I have a dream tonight. I have a dream that one day right here in Rocky Mount, North Carolina, the sons of former slaves and the sons of former owners will meet at the table of brotherhood.

He would come back to that idea.

A. Phillip Randolph of the Negro American Labor Council had first proposed a march on Washington in 1941, more than twenty years earlier, but he couldn't get enough backing to go ahead. Certainly, he couldn't get any white backing.

But on August 28, 1963, nearly a quarter of a million people gathered at the Lincoln Memorial in Washington, D.C. Millions more watched on television. The demonstration was held to show support for the Civil Rights Bill being debated in Congress. It was the largest demonstration Washington had seen and included such notables as singer Joan Baez and actors Paul Newman and Marlon Brando.

King was the main speaker, addressing the crowd near the end of the day. He swung off into the rhythm of down-home Gospel preaching, using the Rocky Mount theme:

> I say to you today, my friends, that in spite of the difficulties and frustrations of the moment I still have a dream. It is a dream deeply rooted in the American dream.
>
> I have a dream that one day this nation will rise up and live out the true meaning of its creed: "We hold these truths to be self-evident, that all men are created equal."
>
> I have a dream that one day on the red hills of Georgia the

sons of former slaves and the sons of former slaveowners will be able to sit down together at the table of brotherhood.

I have a dream that one day even the state of Mississippi, a desert state sweltering with the heat of injustice and oppression, will be transformed into an oasis of freedom and justice.

I have a dream that my four children will one day live in a nation where they will not be judged by the color of their skin but by the content of their character.

I have a dream today.

I have a dream that one day the state of Alabama, whose governor's lips are presently dripping with the words of interposition and nullification, will be transformed into a situation where little black boys and black girls will be able to join hands with little white boys and white girls and walk together as sisters and brothers.

In the White House, President John F. Kennedy watched King on television. "That guy," JFK said, "is really good." Reporter James Reston of the *New York Times* was in the crowd at the Lincoln Memorial and later wrote that "It will be a long time before [America] forgets the melodious and melancholy voice of the Rev. Dr. Martin Luther King Jr. crying out his dreams to the multitude."

One person who didn't agree with King's speech was Black Muslim Malcolm X, who'd earlier referred to King as "just a twentieth-century Uncle Tom." Malcolm X called the gathering at the Lincoln Memorial a "Farce on Washington":

The marchers had been instructed to bring no signs—signs were provided. They had been told to sing one song: "We Shall Overcome." They had been told how to arrive, when, where to arrive, where to assemble, when to start marching and the route to march. First-aid stations were strategically located—even where to faint!

Yes, I was there, I observed that circus. Whoever heard of angry revolutionists all harmonizing "We Shall Overcome . . . some day. . . ." while tripping and swaying along arm-in-arm with the very people they were supposed to be angrily revolting against? Whoever heard of angry revolutionists swinging their bare feet together with their oppressor in lily-pad park pools, with gospels and guitars and "I Have a Dream" speeches?

Malcolm X and Martin Luther King met; it seems, only once, on March 26, 1964, in Washington, D.C., seven months after the march. As civil rights propaganda, the meeting had considerable value, with both men pledging to work together to pressure Congress into passing the pending civil rights legislation. Ideologically, however, Malcolm and Martin remained antithetical personalities.

Born Malcolm Little, he adopted the Islamic faith while serving a six-year prison sentence for armed robbery. Following his release from prison, he joined Elijah Muhammad in the group then known as the "Black Muslims." He changed his last name to "X" to represent an ancestral name lost in slavery. Less than a year after the March on Washington, Malcolm X broke with the Black Muslim movement of Elijah Muhammad and established a nonsectarian, politically oriented black nationalist party, the Organization of Afro-American Unity. In 1965, he was gunned down in a Harlem auditorium. Allegedly, his assassins were followers of Elijah Muhammad.

In 1964, as Congress debated the Civil Rights Bill, eighty-one-year-old Representative Howard W. Smith of Virginia thought he'd found a way to shoot down the measure. He and other Old South colleagues attached to it so-called "killer amendments." The bill carried a list of who would be protected by the law and involved "race, color, religion or national origin." To that, Smith and his good ole boys added the word *sex.* Nobody, they assumed, would vote to protect equality of the sexes. To Congressman Smith's chagrin, not only did the Civil Rights Bill pass, but it carried along with it the "sex" amendment protecting women as well as African Americans.

The director of the Equal Employment Opportunities Commission claimed that the bill hadn't really been meant to prevent sex discrimination. Never mind; it did, and over the next several years women filed more discrimination complaints than did any other single group. On July 2, President Johnson signed the 1964 Civil Rights Bill into law, women's rights and all.

During the summer of 1964, Freedom Summer in Mississippi, while members of SNCC moved through the state trying to get African Americans registered to vote, four literacy volunteers from Northern colleges settled instead in Selma, Alabama. Going against SNCC's cautious plans, these four decided on direct confrontation. It was July 4, and they wanted to celebrate the new civil rights law at the segregated Thirsty Boy drive-in restaurant. But a few minutes after the four arrived there, Sheriff Clark drove up, his squad-car siren wailing for all it was worth. He proceeded to introduce himself with a cattle prod. Clark quickly hauled the four literacy workers off to jail. But that didn't end it, not by a long shot.

It was a time when, if a town didn't have separate movie theaters, it segregated the ones it did have, usually relegating blacks to the balcony, which was known derisively throughout the South as "Nigger Heaven." On this July day, to protest the arrest of the literacy four as much as segregation in general, part of the black crowd at Selma's Wilby Theater decided not to take it anymore. They left "Nigger Heaven" and invaded the white downstairs seats. Whites cried out, "There's niggers in the Wilby!" Sheriff Clark quickly responded, and just as quickly he closed the theater and chased the "offending" blacks outside. That sent some people back to church for the first time in years and the Zion AME hall was packed that night.

Church or not, sanctuary or not, Sheriff Clark didn't like the idea of so many "Nigras" meeting at one time. A posse of fifty special deputies hurled tear gas canisters into the church, and when the congregation ran outside, the "peace" officers attacked them with billy clubs.

The following morning civil rights leader John Lewis led a group of seventy aspiring voters to the Dallas County Courthouse. Sheriff Clark and his deputies met them and herded them into a back alley, out of sight of reporters. Reporters, hell! He chased them off. About twenty would-be voters were left. Clark arrested them—apparently just for being there. As the *New York Times* reported, "The Negroes were marched five blocks to jail." The story added that "repeatedly jolted by cattle prods, they responded with 'Freedom songs.' It was then that Judge James A. Hare issued his injunction banning any "assembly of three persons or more in a public place."

All of this, including the new civil rights law, caused Alabama governor George Wallace to announce that "liberalism is destroying democracy in America."

Back in 1926, black activist and writer Langston Hughes had written in "Negro":

I am a Negro.
Black as the night is black,
Black like the depths of my Africa.

In the sixties that became: Black is beautiful.

In 1960, Dwight Eisenhower was president and many young boys and men sported crew cuts. About half the student population at Chicago's Hirsch High School was white. In 1969, Richard Nixon was in the White House, and long hair was all the rage. That year, the senior class at Hirsch held a mock election to select, for the first time, a "Mr. and Mrs. Afro" (for a while, "afro" was *the* hairstyle for many men and women, black and white). By then, the south side school population was almost a hundred percent African American, the Vietnam War was raging, and blacks were beginning to like who they were.

Between 1960 and 2000 the area around Hirsch changed from a racially mixed, though predominately white, neighborhood to one predominantly black. In 1950, the Grand Crossing community near Hirsch showed a ratio of 94.1 percent white to 5.8 percent black. Following the Supreme Court's *Brown v. Board of Education* decision, white residents began moving out to the white-bread suburbs. By 1960, 86 percent of the Grand Crossing neighborhood was black. And by 1970, it had changed to 98.1 percent black and only 1.5 percent white.

In 2000, when a group of Hirsch sixties-era alumni held its fortieth reunion, no whites attended.

In 1966, Maulana Karenga, a professor in the department of black studies at California State University at Long Beach, created the celebration known today as Kwanzaa. It was to be a cultural observance to promote pride and community self-reliance for African Americans. *Kwanzaa* comes from the Swahili word meaning "first fruits of the harvest" and the celebration runs between Christmas and New Year's Day. During each of Kwanzaa's seven days, a single principle for living, represented by a Swahili word, is offered up for reflection. *Umoja,* or unity. *Imani,* or faith.

At first Kwanzaa struggled for acceptance, but now it's celebrated by millions of Americans. You can, for instance, go to many stores and buy Hallmark and American Greeting Cards wishing you a joyous Kwanzaa. It's become a big business. *Ebony* magazine predicted that in 2000, Kwanzaa businesses would sell about $700 million in cards, gifts, and ceremonial objects. The U.S. Postal Service offered an official Kwanzaa stamp.

It has become so big that some black activists are afraid that the celebration created during the turbulent sixties will go the way of Santa Claus and the Easter Bunny, its original intent lost and its message muddled and commercialized. In fact, to some members of the African American community it's become a little too well accepted by non–African Americans. At some churches the seven-day event is celebrated by both whites and blacks, but some African Americans don't want whites joining them in the celebration. White people, they say, are "coming uninvited" to African American Kwanzaa celebrations.

Kwanzaa, a celebration devised for and by blacks, and begun during the height of racial distress in the 1960s to honor one heritage, is being accepted by another. Problem is, the greater the acceptance, the more multicultural and more commercial it gets, and the more diluted Kwanzaa is likely to be. If some African Americans have their way, a celebration invented to defy segregation may itself become segregationist.

Two 1967 films centered around the issue of sex and race. In one, *In the Heat of the Night,* black big-city detective Sidney Poitier had to help white small-town police chief Rod Steiger solve a crime. Detective Tibbs (Poitier) did just that after realizing that a deputy assigned to drive him around town purposely went out of his way to avoid having Tibbs see a young white woman who frequently hung around the house half naked. Couldn't have that.

In *Guess Who's Coming to Dinner*, Poitier was engaged to pretty (and white) Katharine Houghton, the real-life niece of and reel-life daughter of star Katharine Hepburn. So Poitier and Houghton were about to have dinner with longtime liberals Hepburn and Spencer Tracy, who were longtime liberals offscreen as well. Tracy and Hepburn were a bit shocked, not by their daughter's getting ready to marry a black man, but by the fact that they didn't like the idea. It all worked out, of course.

It especially worked out at next year's Academy Awards presentation. *In the Heat of the Night* won the Oscar for best picture, and Rod Steiger took home the best actor award. Katharine Hepburn won best actress honors.

CHAPTER FIVE

Battles Tied:
The Cold War

With my understanding of the intricate relationships between the peoples of the world and your sensitiveness to the political considerations involved, we will make the most successful team in history.
John Foster Dulles to Dwight D. Eisenhower
after being named secretary of state

The immediate cause of World War III is the preparation of it.
C. Wright Mills

In the sixties, America's population stood at about 177,830,000. About 3.8 million people were unemployed. For those who held jobs, the average salary was $4,743. Strangely enough, the average teacher's salary was slightly higher, $5,174. Minimum wage was a buck.*

• In 1960, a U.S. pharmaceutical company applied for permission to sell the West German–made drug thalidomide. It had been used for years in Europe as a general-purpose tranquilizer among pregnant women for sleeplessness, asthma, and nausea. U.S. Food and Drug Administration researcher Frances Kelsey believed that something was wrong with the drug, and she hesitated about approving thalidomide for American distribution.

She was proved right. Researchers found that more than ten thousand babies worldwide had been born with birth defects after their mothers had taken thalidomide—infants born with

---

* Minimum wage was $1.00 in 1960; $1.15 1961–62; $1.25 1963–66; $1.40 in 1967; $1.60 1968–73.

malformed legs and arms, some with hands growing out of shoulders without arms. Because the drug wasn't generally used in America only ten children were born here with thalidomide-related deformities. And because she'd hesitated, Frances Kelsey was awarded a gold medal for distinguished public service.

• In 1960, Thomas S. Monaghan borrowed five hundred dollars to buy a pizza parlor in Detroit. He renamed it Domino's and started a nationwide chain. Nine years later, he bought an old, crumbling-down abandoned Detroit concert hall, planning on tearing it down to build another pizza parlor. But a local television crew sneaked into the shuttered building and filmed a short piece showing what would be lost if the building were destroyed. The hall once had known nearly perfect acoustics, but the roof had caved in and a large chandelier had fallen onto the front-row seats. Closed as a concert hall, it had been used by a church. Closed as a church, the hall fell into disuse; a street gang once stole hundreds of candles, sneaked into the building, set the candles burning on the seat backs, and then sat around drinking, drugging, and nearly destroying the whole thing. Still, it was obvious that when the hall had been built in 1919, it had been something special.

The Detroit Symphony saw the TV story, decided to get into the act, and filmed a one-time-only performance in the hall to draw more attention to it. The public fought Domino's and the theater eventually was restored. Today, it's called Detroit Orchestra Hall and is the regular home of the city's symphony orchestra. Nearby, however, there is a Domino's.

• In 1961, milkshake-machine salesman Ray Kroc bought out a San Bernardino, California-based, chain of restaurants. Back in 1948 Maurice and Richard McDonald had opened their first hamburger stand, serving precooked food rather than preparing separate orders. Burgers cost $.15—four cents more for cheese. Soft drinks were a dime and milkshakes cost $.20. They sold a lot of shakes, and that was when Kroc got interested; the McDonald brothers had ordered eight of the machines, and Ray was amazed at what he saw. So he bought them out.

Kroc and his Golden Arches were under way, and by the end of 1961, he was operating 323 McDonald's restaurants, selling a total of over five hundred million hamburgers. Later, Maurice and Richard McDonald opened another hamburger stand, but they couldn't use their own name; they'd sold that and everything else to Kroc for $2.7 million.

As president, Dwight Eisenhower tried to cut military spending, but the cuts didn't last long, not in the middle of the "Cold War" between the West (the United States and its World War II allies) and the East (the Soviet Union and a bloc of nations it had overrun during the war and over which it set up puppet governments). The Cold War was an extremely expensive business for both sides—too expensive for the Soviet Union, as it turned out by the end of the twentieth century.

In 1950, the total U.S. budget was about $40 billion, with the military taking about $12 billion of that. Five years later, the military budget itself was up to $40 billion and the entire figure was about $62 billion. By 1960, the military budget had jumped to $45.8 billion, 49.7 percent of the entire federal budget.

Then came cries of a "bomber gap" and a "missile gap," neither of which really existed, but which made good political rhetoric. The result was that by 1962, the United States had amassed more nuclear weapons than we could ever use: fifteen hundred Hiroshima-size atomic bombs, more than enough to destroy every major city in the world. The equivalent of ten tons of TNT for every man, woman, and child on earth.

We had more than fifty intercontinental missiles in the United States, ninety set up in foreign territory, eighty nuclear submarine missiles, seventeen hundred bombers capable of reaching the Soviet Union, three hundred carrier-based fighter-bombers, and more than a thousand land-based supersonic fighter-bombers. As for the Soviet Union, they could muster somewhere between fifty and a hundred intercontinental missiles and fewer than two hundred long-range bombers. That didn't stop us from worrying about what the Russian bear was doing over there in cheery, weary Siberia. Not only worrying about it, we even took a clandestine peek now and then.

At the start of the Cold War, America's intelligence experts relied primarily upon human observers. The Central Intelligence Agency (CIA) would send agents into the Soviet Union or one of its satellite nations or it would question Soviet military and scientific defectors. That worked for a while. Not that our allies' intelligence agencies helped much. The British, French, and West German spy shops had been penetrated so often by so many Soviet agents that they didn't come up with much real information.

By the mid-fifties, the CIA, along with the National Security Agency (NSA), turned to technology instead of agents: tapping telephone lines in Eastern Europe, and monitoring radio signals. Reconnaissance satellites were decades away, so the CIA and NSA used high-flying balloons with cameras to photograph the Soviet defense industry. Balloon overflights of the Soviet Union were difficult to control, since you can't always tell where a balloon is going to drift. Manned aircraft were more reliable, but they were also more vulnerable. We relied on modified B-29s, B-50s, and B-36 bombers until 1956 when the Lockheed Corporation's high-flying U-2 came along. In effect, the U-2 (for Utility Aircraft) was a jet-powered sailplane with small "pogo" wheels attached to each wingtip* to stabilize the fuel-heavy aircraft during takeoff. The CIA ordered forty-eight single-seat and five two-seat training U-2s. Later models carried, not only photographic equipment, but air-sampling devices as well to detect atmospheric nuclear tests. Almost immediately, the National Photographic Interpretation Center began reaping tons of hard data.

On May 1, 1960, the Soviet Union celebrated May Day with a workers' holiday and a military parade through Red Square. Meanwhile, American civilian pilot Francis Gary Powers was in a U.S. U-2 spy plane some seventy thousand feet above the Soviet Union, busily clicking away with the aircraft's special cameras, photographing Soviet missile bases. His bosses had told Powers that he'd be flying so high and so fast that Russian missiles couldn't bring him down. The

---

* These wheels were jettisoned once the aircraft was airborne.

bosses were wrong,* and down came Francis Gary Powers near the Soviet city of Sverdlovsk.

President Eisenhower was so confident that Powers had died when the reconnaissance plane went down that he claimed the U-2 was nothing more than a "weather plane." Ike denied any deliberate attempt either to violate Soviet airspace or to spy. But Powers was very much alive—he hadn't used the poison pin the CIA had thoughtfully provided. Six days after Powers and his U-2 were shot down, Nikita Khrushchev announced to the Supreme Soviet that he not only had the wreckage of the plane, but he had the pilot as well. Live and in glorious black and white, Francis Gary Powers appeared on Soviet television to admit the truth.

Khrushchev was in his glory; joking about the claims Powers was on a mission to gather weather data. "The whole world," he said, "knows that Allen Dulles [head of the CIA] is no great weatherman." Khrushchev displayed gold rings and watches that Powers, like all other U-2 pilots, carried with him to barter with the natives in case his plane crashed. "Perhaps," Nikita joked, Powers "was supposed to fly still higher to Mars, and seduce the Martian ladies!" Khrushchev even had the photographs Powers had taken on his "weather mission." "Here," he cried, "look at this! Here are the airfields—here! Fighters in position on the ground. Two little white strips. Here they are!" At least it proved how good the CIA's cameras were.

After first denying the U-2's real mission, Eisenhower later publicly admitted its purpose and told his son, John, "I am not going to shift the blame to my underlings!" In his usual homespun way, Ike said that "When you get your fingers caught in the cookie jar there's no use of pretending that you were out in the stable somewhere." He publicly canceled all U-2 flights over the USSR, but he never apologized.

Ike and Khrushchev were scheduled to attend a summit meeting in Paris, but the meeting was a disaster. The Soviet leader thundered and shouted so much that Charles de Gaulle, the host, tried to calm

---

* Several other U-2s would be shot down over China and Cuba, a total of ten aircraft lost.

him down. "The acoustics in this room," de Gaulle said, "are excellent. We can all hear the chairman." Privately, Khrushchev told de Gaulle that he couldn't understand why Ike would admit that the U-2 was on a spy mission. In his place, he'd try to bluff it out; the American's candor was an embarrassment.

Khrushchev made impossible demands and embarrassed Eisenhower. When Ike rejected the outrageous Soviet demands, Khrushchev aborted the summit.

In 1961, sixteen years after Soviet troops (with the acquiescence of the Western Allies) pounded their way into Adolf Hitler's wartime capital, West Berlin had become an isolated outpost of capitalism right in the middle of Communist East Germany. In June of that year, U.S. president John Kennedy and Soviet premier Nikita Khrushchev met for the first time. In a Vienna summit meeting, Khrushchev showed a calculated display of aggression. He demanded the withdrawal of Western powers from Berlin within six months' time, and he threatened war if they refused to go.

It was Kennedy's first summit meeting, and he was badly shaken. He believed that Khrushchev just might be crazy enough to trigger a nuclear holocaust. When he returned to Washington, JFK called up reservists, announced a civil defense program to build nuclear fallout shelters (again!), and told the American people that Berlin was the "great testing place of Western courage and will."

The North Atlantic Treaty Organization (NATO) began working on plans to deal with a Soviet attack on West Berlin, maybe even another blockade such as in 1948. Apparently, what no one expected was a wall. It began in the dead of night on the warm summer weekend of August 12–13, 1961. The East German news agency announced that since "deceit, bribery, and blackmail" had induced "unstable elements" to leave East Berlin for the West, "effective control was going to be established around the whole territory of West Berlin." What that really meant was that East Germans and East Berliners in particular were escaping to the West, sometimes by simply walking across the border or even riding the subway to freedom.

With the announcement from East Berlin that a wall was coming, hundreds of anguished and desperate people began a mad dash for the West. In places where the East-West border followed the line along the backs of houses, some East Berliners leapt out of high windows into sheets rushed to the scene and held up by the West Berlin fire brigade. All told, about a thousand East Berliners scrambled their way to the West before the barrier was completed. On August 22, a man named Günter Litfen was shot while trying to get across to the West. He was the first person to die trying to cross the Wall. He would not be the last.

The Western Allies made no effort to intervene to stop the Wall from being built. In fact, while they publicly denounced it, privately many Western leaders considered the Berlin Wall a solution rather than a problem: It became a resolution to an ongoing crisis, stabilizing for a quarter of a century the East-West flashpoint that was Berlin. JFK said it was "a hell of a lot better than a war." Better or not, the Berlin Wall was there, and it became a visual symbol of the Cold War, with the walled-in people of East Berlin paying the price for the West's freedom.

It took East German soldiers, police, and construction crews two days to build a barbed-wire fence through the center of the divided city. Then they built another one, a more substantial wall: eight feet tall, made of cinder blocks, and topped with barbed wire.*

It was virtually an admission by the Soviets that their system was so inadequate, so hated, that they had to prevent people from escaping. East Berliners, and East Germans in general, were nothing more than prisoners who had to be locked up to keep them from going west to enjoy freedom and something more than austerity.

On June 26, 1962, almost a quarter of Berlin's two and a half million people turned out to greet U.S. president John F. Kennedy as he began a four-day visit to West Germany. Later that day, in an open square near the infamous Berlin Wall, an estimated 150,000 people cheered wildly as Kennedy spoke out against the Soviet Union. Their cheers became a tumultuous roar when JFK declared "Ich bin

---

* A section of the wall now is on exhibit at the John Fitzgerald Kennedy Library and Museum in Boston.

ein Berliner." The sentiment was proper, even if the words weren't. The people of that once war-torn, now divided, city use the word *Berliner* to describe a pastry. In effect, Kennedy declared, "I am a jelly doughnut."

In Europe, the Cold War became an ideological battle that ended years later with the collapse of communism in the Soviet Union. It's likely that the Cold War had a greater influence on American foreign policy than it did on the Soviets'. This is particularly true regarding the American ideology of anticommunism, which, when linked to the strategy of containment in the Third World, globalized the Cold War beyond what it might have been.

Generally, we thought of the Cold War as something "bad." But was it? It kept the West and East at each other's political throats for more than a generation, but some political scientists believed that this prevented the two factions from fighting a more deadly (and more costly) hot war. Therefore, they argued, the Cold War was good, which meant that World War II was not our last "good war."

CHAPTER SIX

Battles Lost:
Vietnam

The execution of a coup is not like organizing a tea party. It's a very dangerous business.

General Maxwell Taylor, on the assassination of
South Vietnamese president Ngo Dinh Diem, November 1963

The establishment bastards have bailed out.

President Lyndon B. Johnson, March 26, 1968

On November 9, 1965, Ferdinand Marcos was elected president of the Philippines, and his wife began collecting shoes. On that same day in the United States, the lights went out all along the East Coast. It was 5:17 P.M., the height of rush hour. The blackout started with a 1.1-million-kilowatt surge of power in the Canadian province of Ontario and spread. One circuit blew, then, as automatic breakers cut in, more and more circuits blew until eight states and the Canadian provinces of Ontario and Quebec were in the dark: one-sixth of North America, thirty million people. In New York City alone, an estimated eight hundred thousand people were stalled in subways. Thousands more were caught between floors in elevators. It was nearly seven the next morning before power was restored in Manhattan.

New York governor Nelson Rockefeller called out the National Guard to help direct traffic and prevent looting. Actually, the crime rate during the blackout was even lower than usual, which may or may not have some significant meaning.

Nineteenth-century American men often wore "body bags"—their nickname for undershirts. In the Vietnam War the term *body bag* took on a more terrible definition: a bag in which a soldier's remains were flown from the front to a rear-echelon hospital by "mede-vac"—"medical evacuation" by helicopter.

Wherever "the front" was, because that's another term that took on a different meaning in Vietnam. It was, as Marine Corps officer Philip Caputo wrote, a war "without a front, flanks, or rear . . . a formless war against a formless enemy who evaporated like the jungle mists, only to materialize in some unexpected place." No more did a line drawn on a map, east to west or north to south, separate one side from the other as had been the case in America's other wars— the North's trenches around Richmond in the Civil War (probably the first instance of trench warfare), doughboys and Tommies going "over the top" in World War I hoping to take the enemy's trench system that constituted the Allied-German front; no more thirty-eighth parallel of Korea.

First use of the term *front line* probably came in the fourteenth century. Now, of course, it's no longer a strictly military term but one that often refers to civilian occupations and interests. An environmental activist, for example, could be on the "front line of the struggle."

Since the war no longer had a front, Vietnam War battle reports emphasized "body count"—casualties.

As early as 1900, the infantryman in the lead when his squad was on patrol was the "point man" and said to be "on the point," not to be confused with "on point," which is the stance a bird dog takes when he sees his quarry; although they both lead a patrol, so maybe it's the same after all. In the Vietnam era *point* took on added, not necessarily military meaning, as in the *New York Times* story about the death of former vice president Spiro Agnew: "Nixon Administration's Point Man Dies."

The first American military advisors to Vietnam, the U.S. Military Assistance Advisory Group (MAAG), arrived in September 1950. In 1964, MAAG became part of the U.S. Military Assistance Command, Vietnam (MACV), and very soon, growing numbers of American combat troops began to arrive.

On July 21, 1954, the Big Four countries signed the Geneva Accords, signaling an end to the Indochina War after French troop withdrawal. The agreement temporarily divided Vietnam into two parts. In May 1959, the government in North Vietnam resolved to carry out the reunification of Vietnam by all "appropriate measures." It took control of the growing Communist rebellion in the South and sent forty-five hundred Communist Southerners back into South Vietnam. They set up supply lines along what came to be called the Ho Chi Minh Trail and stepped up terrorist attacks. In September 1960, the Vietminh attacked South Vietnamese troops. What had been a minor conflict became a major civil war.

On January 19, 1961, in a meeting the day before he was to leave the White House, President Dwight D. Eisenhower told President-elect John F. Kennedy that the new chief executive might have to intervene in Southeast Asia. Nine days after his inauguration, Kennedy approved the joint Defense and State Departments' Counterinsurgency Plan (CIP). It was his first action dealing with Vietnam as president. The CIP was designed to shift South Vietnam's military emphasis away from defense against a conventional invasion by North Vietnam and toward internal security against the Communist-supported insurgency.

As a senator, John Kennedy had warned that no amount of military aid could conquer "an enemy of the people which has the support of covert appeal [*sic*] of the people." As president, he approved what he'd earlier said would do no good.

An old soldier familiar with the problem once observed, "There's no such thing as going just a little bit over Niagara Falls." All too soon, America would be in a barrel, headed for the falls.

In November 1961, a nineteen-year-old Seattle-born man joined the U.S. Army, and after basic training, the army transferred him to Fort Campbell, Kentucky. A year later, he earned the right to wear the "Screaming Eagles" patch of the 101st Airborne but was discharged after he was injured during a parachute jump.

He'd been born Johnny Allen Hendrix but was later renamed James by his father, James "Al" Hendrix. Called Jimmy when he joined the army, he later changed the spelling to "Jimi." Hendrix himself didn't go to Vietnam, but his music did: "All Along the Watchtower" and "Star-Spangled Banner."

Jimi Hendrix's military career lasted only a couple of years, which was more than twice as long as that of another musician, Jerry Garcia. In late January 1960, Jerry was unhappy in school, unhappy at home, and had no prospects of a job, so he joined the army. His mother had to sign for him—he was just seventeen years old—and on April 12, at the Oakland, California, recruiting office, Jerry raised his hand and said I do. Almost immediately, both the army and Jerry realized it had been a mistake. The army called him lazy, and he called himself "pathologically antiauthoritarian." After he had, somehow, made it through basic training at Fort Ord, about 125 miles south of San Francisco, the army assigned Garcia to the Presidio of San Francisco. He was more interested in the Haight-Ashbury area of San Francisco than he was in the Presidio, so he went AWOL, absent without leave. Now, the military doesn't appreciate your going AWOL, and they sent a couple of U.S. marshals after Jerry. He was court-martialed in October and found guilty. It looked as if things weren't going to go too well for Jerry, until his company commander asked Garcia if he wanted out of the army. Jerry's answer was a fast "Yes!" And on December 14, 1960, he was released from service, eight months and two days after he'd joined.

With the assassination of John F. Kennedy, the American armed forces found themselves serving under a man whose stated interest was the Great Society, not the great army or navy. The new president referred to his predecessor's advisors as "you Harvards," and called that country in Southeast Asia "Veet-Nam." Lyndon B. Johnson now called the White House home.

There's a story that, in 1964, two American military advisors were sitting in a restaurant in Vietnam and discussing the situation in Southeast Asia. One said that they'd need more help to get the job done. The other advisor, who knew what was planned, said not to worry, that help was on its way.

On December 5, 1964, two reinforced Viet Cong battalions attacked the tiny outpost of Nam Dong in north central Thua Thien province. U.S. Special Forces, the "Green Berets"—technically they were still military advisors—and a handful of indigenous allies fought off the attack. In doing so, Capt. Roger H. C. Donlon of the 7th Special Forces became the first American to be awarded the Medal of Honor in Vietnam. President Johnson presented Donlon with the medal in a White House ceremony. As often as possible, both President Johnson and President Nixon used Medal of Honor ceremonies to spark support for the war.

Altogether, seventeen Green Berets were awarded the Medal of Honor in Vietnam and eighty-eight received the army's second-highest honor, the Distinguished Service Cross. Often, though erroneously, called the Congressional Medal of Honor because it's awarded by the president "in the name of the Congress of the United States," it was established in 1862 during the American Civil War. For their actions in Vietnam, 239 military personnel* received the medals.

In 1965, in his usual good ole boy, blood-stirring manner, President Johnson told America that "The people of South Vietnam have chosen to resist aggression from the North." On March 8, our official "advisory" role in Vietnam came to an end. On that day, the first U.S. combat troops landed in South Vietnam, wading ashore at Orange Beach, south of Da Nang. They were the first of many to come. About that same time, the Viet Cong bombed the U.S. embassy in Saigon. Which brings into question national security adviser Walt Rostow's prediction, "The Viet Cong are going to collapse within weeks."

Troops in Vietnam sometimes returned to base at night, then reversed their route the next morning, sort of like commuting to Saigon's suburbs. Most American troops in Vietnam never saw combat. The Pentagon claims it didn't keep statistics on it, but admits that well over fifty percent of U.S. troops in Vietnam served in rear-echelon areas, base camps, and other protected areas generally safe from enemy attack. This includes clerks, cooks, maintenance personnel, and other essentially noncombatant types.

They spent a lot of their time comfortably ensconced in cities such as Saigon, Da Nang, and Rha Trang. Life there wasn't much differ-

---

* Some sources give the number of Vietnam Medal of Honor winners as 241.

ent from the way troops serving in Germany or Korea lived, except that in those places cold weather could be the worst enemy. Heat was a problem in Vietnam until air conditioners became more readily available, then life became bearable. For these rear echelon troops, most of the action came after hours in bars and brothels. It was the grunts on patrol or at small firebases who suffered.

During the 1960s, American baby boomers embraced the peace sign, but just where it came from isn't certain. One version had it that in the late fifties, British aristocrat and longtime peace advocate Bertrand Russell hired a commercial artist named Gerald Holtom to create a symbol to unite leftist peace marchers. Either Russell or Holtom chose the Teutonic rune of death. Runes are sometimes referred to as "matchstick signs" and form the basis of the Futhark alphabet the Vikings used.

Another version of the sign's origin has it that Russell and Holtom combined the semaphore letters *N*—the two signal flags are held straight down—and *D*—both flags held down at about forty-five-degree angles—inside a circle. *N* for nuclear, *D* for disarmament, and the circle designating Earth. Now, Bertrand Russell was chairman of the Campaign for Nuclear Disarmament, and the CND used the new symbol on flags and banners and signs.

Yet a third accounting of the peace sign's origins is that it's the cross of Christ with the arms drooping in despair.

During the 1970s, the South African government considered forbidding the use of the peace sign, believing it to be both anti-Christian and pro-Communist. After American antiwar activists appropriated the sign in the sixties, some nontraditional fundamentalist Christians called it a "Witch's Foot" or a "Broken Cross" and declared it a work of Satan.

Satan, cross, signal flag, or rune, by the 1980s, the peace sign had been appropriated again. Environmentalists placed the sign in the canton, the upper lanyard-side corner, of the "stars and stripes," and changed the colors to blue, green, and white.

There is, of course, another peace sign, one given with the index and middle fingers forming a *V*, the hand aimed forward. It looks like Winston Churchill's V-for-victory sign from World War II, and that may be where it started. Notice above: "the hand aimed forward." There's a story from World War II of a bunch of American sailors trading jibes with a bunch of English sailors: We've been at this war for years, mate, and you finally decide to join in. Yeah, but if we hadn't joined in, you guys would be sinking. Then, the Brits give the Yanks what the Americans believe to be Churchill's V-for-victory sign, and the Yanks stop jeering and start cheering. Problem was, the Americans didn't look closely enough, or they didn't know enough. The English sailors used the same two fingers but had their palms facing inward, which is something entirely different. What does it symbolize? Try it. Index and middle finger in a V, facing you. Then, drop the index finger. We sometimes call it "flipping the bird." Apparently, the American sailors never got the Brits' point.

For your average "grunt" or "crunchy" or "ground pounder" (the guys who did the down-and-dirty fighting), all wars amount to kill or be killed, wound or be wounded. It seemed to happen especially frequently to "FNGs," or fuckin' new guys, also known as "cherries," who didn't know enough to keep their damn heads down. If you were an inexperienced draftee who'd been run through a quickie training course to make you an NCO, you were a "Shake 'n Bake," a name also sometimes given to a newly commissioned officer with no experience.

A soldier's most prized possession may have been his P-38—not the twin-boom, twin-engine long-range fighter plane from World War II, but a can opener. These standard army can openers have been around since the 1940s, where they were equally cherished. It's difficult opening a can of C Rations without a can opener, and the P-38s were so small, about the size of a nail clipper, they'd frequently be lost. Ground pounders took to wearing them on their dog-tag chains, and a lot of veterans still have their P-38s, mementoes of times gone by. Besides, you never can tell when you might need to open a can of beans and franks.

The old phrase *shoot oneself in the foot* became real for those who didn't want to wait for the "million-dollar wound"—the wound that would send them home without doing too much lasting injury to themselves—and turned it into a do-it-yourself situation. The term *million-dollar wound* came out of World War II but became better known in Vietnam.

In World War II, sailors and troops in the Pacific Theater listened to English-language radio broadcasts by "Tokyo Rose." Troops in Europe had "Axis Sally"—Mildred E. Gillars, a native of Portland, Maine. "Lord Haw-Haw," whose real name was William Joyce, was a British subject—his mother was English, his father was Irish-American. Both Gillars and Joyce broadcast German propaganda to England.

During the Vietnam War, English-speaking Trinh Thi Ngo broadcast over Radio Hanoi. Her American listeners called her "Hanoi Hannah." "My work," she said in a 1994 *New York Times* interview, "was to make the GIs understand that it was not right for them to take part in the war." As with Tokyo Rose, Axis Sally, and Lord Haw-Haw, it's doubtful Hanoi Hannah had any real effect other than to provide American troops with music and give them an occasional laugh.

America had its own version of Hanoi Hannah, a green-eyed blonde named Chris Noel—she swears that's her real name. For five years, beginning in 1966, Armed Forces Radio broadcast *A Date with Chris.* Or, as entertainer Bob Hope called her, "Miss Christmas."

Originally, her show (like many others produced by Armed Forces Radio at the time) was recorded on large 33⅓-rpm discs and played back in Vietnam, Europe, and on American ships overseas. But then she got a telegram, asking her if she'd be willing to go to Vietnam to "help build morale." And of course she said yes.

She traveled "the entire scope of Vietnam" and "stood there and stared at them and they stared at me." These days, some of the troops she met in Vietnam invite her to "travel throughout the United States to come and see them."

As for Hanoi Hannah, "as much passion as I had for what I did for America," Chris Noel remembered, "she had for what she was doing for Hanoi, for the North Vietnamese." Armed Forces Radio hoped Noel's radio broadcasts would attract the audience that had been listening to Hanoi Hannah, and it may have worked, at least from the North Vietnamese angle. They put a ten-thousand-dollar price on her head for anyone who would kill Noel. Evidently, the feeling was that killing Chris Noel would "demoralize the troops and that it would be in their favor." No one ever collected the bounty, and she returned to Hollywood, where she appeared in several television shows, including one that must have made her feel right at home: *China Beach*, the story of a U.S. Armed Forces hospital and recreational facility at Da Nang.

Some deaths in Vietnam came as the result of "friendly fire," combatants killed by their own troops. Called "own fire" or "amicide"* in World War II, it happened a lot more frequently than the Pentagon or several presidential administrations would like to admit.

Not so friendly fire was "fragging," an attack on one's own officer or NCO. It comes from *frag*, or a fragmentation grenade, frequently the weapon of choice in instances of fragging. You'd casually pull the pin on a grenade and just as casually toss it into the tent or hooch where an incompetent or overzealous officer or NCO might be sleeping.

The phenomenon of fragging has been around for most wars and usually was a consequence of a massive breakdown in morale and discipline. Most, but certainly not all, fragging incidents involved rear-echelon troops rather than grunts in the bush.

Beginning in 1969, the number of fragging incidents rose. In that year, from 96 to 126 incidents of fragging occurred, resulting in from 37 to 39 deaths. Fragging peaked in 1970–71, a period of widespread demoralization among U.S. troops. In 1971, there were upwards of 335 fragging incidents, although the death toll was down to 12. Obviously, such figures are uncertain; after all, one object of a fragger was to get rid of a fraggee without being caught. Another thing that makes fragging figures uncertain is that several officers and NCOs were the objects of repeated attempts. By official Pentagon count there were 788 fragging incidents in Vietnam with 86 deaths and 714 wounded. Unofficial counts put the total fragging deaths as high as a thousand.

* From the Latin words for "friend" and "killing."

During the Vietnam War, killing became "waxing" or "zapping." Zapping also referred to the shooting down of airplanes or disabling of tanks. Of course, helicopter gunships could also get zapped, in which case they'd be broken down into "slicks," unarmed transport helicopters. You could say that "Charlie zapped a slick," which meant the Viet Cong shot down a troop-transport helicopter. "Frogs" were choppers with machine guns, and "hogs" had M79 grenade launchers.

The late Bernard Fall, one of the top journalists covering the Vietnam War, referred to all of this as "Batman language," the kind of BAM! ZAP! CLUNK! lingo used in the sixties-era television show *Batman.*

When troops in Vietnam spoke of "the agency" or "the company" it was well known that they meant the CIA, the Central Intelligence Agency, although CIA agents themselves weren't known to use those terms. A-Teams (yes, there was a TV series by that name) were special twelve-man Green Beret units. The Green Berets themselves were members of the army's Special Forces, which in earlier times had been the Rangers. They were trained in techniques of guerrilla warfare (military operations conducted in enemy-held or hostile territory) and shouldn't be confused with "Special Services," which provided entertainment and entertainers during the war, and don't let them assign you to one when you want the other.

"Farm Gate" wasn't a rural version of the later "Watergate," rather it was a U.S. Air Force combat detachment whose mission was air support of ground forces. They also went under the name "Jungle Jim," and were the 4400th Combat Crew Training Squadron. Like all troops, they enjoyed a "walk in the sun," a time when ground troops could move about freely without risk of combat.

A grunt's favorite term may have been *DEROS*, short for the "date eligible for return from overseas," the date that a crunchy's "tour of duty," his time "in country" (in Vietnam) was to end. It was perhaps the most important date in a soldier's life, with grunts frequently asking each other, "What's your DEROS?" If you were lucky, and lived through it all, you'd board a "freedom bird," an airplane that would take you back to "the world" at the end of your tour of duty. As in other wars, a "short timer" was someone nearing the end of his tour, a time when a grunt should be even more careful and try to stay out of trouble of any kind. Being a short timer was "number one," which was very good and not to be confused with "number ten," which was very bad.

Prior to going home, troops looked forward to "I and I," their nickname for "R and R"—rest and recreation—with the emphasis here on intoxication and intercourse, which event frequently ended with a problem whose initials were all too familiar: VD. Grunts often noted PCOD, the "pussy cutoff date," a date several weeks before one's DEROS, when it became wise to abstain from sexual indulgence lest one catch VD, since anyone afflicted with VD wasn't permitted to leave Vietnam until cured.

VD, of course, was not to be confused with *VC,* short for Viet Cong, itself short for *Viet Nam Cong Son,* or Vietnamese Communists, also known as "Victor Charlie."

We've become so accustomed to acronyms that our language may soon be FUBAR, an acronym that grew out of another acronym, SNAFU—"situation normal, all fouled (or fucked) up." FUBAR means "fucked up (or fouled up) beyond all repair (or recognition)."

Napalm wasn't exactly an acronym but rather a shortening of the names of two chemicals, naphthene and palmitate. Together, they form an incendiary substance, a jellied, gasoline-based compound that burns at about two thousand degrees Fahrenheit. Napalm kills by burning or by asphyxiation; once set off, napalm causes massive deoxygenation and produces lethal amounts of carbon monoxide. It is indiscriminate and will burn anything or anyone it contacts— one source says that napalm "reduces the need for accuracy." The stated purpose of napalm attacks was to destroy forests and undergrowth used by the enemy to conceal troops and supply lines. As Gen. Paul D. Harkins—the one-time head of the Military Assistance Command, Vietnam (MACV)—put it, napalm "really puts the fear of God into the Viet Cong," adding, "and that's what counts." In a memo dated September 12, 1962, CINCPAC (Commander in Chief, Pacific) told Harkins, "[W]e want to destroy or drive sick, starved, blistered, and blasted Viet Cong from Zone D so that we scoop them up outside of their net or prevent them from setting foot in the area again."

Novelist John Steinbeck, who frequently corresponded with Johnson administration officials, approved of napalm and wanted to use small napalm bombs to attack North Vietnamese and Viet Cong troops:

> What I suggest is a napalm grenade, packed in a heavy plastic sphere almost the exact size and weight of a baseball. The detonator could be of very low power—just enough to break the plastic shell and ignite the inflammable. If the napalm is packed under pressure, it will spread itself when the case breaks. The detonator (a contact cap) should be carried separately and inserted or screwed in just before throwing. This would allow a man to carry a sack full of balls without danger to himself.

According to Steinbeck, "People who will charge rifle fire won't go through flames."

While the war continued, more and larger crowds marched outside the White House crying, "Hey, hey, LBJ; how many kids did you kill today?" It rocked the Johnson Administration. Protestors also demonstrated outside Dow Chemical Company plants.

Being the chief producer of napalm used in Vietnam, Dow became a symbol for "war profiteer," which confused the hell out of Dow officials. Company executives recalled that during World War II, producing weapons to help America's military effort was patriotic. Now, such production was not only being questioned, it was being called inhumane.

From 1962 to 1971, an herbicide known as "Agent Orange" was used to defoliate more than five million acres of Vietnam territory. Beginning with Operation Ranchhand, the U.S. Air Force spread some eleven million gallons of the chemical, which got its name from the color of a band that marked drums it came in—others were "Agent Blue" and "Agent White," which of course came in drums marked accordingly. U.S. forces primarily used Agent Blue to eradicate rice crops suspected of being farmed by the enemy. And they used Agent White to kill brush and weeds to deny cover to the Viet Cong and the North Vietnamese Army.

Agent Orange stripped land needed for village crops as well as for hiding the enemy. Crews had a motto: only you can prevent forests. Almost as soon as Agent Orange was sprayed, it began killing trees, crops, and large animals.

Agent Orange contains dioxin, a chemical that causes cancer in laboratory animals, and after the war thousands of American Vietnam veterans claimed that they'd been injured or made ill in these attacks, a different form of friendly fire. A 1984 court settlement awarded $180 million to U.S. soldiers who suffered health ailments from exposure to Agent Orange. In 1997, the Department of Veterans Affairs began compensating the children of Vietnam vets who suffered from the birth defect spina bifida due to their parents' exposure to the chemical in Vietnam.

It isn't only American troops and their families who today suffer the aftereffects of Agent Orange and its cousins White and Blue. The Vietnamese also continue to suffer. It's been nearly three decades since the last American plane flew over Vietnam "spraying a white fog" of death and destruction, but the Vietnamese say that its devastating effect lives on in their own country in birth defects among children born in the sprayed areas. How many children, how extensive the birth defects, are unknown. It perhaps is a reminder that the actions we take at any given moment may have extensive and long-lasting effects. As President George H. W. Bush said long after the fighting ended, "Vietnam: that war bleeds us still."

Many American veterans of the Vietnam fighting claim to have suffered a psychological problem called "posttraumatic stress disorder," PTSD, as it's shortened. It's the condition known in other wars by other names: "nostalgia" or "irritable heart" in the Civil War, "battle fatigue" in World War I, "combat stress" or "combat fatigue" in World War II and Korea, and "Gulf War syndrome" in the conflict of that same name. Its symptoms pretty much all sound the same: shortness of breath, palpitations, headache, excessive sweating, dizziness, disturbed sleep, forgetfulness, fainting, and difficulty concentrating. After Vietnam, much was made of this disorder, with newspapers frequently carrying headlines that read: "Viet Vet Goes Berserk."

The one-year tour of duty in Vietnam was partly intended to insure against the development of incapacitating stress reactions. It was far from successful. It's estimated that from five hundred thousand to seven hundred thousand Vietnam veterans were afflicted by PTSD, about twenty to twenty-five percent of all those who served. Regrettably, not everyone who claimed to suffer combat fatigue, or whatever the particular generation called it, even served in the war, much less suffered from that service. In the 1993 movie *Falling Down*, Michael Douglas, the protagonist, is approached by a panhandler who asks for a handout. "I'm a Vietnam vet," the panhandler says. Douglas looks at the man, who obviously was too young to have been a Vietnam vet, and asks, "What were you, a drummer boy?"

In the twenty-first century, of course, you don't have to be a war veteran to suffer PTSD. Survivors of other traumatic experiences, from crime victims to firefighters and police officers, sometimes now lay claim to PTSD.

As Civil War general William T. Sherman said: "War is hell." Which is true, no matter if it's war at home or abroad.

Sometime after the end of the war, rumors began circulating about an extraordinary number of suicides among Vietnam veterans. It was said that from 50,000 to 150,000 Viet vets had taken their own lives. That's about six to sixteen times higher than the norm for Americans. If this were true it would mean that more Americans *killed themselves* than died at the hands of the enemy. This would give a whole new meaning to the words of cartoon character Pogo: "We have met the enemy and he is us."

Luckily, it just ain't so. The Centers for Disease Control (CDC) studied the problem and determined that by 1987, there were some nine thousand suicides among Vietnam veterans, that within the first five years of discharge, veterans committed suicide about 1.7 times more often than did the average American. After the initial five years following discharge, however, the rate slowed considerably. In fact, it slowed to below society's norms. Still, since the end of the Vietnam War, about 12,000 veterans have taken their own lives.

Probably the same rumormongers who claimed to know of large numbers of Viet vets committing suicide started the gossip that disproportionate numbers of Vietnam veterans were homeless. About forty percent of all homeless men are veterans, including the twenty-five thousand or so veterans of World War I who still are alive, the eight million veterans of World War II, and the millions of veterans who have come along in the intervening years. According to a 1996 study, it turns out that veterans who served in combat are less likely to be homeless than those who were not in combat. And, in general, men who served during the Vietnam era are less likely to be homeless than women—only about 1.6 percent of homeless veterans are women who served after the war.

On August 4, 1964, President Johnson went on nationwide television to announce a change in the Vietnam War. Two days earlier, LBJ claimed, North Vietnamese patrol boats had attacked the U.S. destroyer *Maddox* in international waters off Hanoi in the Gulf of Tonkin. He and Secretary of Defense McNamara claimed that it was an "unprovoked attack." Because of this, on August 7, Congress passed the Gulf of Tonkin Resolution, unanimously in the House and with only two dissenting votes in the Senate. It gave Johnson the power to take military action in Southeast Asia—to initiate hostilities without the actual declaration of war by Congress as required by the U.S. Constitution.*

During an interview on NBC television, Secretary of State Dean Rusk said that he'd not yet "been able, quite frankly, to come to a fully satisfactory explanation" as to why the North Vietnamese would attack *Maddox*. "There is," Rusk added,

a great gulf of understanding between that world and our world, ideological in character. They see what we think of as the real world in wholly different terms. Their very processes of logic are different. So that it's very difficult to enter into each other's minds across that great ideological gulf.

No wonder Dean Rusk couldn't find a "fully satisfactory explanation" for the attack. The Gulf of Tonkin incident had never happened, certainly not the way Johnson and McNamara said it had.

* When the U.S. Supreme Court was asked to declare the war unconstitutional, the court refused even to consider the issue.

As we later learned from the Pentagon Papers, the Department of Defense history of Vietnam, two months prior to the alleged attack, U.S. government officials met in Honolulu to discuss the Gulf of Tonkin Resolution. Let's see. They met to discuss the resolution before the event took place.

In the spring of 1964, Secretary of Defense McNamara visited Vietnam, and he came away convinced that a victory by the Communist-led Viet Cong was imminent. Unless the United States stepped up its military involvement. One option was to launch air strikes against the North. But would Americans go along with the plan? Washington would require a forceful pretext to begin the proposed attack on North Vietnam.

In that June-July meeting in Hawaii, Johnson administration officials acknowledged that "public opinion on our Southeast Asia policy [is] badly divided in the United States . . . and that, therefore, the president needed an affirmation of support." What better way to get that affirmation than by claiming innocent Americans had been suddenly and inexplicably attacked by the nasty North Vietnamese?

On August 2, the destroyer *Maddox* was patrolling off North Vietnam, supporting secret hit-and-run raids against the North by South Vietnamese commandoes. *Maddox* regularly patrolled in sight of the North Vietnamese shore and frequently inside the North's proclaimed territorial waters. The commando raids had occurred two days earlier, on July 31.

Now, three North Vietnamese patrol boats ventured out to attack *Maddox*, and the destroyer answered by calling in air support from the carrier *Ticonderoga*. Carrier planes destroyed one PT boat and crippled a second; *Maddox* was undamaged and continued its patrol. Then, on the night of August 4–5, *Maddox* and another destroyer that had joined it claimed to have made radar contact with three enemy vessels.

The PT-boat attack on *Maddox* that first night hadn't amounted to much and the radar contact on the second night probably didn't happen. Either somebody, somewhere, misinterpreted radar data or—hold on to your hats, boys and girls!—the second attack was invented to justify an escalation of U.S. military involvement. Didn't matter. The Johnson administration launched air attacks against North Vietnam. And LBJ went on TV to announce the "unprovoked attacks." Because of the attacks, he said, American planes would begin bombing the North.

On September 9, 1965, Vietnamese troops shot down then-commander, later admiral, James Bond Stockdale while he was on his two hundredth mission. A squadron commander aboard the *Ticonderoga*, he'd earlier led the attack assisting the *Maddox* when the destroyer came under attack in the Gulf of Tonkin. Once Stockdale was taken prisoner by the North Vietnamese, Hanoi tried to turn him into a propaganda tool as the highest-ranking POW; however, throughout nearly eight years of torture, Stockdale defied his jailers. Captain Eugene "Red" McDaniel, himself a long-term POW, said that Stockdale survived without blurting out military secrets under torture because he lived as if he were on a highly sensitive naval operation, not a prisoner of war. "Resolve and commitment and moral leverage," Red McDaniel quotes Stockdale as saying, "are the only glue that ties America's sons to their leaders. Finesse and trickery are not worthy of us." Stockdale did resort to a bit of trickery; using messages tapped out on prison walls, Stockdale encouraged other POWs to resist.

Air Force Colonel George Day, a forward-air-control pilot, was shot down over North Vietnam and held prisoner for sixty-seven months, from August 1967 to March 1973. Day retired with more than forty combat decorations and medals, including the Medal of Honor.

Captain Lance J. Sijan was the first graduate of the U.S. Air Force Academy to be awarded the Medal of Honor, and he was one of the last to receive the medal for action in the Vietnam War. He'd been shot down over Hanoi on November 9, 1967, hurt so badly that when a Jolly Green rescue helicopter tried to hoist him to safety, Sijan couldn't crawl the twenty feet to be picked up. The chopper pilot radioed Sijan that a parajumper was coming down to help, but the downed pilot radioed back: "Negative, Jolly! There's bad guys down here, real close." He tried to escape but was unable to get away and was captured by the "bad guys." He died in 1968 while held captive in a Hanoi prison and was awarded the Medal of Honor posthumously.

Perhaps the last person to receive the Medal of Honor for extraordinary valor during the Vietnam War was Alfred Rascon, a medic with the U.S. Army's 173d Airborne Brigade. On March 16, 1966, Rascon was badly wounded during Operation Silver City. In that same operation, according to other members of Rascon's unit, the medic saved the lives of two other soldiers and turned around a losing situation.

Rascon almost didn't make it himself. He'd been wounded six months earlier, near Ben Cat, and while other members of his patrol continued with their reconnaissance patrol, Rascon stayed behind at the landing zone to supervise the helicopter evacuation of another soldier.

Rascon was a native of Chihuahua, Mexico, and still a Mexican citizen when he went to Vietnam. Only after the war did he take up U.S. citizenship. On February 8, 2000, President Bill Clinton draped the Medal of Honor around Alfred Rascon's neck, thirty-four years after the action that saw him earn the medal.

With the end of World War II, America began preparing for World War III, and for the U.S. Army, part of that preparation was the birth of the 1st Cavalry Division (Airmobile). The idea, reflected in training and arming of the unit, was that the next war would be fought on the plains of Europe in a series of small, dirty battles. In mid-1962, Defense Secretary McNamara ordered the army to determine if the new UH-1 Huey helicopter and the CH-47 Chinook transport helicopter were viable for the battlefields of the future. In February 1963, the 11th Air Assault Division (Test), the 10th Airborne Transport Brigade (Test), and the Aviation Group (Test) were formed at Fort Benning, Georgia. Field trials would be made to determine whether platoon- and company-size elements could be used. By June 1964, the army had added two more brigades of infantry, along with artillery and support units, and training was under way.

That fall, it pitted the 11th Air Assault (test) Division against the Air Assault II in war games in the Carolinas. Helicopter warfare worked, and a year later it was used in the battle of Ia Drang.

It was at Ia Drang, in the central highlands of South Vietnam, that for the first time U.S. troops met regulars of the People's Army of

Vietnam (PAVN), in a fierce six-day battle. It began on November 14. Helicopters dropped some 450 men of the 1st Battalion, 7th Cavalry,* into Landing Zone X-Ray, in the Ia Drang Valley (In Vietnamese, *Ia* means "river"), fourteen miles west of Plei Me, near the Laos border. The unit suspected that North Vietnamese forces were hidden in the mountainous area nearby, and they were right. Almost immediately, upward of 2,500 Communist troops surrounded the Americans. More PAVN troops would arrive in the coming days.

As the battle developed, U.S. soldiers desperately defended a perimeter that at times was only three hundred yards across. Several times PAVN troops almost overran the Americans with a series of flanking operations. The American battalion, which included a good number of Korean War veterans, held its position, beating back first one North Vietnamese assault, then another. The fighting ebbed and flowed and finally the enemy flowed away, over the Cambodian border.

American troops inflicted heavy casualties on the North Vietnamese, possibly as many as 2,500 casualties; North Vietnam later claimed that what they learned at Ia Drang would have been worth the loss of a hundred thousand men. America lost at least 234 dead and nearly 300 wounded, and we may not have learned much at all.

Meanwhile, about two and a half miles away, another American battalion dropped into Landing Zone Albany. They were chopped to pieces as they traveled on foot to the Ia Drang battle site. More than 150 American soldiers died in that fight. Maybe helicopter warfare didn't work, after all.

The two actions, while not gaining or losing much territory, were important as a preview of tactics American ground forces would use in the Vietnam War, helicopters ferrying large units into combat. The 1st Battalion's success—the boys in the Pentagon tried to forget further losses—confirmed Washington's belief that a "war of attrition" would work, with its key instrument of the search-and-destroy mission.

---

* The modern-day version of the 7th Cavalry with whom George Armstrong Custer rode into history at the Battle of Little Big Horn in 1876.

After Ia Drang, American military commanders repeated the tactic, expanded on it, tried to refine it, and used superior weapons and massive firepower. Sometimes it worked, sometimes it didn't, and often it didn't amount to much at all. American and South Vietnamese troops might inflict heavy losses on Communist troops, but the enemy always seemed to come back. North Vietnamese commanders themselves drew lessons from Ia Drang: They tried not to fight U.S. troops head-on and rarely took the bait of America's search-and-destroy missions.*

Finally, in 1969, two years after the battle of Ia Drang, U.S. forces gave up on the search-and-destroy technique. Well, didn't give it up entirely. Americans stopped using the tactic themselves, but we convinced the South Vietnamese army that it was the way to go.

Nineteen sixty-seven saw 9,353 Americans die in Vietnam, bringing the total U.S. troops killed since January 1, 1961, to 15,997. In January 1968, American troops in Vietnam totaled 468,000, and the death count was about to rise dramatically.

In 1968 America tried to shoot itself in the foot. In January, the U.S. military suffered a blow when North Korean gunboats captured the American ship *Pueblo* off the Korean coast. The *Pueblo* had only two machine guns for defense, but it had a lot of special equipment and likely shouldn't have been where it was. *Pueblo* was a spy ship, and that special equipment let the American intelligence system listen in on what was going on with the North Korean military. Whatever that was. The North Koreans had been insolent since the 1953 armistice halted the Korean War. But they hadn't exactly been belligerent either.

The *Pueblo*, however, didn't just listen to North Korean radio signals. It received and transmitted U.S. military signals. In fact, *Pueblo* was the only American ship equipped to intercept and decipher all U.S. naval codes. Its radios could communicate with American naval units around the world.

---

* Also known as "reconnaissance in force" and "preemptive" operations.

The *Pueblo*'s captain, Lloyd Bucher, gave up without a fight, later claiming that to have fought would have meant his men would have been slaughtered by the better armed and more numerous North Koreans. Still, an American sailor was killed and three others were injured while trying to destroy documents and equipment. They didn't get very far, and the North Koreans seized ten bags of documents and a lot of equipment, which until then had been secret. The Koreans escorted *Pueblo* under guard into Wonsan harbor, and *Pueblo* commander Lloyd Bucher broadcast a "confession," admitting his ship had been spying on the North Koreans.

Meanwhile, at the United Nations, U.S. ambassador Arthur Goldberg lied through his teeth. The *Pueblo*, he claimed, had been in international waters, which no one, least of all Goldberg, believed.

The Senate Foreign Relations Committee wanted to know whether the *Pueblo* really had been spying in North Korean territorial waters. And if so, why hadn't the navy sent along an armed escort, especially during this time of high tension in Southeast Asia?

The Johnson administration demanded that the Communists release the crew, but North Korea refused and threatened to try all eighty-two of them as criminals. Congress called for some kind of retaliation, so the navy sent the carrier *Enterprise* steaming toward the Straits of Korea.

This had become a full-blown international crisis. When the Johnson administration asked Soviet foreign minister Andrei Kosygin to use his good offices to get the government in Pyongyang to release the American crew, they were told no: The ship had been in North Korean waters, no matter what Ambassador Goldberg said.

In the end, President Johnson saw the *Pueblo* incident as just that, an "incident." It wasn't a test of will. It was piracy, and so he let it go unpunished.

It would be almost a year before *Pueblo*'s crew was released. The navy, which of course had sent the spy ship into North Korean waters without an escort and which had given the ship only two machine guns for defense, blamed Commander Bucher for having given up without a fight. Forget that when Bucher called for help, the navy didn't respond. When he and the crew finally got back home, navy investigators wanted to court-martial somebody, at least Bucher. Actually, they wanted to leave Bucher testicularly disadvantaged, if possible. The secretary of the navy declined to court-martial Bucher on the grounds that he'd suffered enough. Instead, the navy censured him and his service career was ruined. Perhaps, as one critic put it, if Bucher had insisted on fighting the North Koreans, and he and all of his men had gone down in the skirmish, the navy might have given the captain a medal, not hounded him off his ship.

Lloyd Bucher retired from the navy in 1973 and became a water-color artist in a San Diego suburb.

At the end of January 1968, South Vietnam relaxed for the Tet lunar New Year celebration, a week-long holiday when the Vietnamese buy new clothes, visit their families, prepare special foods, and drape their houses with flowers. During previous Tet observances, both sides in the conflict had observed a truce, and in January 1968, they again promised to suspend the fighting for a week.

South Vietnamese troops sat back and relaxed during what they assumed was a mutually agreed-to truce for Tet. The U.S. command believed that it could breathe easily for a few days. Communist forces, however, didn't honor the truce.

It was midnight in Vietnam and dusk in Washington when the news of the Tet Offensive stuttered into the National Military Command Center (NMCC) on the "E" ring of the Pentagon outside Washington, D.C. At 2:45 A.M. on January 31, a team of nineteen National Liberation Front (NLF) sappers blasted a hole in the wall surrounding the U.S. embassy in Saigon, then dashed into the courtyard. They hauled down the American flag, and for an hour the NLF colors flew over the embassy.

The intruders ran into the courtyard and, for the next six hours, held captive the American embassy, perhaps the most important symbol of the American presence in Vietnam. Likely, the only thing that stopped the VC from killing everybody in the embassy compound was the heavy door guarding the building and the rapid response of American troops. As it was, the Viet Cong sappers hid behind large concrete planters and pounded the building with rockets until they finally were killed or severely wounded.

The battle for the American embassy was only part of the well-planned Tet Offensive. If it had been just that, humiliating as it was, the war would have continued without much change. But it was more than just a suicide attack on the embassy in Saigon. NLF and Viet Cong troops attacked thirty-six of forty-four South Vietnamese provincial capitals, attacking South Vietnamese and U.S. military bases and government installations. They'd hoped that what they called the "General Offensive, General Uprising" would spur a large number of Republic of Vietnam (ARVN) troops to defect and cause a widespread public revolt around the country. That didn't happen.

When the allies took three weeks to stop the North Vietnamese, American public opinion turned against the U.S. involvement in the war. Don North was an American reporter in Saigon at the time. "If the Vietnam War had a defining moment," he wrote more than thirty years later, "it had to be the Tet Offensive of 1968." Like Pearl Harbor and the Cuban Missile Crisis, the Tet Offensive "sticks in our collective memory."

Communist troops suffered frightful losses as they died at an almost suicidal rate—forty-five thousand of the eighty-four-thousand-man army sent to rouse the South. The South Vietnamese lost about twenty-three hundred and American casualties were set at about eleven hundred.

Militarily, the Tet Offensive was a decided failure for the Communists but, far and away, it was a political success. It shocked the American public, which had assumed that a U.S. victory was right around the corner. In itself this created a "credibility gap." How could the American public believe an administration that claimed to see a light at the end of the tunnel of war when, so clearly, the Communists could and would send thousands upon thousands of troops into South Vietnam, realizing they might die?

The Tet Offensive raised to a new level public distress over the Johnson administration and its military experts. Clearly, it dashed American hopes of a successful end to the war. As South Vietnamese army general and deputy prime minister Tran Van Don put it, after the Tet Offensive "the heart went out of the American war effort, and the United States began its disengagement policy."

Despite the Tet Offensive, former President Eisenhower wanted America to continue bombing North Vietnam. "Who wants to stop it?" he asked Richard Nixon. "The Communists want to stop it because it is hurting them. Therefore, we should continue it."

• • •

When Americans questioned the war's cost in both lives and money, Vice President Hubert Humphrey defended his boss, Lyndon Johnson. "No sane person in the country likes the war in Vietnam. Neither does President Johnson."

General William Westmoreland, however, called for another 206,000 men to fight the war. Johnson recalled General Westmoreland, signaling a decision against major escalation of the war.

During the Tet Offensive American forces liberated the delta village of Ben Tre but, in doing so, destroyed the village, which led an American officer to say candidly to reporter Peter Arnett, "It became necessary to destroy the town in order to save it."

A generation of Americans fought in Southeast Asia, and many of them died there. The statistics of the long Vietnam War are staggering. Nine million eighty-seven thousand American military personnel served on active duty during the Vietnam era, from August 5, 1964, to May 7, 1975. Of that number, 3.4 million served in the Southeast Asian theater of Vietnam, Laos, and Cambodia, including flight crews based in Thailand and sailors in adjacent South China Sea waters. About 1.7 million men who served at the time were draftees—the Marines drafted 42,633 men—but only 38 percent of that number actually went to Vietnam. The last man was drafted on June 30, 1973.

About 2.7 million people served within the borders of South Vietnam, not including 50,000 personnel, mainly military advisors, who served between 1960 and 1964. Between 1 million and 1.6 million men and women either fought in combat, provided close support, or were fairly regularly exposed to enemy attack during the length of the war. This includes 7,484 women, about 6,250 of whom were nurses. Eight nurses died in Vietnam, including one listed as KIA, killed in action.

At latest count, the American death toll stood at 58,202, including men formerly classified as MIA. Of the total number killed in Vietnam, 47,378 are listed as hostile deaths, the rest nonhostile. Draftees accounted for 30.4 percent of combat deaths in Vietnam, 17,725 men.

• • •

Of the 16 million American men who fought during World War II, 10 million of them were drafted. Only 43,000 refused to go when called, three times the number of conscientious objectors (COs) as in World War I. Six thousand or so World War II COs went to prison rather than fight, four times the number in the War to End All Wars. During World War II, one out of every six men in federal prison was a conscientious objector.

However, the Pentagon's claimed number of men—those 43,000—who didn't show up for the draft may not be exactly accurate, and the real figure may be much higher. As many as 350,000 men may actually have been draft evaders during World War II, including those who refused to go, some who stayed out on technical grounds, and some few deserters.

The government in Washington never treated the Vietnam War as a "total war," and because of this local draft boards had a great deal of leeway in deciding who got deferments. Thanks to the post–World War II baby boom, there were a lot of young draft-age men, and this, too, gave local draft boards more leeway. At first, if a young man could make a good enough case to his draft board that he had a productive or vital civilian job, or that he was doing all right in college, then he'd be exempt from service.

From 1960 to 1975, some 26.9 million men were legally liable for the draft. Of that number, about 8.7 million volunteered and 2.2 million were drafted; some 15.4 million were either disqualified or deferred, meaning that about half a million men technically were draft dodgers. However, only about 210,000 were charged with draft evasion and only 8,700 of those were convicted of the charge.

During Vietnam, some COs performed alternative service with the FCNL, the Friends Committee on National Legislation, basically a Quaker organization. In a 1988 interview in the *Sunday Oregonian*, CO David Hartsough told how he used his alternative service to try to "dig out the facts" about the Tonkin Gulf incident and spent a couple of days making phone calls to higher and higher levels at the Pentagon. "Finally," he remembered, "I got referred to a general . . . and the general said, 'Wait a minute. Let me put you on hold.'" The "hold" apparently didn't work, and Hartsough heard the conversation:

So he put me on hold, and then he called this other general. He said [to the other general], "This man Hartsough has been calling the Pentagon for the last two days asking all these questions, and his questions are of more than just *passing** interest. If I had anything to say about it, I'd draft him and send him over to Vietnam immediately." And I could hear this while I was on hold.

He got back on and said, "We're not going to answer your questions."

About a week later, the FCNL was notified that COs could no longer do alternative service work with them.

Probably the most famous conscientious objector of the Vietnam War was Cassius Marcellus Clay Jr., the heavyweight boxing champion of the world. He was drafted in 1966 but by then he'd converted to Islam and changed his name to Muhammad Ali. He claimed that being a Muslim—at the time, the term was *Black Muslim*—he was a minister of religion and, therefore, should be exempt from the draft. He applied for conscientious-objector status. When he was rejected, he refused to report for duty. The World Boxing Association stripped Ali of his title, and in June 1967, he was convicted of violating the Selective Service Act. The government fined him ten thousand dollars and sentenced him to five years in prison. Ali remained free on bond while he appealed the conviction, and four years later the U.S. Supreme Court unanimously reversed his conviction. Muhammad Ali never went to jail, but professional boxing, which may be the most corrupt of all major sports, proved just how "patriotic" it was.

In refusing to go to Vietnam, Ali explained that "I ain't got no quarrel with them Viet Cong," adding, "No Viet Cong has never called me a nigger." It became the cry for many antiwar African Americans.

In many cases during the Vietnam War, a guy didn't have to claim to be a CO or to run off to Canada to evade the draft: Friendly physi-

---

* Emphasis in the original.

cians gave anxious young men medical and/or psychological deferments. Thanks to "draft counselors," some men learned how to claim that they belonged to subversive organizations or to fake medical symptoms at their preinduction examinations. A sixties draft-resistance poster showed three young ladies—activist singer Joan Baez and her two sisters—all wearing the latest fashions, with the declaration: "GIRLS SAY YES TO BOYS WHO SAY NO."

Many men, including future politicians Dan Quayle and George W. Bush, joined the National Guard, the Air National Guard, or the Reserves, knowing the odds of their being called to active duty were slim. Fearing a political backlash, President Johnson never mobilized the Guard. Very early in the war, the Joint Chiefs of Staff recommended the mobilization of large numbers of guardsmen and reservists. The secretary of defense turned it over to the president, and Johnson turned it down. Later on, in 1966 and '67, the Joint Chiefs tried again, and again President Johnson rejected the idea.

Calling up the Guard, of course, would have been highly disruptive, not only to an individual's life, but to the life of a community in general. Think of the Gulf War (1990–91) when about a fourth of all reserves were mobilized. During the Berlin Crisis of 1961, four Army National Guard divisions and many Air National Guard squadrons were mobilized, along with many reservists. Many of these were not released for almost two years. There was so much public criticism of this that Lyndon Johnson decided not to activate the Guard and Reserves for Vietnam.

However, more than 340,000 national guardsmen served on active duty during the Vietnam War, mainly in Europe. Over a seven-year period (1965–72) elements of the Guard were called up on 543 occasions, either by individual states or the federal government. They fought forest fires, protected civil rights marchers, suppressed prison riots, provided flood relief, delivered mail during postal strikes, and even helped find lost children.

Only 8,728* members of the Army National Guard or the Air National Guard served in Vietnam under combat conditions, too few,

---

* One source gives this at 6,140.

under the Defense Department's definition of it, to qualify as "mobilization." Still, of that small number, 94 guardsmen were killed and three are still listed as missing in action (MIA). When North Korean forces seized the spy ship *Pueblo* in 1968, the Joint Chiefs asked for as many as 54,000 national guardsmen and reservists to be called up. President Johnson agreed to activate about 30,000 of them (nearly 23,000 guardsmen, the rest air guardsmen and reservists) and, as he had predicted, this caused quite a stir among the public.

Some national guardsmen and reservists volunteered for duty in Vietnam. The first air force Medal of Honor to be awarded—the first not only in Vietnam but the first since the separate air force version of the decoration had come in to being in 1950—went to air national guardsman Maj. Bernard F. Fisher. Piloting an A1E Skyraider on March 10, 1966, Fisher landed under fire on a field in enemy territory to rescue a fellow airman. Another air guardsman, Lt. Col. James R. Riser, became the first living man to be awarded the Air Force Cross* for heroism while a prisoner of war in 1965. Captain Jerome R. Daly, of the Pennsylvania National Guard was named "army aviator of the year in 1967." Despite this, members of the National Guard and the reserves were criticized as refugees from the war. At one point, the waiting list to join the Guard reached one hundred thousand.

About 65 percent of all American troops in Vietnam were volunteers, although many of them enlisted because the draft board was breathing heavily down their necks. That's almost exactly opposite the percentage of draftees versus volunteers in World War II, when only 35 percent were volunteers and 65 percent were drafted.

The claim that America fought the Vietnam War with troops much younger than those of World War II is misleading. According to historians James F. Dunnigan and Albert A. Nofi, the average age of American troops in Vietnam was twenty-two, only four years younger than World War II's average soldier, not the nineteen year age others claim. Warrant officers and officers were a bit older in Vietnam, but the draft normally took a young man at age twenty. Add to that

---

* The second highest decoration in the air force.

the months of training prior to shipping out, factor in their length of service before going to Vietnam, and the figure still isn't as young as some claim.

The average age of soldiers with the military occupational specialty (MOS) 11B (infantry rifleman) who died in the war was about 22.5 years. The "Eleven Bravos," as they were called, accounted for 31.76 percent of American deaths in the war. The average age of American military personnel who died in Vietnam was 23.11 years, with 61 percent being 21 or younger. Only a few hundred of the fifty-eight-thousand-plus American deaths in the war were of those older than 30. At least five men killed in Vietnam were under 17 years of age (they used false identification to get in, sometimes with the knowledge of their parents). One, a Marine, apparently was only 13, almost matching the age of World War II's youngest combatant, Calvin Graham of Fort Worth, Texas, who was only 12 years old when he enlisted in the navy.

Critics of the Vietnam War make at least two other claims that are untrue: that American troops in Vietnam were uneducated and that a disproportionate number of U.S. troops in Vietnam were African American. First, the education claim. During World War II, only 24 percent of enlisted men were high school graduates, and 20 percent of all forties-era draftees and volunteers were functionally illiterate. In Vietnam, 20 percent of enlisted men had at least some college. However, the military itself believed the education level was too low. "Project 100,000" was begun as a remedial education program to include, as the name implies, a hundred thousand men each year. Those taken into the program fell into "Mental Category IV," the second lowest of five groupings based on induction test scores. The object was to bring them up to standards and then put them in uniform. Over the life of "Project 100,000" about 157,000 men were drafted and another 200,000 volunteered. "New Standards" men, they were called, and they seemed to do just about as well in Vietnam as those who had originally passed the tests. In fact, a lower proportion of New Standards troops died in Vietnam than did their better-educated fellow troops. Maybe Project 100,000 taught them how to duck.

116

As for race, blacks made up 10.6 percent of America's population during the 1940s, but the then-segregated military never came close to having that percentage of black forces. After President Harry Truman ended segregation in the armed forces, the number of blacks who were career military personnel increased beyond the percentage in nonmilitary life. As a result, when America became involved in the Vietnam War, a large number of troops in Vietnam were black. About twenty percent of NCOs in the army were African American, although the percentage of black officers was lower than the percentage of blacks in the overall population.

During Vietnam, African Americans comprised between 10 and 12 percent of the American population, about the same percentage then as at any other time since the American Revolution. As the war continued, and the armed forces expanded, the percentage of African Americans serving in Vietnam decreased markedly, simply because the draft brought in proportionately more whites. In 1972, for example, overall 11.2 percent of American military personnel were African American. By then, of course, the perception had become pervasive that frontline troops were mostly black.

Compared to the Civil War and World War II, Vietnam saw a larger percentage of black deaths. The Civil War saw 2.7 percent of black troops die, and in World War II the figure was 3 percent. During both of those wars, segregation was the official policy in military and civilian life. From 1964 to 1966, about a fifth (20 percent*) of those killed in action in Vietnam were African Americans; 80 percent were Caucasian. Over time, as the percentage of black to white troops fell in Vietnam, the overall percentage of blacks who died there wasn't much higher than the percentage of blacks in the general population at the time and was about the same percentage as that of blacks in the military.

Amputation or crippling wounds to lower extremities were 300 percent higher in Vietnam than in World War II and 70 percent higher than in Korea. Mainly, this was due to the increased number

---

* Other sources put this at 7,241 African Americans who died, or 12.5 percent.

of land mines and booby traps used. U.S. and South Vietnamese military forces relied heavily upon land mines to fight the war. In 2000, the United Nations reported that from 80 to 110 million potentially lethal land mines, deployed in sixty-two nations, remain buried. As many as 350,000 land mines may still be buried in Vietnam. Many of them, despite the manufacturers' claims that the mines will deteriorate and no longer be active, remain lethal; year after year "inactive" land mines take civilian lives and limbs. Not to mention those men, women, and children who fell victim to mines and were maimed during the war.

Seventy-six percent of all men sent to Vietnam came from lower-middle working-class backgrounds, with three-fourths having family incomes above the poverty level. Eighty-two percent of Vietnam veterans who saw heavy combat strongly believe the war was lost because of lack of political will. Seventy-five percent of the general public agree.

While we add and subtract the number of Americans who fought, died, and had their lives destroyed by the war in Vietnam, all too often we forget about the Vietnamese themselves. The price they paid makes ours seem small. South Vietnamese armed forces lost more than 200,000 killed in action, with another 2 million–plus civilian casualties, all of this from a population of about 17 million. Add to that about 110,000 who became drug addicts (how they got to be addicts is another story in itself), 400,000 who suffered amputations, a half million women and girls who became prostitutes, and 800,000 children who were orphanned. The North Vietnamese army lost over 900,000 lives, mainly while fighting in the South. No official total number of North Vietnamese troops killed is available. The same is true of North Vietnamese civilians. As one North Vietnamese officer wrote, "It is the duty of my generation to die for our country."

World War II was America's most expensive war, costing about $560 billion, including payments for veterans' benefits and interest on debts. All things considered, the American Revolution cost a mere pittance: about $124 million. Our first "billion-dollar war" was the

American Civil War, on which we spent about $8 billion brother-killing-brother. World War I cost about $66 million and the Korean War ran us about $70 million. Counting payments for veterans' benefits and interest on debts, the Vietnam War ran about $121.5 billion.

Early on March 16, 1968, troops from Charlie Company—C Company, 1st Battalion, 20th Infantry, an element of the 11th Light Infantry Brigade of the 23d "Americal" Division—swarmed into the hamlet of My Lai 4, one of several villages in the Son Tinh district of Quang Ngai province. It was an area known to be sympathetic toward the Viet Cong; the troops called the area "Pinkville" (as in Communist "red") and it was even colored pink on their maps. The GIs expected to meet the 48th Viet Cong Battalion at My Lai. Instead of enemy troops, they found women, children, and old men, many of them still busy cooking breakfast rice over outdoor fires. No armed VC, no signs of the enemy. But who could tell a "good gook" from a "bad gook" without uniforms? They all wear black pajamas, don't they?

The troops were frustrated and angry and more than just a little afraid. After all, they'd been hit several times recently by sniper fire and booby traps. They were commanded by twenty-four-year-old 2d Lt. William C. Calley, and that morning they'd been dropped by helicopter on a search-and-destroy mission. Instead of a mission, it became a massacre, the worst atrocity ever committed by American troops.

When a search of the hamlet failed to uncover any Viet Cong troops—only a few weapons were discovered—Lieutenant Calley ordered his men to round everybody up in the center of the village and kill them. Calley's troops mowed down the villagers with automatic-weapons fire, killing some on the spot. Others they herded into ditches, where they raped the women and then killed them. The soldiers rounded up fifteen to twenty of the villagers near a temple, where some of the locals were kneeling and crying and praying. As one investigator later put it, "Various soldiers . . . walked by and executed these women and children by shooting them in the head." Some tossed grenades into hootches (huts) and set them on fire. Sometimes the hootch occupants were still inside.

The civilian death toll was at least 150 and may have been much higher, perhaps as high as 560. A likely figure is 347, but we just don't know.

Some of the troops protested—one called it "point-blank murder"—and refused to take part in the massacre despite threats from Calley that he'd court-martial them if they didn't. Rather than massacre the civilians, one soldier shot himself in the foot. Helicopter pilot WO1 Hugh C. Thompson Jr. personally prevented the murder of some of the villagers by threatening to fire on the troops with the chopper's minigun. He managed to rescue a handful of children.

In an interview with CBS Television's Mike Wallace in 1969, Pvt. Paul Meadlo told what he saw and did at My Lai.

> Wallace: You killed how many? At that time?
>
> Meadlo: Well, I fired . . . on automatic, so you can't . . . you just spray the area . . . so you can't know how many you killed 'cause they were going fast. So I might have killed ten or fifteen of them.
>
> Wallace: Men, women, and children?
>
> Meadlo: Men, women, and children.
>
> Wallace: And babies?
>
> Meadlo: And babies. . . .
>
> Wallace: Why did you do it?
>
> Meadlo: Why did I do it? Because I felt I was ordered to do it, and it seemed like that, at the time, I felt like I was doing the right thing.

At the end of the day, Lieutenant Calley filed a report on the operation, indicating that his men had killed 128 enemy troops. For this, he received a citation, and for a year and a half nothing more was heard of My Lai.

Even from the first, however, Calley's superiors knew the truth of what had happened. In fact, company commander Capt. Ernest Medina, who'd given nebulous orders to "clean the village out," was present in My Lai at the time of the incident. The battalion commander, the task-force commander, and the brigade commander all knew about the massacre almost as soon as it happened. None of them, not even division commander Maj. Gen. Samuel W. Koster, did anything about it.* When several GIs tried to report the incident, their efforts were quashed. Outsiders who heard rumors of the deaths were brushed off or ignored. True, Communist propaganda told about the massacre, but after all, it was the enemy who made the claims, and we were the good guys, right?

The My Lai massacre finally came to light when a soldier named Ronald Ridenhour, who hadn't been at the village during the shooting, wrote a letter to the chairman of the Armed Services Committee, reporting what he'd heard from several sources. He called it a "dark and bloody" event. His letter went to Secretary of the Army Stanley Resor, who passed it on to army chief of staff Gen. William Westmoreland. The general immediately ordered the Criminal Investigation Division (CID) to look into the matter.

Under Lt. Gen. William R. Peers, the CID investigated the incident—what happened, who took part, and why it was covered up. Included in the investigation were photographs taken by army photographer Sgt. Ronald Hoeberle, who'd been with the troops at My Lai.

The army charged twenty-five soldiers (fourteen of them officers), including twelve for war crimes (two officers and ten enlisted men), with covering up the massacre. Lieutenant Calley was also charged, as were two chaplains who'd heard about the massacre but hadn't reported it. In the end, however, only four men went on trial, one of them Calley. Charges against the others were dismissed on technicalities. Of the four who were tried, three men were acquitted due to technicalities. Only Calley was convicted. He was sentenced to life in prison; however, President Nixon reduced Calley's sentence to twenty years and then to ten. Finally, the sentence was set at two years of house arrest, and then he was paroled.

Far-right supporters of the Vietnam War claimed the atrocity was an aberration, that Calley was the victim of a "leftist" antiwar movement. To those who opposed the war, Calley and My Lai epitomized

---

* Koster was indicted but charges were dismissed. The army reduced him in rank and issued a letter of censure, effectively ending his career.

the war's immorality and injustice. Makes you wonder, though how we'd feel if a band of Viet Cong massacred hundreds of innocent Americans.

In 1928, representatives of forty-eight nations agreed to the Geneva Convention Relating to the Treatment of Prisoners of War. The convention's ninety-seven articles governed all aspects of military captivity, including notifying the International Red Cross that an individual is being held prisoner. POWs were to be served food equal to that served to troops of the detaining country and were not to be kept in solitary confinement. While in other wars there had been frequent lapses in the way nations treated prisoners, in the Vietnam War American prisoners routinely were ill housed, poorly fed, and often subjected to beatings and torturous interrogation.

The Hanoi regime never gave formal notification of men taken prisoner, so it's never been known exactly how many POWs they held or how many POWs died while being held or how many POWs they may still hold. Originally, Hanoi denied holding POWs. War criminals, yes; POWs, no. When the North Vietnamese finally admitted holding American prisoners, they did so only for propaganda purposes. And according to them, when the war was over, all American prisoners were released.

Immediately, friends and families of some 2,273 Americans wanted to know where their sons and husbands and brothers and lovers were. They demanded a full accounting of all men missing in action. Vietnam, some people claim, continues to hold Americans. Fifty-five of those declared still missing in action are known to have been taken prisoner; the rest were last seen under circumstances that strongly suggest they should be classified as "presumed dead."

The MIA issue developed a whole industry. First came bracelets sold with a POW or MIA's name on it. Second came bracelets with names the bracelet sellers fabricated just to make money. Then came the development of the POW/MIA flag, now flown over most U.S. cities and many American homes and businesses.

Some POWs may have been killed by American bombs. The North Vietnamese put some prison camps in areas likely to be struck. The infamous "Hanoi Hilton" comes to mind. Following the

November 21, 1970, unsuccessful attempt to rescue prisoners at the Son Tay prison camp outside Hanoi—code-named "Operation King-pin"—North Vietnam concentrated POWs in the Hao Lo prison, a former French colonial jail. To Americans prisoners, it became known as the Hanoi Hilton. Between 1964 and 1973, the Hanoi Hilton housed more than 700 U.S. POWs.

More than 8,000 American troops were listed as MIA following the Korean War, nearly three and a half times as many as after Vietnam. Following World War II, American MIAs totaled 78,773. We still don't know where some of them are or what happened to them.

While we're justifiably concerned over America's Vietnam MIAs, Vietnam itself had an even bigger problem. On June 1, 1993, Vietnam's foreign minister, Nguyen Manh Cam, appealed to U.S. senator John F. Kerry for help in locating its own missing of more than 300,000.

Students rioted all over America; black ghettos in Detroit and Newark and Watts went up in flames. The antiwar movement pushed for America to get out of Vietnam, and although not everyone agreed with them, the war didn't sit very well in many segments of the nation. Many Americans felt that the time had come in Vietnam: either win the damn war or get the hell out. Here we were, three years into a ground war, and the Joint Chiefs of Staff apparently didn't have a plan for victory.

President Johnson didn't subscribe to the goal of traditional victory. He instructed his ambassador to Vietnam, Ellsworth Bunker, to work toward an eventual U.S. disengagement without losing the war.

The photograph of a young girl running naked from her village after being burned by napalm and an Associated Press photograph of Vietnam national police chief Nguyen Ngoc Loan* executing a suspected Viet Cong officer following the Tet Offensive, clearly

---

* The girl, Kim Phuc, later moved to Canada, and, in 1975, Loan left Vietnam to live in the United States.

aroused the American people. Women and children were being injured or killed, and we were backing a government whose members didn't think twice about coldly killing someone in the middle of a city street. Violence was triumphing over law.

By October 1968, much of the U.S. public had become disenchanted with the Vietnam War. When American troops first waded ashore in Vietnam in 1965, sixty-one percent of the American public approved. But by October 1967, that approval rate had dropped to only about forty-four percent; forty-six percent were against it.

Ninety-seven percent of Vietnam-era veterans received honorable discharges. Of those veterans who saw heavy combat during the war, ninety percent say they're proud to have served their country. Sixty-six percent of Vietnam vets say that they'd do it all over again if they were called.

Now, nearly thirty years after the war's end, eighty-seven percent of the American public says it holds Vietnam veterans in high esteem.

By the year 2000, roughly eighty percent of all Vietnamese were under age forty. Like most Americans, today most Vietnamese weren't alive at the time of conflict between the two nations.

CHAPTER SEVEN

Shots Ring Out:
JFK, RFK, and MLK

Above all he [John F. Kennedy] gave the world for an imperishable moment the vision of a leader who greatly understood the terror and the hope, the diversity and the possibility, of life on this planet and who made people look beyond nation and race to the future of humanity.
Arthur Meir Schlesinger Jr., *A Thousand Days* (1965)

Good morning, Mr. President.
Caroline Kennedy to her father on November 9, 1960, the first time anyone ever addressed John F. Kennedy as president

Originally, Congress set the vice president's annual salary at five thousand dollars, a fifth of the president's. Even that was too high, according to some congressmen, and they proposed a sort of piecework system, paying on the basis of work done. At least a couple of vice presidents agreed that there wasn't much to the job. John Nance Garner, Franklin D. Roosevelt's first VP, said the job wasn't worth "a pitcher of warm spit." Or something like that. Garner's actual words were more like "a pitcher of warm piss," but that would have been too gross for the time.*

Lyndon B. Johnson remembered that "The vice presidency is filled with trips around the world, chauffeurs, men saluting, people clapping, [and] chairmanship of councils, but in the end it is nothing." He added: "I detested every minute of it."

John Fitzgerald Kennedy—he would become JFK to the world's headline writers—was born on May 29, 1917, at 83 Beale Street in Brookline, Massachusetts. He was the second of nine children.

---

* A story about President Harry Truman has a friend of Mrs. Truman complaining about the president's frequent use of the word *manure* in everyday, non-farm conversation. "Can't you get him to use another word?" the friend asked Bess Truman. "You don't know," Mrs. Truman replied, "how long it took me to get him to say 'manure.'"

Photographs taken of young Jack when he was about six months old show a grinning baby, happily playing with his toes. He grew into a rail-thin sickly child—whooping cough, tonsillitis, measles, chicken pox, scarlet fever, and appendicitis—so sickly that his older brother, Joe, used to tease him and say that a mosquito took a big risk in biting Jack.

JFK's father, Joseph Patrick Kennedy, was U.S. ambassador to England's Court of St. James's from 1937 to 1940. That naturally contributed to John's ideas and thinking and even how people reacted to him.

Kennedy's days were those of a golden child, of wealthy and adoring, if sometimes too strict, parents. He attended Choate, a Wallingford, Connecticut, private preparatory school for young boys. Pulitzer Prize–winning Historian Doris Kearns Goodwin says that "The students were mostly Protestant, though in recent years a few Catholics had been admitted, including the two sons of Ambassador Joseph Kennedy, Joe Junior and John Fitzgerald Kennedy." He ranked sixty-fourth in his 1935 Choate graduating class of 112. In England, JFK attended the London School of Economics, but while there, he contracted jaundice.

JFK enrolled at Princeton University on September 23, 1935; however, the jaundice he'd contracted in London delayed his entrance, and after a recurrence of the illness, he dropped out on December 12. A year later, he entered Harvard. On his twenty-first birthday, May 29, 1938, Kennedy received a one-million-dollar trust fund from his father, and in 1939, he toured Europe. Instead of attending classes in the second semester of his junior year at Harvard, John served as secretary to his father the ambassador in London; he was in London on September 1, 1939, when Germany invaded Poland and started World War II.

Back in America, JFK graduated from Harvard in June 1940, where, once more, he'd been an average student. As a Harvard undergraduate he played football, golf, was on the sailing and swim teams, and was an editor of the *Harvard Crimson*. As president, Jack Kennedy once gave a commencement address at Yale University, which presented him with an honorary doctorate. "I have the best of all possible worlds," Kennedy declared, "a Harvard education and a Yale degree."

For a while, in the fall of 1940, Kennedy studied at Stanford Graduate School of Business at Palo Alto, California. It was while he was at Stanford that his first book, *While England Slept*, was published; it was an expansion of his senior thesis at Harvard and analyzed England's lack of preparations for the Second World War. One critic said it should have been titled *While Daddy Slept*, in reference to Papa Joe Kennedy's accommodating attitude toward the Nazi onslaught of Europe.

In the fall of 1941, two months before Japan bombed Pearl Harbor, he was commissioned an ensign in the U.S. Navy, but he wasn't called up for duty until 1942. After attending PT (patrol boat) training school, Kennedy was sent to the South Pacific, where (as lieutenant, j.g.) he assumed command of PT-109. Five months later his boat was rammed and sunk by the Japanese destroyer *Amagiri* in a high-traffic area of the Solomon Islands known as "the Slot." Two crewmen died in the incident, but Kennedy helped rescue at least one badly injured crewman. The survivors hung on to their wrecked boat until they could reach an atoll named Bird Island. JFK scrawled a message on a coconut, talked a cooperative native into taking the coconut to a nearby Australian coast-watcher, and Kennedy and crew were rescued. JFK was proclaimed a hero; in an after-hours interview during his presidential campaign, a reporter asked Kennedy how he'd become a hero. "It was easy," JFK said, "they sank my boat." A tie clip fashioned like PT-109 became a campaign memento in 1960, and that message-bearing coconut the islander had taken to the coast-watcher ended up on Jack's Oval Office desk. Who could ask for a more appealing story, and of course Hollywood (after Kennedy was elected president) ate it up, turning the incident into a movie, wide screen and in glorious color.

To top it off, while Kennedy recuperated from a back injury he'd received when his boat was rammed and sunk, he wrote another book. Well, maybe. Some critics say he wrote only parts of it, that longtime advisor Theodore "Ted" Sorensen wrote it for him. In any event, the book, *Profiles in Courage*, won a Pulitzer Prize, and JFK's name is on both the book and the award.

After recuperating and being discharged from the navy, Kennedy worked as a journalist for a short while and then got down to his life's true work. He was twice elected congressman from Massachusetts, where he sometimes was referred to as "Mattress Jack," because of his sexual appetite.

He went on to the U.S. Senate, where he served from 1953 to 1961. He was assigned room 362 in the Senate Office Building. Directly across the hall in room 361 sat his future opponent, Richard M. Nixon. "It was," Kennedy's secretary Evelyn Lincoln recalled, "a busy corridor between those two offices." In 1961, of course, JFK changed offices and jobs.

Let's face it, even during the presidential primaries Kennedy's youthful good looks attracted a lot of votes: the "Kennedy image." His primary rival, Hubert Humphrey was, according to historian William L. O'Neill, "overweight, [had a] big balding dome, square little chin, and rat-trap mouth." O'Neill, who by far isn't a Kennedy fan, says that Humphrey "didn't look like a President [but] offered a rather comic appearance." It didn't hurt that Kennedy had at his side perhaps the most beautiful first lady ever to hang a little black dress in a White House closet.

Jacqueline Lee Bouvier Kennedy was twelve years younger than Jack, and like JFK, she'd been born wealthy, grown up wealthy, and lived wealthy. She was just twenty-four years old when they married. Like most of the great events of their lives, the way they met was something out of a Hollywood script. Jackie was an inquiring reporter-photographer for a Washington newspaper when she interviewed Congressman Kennedy. It may not have been love at first sight, but it was close enough. It's pretty certain that once the American public saw Jack and Jackie together, they fell in love with both of them.

In 1950, Joseph Kennedy, financially backed Republican Richard Nixon. But as John Kennedy once described him, "Hell, he's a businessman. He gave [money] to everybody." Ten years after Joe Kennedy had backed Nixon, Joe's son John ran against Nixon and defeated Tricky Dick for the presidency.

On January 2, 1960, John Fitzgerald Kennedy formally announced that he was running for the Democratic Party's nomination for president of the United States. It was a cold day in Washington, D.C., and only a small crowd of reporters, family members, and Kennedy's senatorial staff gathered in the Senate Caucus Room to hear the announcement.

Early on, he fought and beat Minnesota's Senator Hubert Humphrey, the odds-on nominee at the beginning of the race, and at one point Humphrey claimed Joe Kennedy was busy buying votes for his son. It was a charge John had first faced back in 1952 when he'd won a U.S. Senate seat. Shortly after that election, he attended the annual Gridiron Club meeting in Washington at which reporters teased him about the charge, introducing him with a song they called, "The Bill Goes to Daddy." Kennedy brought down the house by reading from a telegram he said had come from his father: "Dear Jack. Don't buy a single vote more than necessary. I'll be damned if I'll pay for a landslide!"

During the Democratic convention, Lyndon Johnson, who himself hoped to be the party's candidate, invited Kennedy to visit the Texas delegation to debate him in front of the wildly pro-Johnson audience, and surprisingly Kennedy accepted the invitation. He did more than accept, he stunned the crowd when he said that he'd come to endorse Lyndon Johnson. He admired the big Texan, Kennedy said, had great affection for him, and strongly supported him—to remain Senate Majority leader.

John F. Kennedy stunned the nation by winning the nomination on the first ballot. Kennedy then stunned convention delegations by naming Lyndon B. Johnson as his vice-presidential running mate. Later, someone, who apparently couldn't conceive of the Texan playing second fiddle, asked the then vice-presidential nominee about the LBJ button Johnson was still wearing. Johnson quickly said, "It means, 'Let's Back Jack.'"

Vice President Richard Nixon had little trouble getting the Republican nomination. Meeting in Chicago in July, the GOP named Nixon as its presidential candidate and Henry Cabot Lodge of Massachusetts as his running mate. Perhaps the most trouble Nixon had came from his boss, Dwight Eisenhower. About a month after Nixon received the Republican nomination, a reporter asked Ike what presidential decisions Nixon, as Ike's vice president, had participated in. Eisenhower smiled and said, "If you give me a week

I might think of one." Ike later telephoned Dick Nixon to say he'd only been joking.

In his farewell address on January 17, 1961, America's thirty-fourth president*, Dwight D. Eisenhower, reminded us that in the past, U.S. industry had geared up for war only when the battle had begun. But now the world was fighting a Cold War, he said, and "a permanent armaments industry of vast proportions" existed, employing 3.5 million Americans. An old soldier himself, Eisenhower warned that "We must guard against the acquisition of unwarranted influence, whether sought or unsought, by the military-industrial complex." It was a new thought in a changing world.

Three days after Ike's farewell address, the nation's new president John F. Kennedy, called on his "fellow Americans" to "ask not what your country can do for you; ask what you can do for your country." And to his "fellow citizens of the world," he said, "ask not what America will do for you, but what together we can do for the freedom of man."

Inauguration Day was cold in Washington, D.C. A heavy snowfall had prevented former president Herbert Hoover's plane from landing. Despite the cold, the forty-three-year-old Kennedy stood hatless and without his topcoat; his seventy-year-old predecessor wore a heavy coat, a scarf, and a hat.

Seated on the inaugural stand was former first lady Edith Bolling Wilson, Woodrow Wilson's widow. To help ward off the cold, the eighty-nine-year-old Mrs. Wilson carried a flask of bourbon from which, from time to time, she sought comfort.

Another former first lady, Eleanor Roosevelt, had also been invited to the inauguration, but she turned down the invitation. It would have meant sharing the platform with Joe Kennedy, the new president's father, and Joe and Eleanor shared a longtime hatred of each other. The reasons why they hated each other aren't quite clear, but

---

* Eisenhower actually was the thirty-third person to be president; Grover Cleveland served two, nonconsecutive terms, and is counted as both the twenty-second and twenty-fourth.

it may have been because of an incident that had occurred during the final days of Joe Kennedy's ambassadorship to England.

Eleanor Roosevelt claimed that Joe Kennedy had visited FDR at the president's Hyde Park retreat, but within ten minutes of the start of the visit an aide rushed up to Eleanor, telling her she had to get Joe Kennedy out of there. So Mrs. Roosevelt rushed back into the room, where she found FDR white faced and furious. Eleanor asked Joe to step outside for a moment, and the president told his wife that "I never want to see that man as long as I live." Joe Kennedy had tried to persuade Roosevelt to cut a deal with Hitler to end the war.

As John Kennedy took the oath of office as the nation's thirty-fifth president, Richard Nixon stood less than ten feet away from him. After the inauguration, Nixon told a Kennedy aide that he wished he'd said some of the things Kennedy had in the ceremony. "What part," the aide asked—"that part about 'Ask not what your country can do for you, but what you can do for your country?'" No, Richard Nixon replied: "The part that starts, 'I do solemnly swear.'"

The nation's political experts were stunned in 1960 when the *New York Times* endorsed John Kennedy for president; the newspaper usually endorsed Republicans. After the election, in a play on the paper's ongoing advertising campaign, Kennedy remarked, "I am one person who can truthfully say, 'I got my job through the *New York Times.*'"

One thing John F. Kennedy had bestowed on him was the nickname "Mattress Jack," and by all accounts it was well and truly deserved. While a twenty-four-year-old navy ensign, he'd had an affair with former Danish beauty queen Inga Marie Arvad, the wife of Hungarian movie director Paul Fejos. As a prewar journalist, Inga interviewed and socialized with Adolf Hitler and other leading Nazis.*

Jack apparently met and bedded Washington party girl and Elizabeth Taylor look-alike Ellie Rometsch, who had been born in what

---

* Joe Kennedy arranged for Jack to be transferred from Washington, D.C., to a desk job at the Charleston Naval Base in South Carolina, and even there the Jack Kennedy–Inga Arvad romance continued for a couple of months, during which FBI Chief J. Edgar Hoover kept the couple under surveillance, making explicit recordings of the lovers at play.

became East Germany and who, as a child, had been a member of a Communist Party youth group. She was also a prostitute.

Kennedy bedded his senatorial aide, Pamela Turnure, but according to reports Turnure's old-fashioned landlords, Flo and Leonard Kater, tried to stop Jack's extramarital shenanigans with their tenant. The Katers bombarded Washington newspapers with stories about the sexy senator, but for the most part the papers ignored the claims. After JFK was elected president, he took Turnure to the White House, and her former landlords—by then she'd found an apartment whose owners didn't care what went on—showed up at the inauguration with a sign that read: "Do You Want an Adulterer in the White House?"

Actress Marilyn Monroe certainly was John Kennedy's most glamorous bedmate. In addition to her other activities, according to the star's longtime publicist Patricia Newcomb, Marilyn "made Jack laugh." Of course, Marilyn didn't make the first lady laugh when the actress showed up at the president's forty-fifth birthday in a twelve-thousand-dollar gown that Adlai Stevenson described as "skin and beads," adding, "I didn't see the beads!" The dress was made of rhinestones sewn to a flesh-colored mesh and was so tight it had to be glued to Marilyn's breasts and she had to be sewn into the outfit.

Jack Kennedy also seduced (or maybe he was seduced by) another blond bombshell, Jayne Mansfield. The Reverend Billy Graham once complained that "This country knows more about Jayne [Mansfield]'s statistics that about the second Commandment."* Statistically speaking, Jayne and Jack are said to have done more than tripped the light fantastic, so to speak, only three times.

Another infrequent Kennedy bedmate was actress Angie Dickinson, who supposedly celebrated Jack's 1960 nomination by skinny-

---

* According to Judeo-Christian tradition, the second commandment says, "Thou shalt not make thee any graven image. . . ." Perhaps Reverand Graham meant commandment number seven, which says, "Thou shalt not commit adultery." Most Prostestant, Anglican, and Orthodox Christians follow Jewish tradition in separating the commandments. The Roman Catholic and Lutheran churches, however, follow Saint Augustine's division, combining some and dividing others.

dipping with the candidate and celebrated his inauguration by romping in bed with him. Dickinson reportedly commented that her romantic rendezvous in Jack Kennedy's bed was "the most remarkable sixty seconds of my life."

The president was also reported to have bedded another actress, Lee Remick, as well as several movie starlets and starlet wannabees. JFK's brother-in-law Peter Lawford usually procured them for Kennedy.

Years before one presidential candidate admitted to smoking but not inhaling, marijuana, grass, weed, or dope—call it what you will—made it into a White House bedroom. The president's bedroom, in fact.

Mary Pinchot Meyer was a successful painter who began an affair with Jack Kennedy in March 1961, and it continued off and on until his death. Mary was a sister-in-law of longtime Kennedy pal and later *Washington Post* editor Ben Bradlee. Jack managed to sneak Mary into the White House more than thirty times. She once walked in carrying "a small box with six joints," according to Mary's friend James Angleton, who also happened to be director of covert operations at the CIA. Based on a conversation with Meyer, Angleton said that, right there in the Kennedys' White House, Mary and JFK shared a doobie. As they did, JFK laughingly commented that in just a couple of weeks, he'd be hosting a White House conference on narcotics. Ah, well. They smoked two more joints, and by then Kennedy was relaxed, his eyes closed. Mary Meyer suggested a fourth smoke, but JFK refused. "Suppose the Russians drop a bomb," he said.

Meyer was also a good friend of LSD guru Timothy Leary. Supposedly, Jack and Mary tripped out at least once on Tim's favorite flavor of acid.

Mary was murdered just ten months after JFK, and to this date, her killer hasn't been found. Jackie Kennedy's secretary was yet another of Jack's lovers, as were two other White House secretaries who frequently joined JFK in his noontime swimming sessions. The sessions ostensibly were designed to provide mild exercise and comfort to the president's back, but he used the time and pool for another exercise, which could also be said to be comforting. "It was common knowledge in the White House," staffer Larry Newman claimed, "that

133

when the president took lunch in the pool . . . nobody goes in there." Often, Newman said, Bobby and Teddy Kennedy would join brother Jack in a little aquatic romp. JFK referred to the two skinny-dipping young secretaries as "Fiddle" (Priscilla Weir) and "Faddle" (Jill Cowan).

Jackie, who had been "trained" by both Jack and her father, Black Jack Bouvier,* to accept adultery as an ugly fact of family life, knew about the secretaries and called them "the White House dogs." "Trained" or not, Jackie knew about many of Jack's extramarital affairs. Once, so the story goes, she handed her husband a pair of panties that she'd found in the presidential bed. "Here," she told him, "find out who owns these. They're not my size."

More salacious was the story that mob-connected Judith Campbell (later Judith Campbell Exner after she married pro golfer Dan Exner) was so captivated with Jack Kennedy that she believed he would—any day now—divorce Jackie and marry her. In the spring of 1962, while Jack and Bobby were trying to get rid of longtime FBI director J. Edgar Hoover, Hoover sent a memorandum to Bobby that can only be seen as a form of blackmail to keep his job.

Hoover had heard about Judy Campbell, apparently in connection with an FBI investigation of West Coast mob leader John Rosselli. Not content with letting the Kennedys know what he knew, Hoover leaked the Campbell story to Walter Winchell, who brought up Judith's name in his nationally syndicated column.

Hoover also leaked another story to the press, a claim that, in 1946, Jack Kennedy met and married Florida socialite Durie Malcolm. *Newsweek* magazine started to run the story, but Bobby ordered the FBI to release its file on the subject to the magazine's editor and Kennedy family friend Ben Bradlee (yes, the same Ben Bradlee who, as editor of the *Washington Post*, would unleash the Watergate story that led to Richard Nixon's downfall). *Newsweek* debunked the

---

* Jack Bouvier was involved with several women other than his wife, Janet. The *New York Daily News* even published a photograph of Jack, Janet, and a woman named Virginia Kernochan with whom, the day the photo was taken, Jack disappeared for the better part of the afternoon. He was an alcoholic, and on the day of Jackie's wedding to John Kennedy, Bouvier was too drunk to give her away.

Kennedy-Malcolm story, but the tale didn't die, just sort of languished on the back burners of gossip mongers. In 1997, Kennedy critic Seymour Hersh brought up the Malcolm story again, claiming that Jack and Durie had actually been married but that Papa Joe had nearly blown his top—he quotes a former Kennedy insider as saying that "The Old man had a shit fit and got it [the marriage] nullified."

Hersh admitted that there was no physical record of any Kennedy-Malcolm marriage—no marriage license, for instance—but he insisted that's because family aides literally tore up court records. Hersh also said that there was no record of a divorce (other than of Durie's previous two divorces). If, as Hersh claimed, the marriage really took place and that there really never was a divorce, that would have made Jack Kennedy a bigamist, his marriage to Jackie null and void, and their two children legally bastards.

In her eighties as the twentieth century ended, Durie Malcolm told the London *Sunday Times* that there was no truth to the story of marriage and bigamy. "I wouldn't," she said, "have married Jack Kennedy for all the tea in China." Why? she was asked. "If you want to know the truth, I didn't care for those Irish micks, and old Joe was a terrible man."

During the 1960 presidential campaign, Jackie Kennedy got a bit of advice from her mother, Janet Bouvier. She thought Jackie's designer fashions intimidated the public. "Why can't you look like Muriel Humphrey," she asked, "or Pat Nixon?" Of course Jackie didn't change her mind, and of course she gained a lot of good press (and good will) for her candidate husband.

Nineteen sixty-three was a year of black demonstrators being attacked with fire hoses by Birmingham, Alabama, authorities—hoses carrying enough pressure to strip the bark off a tree. The U.S. nuclear-powered submarine *Thresher* sank in eighty-four hundred feet of water two hundred miles off the East Coast, killing all 129 men aboard. Pope John XXIII died at the age of eighty-one, and the Catholic Church elected Cardinal Giovanni Battista Montini as his successor; he assumed the name Pope Paul VI. Washington and Moscow installed a hot line to provide direct emergency communication.

Julia Child prepared boeuf bourguignon, demonstrating to American television audiences the art of French cooking. *The Beverly Hillbillies, Bonanza,* and *The Andy Griffith Show* were among our favorite TV shows, along with *The Dick Van Dyke Show* and *The Huntley-Brinkley Report.* Mary Tyler Moore won an Emmy Award as Best Actress in a comedy series. *Tom Jones* won an Academy Award as Best Picture. Sidney Poitier won as Best Actor in *Lilies of the Field.* Kodak introduced its Instamatic cameras with film cartridges; Trimline phones made their first appearance. "The Amazing Spider-Man" swung into comic-book action. A British singing group scored its first American success with "I Want to Hold Your Hand"—the Beatles.

Back in Alabama, a bomb exploded at Birmingham's Sixteenth Street Baptist Church, killing four black schoolchildren and injuring nineteen others.* In ten days of televised testimony before the Senate Permanent Investigations Subcommittee, Joe Valachi detailed the inner workings of the Mafia. In South Vietnam, army officers overthrew the regime of Ngo Dinh Diem and then murdered him and his brother, Ngo Dinh Nhu. And President John F. Kennedy went to Texas for a two-day campaign tour to bring peace to Texas Democrats whose feuding threatened to deliver the state to the Republicans. The evening before going to Dallas, he said to Jackie:

> If anybody really wanted to shoot the president of the United States, it's not a very difficult job. All one has to do is get on a high building some day with a telescopic rifle and there is nothing anyone can do to defend against such an attempt.

President and Mrs. Kennedy rode in the White House Lincoln Continental, its bubble top removed by the Secret Service after Kennedy commented on the sunny skies and mild weather. Texas governor John Connally and his wife Nelly rode in the car's jump

---

* In May of 2001, former Ku Klux Klansman, Thomas Blenton Jr. was convicted of murder in the 1963 bombing.

seats in front of the presidential couple. The crowds cheered wildly, and Mrs. Connally leaned back to tell the president, "Well, you can't say Dallas doesn't love you." They were en route to the Dallas World Trade Center, where Kennedy was to address a group of businessmen. "We are in this country," his speech read, "watchmen on the walls of freedom."

At 12:23 P.M., the motorcade approached an underpass to the freeway. The president's limousine made its turn in front of the Texas School Book Depository. In direct violation of Secret Service procedure, which requires vehicles to maintain a speed of at least forty-four miles per hour, the limousine slowed down to only a few miles per hour as it passed through Dealey Plaza. And shots rang out.

United Press International reporter Merriman Smith won a Pulitzer Prize for his account of the events: "Suddenly we heard three loud, almost painfully loud, cracks. The first sounded as if it might have been a large firecracker. But the second and third blasts were unmistakable. Gunfire."

It was all caught on film, not just by one amateur photographer, but by more than a dozen 8mm cameras cranking away: Kennedy turned and waved his hand in greeting, and then, almost as if something hurt, his hand quickly flew to his throat.

Partly, it was a neurological response to a bullet through his throat. The president's arms flexed near his chin. JFK was strapped into a brace for his bad back, and he remained propped upright; his head lolled slightly to the left. Slowly he leaned back toward Jackie, as if he was tired and wanted to rest his head on her shoulder.

Both Kennedy and Governor Connally were hit, and the governor fell into Nelly's arms. Jackie Kennedy leaned toward her husband, looking at him quizzically. Then, brutally, unbelievably, an invisible and terrible second impact jolted the president's head. His head jerked up, and in those amateur films there's a fractional second of crimson flashing from the president's head. Jack Kennedy's body—it was "a body" by then; he no longer lived—toppled onto his wife. President John F. Kennedy's death was quick and, according to experts, probably painless.

It was 12:30 P.M. in Dallas, 1:30 P.M. in the nation's capital, when America's thirty-fifth president died.

Secret Service agent Clinton Hill was riding in the back-up car and saw what was happening. He jumped out, ran forward, and mounted the limousine's rear bumper. Jackie reached back for something, but Hill pushed her back inside the car. Mrs. Kennedy had been reaching for a fragment of the president's skull blown away by the shots.*

Later, in a television interview with CBS's Mike Wallace, Agent Hill blamed himself for not getting there fast enough. "If [I] had reacted about five tenths of a second faster or maybe a second faster, I wouldn't be here today." "You mean," Wallace asked, "you would have gotten there and you would have taken the shot."

"The third shot, yes, sir."

Agent Clint Hill felt that he should have saved the president. "It was my fault," he believed. "I guess I'll have to live with that to my grave."

Jackie covered Jack's body with her own and cried: "Jack, Jack! Can you hear me? I love you, Jack!"

Secret Service Agent William Greer, the limousine driver, sensed that something was wrong, turned in his seat to see what was happening, and—inexplicably—slowed the car to almost a standstill. Greer then slammed his foot onto the accelerator and raced out of Dealey Plaza.

Again, Merriman Smith: "Everybody in our car began shouting at the driver to pull up closer to the president's car. But at this moment, we saw the big limousine and a motorcycle escort roar away at high speed."

Governor Connally shouted, "My God, they're going to kill us all!"

Smith: "We screamed at our driver, 'Get going, get going.' We careened around the Johnson car and its escort and set out down the highway, barely able to keep in sight of the president's car and the accompanying Secret Service follow-up car."

---

* The day after the assassination, a college student found a piece of skull bone near Elm Street, opposite the grassy knoll. Some who believe the body autopsied in Bethesda was not that of President Kennedy claim that the bit of skull bone didn't fit the skull of the body at Bethesda. It's likely that in all of the handling, possibly even having been driven over by cars, the bone fragment lost bits and pieces before pathologists tried to fit it in place.

Shots Ring Out

● ● ●

When the shots were fired, Secret Service agent Rufus Youngblood pushed Vice President Johnson to the floor of his car and jumped on top of him. Johnson wasn't sure what had happened and tried to get up. "An emergency exists," the agent told Johnson, then said, "When we get where we're going, you and me are going to move right off and not tie in with the other people." Hearing what was going on over his handheld radio, Youngblood had a pretty good idea how serious things were, and he wanted to get LBJ inside a building as soon as possible. Johnson stopped trying to get off the floor and said to the agent, "Okay, partner."

Howard Brennan was a forty-five-year-old steamfitter who was near Dealey Plaza when Kennedy was shot. Before the presidential limousine turned into Elm Street from Houston Street, Brennan glanced up at an office building and noticed a man in a corner window. The man moved away, then returned "a couple of times." The man didn't seem excited about the presidential motorcade; "His face was almost expressionless. . . . He seemed preoccupied."
And then a shot rang out.

I looked up then at the Texas School Book Depository Building. What I saw made my blood run cold. Poised in the corner window of the sixth floor was the same young man I had noticed several times before the motorcade arrived. There was one difference—this time he held a rifle in his hands, pointing toward the Presidential car. He steadied the rifle against the cornice and while he moved quickly, he didn't seem to be in any kind of panic. All this happened in a matter of a second or two. Then came the sickening sound of a second shot. . . . I wanted to cry, I wanted to scream, but I couldn't utter a sound.
He was aiming again and I wanted to pray, to beg God to somehow make him miss the target. . . . What I was seeing, the sight became so fixed in my mind that I'll never forget it as long as I live. . . . Then another shot rang out.

• • •

Flash (five bells ring on Associated Press teletypes all around the world): PRESIDENT DEAD.*

In his Justice Department office in Washington, Bobby Kennedy had been holding a meeting on organized crime. About forty top law-enforcement officials had gathered to discuss the state of their battle against the Mafia. Shortly before noon, Bobby adjourned the meeting and invited two of the officials—New York district attorney Robert Morgenthau and his assistant Silvio Mollo—out to his house Hickory Hill, for lunch. Morgenthau remembered that while Bobby took a quick prelunch swim, then changed into dry clothes, workmen who were hanging shutters on the house were listening to a transistor radio, but he couldn't make out what they were hearing.

At FBI headquarters, J. Edgar Hoover got the United Press International report about the shooting. He called the attorney general's office and the operator patched Hoover to Hickory Hill. Ethel Kennedy answered and was told that J. Edgar Hoover wanted to talk with the attorney general. Ethel replied, "The attorney general is at lunch."

"This is urgent," the operator said.

So Ethel motioned to her husband and told him, "It's J. Edgar Hoover."

As Bobby answered the call on a pool-side phone, one of the workmen who'd been hanging shutters and listening to the radio started running toward the Kennedys, shouting something.

"I have news for you," Hoover told Bobby. "The president's been shot."

Bobby asked if it were serious, and Hoover told him that he thought it was. "I am endeavoring to get details. I'll call you back when I find out more."

Bobby hung up, stared at Ethel and Morgenthau and then what Hoover had just told him hit him. He almost collapsed. "Jack's been shot."

---

* Well, not all. In Chicago, a teletype operator, whose daily task was to type up stock-market reports, continued with what he'd been doing, and then—finally—he typed up the flash.

• • •

Millions turned on their television sets and watched Walter Cronkite remove his horn-rimmed glasses, almost choke on his own tears, and tell us that President Kennedy was dead. The death, almost in front of us, likely impressed us more than any other event in our lives to that moment.

Reporters interviewed police officers, interviewed witnesses, and interviewed themselves. They told us about the Texas School Book Depository Building, the grassy knoll, and a railroad overpass—all claimed by some or many to be the location where at least one gunman stood, sat, or lay before shooting the president. The police blundered and the public lost confidence and trust in our legal system. We saw the man who many said was the lone gunman and many others said was a "patsy" and some even said was a government agent. Police pulled and pushed twenty-four-year-old Lee Harvey Oswald through a crowd of reporters and cameramen and other police officers at the Dallas Police Department headquarters.

When Oswald was two years old, his mother shipped his older brother Robert and half-brother John Pic off to an orphanage, saying she just couldn't cope with them. Marguerite tried to send Lee off also, but orphanage officials said that he was too young. So Marguerite shuttled Lee back and forth between his sister and various housekeepers and baby-sitters; for a while she had a couple move in with her to help take care of Lee, but then fired them because they'd been whipping the boy to control his "unmanageable" disposition. She juggled jobs and homes—they moved five times before Lee was three years old—and in general, found life difficult. Finally, the day after Christmas 1942, Mama Oswald packed up the now three-year-old boy and shipped him off to join his brothers Robert and John at the Bethlehem Children's Home.

In early 1944, Marguerite unexpectedly checked all three boys out of the orphanage and moved them to Dallas, where she was living with a new boyfriend, Edwin Ekdahl. Marguerite and Edwin married in May 1943, but didn't live happily ever after. Ekdahl worked for a utility company and his job required extensive travel, so they put Robert and John in a military boarding school and took Lee with them on Edwin's frequent business trips. These trips and short relocations were so frequent that Lee missed most of his first year in school. Educationally, it was all downhill from there.

It seems, however, that the six-year-old boy had found a friend in his stepfather. The same can't be said for Marguerite. She and Ekdahl fought often, mainly over money. She wanted more of it.* In 1946, the not-so-loving couple separated and Edwin walked out. Marguerite took Lee and moved to Covington, Louisiana. When it was time for Lee to return to school, he'd missed so much of his first year that officials put him in with the younger kids who were just starting out; he was a year older than his classmates, bigger than they were, he'd been around the block a lot more than they had, and already was a bully—at age seven classmates considered him a tough guy and none of them wanted him for a friend. Lee finally finished first grade, but before he could start the second, the family moved again.

Now divorced, Marguerite had to take Robert and John out of boarding school because she couldn't afford the tuition. During the summer, the family moved to Benbrook, Texas—the twelfth move for Lee since his birth. In the fall, they moved to Fort Worth—move number thirteen—and Lee was enrolled in the third grade. With her marriage to Ekdahl over, Marguerite gave all her attention to the boys, especially Lee. She spoiled him, protected him, let him have his way, didn't make him go to school when he whined that he didn't like it, and until Lee was eleven years old Marguerite shared her bed with him. Homelife, half-brother John Pic remembered, was depressing.

When he was fifteen, Lee and his mother moved to New Orleans to avoid his being committed to a youth center for troubled boys. The psychiatrist who examined him reported that Lee Harvey Oswald "had potential for explosive, aggressive, assaultive acting out." In the fall of 1955, when Oswald was enrolled in his eleventh school, he forged his mother's name and wrote school authorities a note saying they were moving to San Diego, that Lee "must quit school now." He was sixteen. His aunt Lillian Murret later explained that he "didn't

---

* Following the assassination of JFK and her son Lee, when asked to sit for an interview or to be photographed, she'd almost always refuse unless she were paid.

think he had to go to school. He said he was smart enough and that he couldn't learn anything at school, that nobody could teach him anything." A few days after he dropped out of school, Lee wrote a letter to the Socialist Party of America, announcing,

> I am sixteen years of age and would like more information about your youth League. I would like to know if there is a branch in my area, how to join, ect [sic]. I am a Marxist and have been studying Socialist principles for well over fifteen months.

On October 18, 1956, Lee Harvey Oswald turned seventeen. A week later he joined the U.S. Marine Corps, apparently as much to get away from his mother, Marguerite, as anything else—both older brothers had done the same thing. At the Marine Corps recruit depot in San Diego, he took a series of tests, scoring slightly below average. They taught him to fire the M1 rifle, and he scored higher than average: 212, two points over the score required for a "sharpshooter" qualification, the second highest qualification in the Corps.

It's uncertain how Oswald was oriented sexually. Both in basic training and later, some other Marines believed he was homosexual. "He had a lot of feminine characteristics," one recalled, while another claimed that he stayed away from Lee because he thought he was gay. Members of his unit sometimes taunted him as "Mrs. Oswald," and once they threw him fully clothed into the shower to provoke him. Unlike his years as a teenage bully, Lee no longer was larger than those around him. At five feet nine inches he initially didn't fight back but walked away from any provocation.

He seldom went to bars with other Marines, but several in his unit recalled that while they were stationed in Yamato, Japan, Oswald visited a transvestite bar, a club with which he seemed familiar.* In California, he once went south of the border to Tijuana, Mexico, with

---

* According to Oswald's wife, Marina, Lee had told her that he had had eight sexual relationships while in Japan. He described three: one woman nearly twice his age, one extremely thin and promiscuous, and one who apparently was very fat, but who also cooked for him.

a group of other Marines and while there he guided them to a run-down gay bar, the Flamingo.

In the autumn of 1958, doctors treated him for a mild case of venereal disease. A notation in his military file said that his contraction of VD was "in line of duty, not due to own misconduct." Some critics see this as meaning his extracurricular activities, whatever and with whomever they were, had the blessings of the military. Others, however, believe the "not due to own misconduct" notation was the doctor's way of giving Oswald a break and avoiding having the young Marine's pay jeopardized; it was, they say, a routine practice.

Oswald served in the Marine Corps for three years, until 1959, when he asked for and was given an early discharge. A week before his discharge, he'd applied for a passport, claiming he would be attending Albert Schweitzer College in Switzerland and Turku University in Finland—this from a young man who had quit school at age sixteen without graduating from high school. In Fort Worth, Texas, for a post–Marine Corps visit with his mother, he said that he was going to work for an import-export business and was about to board a ship for Europe. By October 10, Oswald was in Helsinki, Finland, and he applied for a visa to visit the Soviet Union; he was nineteen years old, didn't list his Marine Corps service on his application, claimed he currently was unemployed, and said he was a student. Two days later, the Soviets issued him a visa. He went to Moscow, and two days after he arrived there, he got into a conversation with his official guide, Rima Shirokova. At the time, all visitors to the Soviet Union had to have an official guide from the USSR tourist agency Intourist, which according to many sources was made up entirely of informants or agents for the KGB. He told Shirokova that he wanted to defect and become a Soviet citizen. Some sources claim his "defection" was a ruse to cloak his alleged connection to the CIA or the FBI or the Office of Naval Intelligence.

Two days after his real or faked defection, Oswald celebrated his twentieth birthday. As a gift, Intourist representative Rima Shirokova gave him a book and inscribed it: "Dear Lee, Great Congratulations! Let all your dreams come true." The book was by Dostoevski: *The Idiot.* What Oswald didn't know was that the KGB

144

external surveillance team in Moscow had given him the code name *Nalim*, a Russian fish.

The KGB vetoed Oswald's request to stay in Russia, and on October 21, with his six-day visa running out, the Soviet Ministry of Foreign Affairs summoned him to their office. Officials told him that his request was denied, and a ministry spokesman gave him two hours to get out of town.

That night, Intourist guide Rima Shirokova went to Oswald's hotel to pick him up and escort him out of town. When he didn't answer her knock, she had the hotel clerk open the door. They found Lee with his wrist cut and blood all over.

Rima Shirokova rushed Oswald, by ambulance, to a hospital where blood transfusions stabilized him. Prompted by his attempt at suicide, the KGB ordered a mental evaluation; the doctors' report concluded that Oswald was "mentally unstable." The agency had the choice either to physically force Oswald onto an airplane to get rid of him, or let him stay in Moscow temporarily without granting him citizenship.

At that time the Cold War was warming up and it was this circumstance that allowed Oswald to remain in the Soviet Union. Thanks to a recent meeting between U.S. president Eisenhower and Soviet premier Khrushchev, and in the "spirit of Camp David," senior Politburo member Anastas Mikoyan personally gave the order that Lee's request for asylum be given careful consideration.

Meanwhile, Shirokova had found his diary, complete with the misspellings of someone who'd scored "slightly below average" on his Marine Corps test. Oswald might have been dyslexic and frequently transposed letters within words:

> I am stunned. . . . Eve. 6.00 Recive word from police official. I must leave country tonight at. 8.00 p.m. as visa expirs. I am shocked!! My dreams! I retire to my room. I have $100 left. I have waited 2 years to be accepted. My fondes dreams are shattered because of a petty official; because of bad planning I planned too much! 7.00 p.m. I decide to end it. Soak rist in cold water to numb the pain. Than slash my left wrist. Than plaug [plunge?] wrist into bathtub of hot water. I think "when Rimmy

comes at 8. to find me dead it will be a great shock." somewhere a violin plays, as I wacth my life whirl away. I think to myself. "how easy to die" and "a sweet death."

As with nearly everything else about Lee Harvey Oswald, this document (which he called his Historic Diary and in which he gave an on-again, off-again account of his life in Russia) sometimes is called a fake. Handwriting experts used by both the Warren Commission and the later House Select Committee believed, however, that the diary was written by Oswald.

Out of the hospital, and in a new hotel, Oswald waited while officials decided what to do with him. After three days of waiting without hearing any decision, he stormed into the American embassy, declared that he was a Marxist, tossed his passport across the consul's desk, and tried to renounce his U.S. citizenship. He would, he claimed, give the Soviets all the information he'd picked up as a Marine radar operator, never mind that as a Marine private first class, all he had was the lowest-level security clearance, "confidential."

It was a Saturday, and American consul Richard Snyder tried to stop Oswald from making a permanent decision by telling him that it was too late in the day to take care of the paperwork. Come back on Monday. American bureaucrats in Russia it seemed, didn't work Saturdays any more often than did American bureaucrats in America. Lee walked off in a huff but didn't show up on Monday to finish the revocation.

Finally, two and a half months after he'd said he wanted to defect, the Soviet Ministry of Foreign Affairs gave him identification number 311479, declaring him a stateless person. They decided to send him to Minsk, an industrial city of about five hundred thousand people, some 450 miles southwest of Moscow. The next day he was contacted by a Soviet agency sometimes referred to as the Russian Red Cross, although it's not connected with the international agency by that same name. They gave Lee five thousand rubles (about five hundred dollars), out of which he paid his hotel bill and bought a train ticket to Minsk, where he was greeted by another Intourist guide, Roza Kuznetsova.

The local KGB in Minsk kept Oswald under surveillance but couldn't detain him or arrest him; they couldn't blackmail him or try to recruit him as a spy. Still, while he was in the city, the Minsk KGB kept a case file on Oswald, number 31451, five thick volumes and a thin folder tied together with shoelaces. The KGB wasn't impressed by Oswald, but neither was the CIA. The Langley, Virginia, agency didn't open a file (termed a 201) on him until almost a year after he'd defected.

The Russians called him "Alik," because "Lee" sounded too Chinese, and they went out of their way to help him settle into his new homeland. Intourist guide Roza Kuznetsova took him almost every night to the movies (where she acted as his interpreter), to the opera, and to the theater. He had friends in Minsk, which was something that had pretty much escaped him in the United States. In his diary, Oswald wrote, "I am living big and am very satisfied." Lee (or Alik) ate it up. He loved the attention his celebrity brought him.

Oswald's KGB file listed him not as Lee, not even as Alik, but under another code name, Likhoy—Russian for "valiant" or "dashing." Not so much a description of Oswald as it was a play on his names: Lee Harvey = Likhoy. They tried using informants to engage Likhoy in anti-Soviet conversations, and they put him in contact with people who pretended to possess secret information that they'd be glad to pass on to their new American friend. At least once they even drugged him, trying to make him talk; it didn't work. Maybe he had nothing to say.

Lee Harvey Oswald was the only American defector in Minsk and became a minor celebrity. Kuznetsova introduced him to the mayor, who provided him with a rent-free apartment, the kind of home that would have taken a Russian several years to get. On January 13, Lee began work as a metalworker at the Byelorussian Radio and Television Factory. It wasn't exactly what he—an American defector who knew all kinds of Marine Corps secrets—had had in mind, but it was a start. Within six months, thanks to a continuing Red Cross subsidy, he was bringing home to that rent-free, one-room apartment—in a middle-class neighborhood with a view of the Svisloch River—a comfortable $150 a month.

In mid-1960, he met Ella German, a "black-haired Jewish beauty with fine eyes, skin as white as snow, a beautiful smile, and a good but unpredictable nature." Oswald admitted that he probably fell in love with Ella the first minute he saw her. They dated through the fall, and they spent New Year's Eve with her family. Going back to Minsk, Lee proposed to Ella, but she shocked him by saying no. "My love is real but she has none of me. . . . I am stunned she snickers at my awkwardness." With that, he began to wonder whether he should remain in Russia: "I have had enough." And when the Minsk visa authorities asked him if he still wanted to take out Soviet citizenship papers, Oswald said no, and asked only that his temporary papers be extended a year.

By then, Lee Harvey Oswald had developed an attitude problem. He became lazy, and took to propping his feet on a table at work, where he complained about his job and told everyone that he wasn't making enough money. The Soviet system wasn't a classless society, he had learned, but a system that was much more regimented than he'd first believed; he saw that the Soviets promoted from within the Communist Party while forcing nonmembers into oppressive workers' collectives.

A month after Ella German rejected him, Oswald wrote the American embassy in Moscow: "I desire to return to the United States." American consul Richard Snyder, who'd earlier told him to come back later, now urged U.S. officials at the embassy to do everything they could to help Oswald. After all, he was still an "American citizen." Snyder and Oswald exchanged letters: Come to the embassy, Snyder wrote. I can't without Soviet approval, Oswald replied.

It was about then that Lee met Marina Prusakova, a striking nineteen-year-old pharmacology student working at a Minsk hospital. Since the summer of 1957, while he was still a U.S. Marine, Lee Oswald had been studying the Russian language, and Marina commented on how well he spoke it. He has an accent, she admitted, but he spoke Russian so well, maybe his accent meant that he was from another part of the Soviet Union, somewhere in the Baltic states, say? However, others who knew him in Minsk claimed that Oswald's Russian was so limited—he knew only a couple of hundred words—that they generally spoke to him in English.

A month after meeting Marina, Lee used his halting Russian to propose to her, and less than two weeks after he proposed, they were married in the Minsk registry office. In his diary, Oswald admitted that he married Marina to "hurt Ella." Marina later said that one reason she married Lee was that he had his own apartment. She later denied however, marrying him just to get a passport; what kind of girl did he think she was? In fact, she claimed to have been "slightly startled" when he told her he wanted to return to the good ole US of A.

It was also about then that Lee told Marina about his real ambition: He wanted to be a spy. "I'd love the danger," he claimed. Marina said later, "I think that he had a sick imagination [and] I already considered him to be not quite normal."

On July 8, Oswald unexpectedly turned up at the American embassy in Moscow. Once again he was there on a Saturday and once again embassy officials told him to come back the following week. This time, however, he did return.

Marina joined him from Minsk and waited outside while Lee went inside to see Richard Snyder. This time, instead of slamming his passport on Synder's desk, Oswald was remorseful, sorry about all those anti-American statements he'd made. True, he'd applied for Soviet citizenship, but he didn't like Minsk, didn't like his job in the television factory, didn't like much of anything about Russia. Make it all go away, he asked, let me go home. And Snyder believed him; Lee Harvey Oswald had learned his lesson, the consul felt.

When Oswald returned to the embassy on Tuesday, Marina went with him. Just as had Lee, Marina lied to embassy officials. In reality, she was a member of the Communist youth league—the Komsomol—but under urging from Lee, she denied any ties to the group.

On Wednesday, Lee and Marina returned to Minsk and began working to get permission to leave the Soviet Union. Lee later wrote the American embassy, claiming the Soviets were trying to get Marina to change her mind to convince her to stay in Russia. If there really was any attempt to keep Marina—and there's no proof that there was—it didn't work, and on August 20 the happy couple received word from Soviet officials that they could leave in December.

October 18 was Lee's twenty-second birthday. Marina was pregnant, and, as he wrote in his diary, "We are becoming anoid [sic] about the delay Marina is beginning to waiver." By Christmas Day, however, he believed that things were different: "It's great (I think!)" Finally, they received permission to leave. A long-time KGB agent claimed that there never was any real problem, that "We realized that Oswald was a useless man." And since Marina had no real ties to anybody with any kind of power—her uncle was the closest; he was in the militia but it amounted to being a local policeman—"There was no reason to keep her." The only problem became one of permission from the U.S. State Department for Marina to immigrate.

In January, Marina gave birth to a daughter, June, which may have stimulated American officials. Both the CIA and FBI investigated her, said she was okay, and the State Department informed the embassy in Moscow that Marina was eligible for an immigrant visa. In May 1962, the Immigration and Naturalization Service gave its final approval for Marina Prusakova Oswald (and of course baby June) to come to the United States of America. Hail, Columbia.

Oh, hell. Lee didn't have money for airfare. No problem, the State Department loaned him the money: $435.71.

Finally, they were back in the United States. Lee Harvey Oswald was twenty-two years old, married to a woman whom he refused to let learn English, and he was the father of a little girl. He was also broke, owed the government money, didn't have a job, and had to live in his brother Robert's Fort Worth home. Marina, however, was getting along well, thank you, with or without English. For the first time she got a hair permanent, bought her first pair of shorts, and went on a whirlwind tour of Dallas with Robert and his wife, Vada. Then Marguerite Oswald came back into the picture.

By the end of Lee and Marina's first week in Texas, Lee and his mother were back to arguing. Lee claimed that mama "thinks that she's the one who got us out" of the Soviet Union and didn't want to give him credit.

Meanwhile, Marguerite was after Lee to write a book about his exploits in Russia. She won, and within a week he approached a public stenographer, Mrs. Pauline Bates. He hired her to type a manuscript from bits and pieces of paper on which he had written his recollections of Russia, notes that he'd smuggled out of the Soviet Union. The title of his manuscript: *The Collective*. It's said to be a "dreary and pedestrian commentary on the lives of the average Russian workers."

However, Pauline Bates was so intrigued by Lee Oswald and his story that she even gave him a discount on her fee. Still, by the time she'd typed about ten pages, roughly a third of Oswald's notes, he told her that they'd have to stop, that he'd run out of money. Mrs. Bates offered to work for nothing, but Oswald turned her down. "No," he said, "I don't work that way. I've got ten dollars"—and he pulled the money out of his pocket, threw it on the table, and walked out.

Oswald's life back in the United States was as erratic as had been his life in Russia, and as had been his life in America the first time around. He, Marina, and June moved to Dallas, where he got a $1.35-an-hour job with a graphic arts firm, Jaggers-Chiles-Stovall. The company did some minor work with the U.S. Army's map service, but neither company officials nor Lee Oswald, it appears to have handled anything classified. While he was working at Jaggers, Oswald may have forged a Selective Service notice of classification and a Marine Corps certificate of service under the name Alek Hidell.

By the fall of 1962, Lee had bought a book entitled *How to Be a Spy* and begun studying. He may have been preparing himself for a new career. He rented a post office box in Dallas and began the occasional use of a false address and a phony name. He used the fake name and post office box to send a $21.45 money order to a Chicago-based mail-order house, Klein's Sporting Goods. Under the alias A. Hidell, he ordered an Italian military rifle, a 6.5mm Mannlicher-Carcano, complete with a four-power (4x) scope. He also bought a Smith & Wesson .38 special revolver from the Los Angeles–based Seaport Traders. It cost a total of $29.95—$10 in cash and the balance of $19.95 paid COD when delivered to his post office box. He signed the order form "A. J. Hidell" and even forged the name of a witness.

So, for a total of only $51.40 (plus the cost of the P.O. box) Lee Harvey Oswald (or A. J. Hidell) had the rifle that experts say murdered President John F. Kennedy and the revolver that those same experts say killed Dallas policeman Jefferson Davis Tippit after the officer tried to stop a man who answered the description of the president's murderer.

On the day John Kennedy was assassinated, Richard Milhous Nixon—the man JFK defeated for the presidency in 1960 and who would win the job in 1968—was in Dallas, Texas, on business. He left town at 9:05 A.M., about three and a half hours before Kennedy was shot. Nixon learned about the assassination after he arrived at New York's Idlewild Airport—soon to be renamed Kennedy International. Richard Nixon was in a cab, at Twenty-first Street and Thirty-fourth Avenue in Queens, when a stranger who apparently didn't recognize the former vice president stuck his head in the taxi's window and asked the driver if his radio was on; he wanted news about JFK's death.

Near Gettysburg, Pennsylvania, state police rushed to throw a cordon around the farm where Richard Nixon's former boss Dwight Eisenhower lived. They were afraid that Ike might also have been in a sniper's gunsights. But Eisenhower wasn't there. He was at a United Nations luncheon at New York's Chatham Hotel, when Secretary General U Thant was interrupted in midspeech for an announcement that John F. Kennedy was dead. Eisenhower left immediately for his suite at the Waldorf.

Judith Campbell, who had shared the bed of both John Kennedy and Sam Giancana, was in the Beverly Crest Hotel in Los Angeles, where West Coast mobster Johnny Rosselli had installed her. She was alone when she heard the news about her former lover. Upset, she barricaded herself in her room and refused to take any of Rosselli's phone calls.

Nelson Rockefeller, who had already announced his candidacy to challenge Kennedy in next year's election, was lunching privately at his Fifty-fourth Street home in New York City. With him was another long-time presidential hopeful, Thomas E. Dewey. Rockefeller wanted the two-time Republican presidential hopeful's help in winning the 1964 GOP nomination. Rockefeller's black maid brought them the news.

Senator Barry Goldwater was in Chicago, stopping over on a sorrowful errand; he was supervising the transfer of the coffin carrying his mother-in-law's body. Goldwater and his wife were taking the body from Phoenix, Arizona, to Muncie, Indiana, for burial.

Over the Pacific Ocean, an Air Force VC 137 "banked like a fighter plane" at thirty-five thousand feet and rushed back to America at 625 miles per hour. On board were members of President Kennedy's cabinet.

At the Pentagon, on the orders of the Chairman of the Joint Chiefs of Staff, the military stood at global readiness, suspecting a coup. One of the nation's nine combat commands, on the commander's own initiative, was called to Defense Condition One, or combat alert.

In Chicago, a white passerby approached a young black man who was listening to the radio. "What's the news?" he asked. "He's dead," the man with the radio replied, and gripped the white man's arm: "Pray, man."

All over America—mid-lunch on the East Coast to midmorning out West—we learned that the nation's young president was dead, and we really didn't know how to handle it. We slammed our fists against trees, we cried, we tolled church bells, we lowered our flags to half-staff, and we cried again. Uncontrollably in private and on public streets, and once you knew why the woman next to you was crying you didn't have to ask why, because you were crying yourself.

When the networks broke into their afternoon programming, telephones at local affiliates and network headquarters went on over-load. New York CBS switchboard operator Chris Santana said that "People were actually upset because the soaps weren't on." Let the world explode, but "put it on the six o'clock news." Just don't interrupt the soap operas.

Millions of people around America, however, turned to television for news about the president. Joseph Kennedy tried but he couldn't. By this time, the seventy five-year-old patriarch of the Kennedy clan had suffered a stroke; he couldn't speak, could barely move, and spent much of his days confined to a wheelchair. When Bobby learned that Jack was dead, he asked his brother Teddy to go to their father, who as, historian Richard Mahoney wrote, was "blinking in and out of lucidity in his convalescence in Hyannis Port."

Before Teddy could get to the family enclave, Joe awoke from a nap and motioned for the TV to be turned on. A family worker, who knew about Jack's death, lied and claimed the television set was broken.

When Teddy arrived, Joe, who had seen through the earlier lie, motioned angrily for his son to turn the TV on. Teddy went to the set, but instead of turning it on, he unplugged it. See, he said, it won't work. Joe was crippled but not blind. He pointed to the dangling cord. So Teddy knelt by the set and plugged it back in. As the TV began to warm up, Teddy reached in back and tore wires out of it. Now it really wouldn't work again, and Joe Kennedy didn't know that his second son was, like Joe Junior before him, dead.

Joseph P. Kennedy died in 1969. It's uncertain whether he ever knew—really knew and understood—that Jack was dead.

Within hours of the assassination, Kennedy's body was taken aboard Air Force One at Dallas's Love Field. Lyndon Johnson telephoned Attorney General Bobby Kennedy and asked for legal advice. Despite his personal loss, Bobby told Johnson that, from a legal point of view, Lyndon should take the formal oath of office there in Dallas. So Lyndon Johnson contacted his long-time friend, sixty-seven-year-old U.S. district judge Sarah T. Hughes. Holding a small black Bible, she swore him in as the nation's thirty-sixth president. JFK's widow stood near him, her bright pink suit splashed with her late husband's brains and blood. She hadn't changed, she said later, because she wanted the world to see what they had done.

There, on Air Force One, Judge Hughes said, "Hold up your right hand and repeat after me."

Johnson covered the small Bible with his large left hand and his right arm slowly rose into the air.

Sarah Hughes continued: "I do solemnly swear that I will faithfully execute the office of president of the United States . . ." The short ceremony came to an end, and President Johnson ordered Air Force One into the air, headed homeward.

Around the Washington area, thousands of people stood on the streets and on rooftops and at windows and stared toward nearby Andrews Air Force Base, looking to see Air Force One as it bore Kennedy's body back to the capital. Guards patrolled the gates at the base and watched as hundreds of people rimmed the wire fence, mostly silent, but often in tears.

At 5:58 Eastern time Air Force One landed. The casket was lowered from the plane and placed in a waiting hearse driven by Secret Service agent William Greer, who'd been driving the presidential limousine in Dealey Plaza earlier that day when Kennedy was killed.

Shots Ring Out

Some conspiracy theorists claim it wasn't JFK's body in the casket but someone else's, that somewhere between Dealey Plaza and Parkland Memorial Hospital and Air Force One and Andrews Air Force Base and Bethesda Naval Hospital bodies were exchanged and we really don't know who's buried in Arlington National Cemetery under the eternal flame.

In Dallas, at 11:21 A.M. on Sunday, police planned to move Lee Harvey Oswald to a presumably safer location. As Dallas plainclothesman James Leavelle led Oswald to the fifth-floor elevator that would take them to the basement and on to that "safer location," the cop said, "If anybody shoots at you, I sure hope they are as good a shot as you are." Oswald kind of laughed and replied, "Nobody is going to shoot me."

In the basement, nightclub owner Jack Ruby waited. As Oswald was being led to a waiting car, Ruby stepped from between television cameras and shot Oswald at point-blank range with a .38 snub-nosed revolver. Nobody knows why, not really.

Jack Ruby had been born Jacob Rubenstein in Chicago on March 25, 1911.* After he'd shot Oswald, police found Ruby's 1960 Oldsmobile parked and locked in downtown Dallas; friends say he'd practically lived in the car. Among its contents when police broke into it: his dachshund, Sheba, two sets of lightweight metal knuckles (one set badly worn), several unpaid parking tickets, a paper bag containing $837.50 in cash, an empty wallet, a woman's bathing cap, a left golf shoe with a dollar bill tucked inside, hundreds of photos of a stripper named Jada, a roll of toilet paper, a can of paint, a gray suit, a November 20 newspaper showing Kennedy's motorcade route, and an empty pistol holster.

All through the night Saturday and into Sunday hundreds of thousands of mourners—more than a quarter of a million of them—filed past John Kennedy's body as it lay in state in the capitol rotunda.

---

* Because Chicago did not keep official birth records prior to 1915, Jacob Rubenstein had at least six different birth dates listed for him among school records, driver's licenses, and arrest records. March 15, 1911, is the date Ruby himself used in his adult life.

More lined the route taken on Monday, as the somber procession bore the casket to St. Matthew's Cathedral and on to Arlington National Cemetery.

For days the nation remained stunned. It was, newscaster David Brinkley said, "too big, too sudden, too overwhelming, and it meant too much."

Lee Harvey Oswald's mother, Marguerite, sold her dead son's letters to her to *Esquire* magazine. With the money, she bought a large reproduction of artist James Whistler's best-known work, a gray-and-black portrait popularly known as *Whistler's Mother.*

Marguerite wasn't the only Oswald who made money off Lee Harvey's actions and death. His widow, Marina, received seventy thousand dollars in donations from people around the country, people presumably sorry for her and not in gratitude for what Lee had done. She also hawked Oswald's Russian diary for twenty thousand dollars, got five thousand dollars for a photograph of him holding the rifle he'd used to kill Kennedy, and even tried to get the weapon itself, presumably to market it as a souvenir.

After JFK's assassination and LBJ's assumption of duties as president, a critic commented that the change was one from touch football to rodeos, from clambakes to beef barbecues. Another change was that men's hats returned to favor: During Lyndon Johnson's first full year as president, his Stetson-style hat grew more popular in the East. And, of course, more expensive. You could get one for $17.50 or you could go all the way to $250 for a mink-trimmed model.

As early as 1966, Johnson told White House staff members, "I got my resignation right here in my pocket," and he'd pat his breast. Most, of course, didn't believe him; after all, the presidency was what Johnson had aimed for almost all of his life.

By the beginning of 1968, "crackpot letters threatening the president's life" historian Theodore H. White wrote,

> had jumped from an old average of one hundred a month to an average substantially above a thousand a month. In Syra-

cuse, during a precheck on a presidential trip, the Secret Service found demonstrators preparing paper cups of urine to throw at him, and buttons reviling the Johnson daughters in slogans of absolute filth printed up for the demonstrators to wear.

Demonstrations, threats against him and his family, frustration at the progress, or lack of progress, in the war left Lyndon Johnson "an individual embittered in all his thinking," White writes. He became "isolated in the White House with a corporal's guard of devoted loyalists," or as LBJ himself put it, they were "hunkering our heads down and taking it."

John F. Kennedy wasn't supposed to be the clan's man in the White House. That job was to have gone to John's older brother, Joseph Kennedy Jr. When Joe Junior died in a World War II explosion the political mantle fell onto Jack. When President Kennedy was assassinated, the mantle fell onto the next brother, Bobby, who'd been only nineteen when Joe Junior died and was only thirty-eight when Jack was killed.

During the final year of World War II, Bobby dropped out of Harvard to join the navy. Just after his eighteenth birthday, Bobby Kennedy was sworn in—baby-faced and small—standing between his father and the officer administering the oath. He wore a checked sport coat that looked a bit too large for him, and in fact was. It actually belonged to his older and larger brother Jack.

If Joe Kennedy Jr. was his father's favorite, number-three son Bobby got kinda left out; Joe often referred to Bobby as "runt." Bobby was, however, often protected by Mama Rose Kennedy. When his siblings teased him, Rose would console Bobby, "You're *my* favorite," but when Bobby was young even Mama Rose was worried about him, afraid that he might grow up "puny and girlish."

He didn't have his older brother Joe's good looks or athletic build. He didn't have Jack's self-possessed bookishness. Bobby himself admitted that, as a child, "I guess I was very awkward. . . . I dropped everything. I always fell down. I always bumped my nose or head."

He grew up in the company of his mother and three sisters and attended at least ten different schools. Later, he told one writer,

"What I remember most vividly growing up was going to a lot of different schools, always having to make new friends." He performed, at best, indifferently in all of them. "I was pretty quiet most of the time," he recalled, "and I didn't mind being alone."

Aside from his family, the one constant in Bobby's life was the Catholic Church. While other members, especially his brothers, may have been only technically religious, Bobby took to the church avidly as an altar boy throughout high school. Sister-in-law Jackie Kennedy, who was big with nicknames, called him "Saint Bobby."

At family dinners, Joe Senior argued politics with Joe Junior and Jack, but Bobby usually sat quietly. Later, Bobby became Jack's best friend, but it wasn't always that way. When brother Jack was running for Congress in 1946, Papa Joe sent Bobby to help out, but the candidate was skeptical whether Bobby would be of much help: "I can't see that sober, silent face breathing new vigor in the ranks." In fact, Jack suggested they send Bobby to the movies to get rid of him. Bobby was so much a gloomy scold, Jack began calling him "Black Robert."

Instead, young Bobby—he was twenty-one but looked sixteen—had a positive effect on the campaign. Family friend Dave Powers estimated that Bobby would hit around three hundred homes and apartments per day, that "When he asked people to vote for Jack, you would have thought he was inviting them to enter the kingdom of heaven."

After the campaign, Bobby went back to Harvard, where his big ambition of the time was to make the football team. He did, through "unremitting practice and wild aggression," and won a letter in 1947, when he played the Harvard-Yale game with a cast on his broken leg.

During John Kennedy's presidential race, Bobby was his campaign manager. As such, he often protected his older brother and terrorized campaign workers, "Little brother is watching you," they whispered.

When opponent Hubert Humphrey won the Wisconsin Democratic primary, it was said that most of the votes Jack Kennedy received were from Catholics. The night of the primary, CBS's Walter Cronkite asked Jack about the Catholic vote. Jack Kennedy was furious but his brother the campaign manager was even more so, and

Bobby Kennedy believed in the family saying: Don't get mad, get even. He told Cronkite, "I'm going to see that you never get another interview." Which, of course, didn't happen, and in February 1961, the new president and his equally new first lady had Walter in the White House for a purported first-time view of "the actual conduct of official business" in the Oval Office.

Shortly after Jack was elected president, he chose Bobby to be his attorney general, an appointment that drew criticism from people who believed that Bobby, at age thirty-six, was too young and too inexperienced for the office. Bobby at first refused the job, saying there'd be accusations of nepotism. President Kennedy went ahead with the nomination and jokingly remarked that he wanted to see his little brother get some legal experience as a government lawyer before he had to go out into the real world and try his hands at private practice. Bobby became the nation's youngest attorney general.

Actually, Bobby already had done some work as a government lawyer. After he and Jack returned from their seven-week fact-finding tour of Southeast Asia ten years earlier, Bobby Kennedy began a six-year career that included several government jobs and several more political assignments arranged by his father. One of Papa Joe's political friends was the Republican junior senator from Wisconsin, red-baiting Joseph Raymond McCarthy.

Joe McCarthy drank heavily, and once when he was drunk at Washington's Sulgrave Club in the Dupont Circle area, he got into a fight with muckraking columnist Drew Pearson. McCarthy was flailing away at Pearson when a young U.S. senator stepped in. "Let a good Quaker stop this fight," Richard Nixon said, and forced his way in between the two men.

To say that Jack's death hit Bobby Kennedy hard isn't saying nearly enough. He took down all portraits of his brother, and when he was in a friend's home or office, he'd go around turning over magazines with Jack's picture on the cover. He refused to say "November twenty-second," or "Dallas." Unlike the rest of the world who called JFK's accused killer by his full name, Lee Harvey Oswald, Bobby referred to him only as "Harvey Oswald." Sometimes Bobby wore his brother's clothes—an old overcoat or a jacket from John's PT boat days. There are even rumors that Bobby and Jackie consoled each other with a brief sexual interlude.

With President Kennedy dead, Jimmy Hoffa, whom Bobby had tried to put in jail on bribery charges, said that "Bobby Kennedy is just another lawyer now." FBI director J. Edgar Hoover, who'd been a long-time friend of Lyndon Johnson, felt that he was back in charge, and he ordered his secretary to get rid of the phone on his desk that linked him directly to the attorney general. The Justice Department's Organized Crime Section stopped its investigations; as section head Bill Hundley put it, "The minute that bullet hit Jack Kennedy's head, it was all over. Right then. The organized crime program just stopped, and Hoover took control back." When President Lyndon Johnson saw one of his Secret Service agents wearing a JFK PT-109 tie clasp, Johnson tore it off the agent's necktie and threw it to the ground.

It's hard to pinpoint just why Bobby Kennedy and Lyndon Johnson didn't get along, but clearly they didn't. Ever. It could simply have been a matter of pride; both men had giant-size egos. In 1960, Lyndon Johnson, who'd begun in politics about the time Bobby had begun the first grade, had to put up with someone seventeen years his junior telling him what he should and shouldn't do. When Bobby went to Lyndon to remind LBJ what, as a Southerner, he might face in the election—claims of racism being the least—Johnson thought that the younger Kennedy was trying to keep him off the ticket. Actually, Bobby was just warning LBJ about northern and eastern liberals' knee-jerk objection to a Southerner on the ticket.

After the election, Bobby was not only attorney general but Jack's chief aide and advisor. It's not that Johnson suffered at Bobby Kennedy's hands, more that Bobby treated LBJ with indifference. Lyndon Johnson felt that he was being ignored. And nobody, NOBODY, could ever ignore Lyndon Johnson, no sir.

With Jack Kennedy dead, Lyndon Johnson clearly went after Bobby. LBJ even called in his friend and neighbor J. Edgar Hoover— the FBI chief and his live-in partner Clyde Tolson owned a home down the street from LBJ and Lady Bird—to check into whether

Jack's killer, Lee Harvey Oswald, was connected with Mongoose, the CIA-proposed plan to pay the Mafia to get rid of Cuba's Fidel Castro. Even when Hoover told Johnson that, so far as the FBI could determine, Oswald was on the *other* side, that is, pro-Castro, Johnson didn't believe it. LBJ was, as Johnson's long-time bagman Bobby Baker noted, practically "paranoiac" on the subject of Robert Kennedy. J. Edgar Hoover added to that paranoia by concocting reports about Kennedy, claiming Bobby was holding off-the-record news conferences about a scandal involving Baker.

Hoover's being a Lyndon Johnson fan aside, he and Bobby Kennedy were never even close to being friends. Friends? Hoover tried blackmailing Bobby Kennedy and, in a conversation with former vice president Richard Nixon, described the younger man as a "sneaky little son of a bitch."

Bobby wasn't much better. He openly wondered if Hoover had to "squat to pee" and, because of Hoover's live-in relationship with partner Clyde Tolson, referred to the head of the FBI as "J. Edna."

With the 1964 election right around the corner, Lyndon Johnson realized that, to win, he had to make the voting public believe that he was carrying out Jack Kennedy's unfinished business. And for that, he kept JFK's team of advisors and appointees pretty much intact. He even dangled before Bobby Kennedy the possibility of making Bobby his vice-presidential running mate. Johnson knew he didn't really want Bobby, and Kennedy knew that staying with Lyndon was the last thing on his mind.

Nineteen sixty-four was a year of student demonstrations, and of China's first successful nuclear bomb test.

- The Pentagon's "Operation Plan 34A" marked the first time the U.S. military, not the CIA, took part in attacks on North Vietnam.
- In New York City, 464,000 black students stayed home to protest de facto school segregation in the city; they demanded to be bused to predominantly white schools.
- In Atlanta, Lester Maddox closed his Pickrick restaurant rather than serve blacks; previously, he'd distributed pickax

handles to anyone willing to bludgeon blacks who tried to enter the restaurant.

• The U.S. Supreme Court extended its one-man, one-vote ruling to state legislatures.

• Malcolm X broke with Elijah Muhammad's Black Muslim movement to establish his own nonsectarian, politically oriented Black Nationalist party. "I don't see an American dream," he said, "I see an American nightmare."

• Martin Luther King Jr. donated to the civil rights movement the $54,600 he'd received with the Nobel Peace Prize.

• The Warren Commission concluded that Lee Harvey Oswald had acted alone in killing JFK.

• A Dallas jury convicted Jack Ruby of murdering Oswald.

• In Moscow, American crews uncovered some forty hidden microphones embedded in the walls of the U.S. embassy.

• Less than a year after he'd backed down in the Cuban Missile Crisis, Nikita Khrushchev was out as the head of the Soviet Union.*

• Civil rights workers Goodman, Chaney, and Schwerner were murdered in Mississippi.

• Designer Rudy Gernreich introduced his topless bathing suit.

• "Go-go girls" performed dances such as the frug, the swim, the watusi, and the monkey on raised platforms in discos.

• In San Francisco a bar introduced topless go-go girls and within three months their bottoms had joined their tops as noncostumes.

• Also in San Francisco, Republicans named Senator Barry Goldwater as their presidential nominee; the choice came two months after he'd called for the use of "low-yield atomic weapons" in South Vietnam.

---

* Khrushchev ended his life in obscurity, virtually a prisoner in a small cottage outside of Moscow. When he died on September 11, 1971, the Soviet Politburo denied him a state funeral or burial in the Kremlin wall. Not a single Soviet official attended Khrushchev's funeral.

- In Atlantic City, Democrats named Lyndon Johnson as their presidential nominee. This was three weeks after Johnson had ordered retaliatory air strikes on North Vietnam in response to the North's alleged attacks on American warships.

And in early September Robert Kennedy stepped down as U.S. attorney general. By then, he was already a candidate in New York's Democratic primary for a seat in the U.S. Senate. In October, he faced a group of antagonistic students at Columbia University. They accused him of opportunism, of running on the Kennedy name in a state where he'd never lived. The exchange was so sharp, and Bobby was so good, that his campaign bought a half hour of statewide television prime time to run the exchange.

That same month, during the presidential campaign, Lyndon Johnson promised not to send American fighting men to Vietnam:

We are not about to send American boys nine or ten thousand miles away from home to do what Asian boys ought to be doing for themselves.

By the end of the Eisenhower Administration in 1960, there were 900 American military advisers in Vietnam. By the end of 1963, the number had risen to 16,300.

In the November 1964 election, Johnson overwhelmed Republican Barry Goldwater. Bobby Kennedy easily beat Republican incumbent Kenneth Keating in the run for the Senate. It looked as if Johnson and Kennedy would meet again four years down the line.

In 1967, Michigan governor George Romney made his own run for the GOP nomination. His prospects didn't look good, however. Month after month it seemed that his ratings in the national polls sagged ever further. For some reason, the Detroit riot that summer raised Romney's showing. For political reasons, he'd held back National Guard troops when Democratic presidential hopeful Jerome "Jerry" Cavanagh had asked for help at the start of the riot. When Romney himself asked Democrat Lyndon Johnson for help, LBJ hesitated, also for political reasons. And it may be this dispute with Johnson that boosted Romney's ratings in the polls.

Just before Labor Day, Detroit radio and TV talk show host Lou Gordon was set to kick off a new television show to be syndicated in Philadelphia and Boston. Gordon and George Romney were friends, and George even filled in as Lou's guest-host on a earlier show when Gordon went on vacation.

On Thursday, August 31, Romney had a full slate of events, including a meeting with staff members and an appearance at a state fair. While he and one of his grandchildren were at the fair, the little girl disappeared. Romney's first thought was that she had been kidnapped. Anxious state troopers fanned out over the fairground, looking for the child, and there she was, happily riding around and around on the Ferris wheel. No kidnapping here, just a little girl who'd grown bored with Grandpa's politicking and decided to have some fun.

With that taken care of, but with what a witness called "cowflop and dirt from the state fair still sticking to his shoes," George Romney raced to the studios at WKBD-TV. Because he was running late, and because Lou Gordon wanted to make a big splash with his new show, Romney had to wait for Lou to wrap up with his first guests, a couple from the Swingers, a national husband- and wife-swapping organization.

Finally, the Swingers were gone and George settled in for a relaxed conversation with his old pal Lou. The first question dealt with Vietnam, which Romney had recently visited. Lou Gordon's question was what's called in television a "softball." It was Romney's answer that caused all the excitement.

Gordon: "Isn't your position a bit inconsistent with what it was, and what do you propose we do now?"

Romney: "Well, you know, when I came back from Vietnam, I just had the greatest brainwashing that anybody can get when you go over to Vietnam. Not only by the generals, but also by the diplomatic corps over there, and they do a very thorough job. . . ."

Gordon treated it as a sort of throwaway line. He didn't think it was much and George Romney didn't realize that by saying he'd been brainwashed in Vietnam he'd just sent his presidential aspirations swirling around and around in the political toilet. Several days later, however, as Gordon reviewed the transcript of his show, the word *brainwashing* caught his eye, and he telephoned the *New York Times* man in Detroit, Jerry Flint. Jerry read the transcript and even watched the show. He reported the story, but buried the "brainwashing" comment way down in the text.

Getting a statement like that buried way beneath the headline was good luck for George Romney, but perhaps bad luck for other candidates. Then Lady Luck switched sides. A *Times* deskman, whose job it was to edit Flint's story, caught the brainwashing comment and moved it higher into the story. So on September 5, one day after the Lou Gordon tape actually aired—right there! on page twenty-eight of the *New York Times*—the headline blurted out, "Brainwashing on Vietnam Trip."

The TV networks took a thirty-second clip from *The Lou Gordon Show*, and with the background and circumstances shorn away, there sat George Romney admitting he'd been brainwashed. The Democrats were happy, because they realized that, until that moment, George would have made an appealing candidate. Some Republicans were happy, because they didn't want Romney on the ticket. And Nelson Rockefeller, who'd already declared his presidential candidacy, just loved to see George swinging in the breeze.

On February 1, 1968, a man registered as a guest at the Howard Johnson Inn in Nashua, New Hampshire, using the name "Benjamin Chapman." The next day, "Chapman" appeared before a news conference at the Manchester Holiday Inn. Standing before the news media, he announced, "Gentlemen, this is *not* my last press conference." Benjamin Chapman didn't exist. His real name was Richard Nixon. Nixon announced that he'd be challenging Nelson Rockefeller and George Romney for the Republican presidential nomination.

In New Hampshire, which hadn't heard Richard Nixon utter a word about Vietnam—brainwashed or not—voters decided that Romney just wasn't for them. A poll showed that New Hampshire Republicans would go for Nixon 64.2 percent to 12 percent for Romney. A five-to-one preference. How did Richard Nixon take it all? "I guess the poll shows that New Hampshire Republicans think George Romney is too dumb to be President of the United States."

Not, you understand, that we'd ever vote for a candidate who was "too dumb to be president."

On March 12, 1968, peace candidate Eugene McCarthy captured an amazing 42 percent of the New Hampshire Democratic primary. President Johnson won the race, but he got only six percentage points more than McCarthy.

Four days later, on March 16, Robert Kennedy announced that he was in the race for the White House. "I do not run for the presidency merely to oppose any man," he said, at which point he paused and some in the crowd giggled, "but to propose new politics." He congratulated Eugene McCarthy on the senator's near-victory over LBJ and suggested that McCarthy and Kennedy run "in harmony." Whatever that meant.

Bobby Kennedy had no campaign staff, no strategy for a national race, not this time. Entering the race late, he wouldn't be on the ballot in some primary states. But he was John F. Kennedy's brother and to many JFK's heir apparent.

Bobby Kennedy opened his campaign with a stinging rebuke of the Johnson administration's Vietnam policy. He admitted his part in the military buildup during JFK's administration but said that "past error is no excuse for its own perpetuation." If elected, he added, he would actively seek a peace settlement.

On March 31, President Johnson addressed the nation, saying he was unilaterally halting the U.S. air and naval bombardment of North Vietnam. This would, he told the audience, hopefully "lead to early [peace] talks. I am taking the first step to deescalate the conflict." Oh, and one more thing, before he signed off: a decision that he'd almost revealed almost two months earlier.

Back on January 17, during his fifth State of the Union address, President Johnson had declared that the U.S. bombing of North Vietnam "would stop immediately if talks would take place promptly and with reasonable hopes that it would be productive." LBJ had demanded reciprocity, saying that "The other side must not take advantage of our restraint as they have in the past."

As his formal State of the Union speech, the one that his writers and aides had seen, came to a close, LBJ had reached into his pocket, looking for a note he'd intended to read to the gathered members of Congress and the nation. But the note was missing, and LBJ had gone on to finish the address as it appeared on the TelePrompTer.

Back in the White House residence, Johnson had railed at his wife, Lady Bird: She was supposed to have put the note in his pocket. No, she railed back, *you* were supposed to do it. In any event, the unread message finally was found; someone had laid it on a nearby table.

Six weeks later, on March 31, Johnson finally read that note: "I shall not seek, and I will not accept, the nomination of my party for another term as your president. "

Bobby Kennedy: "I don't know quite what to say."

Republican senator Everett Dirksen: "I went and had another drink."

Demonstrators outside the White House displayed a sign: "Thanks, LBJ."

George Romney had brainwashed himself out on the Republican side and Lyndon Johnson had removed himself from the Democratic side. That left Nelson Rockefeller and Richard Nixon on the right and Vice President Hubert Humphrey, and Senators Eugene McCarthy and Robert Kennedy on the left. The campaign of 1968 was getting interesting, to say the least.

Dr. Martin Luther King Jr. presented a rather unimposing figure. He was five feet seven inches tall and weighed 173 pounds, a heavy-chested man. He dressed with funereal conservatism; five of his six suits were black, as were most of his neckties. He didn't have much of a sense of humor.

He spent a lot of time in jails, sent there by officials who didn't want him marching through their streets or trying to get their schools and restaurants and buses desegregated. J. Edgar Hoover called King "the most notorious liar in the country" and claimed that the SCLC was "spearheaded by Communists and moral degenerates," charges that were never proved. King, according to Bobby Kennedy, "sort of laughs about a lot of these accusations, makes fun" of them.

There's no doubt that Martin Luther King Jr. was both a well-loved and deeply hated man. Nearly every day he received dozens of letters praising him: He was "Moses, sent to lead his people to the Promised Land of first-class citizenship," one letter-writer claimed. And nearly every day he received threats: "This isn't a threat but a promise—your head will be blown off as sure as Christ made green apples."

In the eight years since Rosa Parks had refused to give up her seat on a Montgomery bus to a white man, African Americans had gained a little and lost a lot. Now suddenly, they were to lose a lot more.

Memphis, Tennessee, sanitation workers were members of AF-SCME, the American Federation of State, County, and Municipal Employees, a booming national union that had turned Northern cities upside down, then moved into the South to do the same thing. In August 1966, sanitation workers' Local 1733 voted to strike for better conditions, but a court injunction (based on a Tennessee law that banned all strikes by city workers) stopped the job action dead in its tracks.

Then, on a rainy day early in 1968, one day before the Tet Offensive halfway around the world, trouble broke out in Memphis. Twenty-one black street repairmen were sent home with only two hours of "show-up" pay. Their white supervisors, however, remained and collected a full day's pay. Black workers believed they were being perceived as less worthy than their white bosses.

In addition, they received no health benefits; should they get sick or hurt, they paid the doctor. Two days after the rainy-day incident, in the middle of another heavy storm, an outmoded garbage truck with a hydraulic compacting ram short-circuited and crushed two black sanitation workers inside. The union blamed the city, saying that safety had never been a concern of the sanitation department.

Within days, the union had drawn up a list of grievances, and at a union meeting, members loudly called once more for a strike. They wanted the city to recognize the union, they wanted a pay hike, they wanted overtime pay, they wanted health benefits, and they wanted improved safety conditions. On February 12, Lincoln's birthday, they went on strike, a wildcat strike, because the national

AFSCME office hadn't approved it. That was a problem, because the Memphis local had no funds to help out its striking members. The court injunction didn't help matters, either, not to mention the law forbidding their strike.

Three months later, the thirteen hundred garbage workers were still striking, and Memphis's black neighborhoods had rallied behind them. On March 28, Dr. Martin Luther King Jr. was in town to lend his support and authority to the protest. As soon as he arrived, he dropped his usual exhortations to nonviolence, stepped straight out of his car and straight into a marching mode, linking arms with Rev. Ralph Abernathy and local ministers. And with some fifteen thousand people behind them—most of them black—they marched west on Beale Street, past Handy Park. All the time, crowds of whites gathered along the way to jeer and curse them. Near Second Street, someone broke a store window, and despite attempts to turn the marchers away, some of them took the window breaking as a signal to smash other storefronts.

As the protest line disintegrated, King jumped into a passing car and took refuge at the Holiday Inn–Rivermont Hotel. The next day a Memphis newspaper carried the headline "Chicken A La King."

With King no longer in the group, a line of white Memphis police officers and national guardsmen waded into the broken march. The cops wore gas masks; the marchers did not. With tear gas and clubs and chemical sprays the police broke up the demonstration. Seventy-four people were injured and one, high-school junior Larry Payne, was killed. Police said they'd suspected him of looting a Sears store, and a police officer shot him dead in the basement of a housing project. Throughout the night, national guardsmen patrolled the town in armored personnel carriers. The situation was so tense that the New Orleans to Chicago trains were ordered to skip their usual Memphis stop.

The following day, about four hundred people marched to City Hall, without incident. By then, Memphis was an occupied city, and guardsmen with fixed bayonets lined the streets. The sanitation workers strike continued.

Martin Luther King returned to Memphis on the third, and as television cameras watched, he checked into room 306 at the Lorraine

Motel. He was, according to his staff, moody and withdrawn. That night King attended a sanitation workers' meeting at Mason Temple, and his speech was of a messianic vision:

> Like anybody, I would like to live a long life. Longevity has its place. But I'm not concerned about that now. I just want to do God's will. And He's allowed me to go up to the mountain. And I've looked over, and I've seen the promised land. I may not get there with you, but I want you to know tonight that we as a people will get to the promised land. . . .

On April 4, he had a day of meetings, and that night, at six o'-clock, he stood on the second-floor balcony of the Lorraine Motel, chatting with some friends, including Jesse Jackson and Ben Branch, who were in the courtyard below. King asked someone, a musician, to play "Precious Lord, Take My Hand" at the rally he was about to attend. Then, a shot was fired and Martin Luther King Jr.'s head gushed with blood.

Ralph Abernathy was inside the room and rushed out. Jackson and Branch and the others in the courtyard were nowhere to be seen; apparently, they'd taken cover. "Martin," Abernathy cried out, "It's all right. Don't worry." King appeared calm, then, Abernathy said, "I saw the understanding drain from his eyes and leave them absolutely empty." He told the Reverend Billy Kyle to "go call an ambulance!" But when Abernathy looked inside, Kyle was lying facedown on the bed, screaming. "This is no time to lose our heads," Abernathy told him. "Get an ambulance."

"I can't get a [telephone] line," Kyle yelled. "Something's wrong with the phone."

Nothing was "wrong" with the phone, only with the motel phone switchboard operator. When she heard the shot that killed Martin Luther King, without even knowing what it was or who was killed, she'd had a heart attack and later died, making all phone calls impossible at the moment.

Andrew Young joined Abernathy on the balcony and he knelt beside King. He looked down at Martin and cried out, "Oh, God! Ralph. It's over!"

Someone, somewhere, finally called an ambulance, but it took a quarter of an hour to arrive. An hour later, at St. Joseph's Hospital, doctors pronounced Martin Luther King Jr. dead.

Memphis blacks were beyond outrage. The man many of his followers (and even some of his critics) called "De Lawd" was dead. The city stumbled and burned and sniper fire jarred the night. The stumble continued across the country. Within three hours Washington, D.C., was ablaze in a long thin rectangle that stretched north from Pennsylvania Avenue to Florida Avenue and encompassed the city's chief downtown shopping area.

Deeply disturbed blacks believed that the white business community was not properly honoring Dr. King. Stokely Carmichael, who rejected King's faith in white liberals and nonviolence, wore a gun strapped to his waist and walked the streets. He courteously asked shopkeepers and theater owners and restaurant managers to close in honor of the man who'd been brutally murdered. But Carmichael couldn't control his followers, who muttered and scattered and by ten at night began breaking store windows. Looting began and fires were set.

Still the rage spread. In Boston north of Grove Hall, then downtown Blue Hill Avenue. In Detroit and Philadelphia and San Francisco. And Chicago. On April 15, Chicago Mayor Richard Daley ordered his police to "shoot to kill any arsonists or anyone with a Molotov cocktail in his hand" and to "shoot to maim or cripple anyone looting any store in our city." No official death toll was given after the Chicago riot, although published accounts said from 9 to 11 people died—4 of them blacks killed by police, who wounded 48 others and arrested 350.

In more than 125 cities, riots—uncontrolled by blacks or whites—hit America. Governors across the country called out the National Guard, but 34,000 members of the Guard could do little to control the bitter despair. "The Man, baby, the Man," blacks cried out. At 4:02 Friday afternoon, President Johnson signed an order calling in the U.S. Army. Within the hour helmeted troops, rifles loaded and bayonets fixed, stood in place. Just in time too. By the time they took up their positions, the rioting and looting had come within two blocks of the White House. For the first time since the American Civil

War, troops in full battle gear had been called on to defend the halls of Congress.

Life photographer Gordon Parks was driving past actor Marlon Brando's Hollywood apartment when he heard the news of Dr. King's death. In a state of shock, Parks stopped the car and went into Brando's high-rise, where he found Marlon stretched out on a couch. Parks was in shock, but Brando apparently hadn't even heard the news. "You know Dr. King is dead?" the photographer asked the lounging actor. Now Brando was excited, but not enough to get up. He just "called his assistant" and said, "Order me some guns from my gunsmith." Brando also telephoned the California headquarters of the Black Panthers, then told Parks, "I feel like shooting my way all the way to Washington, D.C."

Finally, Brando calmed down and Parks went back to his hotel, where he got a call from *Life* magazine giving him his next photographic assignment: Dr. Martin Luther King's funeral.

Bobby Kennedy was campaigning in Indiana. He received the news that King had been shot as he flew from Terre Haute to Indianapolis. When his plane landed, he learned that the civil rights leader was dead. He seemed "to shrink back as if struck physically," his friend and aide Arthur Schlesinger remembered. He gasped, "Oh, God. When is this violence going to stop?"

He was scheduled to go to a rally in the black section of town but several people—including his wife, Ethel, and the Indianapolis police chief—thought it wouldn't be safe and wanted him to go immediately to his hotel. Kennedy decided he had to attend the rally, and as his car reached the unpaved parking lot where the gathering was to be held, it became clear that the crowd there had not yet heard the news about Martin Luther King.

Bobby climbed onto a flatbed truck that served as a dais and grabbed a portable microphone. "I have some terrible news for you," he told the unsuspecting crowd. "Martin Luther King has been shot." A gasp went up from the crowd and Kennedy stood there "hunched in his black overcoat, his face gaunt and distressed and full of anguish." Martin Luther King had "dedicated his life to love and to justice for his fellow human beings," Kennedy said.

> He died because of that effort. In this difficult day, in this difficult time for the United States, it is perhaps well to ask what kind of a nation we are and what direction we want to move in. For those of you who are black—considering the evidence . . . that there were white people who were responsible—you can be filled with bitterness, with hatred, and a desire for revenge. . . . Or we can make an effort, as Martin Luther King did, to understand and to comprehend, and to replace that stain of bloodshed that has spread across our land, with an effort to understand with compassion and love. For those of you who are black and are tempted to be filled with hatred and distrust at the injustice of such an act, against all white people, I can only say that I feel in my own heart the same kind of feeling. I had a member of my family killed. . . .

That summer, author James Baldwin told Chicago television host Jim Tilmon:

> There's more than one way for a generation to be slaughtered. They can be slaughtered in the streets with tanks, with guns. They can be thrown into jail. They can be, as our generation in so many ways has—and [as] previous generations have been—demoralized and emasculated and beaten down. I think it is up to their elders to force the situation to such an extent [that] this must, this has to be prevented.

On May 7, primary election day in Indiana, Bobby Kennedy got into a full-contact "touch" football game so rough that two players were injured. That night he won the primary with 43 percent of the vote. Eugene McCarthy received only 27 percent. Hell, Indiana governor Roger Branigan, running as a favorite son hoping to control convention delegates, beat McCarthy with 31 percent of the votes.

That same night, in the District of Columbia, Kennedy defeated Hubert Humphrey by a margin of 62.5 percent to 37. Then came the Nebraska primary and Bobby beat them both.

In Oregon, McCarthy claimed that "We began this campaign against the war when no one else would touch it." Aiming his rhetoric at Kennedy, McCarthy continued:

> We are not just running a political campaign, we represent a movement—a movement for peace in Vietnam, a movement for reconciliation at home. We must not let Kennedy's personal ambitions halt that movement. And I don't think he can.

On May 28, he beat Kennedy by six percentage points, and with that defeat, Bobby Kennedy became the underdog. For a while.

On board a plane heading for California, campaign workers and reporters celebrated Kennedy bodyguard Bill Barry's birthday, a cake decorated with the faces of both Barry and Kennedy. The champagne flowed and everyone laughed and sang until, suddenly, a balloon popped loudly. Bobby's hand slowly rose to his face and covered his eyes and for ten or fifteen seconds the plane was shocked into quiet. Then the party resumed.

When they landed in Los Angeles, Bobby got off the plane while campaign workers and reporters continued drinking and laughing and singing, whatever songs they knew—folk songs, patriotic songs, campaign songs, and even a parody on an old church hymn: "What a Friend We Have in Bobby."

Back in February 1967, when Lyndon Johnson was still expected to run in '68, the president pulled ahead of Bobby Kennedy in the polls, twenty-two points ahead. In a face-to-face meeting Johnson told Kennedy, "You'll be dead politically in six months."

Jackie Kennedy and her sister-in-law Ethel, Bobby's wife, didn't always get along, and perhaps it was only that their husbands were members of a strong clan that kept them even talking to each other. For instance, right after Bobby declared his candidacy for president, Jackie said to Ethel, "Won't it be wonderful when we get back into the White House again?" And Ethel answered, "What do you mean *we?*" In March, after Bobby announced his candidacy, Jackie Kennedy told Arthur Schlesinger, "Do you know what I think will happen to Bobby? The same thing that happened to Jack."

Surrounded by a group of reporters, including columnist Jimmy Breslin, one-time New York mayor and presidential hopeful John Lindsay was asked if he thought Bobby Kennedy had the "stuff to go all the way" to the White House. "Yes, of course I do," Lindsay replied but added, "He's not going to go all the way. The reason is that somebody is going to shoot him. I know it and you know it, just as sure as we're sitting here. He's out there waiting for him."

Several weeks later, an informant told the FBI that the Mafia had put a contract out to assassinate Kennedy "in the event it appeared he might receive the Democratic nomination." The FBI had also picked up unconfirmed reports of a conspiracy among Jimmy Hoffa and his cronies in the Lewisburg Federal Penitentiary about "a contract to kill Bob Kennedy." That brought on talk of giving Kennedy protection—at the time, candidates weren't normally provided with FBI or Secret Service guards. J. Edgar Hoover made it clear that he would do nothing to protect Bobby. Hoover's second in command and first in bed, Clyde Tolson, followed J. Edgar's lead. "I hope," he said, "someone shoots and kills that son of a bitch."

By the time the campaign got to California, Bobby Kennedy was in the eighty-fifth day of his run for president. He'd had good times and bad, won primaries and lost them. It all got down to the June 5, California primary. By eight o'clock, Kennedy supporters had packed the Royal Suite on the fifth floor of the Ambassador Hotel, waiting for what they hoped—some expected—to be the good word. By nine o'clock, CBS television had made the first projection: Bobby Kennedy would win 52 to 38 over McCarthy. There were cheers and singing and happiness, Californians and Bostonians, staff members, family, and old friends: "Happy days are here again," as the old Democratic Party favorite song goes.*

---

* Words by Jack Yellen, music by Milton Ager, copyright 1929. This was played at the 1932 Democratic presidential convention and became a campaign song for Franklin D. Roosevelt and just about every Democratic presidential candidate after that.

It wasn't over yet, he and his advisors felt, but that night in Los Angeles things looked pretty good for Bobby Kennedy. He appeared on ABC and CBS and NBC, then waited for Eugene McCarthy to concede defeat—a well-worn ritual that most political candidates follow.

Around midnight, in the first-floor ballroom, campaign workers and curiosity seekers squeezed in to see and hear and maybe touch Bobby Kennedy, the man of the hour and perhaps the man of the year. Balloons and confetti floated in the air, and television camera cables snaked over the floor; still cameras flashed, and the crowd stomped and cheered and stomped and cheered some more when Kennedy finally stood before them.

For perhaps the first time in quite a while, he was reflective:

> What I think is quite clear is that we can work together in the last analysis, and that what has been going on in the United States over the last three years—the division, the violence, the disenchantment with our society: the divisions whether it's between blacks and whites, between the poor and the more affluent, or between age groups or on the war in Vietnam—is that we can start to work together. We are a great country, an unselfish country and a compassionate country. I intend to make that my basis for running.

"And so," he said, "it's on to Chicago and let's win there."

His staff was confused about how they'd get to a press conference in another hotel. Two routes were available. One: He could leave the platform, turn left, reach the hotel's main corridor, then the stairwell, and out to his car. Or: He could turn right off the platform, go out through the kitchen, then back to the stairwell, and down. Kennedy turned right, for a very simple reason: He wanted to stop off in the kitchen, maybe for a quick bite to eat.

It was 1:44 A.M. and security guard Thane Eugene Cesar held Bobby's right elbow as they headed through the serving pantry. A Palestinian immigrant named Sirhan Sirhan stepped up, aimed a .22 caliber pistol at Bobby from less than an inch away, and shot Kennedy in the back of the head, near the right ear. Sirhan then turned the weapon on the crowd and injured five others before he was subdued.

"I'm hurt," Bobby Kennedy whispered, "I'm hurt." He was conscious for a few seconds, lying face up on the pantry floor, with blood pooling around his head. "No, no, no!" he cried.

Busboy Juan Romero, who only moments before had shaken Kennedy's hand, knelt next to Bobby, touching him as Kennedy looked up pleadingly. Someone put rosary beads in Bobby's hand and he gripped them tightly. Ethel Kennedy pushed her way through the crowd, trying to reach her husband. A friend leaned over to listen as Bobby Kennedy's lips moved: "Jack, Jack."

And then Kennedy lapsed into unconsciousness. He never recovered.

In Washington, D.C., on the morning Bobby Kennedy died, President Lyndon Johnson—without Congressional authority—appointed a commission to investigate physical violence in America.

On June 8, while Bobby Kennedy's body lay in state in St. Patrick's Cathedral in New York, detectives from London's Scotland Yard arrested James Earl Ray, the man many believe murdered Martin Luther King Jr. Ray had been staying at a boardinghouse in sight of the Lorraine Motel in Memphis when King was shot.

At first, Ray claimed that he was innocent, but in 1969, he pleaded guilty. Then he changed his mind and claimed that he'd been pressured by his attorney and said the FBI had threatened his father and brother if he refused to sign a confession. Ray never could prove his innocence, and after he'd been convicted of murder, a judge sentenced him to life in prison.

Shortly before his death in 1998, James Earl Ray told a television interviewer, "I was not the triggerman. I didn't know anything about the killing."

During a four-month-long trial in 1969, Sirhan Sirhan's attorney offered a claim of diminished capacity as a defense in the death of Robert Kennedy. Sirhan himself said he couldn't remember the shooting. As evidence against him, the prosecution offered Sirhan's diaries in which he'd written that he hated Bobby Kennedy for Kennedy's support of Israel. Bobby, he believed, had to die before the anniversary of the June 5, 1967, Arab-Israeli War, the war during which Israel took control of the Sinai Peninsula and the Golan Heights.

On April 17, 1969, the jury found Sirhan Sirhan guilty of first-degree murder. The prosecution didn't ask for the death penalty, and Kennedy's brother, Senator Ted Kennedy, pleaded for clemency. But the jury saw things differently; they wanted to give him the death penalty. The judge agreed and sentenced Sirhan to be executed.

On June 29, 1972, however, the U.S. Supreme Court, in *Furman v. Georgia,* ruled that the death penalty could constitute cruel and unusual punishment and violate the Eighth Amendment to the Constitution. The ruling affected the fate of many on death rows around the country, and many death sentences were commuted to life in prison. With that, Sirhan Sirhan escaped execution.

 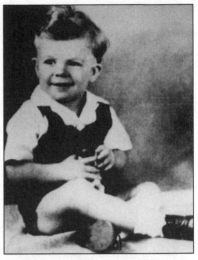

John Fitzgerald Kennedy at about six months of age. (The John F. Kennedy Library)

Lee Harvey Oswald at about two years old. Claiming she couldn't cope with them, Marguerite Oswald tried to place Lee and his two brothers in an orphanage. Lee was not accepted into the home until he turned three. (National Archives)

Lee Harvey Oswald's passport, issued on September 10, 1959, one day before his discharge from the Marine Corps. (National Archives)

President John F. Kennedy and Mrs. Jacqueline Kennedy in Dallas, Texas, moments before he was assassinated on November 22, 1963. (UPI/Bettman)

Dr. Martin Luther King Jr., August 5, 1966, during a news conference at an open-housing march through Chicago's Marquette Park. (Chicago Tribune)

Dr. King, August 28, 1963, leading a quarter of a million people in a civil rights march at the Lincoln Memorial in Washington, D.C. (Hulton Getty)

Mourners pack the streets of Atlanta, Georgia, on April 9, 1968, to see Martin Luther King's casket drawn by a mule team to a memorial service at Morehouse College. (Corbis/Bettman/UPI)

Neshoba County deputy sheriff Cecil Price (left) and Sheriff Lawrence Rainey in 1964, about to be arraigned for the murder of civil rights workers Mickey Schwerner, James Chaney, and Andrew Goodman. Price and Rainey were never brought to trial. (Bill Reed/Black Star)

Students for a Democratic Society (SDS), national council meeting in Bloomington, Indiana, September 1963. Tom Hayden is (literally) on the far left, and Rennie Davis is on the extreme right (politically unlikely, photographically true). (George Abbott White)

Line of Michigan National Guardsmen drive would-be looters away from a burning building during a July 1967 riot in Detroit's West Side. More than 4,000 people were injured and at least 90 died in more than 120 riots in one year. (UPI/Bettman)

An unidentified American soldier in Vietnam, 1968. The writing on his helmet is in response to the frequently seen motto: "Make Love, Not War." (UPI/Bettman)

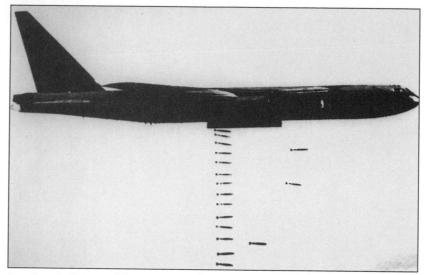

In the mid-sixties, B-52 bomber attacks became common and forced communist troops to place as much of their personnel and equipment underground as possible. B-52s flew so high that they could not be seen or heard until the bombs hit. (National Archives)

On the steps of the Pentagon in 1967, an antiwar demonstrator inserts pink carnations into the gun barrels of army troops. (Bernie Boston, *Washington Star*)

With the whole world watching, Chicago police manhandle protesters outside the Chicago Hilton, headquarters for delegates to the 1968 Democratic convention. The Chicago Crime Commission later concluded that a "police riot" had occurred. (UPI/Bettmann)

Chicago police confiscate Pigasus the Pig, Yippie "presidential candidate," outside the Democratic Party convention. (Fred W. McDarrah)

In 1964, the Beatles came to America, where they saw thousands of screaming fans wherever they went; they had conquered the American music scene. In April, they held the top five positions in the singles chart. Their success paved the way for other British bands in what came to be known as the British Invasion. (Hulton Getty)

"Hitsville U.S.A." With an $800 loan from his parents' savings club, in 1959 Berry Gordy Jr. began Tamla Records. On April 14, 1960, Gordy changed the company's name to Motown to reflect Detroit's Motor City heritage. (Author's collection)

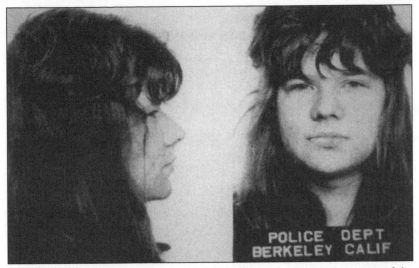

Singer Janis Joplin, police mug shot taken after she was arrested in Berkeley, Calif., for shoplifting on February 21, 1963, a month after she arrived in town. At first unsuccessful as a singer, she tried prostitution. Again, she was unsuccessful, later joking that she was "too ugly" for men to pay her for sex. (Berkeley, California, police dept.)

The Grateful Dead in their home territory, the corner of Haight and Ashbury Streets in San Francisco, 1965. (Herb Greene, *Life* magazine)

An estimated 400,000 people attended the August 15-17, 1969, Woodstock Music and Art Fair at farmer Max Yasgur's 35-acre field outside Bethel, New York. The crowd far overran facilities planned by festival promoters; still it was "three days of peace and music." Today the field is something of a shrine dedicated to "peace and good will." (Author's collection)

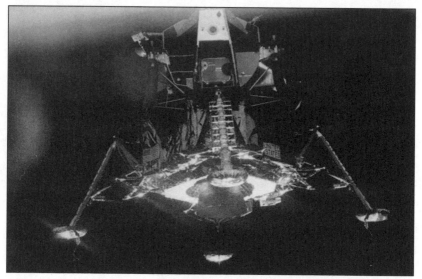

Lunar lander *Eagle* with astronauts Neil Armstrong and Edwin "Buzz" Aldrin on board descends from Apollo 11 on July 20, 1969. Armstrong reported, "The *Eagle* has wings!" Later that day after touching down on the Moon with just twenty seconds of fuel to spare, Armstrong radioed back: "The *Eagle* has landed." (NASA)

CHAPTER EIGHT

The Generation Gap:
Old at Thirty

Don't trust anyone over thirty.
Jack Weinberg, Free Speech Movement of the sixties*

For too long, those who have led us have viewed politics as the "art of the possible." The challenge which faces them and us now is to practice politics as the art of making what appears impossible.
Hillary Rodham, May 1969, president of the Wellesley College Government Association, address at Wellesley's ninety-second commencement

In 1961, Roger Maris of the New York Yankees beat out teammate Mickey Mantle for the American League home run championship. In doing so, he broke Babe Ruth's thirty-four-year-old home run record of sixty, with Roger hitting sixty-one. Maris's record lasted thirty-seven years, until 1998 when it was topped by two players in one season: Mark McGwire of the St. Louis Cardinals with seventy, and the Chicago Cubs' Sammy Sosa with sixty-six home runs.

And, yeah, in 1961, those damn Yankees won the world series. Again. They beat the Cincinnati Reds 4–1.

Maybe it wasn't as big a deal as setting a new home run record, but on September 8, 1965, Bert Campaneris of the Kansas City A's did something unusual. Campaneris started the game at shortstop, moved to second base, then third, and then he played the outfield—all three parts of the outfield, moving from left field to right. He pitched the eighth inning, and in the ninth he stayed in the game behind the plate. He'd played all nine positions in a single game. He finally left after a collision at home plate.

---

* During a 1964 interview, Weinberg, a leader of the Free Speech Movement at the University of California, Berkeley, commented that "We have a saying in the movement that we don't trust anybody over thirty."

On January 15, 1967, the National Football League held the first Super Bowl, with the National Football League's Green Bay Packers meeting the American Football League's Kansas City Chiefs at Los Angeles's Memorial Coliseum. Vince Lombardi's Packers beat the Chiefs 35–10. The Packers won again in 1968, this time beating the Oakland Raiders 33–14 in Miami's Orange Bowl Stadium. Green Bay quarterback Bart Starr was voted Most Valuable Player in both games.

Incidentally, Vince Lombardi, who's generally credited with saying, "Winning isn't everything; it's the only thing," didn't actually say it. It was another long-time coach, Red Sanders, who said it in 1955. What Vince Lombardi said, seven years later in 1962, was, "Winning isn't everything, but wanting to win is."

The merger between the National Football League and the upstart American Football League was something of a shotgun wedding. Negotiations for the nuptials began in a parking lot at Dallas's Love Field in June 1966. At the meeting was Tex Schramm, a reformed journalist who was then president of the Dallas Cowboys. His nickname around the NFL was "Loophole," because he always found one in legal contracts. Lamar Hunt was also at the meeting, one of Texas's oil-rich Hunts, who had been rejected by the NFL when he'd tried to buy the Chicago Cardinals.* So, in 1960, Hunt began his own league, the American Football League, with teams playing in such cities as Oakland and Denver and Buffalo. It was, according to the NFL commissioner Pete Rozelle, "the other league."

In the early years the other league played with the culls and rejects of the NFL, players too old, too slow, too bad, to make it in "the real league." League founder Hunt owned the Dallas Texans. It was the same year the NFL's Dallas Cowboys broke from the starting gate, but the race was never close. Hunt's Texans were driven out of town in three years, and he took them to Kansas City, where they became the "Chiefs."

About the time the Cardinals moved from Chicago to St. Louis, they drafted quarterback Joe Namath and fully expected him to play for them. But New Yorker Sonny Werblin, who had bought the AFL

* The Cardinals eventually moved to St. Louis and even later to Phoenix.

Titans and renamed the franchise the Jets, offered Joe a then mind-boggling $425,000 to play in "the other league." That was ten times the salary such established NFL quarterbacks as John Brodie of the San Francisco 49ers were being paid. Actually, more than ten times, because Brodie was earning only $35,000 at the time. And, of course, Joe Namath signed on the AFL dotted line.

Then Oakland picked off Los Angeles Rams quarterback Roman Gabriel. The AFL even raided Chicago Bears owner-coach George Halas, hiring away a guy named Mike Ditka, and he signed with the Philadelphia Eagles in 1967.

So, the two leagues were going against each other tooth, nail, and checkbook, when they finally waved a white flag. In that airport parking lot, Hunt and Schramm agreed that instead of fighting and spending a lot of money and, in the process destroying each other, they'd join forces: The forty-six-year-old NFL and the six-year-old AFL would merge. They'd become the National Football League, with two conferences, the National and the American on equal footing. The change would become effective with the 1970 season.

In the meantime, the two leagues would meet in a world championship to be called . . . Well, what could we call it?

The story goes that Lamar Hunt was back home one day and his young daughter was playing with a hard-shelled rubber ball. She'd bounce the ball and it would ricochet over her head. "What's that called?" Daddy Lamar asked.

"It's a Super Ball," his daughter answered.

And with an "Aha!" Hunt had the answer to what to call the NFL-AFL championship game. And on January 15, 1967, the first Super Ball–turned–Super Bowl matched the Green Bay Packers against Hunt's Kansas City Chiefs, with the Cheesehead Packers, after struggling in their first series of plays, winning easily 35–10. The football itself may have made the difference. The official AFL ball was just a bit longer, a bit skinnier, than the NFL version. After the game, reporters asked Packers' long-time coach Vince Lombardi about this. The NFL ball "kicks a little better, it throws a little bit better, and it catches a little bit better."

Then came Super Bowl II in 1968 and the Packers won by almost as impressive a score as the first time around, 33–14 over the Oakland Raiders.

So, what about that curly-haired quarterback who wore fur coats and white shoes and had shaggy sideburns down to here? "Broadway Joe," they called Namath, even though he'd come out of a Pennsylvania mill town and went to college in Alabama. He'd had a pretty fair season in '68. The Jets won the AFL championship and headed for Miami's Orange Bowl for the big game.

Super Bowl III on January 12, 1969, would be the last time the two leagues would meet for the world championship. After that it would be all one happy family with two conference, not league, champions meeting.

The Baltimore Colts dominated the NFL in '68, beat and whallopped the Cleveland Browns 34–zip for the NFL championship. Going into the Super Bowl the word was that the Colts and Bubba Smith would murder Namath and the Jets. Oddsmaker Jimmy the Greek put the Colts up by seventeen points.

Then, the Sunday before the game, Namath and teammate Jim Hudson walked into a restaurant in Fort Lauderdale, Florida. Joe wore no coat, no socks. He ordered Johnnie Walker Red scotch and stood in a corner surrounded by gawkers, including field-goal kicker Lou Michaels of the Colts.

Michaels introduced himself to Namath, who didn't even answer, just barely nodded and sipped his scotch. "You do a lot of talking, boy," Michaels said.

This time, Namath answered. "There's a lot to talk about. We're going to kick the hell out of your team."

A few days later, "The Dutchman"—NFL great Norm Van Brocklin—told a gathering at the Miami Touchdown Club that, come Super Bowl Sunday, "Joe Namath will be playing his first pro game." The recipient of the club's Outstanding Player of the Year Award was late arriving at the Touchdown Club gathering and didn't hear the Dutchman's proclamation, which may be why when he stood up to receive his award Joe Namath said what he did. After all, Van Brocklin was known for his sharp wit and wisdom about the game. If he said the Colts would win, they'd win. Well, maybe.

Namath spoke with a Southern drawl, undoubtedly cultivated while playing with Bear Bryant at Alabama. "We're going to win Sunday," he said. "I guarantee you."

The Touchdown Club audience was shocked, and that included Florida governor Claude Kirk Jr. and assorted hangers-on. Not many sportswriters or commentators were at the Touchdown Club shindig, mainly because they usually weren't invited. A reporter for the *Miami Herald* was there and the next day the *Herald* came out with the headline "Namath Guarantees Jet Victory."

By the end of the first half, it was obvious that the Colts weren't going to beat the hell out of the hopeless and helpless Jets. After it was over, with the Jets winning, sportswriter Jerry Green of the *Detroit News* wrote:

> It happened. Space has been conquered and the New York Jets are the professional champions of the universe.
>
> Joe Namath, the Broadway loudmouth, is king of the quarterbacks and the American Football League is equal. . . .
>
> The score was 16–7, and today there are those who call this the greatest upset in the history of team sports.
>
> Maybe so.

Later, while a trainer unwrapped the tape from Namath's legs—his legs would go later and end his career—Joe talked with Green. "I told you so," he said.

And indeed he had. And indeed he lived up to his guarantee.

For the Chicago Cubs, the 1969 season began, as do most Cubs' seasons, with high hopes. Only this time, as third baseman Ron Santo remembered, "We knew that this was the season we were going to win." They reeled off nine wins in their first ten games. From opening day until September 10, the boys from Wrigley Field were in first place. And on August 19, Ken Holtzman even pitched a no-hitter against the Atlanta Braves. At the time, the Cubs held a nine-and-a-half-game lead over the New York Mets, and it looked as if they might end a twenty-four-year postseason drought. But slowly, the lead began slipping away.

On September 11, a black cat somehow wondered out onto the field, and then, naturally, headed for the Cubs' dugout. Maybe it was a sign.

From September 3 to the eleventh, they lost eight games in a row, and at the same time the Mets had a seven-game *winning* streak, the infamous "September swoon." "If I'd known we were going to lose eight straight," Manager Leo Durocher said later, "I would have just played nine pitchers every day and let everyone else go home and rest."

By the end of September, the lead was down to four games, and the Mets continued chipping away. Then, barely three weeks after holding that four-game lead, the Cubs found themselves mathematically eliminated from the playoffs.

So why did the Cubs falter? *Chicago Tribune* sports columnist Robert Markus had a theory: "The Cubs simply had to shoulder their burden too long. It is impossible to endure the kind of pressure the Cubs were under for six months." Maybe it was that black cat.

Or maybe the answer was that the Mets were a better ball club. On the night of September 24, the Mets served champagne, shaving cream, and bath towels. They'd won the National League East division title. The "Amazing Mets," they were called. They beat the Atlanta Braves to become National League champions. They beat the American League champs Baltimore 4–1 in the World Series.

Back in the late eighteenth century, a Sudbury, Massachusetts, merchant came up with an idea to attract customers. With every purchase, he gave away copper tokens, and the tokens were redeemable for goods in his store. The idea of trading tokens or stamps stuck around, but usually you had to use them wherever you received them.

But in 1896, the Sperry and Hutchinson Company—founded by Jackson, Michigan, silverware salesman Thomas A. Sperry and Michigan businessman Shelley B. Hutchinson—began issuing its own, independent, trading stamps. They were given out by a number of different stores and could be redeemed at a number of different sites. S & H Green Trading Stamps became a phenomenal success, working something like frequent flyer miles of later days. By 1921, S & H Green Stamps were given out by some 25,000 stores and could be redeemed in some 600 centers around the country.

By the 1960s, everybody gave Green Stamps, everybody saved Green Stamps, everybody licked them and put them in booklets, and everybody exchanged them for goods at what S & H referred to as "premium parlors." Each stamp had a cash value of one mill, one tenth of one cent, and we got one S & H Green Stamp for every ten cents we spent: Spend a dollar, get ten Green Stamps for our booklets. Fill enough booklets and we could exchange them for various items out of the catalog the company called the "Ideabook"—140 million Ideabooks were printed in 1964 alone. S & H Green Stamps became so popular that Sperry and Hutchinson became the largest wholesale buyer of General Electric small appliances, Coleman lanterns, and Bissell carpet sweepers. You could pool your stamps for charity or community projects. The city of Erie, Pennsylvania, convinced its citizens to donate their stamps and the Erie zoo bought a pair of gorillas that they named, appropriately enough, Samantha and Henry—S & H.

Even Jackie Kennedy got in on the act when she was in the White House. "Do you know," she said to her secretary Mary Gallagher, "all the food we buy here at the White House? Well, [presidential secretary Anne Lincoln] told me that with the stamps the stores give us, we can trade them in for these marvelous gifts!" No word on whether Jackie picked out a toaster or what.

Some lawmakers thought that somehow they were illegal, or if they weren't they should be. Fifty bills were introduced in twenty-four states, trying to penalize the stamps in one way or another. Some areas—the District of Columbia, for instance—banned them outright, and others imposed prohibitive taxes. The Casper, Wyoming, city council passed an antistamp ordinance and ordered Sperry and Hutchinson to get out of town by sunset. Or at least by the end of the month.

The public, however, loved them. Why, we even had a "Green Stamp Song." Nobody knows who wrote it, but it went to the tune of "Greensleeves":

> I found my love in a grocery shop,
>> Selling pickles and egg plants and bottles of pop;
> She ask me to try her asparagus tips,
>> And I fell for the smile on her ruby red lips.
> Green stamps were all she gave,
>> Green stamps were all I took;

185

Green stamps were all I saved,
So I pasted them all in my green stamp book.

In 1964, S & H printed and sold more stamps than did the U.S. Post Office. The company claimed that it printed so many catalogs that if you put them end to end they'd circle the earth one and a half times.

Redemption centers had their own problem: what to do with stamp booklets that had been turned in for merchandise. Redeemed booklets kept being stolen and turning up for reredemption. One center put weights into sacks of redeemed books and tossed them into the ocean, but divers retrieved the sacks and turned them in for other merchandise. Companies that incinerated Green Stamp booklets found that in order to burn enough of them fast enough, they had to have special furnaces. And then they were stuck with the ashes.

But in 1965, the bottom fell out. Supermarkets and gas stations found a new gimmick to get customers: They simply lowered their prices. "Do you want trading stamps, or do you want upper-class quality foods at stampless discount prices?" the St. Louis–based Bettendorf stores asked in an ad campaign. By the end of the year, more than five hundred supermarkets had dropped trading stamps. By 1967, the trading-stamp industry was in a tailspin.

Food prices skyrocketed late in the sixties, and customers opted for lower prices and fewer frills, meaning fewer stamps. Discount stores popped up left and right—Target, Shopper's City, Kmart—and they didn't give stamps.

Still, Sperry and Hutchinson didn't go out of business. In fact, pockets still exist in America where you can get Green Stamps, and you can get them when you rent a car or order flowers on-line. S & H converted the stamps to lick-free stickers (called Greenpoints), and more recently they're recorded on credit card–like plastic. And there's a new way to redeem them: Today, you go on-line. Computers and the internet have taken over Green Stamps.

During the fifteen years between the end of World War II and the election of John F. Kennedy in 1960, American society was transformed. Or it transformed itself, more likely.

Perhaps the biggest change was in the family. During the Great Depression of the thirties, young people remained single longer or deferred marriage. By the sixties they were getting married at an earlier age. The number of married couples skyrocketed from 28.2 million in 1945 to 38.9 million in 1960, a gain of 10.7 million. More people marrying at a younger age increased the number of children born. The birth rate—the number of children born annually per thousand women—rose from about 19 during the Great Depression to around 21 during World War II and to about 25 per thousand during the fifties. The baby boom in all its glory!

During the thirties the number of babies born annually was usually fewer than 2.5 million. In 1943, the number was up to 3 million and in 1946 it hit 3.4 million births. The total passed 4 million in 1954 and remained above the 4-million mark through 1960. That year, according to the U.S. Bureau of the Census, there were 4,258,000 births in America, the number down just a nudge from the peak baby-boomer year of 1957, which had posted 4,300,000 newborns. Baby boom? Oh, yes.

The total number of babies born between 1946 and 1960 was a staggering 59.4 million. And still more were born. The birth rate rose even higher in 1961, to 4,268,000, but after that there was a steady decrease. From then on, baby boomers had no place to go but old age. In 1940, life expectancy was 62.9 years. It gained almost seven years by 1960 and stood at 69.7, and it continues to rise today. Currently it's at 70.2 years, for all races and both sexes; it's shorter for men, longer for women; shorter for African Americans, longer for whites.

In 1946, America's population was about 141 million. By 1960, it was up to 180.6 million, a gain of 39.6 million. Oh, there was some immigration and the death rate declined, but most of the increase we did ourselves. Or to ourselves.

The rise in population saw changes in where and how we lived. The number of people living on farms declined—it's still declining—and the number of people living in urban areas grew. Not necessarily in large cities, however. Of the sixteen cities with populations of 600,000 or more in 1960, eleven declined in size over the decade. Only five—including Los Angeles, Houston, and Dallas in the South and Southwest—grew, and in part they grew by annexing fringe areas.

Between 1940 and 1960, the population of Los Angeles increased from 1.5 million to 2.5 million. In the same period, San Diego saw an increase from 203,000 to 573,000, Houston grew from 385,000 to 938,000, Seattle from 368,000 to 557,000, and Phoenix from 65,000 to 439,000.

If people left rural areas during the fifties and sixties and didn't move into large cities, where did they go? The answer, of course, is the suburbs. Eighty-three percent of America's population growth during the 1950s was in the suburbs, which were growing fifteen times faster than any other segment of the country.

That's for all races. The birth rate among African Americans was even higher. During the fifties, black women averaged nearly four children per mother. The African American population grew from 12.9 million in 1940 to 18.9 million in 1960.

Distribution of races also changed. Historically, blacks had concentrated in the rural South, but during World War II the black migration to northern cities increased dramatically. The fifties saw a record 1,457,000 blacks leave the South for the North and West, looking for jobs and freedom. By 1960, two-thirds of all blacks in America lived in the North, half of them in central cities.

That brought about the phenomenon known as "white flight"— as more and more blacks moved north and into urban areas, more and more whites moved out of the cities into the suburbs. Whites fled to the suburbs and blacks moved into city ghettoes.

That's when the suburbs came of age. Prior to World War II, living in the suburbs was atypical, not the life of your average American. By the sixties, more and more people wanted—and could afford—their own homes out in the suburbs, which meant we had to have our own cars to get to and from work, which meant the nation needed new streets and highways.

Oh, sure, there was a sameness to many suburban homes: Cape Cod, ranch-style, split-level. We even had a song about our homes made out of "ticky-tacky."

But we had new schools (they were, naturally, all-white, as were the suburban communities), new shopping centers, and new churches.

Take the Chicago suburb of Park Forest, where in the 1960s the model family was a twenty-five to thirty-five-year-old white-collar organization man with a wife, one child, and one more on the way. He earned a salary between $6,000 and $7,000, was an engineer, a lawyer, a salesman, an insurance agent, in middle management, or he was a teacher, a bureaucrat, a junior officer in the military. Whatever he was, he and all of his neighbors were middle class.

In the 1960s, according to *Fortune* magazine, suburbia became "the most important single market in the country." It was the home of the consumer. Millions of families with relatively high incomes lived in suburbia. Their high incomes meant lots of discretionary buying, which meant manufacturers and marketers and advertising agencies took aim at them, which meant they bought more cars, more TVs, more diapers, bicycles, barbecues, casual clothing, and became one big market for food. Who could ask for anything more?

When the sixties began, the most popular name for baby boys was David; Mary was the most popular name for girls. By the end of the decade David had dropped to second place behind Michael, which continued as the number one boy baby name through the end of the century. Mary had been the top girls' name but dropped to eighth place, behind number one Lisa, number two Jennifer, and names such as Michelle, Kimberly, Maria, Melissa, and Amy.

In 1960, an estimated 850,000 "war baby" freshmen entered American colleges. The baby boom caused schools to set up emergency living quarters in dorm lounges, hotels, and trailer camps. This influx, including many former servicemen going to school under the GI Bill, changed college life in many ways. No longer were all college freshmen bright-eyed and bushy-tailed students straight out of high school. Some were old (read twenty-five years old or so) and sophisticated—they'd fought and loved in Europe and Asia, had seen many of their friends die there. They were serious about studying. Still, all things considered, they *were* still young, and Pepsi-Cola's big advertising campaign that year was pegged "For those who think young!"

In 1960, the population of the United States was 177,830,000. In 1970, it stood at 204,879,000. The average annual salary was $4,743 in 1960; by 1970, it was up to $7,564.

Now, in the twenty-first century, the baby boom is over, and baby boomers themselves are aging. The baby boom ran from 1946 to 1964, which makes the youngest boomer at least thirty-six years old and the oldest fifty-four. Meanwhile, the boomers' numbers are shrinking. During the boom, an estimated 65 million American babies were born; however, as of April 2000, there were 100,000 *fewer* boomers around. The U.S. Census Bureau called it the first major shrinkage of the group, and of course the baby-boom generation has no place to go but down, at an accelerated pace. Sorry about that, baby boomers.

Chronologically, baby boomers are at least middle aged: more than halfway to their life expectancy, as determined by the National Center for Health Statistics. Since the beginning of 1996, one boomer has been turning fifty every eight minutes, a rate that will continue until the year 2014. By 2031, the boomer ranks will have shrunk to 51 million; by 2046, there'll be only 19 million of them, a mere shadow of the generation's former self.

The baby-boom generation likely will not go gently into the night. Those noisy and demanding boomer children became noisy and demanding adults, and likely they'll become noisy and demanding old codgers.

The so-called "hip generation" of the 1960s had, like so many others, a language of its on. "Acid" was short for lysergic acid diethylamide, LSD, the drug some nonhippies were virtually certain made its users glow in the dark. One might "drop" acid, that is, take the drug, without being a member of "Drop City," which was a mid-sixties-era commune outside Trinidad, Colorado, its members brought together by interests in anarchy, pacifism, sexual freedom, rural isolation, and—as their name implies—dropping LSD.

"Acid gas" came in empty capsules that had been dosed with LSD from an eyedropper, called acid gas because there was nothing in them but air. Police caught on to this about 1965 and acid-gas capsules were discontinued, to be replaced by tablets and by "blotter," a type of acid that appeared in the early 1970s: LSD-soaked bits of paper. At one point, some newspapers aimed at hippies claimed that sections of their paper had been soaked in acid, which led thousands of believers to sniff, lick, and chew the want ads.

Not everybody who was hip wanted to be called a hippie, especially "Diggers," members of a San Francisco–based commune named after a seventeenth-century English movement that defended common people against royal usurpation of rights. The American Diggers were, among other things, a theatrical troupe, a service organization, an urban commune, and (some said) a band of outlaws. But they were not, they claimed, hippies.

For a while, the head Digger was Emmett Grogan, described by some as a real-life Frodo Baggins. Baggins is the hero of J. R. R. Tolkien's classic trilogy, *Lord of the Rings*, which seemed to be every hippie's favorite book. In fact, according to *Publishers Weekly*, *Lord of the Rings* (originally published in 1954) was the leading mass-market paperback seller in 1966.

Tolkien's original story came out in 1937. "In a hole in the ground there lived a hobbit," he wrote:

> Not a nasty, dirty, wet hole filled with the ends of worms and an oozy smell, nor yet a dry, bare, sandy hole with nothing in it to sit down on or to eat: it was a hobbit-hole, and that means comfort.*

It's the story about a race of little people called Hobbits who live somewhere in time, in a place called Middle Earth. Hobbits are intrinsically good and hedonistic, happy little fellows who love beauty and pretty colors, pass the time of day eating three or four meals a day, and smoke burning leaves—some kind of herb—in clay pipes, which certainly reminds you of hippies.

---

* *The Hobbit; Or, There and Back Again*, copyright 1937 John Ronald Reuel Tolkien.

The almost-Hobbit named Emmett Grogan was in his early twenties in the mid-sixties, with blond, unruly hair, and a faceful of freckles. He was in and out of jail a dozen or more times a week, once for slugging a cop in the nose. Grogan had a thing about the police, and they had a thing about him. Officers of the law would roust him out, and Grogan would complain, "Why can't I stand on the corner and wait for nobody. Why can't everyone?" He thought hippie merchants in San Francisco's Haight-Ashbury district should be more like the Diggers—"They just want to expand their sales, they don't care what happens to people here; they're nothing but goddamn shopkeepers with beards."

Grogan had run away from his Brooklyn, New York, home when he was fifteen, gone to Europe, where he worked as a busboy in a hotel in the Alps, then on to Italy, where he studied filmmaking under director Michelangelo Antonioni. Finally, at the age of about twenty-one, he returned to America, where—in as much as he'd neglected to register for the draft before he'd run away at age fifteen—he was greeted by Selective Service officials and, four days later, This is the army, Mr. Grogan. To say the least, Emmett Grogan and the U.S. Army didn't get along too well. For instance, when ordered to clean up the barracks, he proceeded to toss all of the unit's rifles out the window, along with a few bunks and some footlockers that didn't please his artistic senses. He told the sergeant, "I threw out everything that was not aesthetically pleasing." And with that Emmett Grogan was sent to the psychiatric ward of Letterman Hospital in San Francisco, where he stayed for about six months until the hospital realized he was costing them too much. An army doctor, it seems, found out that Emmett had studied film, so he ordered Grogan to the hospital's photo lab for "work therapy." It was, Grogan remembered, a "beautiful, tremendously equipped lab." And basically unused. Except by Emmett Grogan. Who proceeded to make five thousand nine-by-twelve prints of his own big blond face. Not long after that he was released from the hospital as well as the army.

Back to our hippie dictionary. A "cat" was a wild and uninhibited male, while a "chick" was the female equivalent. "Baby" was a term of endearment, often applied by cats to their chicks. "Beautiful" could be applied to anyone, cat or chick, and was also a groovy situation, "groovy" meaning fun, a good time, and swinging—the opposite of "bummer" which was a bad situation, especially a "bad scene" or "bad trip" such as one might experience with "bad acid." Some "acid heads" at Woodstock got hold of some bad acid, had bad trips, and had to be cared for by Wavy Gravy (who years later claimed "I'm a psychedelic relic") and other members of the Hog Farm commune. A bad trip, whether at Woodstock or wherever, could make you "freak out." Actually, a chick or cat could freak out over just about anything and didn't have to be even close to acid. In 1966, Frank Zappa and the Mothers of Invention recorded the first two-disc LP album, *Freak Out!*, and used the term to mean any event or action that brought out "freaks," which was the insider name for "hippies." They weren't necessarily "flower children." That is, hippies who were more into art than political activism.

To flower children, "flower power" expressed the essence of nature and the exact opposite of all things plastic. It was the elemental power of nature against police clubs and Mace, the Vietnam War's napalm and awesome firepower.

Flower power probably orginated in the Haight-Ashbury area, in an area called the Panhandle. Inspired by that hippie-of-all hippies Ken Kesey, a group of young people spent much of their time in the Panhandle. It was, sociologist Lewis Yablonski wrote,

> almost a fantasy land of sights and sounds. Flute players in robes. Micro-minied girls in boots, without bras, obviously aware of a kind of sexual attractiveness, swing down the street. There are consciously dirty teenagers and underfed youths who come from upper-middle-class families. Some seem to be beating their parents up obliquely by literally starving and begging. On the same scene are wiser, older "heads"—philosophers of the movement. These bearded figures (some in their late thirties and forties) smile straight ahead as they walk down the street, many in flowing robes with "hip" crosses round their necks.

"Beatniks" of earlier times, by the way, didn't like being called *beatniks*, a word coined by columnist Herb Caen for members of the Beat Generation. Members of the generation themselves preferred being called "beats."

A "blast" was anything hippies did that was exciting, such as having a blast with some "grass," which wasn't your bovine type of grass but was marijuana or "Mary Jane." Using grass might lead to "free love," a result of the so-called "sexual revolution" of the sixties; birth control pills led to a lessening of inhibitions regarding out-of-wedlock sex.

As a spin-off, the sexual revolution included "gay liberation" and "women's liberation." The word *gay* began to replace *queer* and *fag* or *faggot.* Hippies often called male homosexuals *gay* and referred to female homosexuals as *dykes.*

A policeman who for years might have been called a "cop" now became the "fuzz" or even a "pig." Beginning about the time of the Democratic National Convention in Chicago in 1968, hippies began calling police "fascist pigs."*

"Dude," which had come into fashion in the eighteen hundreds' Wild West, actually came from the German word *dudenkopf,* which means "lazy fellow" or "lazy head." In the 1960s some hippies believed it was impolite to call blacks "spades," so they came to be called "dudes." Today, any cat can be a dude if he works at it hard enough.

In 1960, a group of University of Michigan students concerned with racism, poverty, and social justice formed the activist (some called them "extreme-radical") Students for a Democratic Society (SDS). Among its original members were "red-diaper babies," that is, children of thirties-era American Communists.**

Red-diaper babies grew up with the Communist Party newspaper, the *Daily Worker,* as their family's newspaper of choice. They heard their parents' whispered conversations about the Rosenberg case— Julius and Ethel Rosenberg convicted of giving American A-bomb secrets to the Soviet Union, were executed in 1953—and their rage over Joe McCarthy's self-proclaimed war on Communism. Most chil-

---

* Yippies who demonstrated outside the convention had a pig named Pigasus that they "nominated" for president.
** Many of their parents were members of the Young Communist League in the thirties and forties, proclaiming that "Communism is twentieth century Americanism."

dren of thirties-era American Communist Party members eventually grew away from the party. Stalin, they realized, had been one of the bloodiest butchers of the twentieth century. By the fifties, most red-diaper babies had become disillusioned about Communism.

At least one SDS founder wasn't a red-diaper baby. Instead, Tom Hayden was strictly middle class, middle American. He was born in 1939 and grew up in the Detroit suburb of Royal Oak. He attended a Catholic grammar school but went on to a public high school, where he was editor of the school newspaper. Hayden's final editorial just before he graduated seemed like any other ordinary high school newspaper editorial, unless you looked at it closely. Then, it said something quite different. The first letter of each paragraph gave his readers Hayden's real message: "Go to hell," the letters spelled out.

In 1957, Hayden entered the University of Michigan at Ann Arbor, where, as he later wrote,

> I had to live in a dorm with thirteen hundred guys that was worse than a public housing project. There were no written rules . . . [only] absolute, arbitrary authority.

Following his junior year, he drove a motorcycle and hitchhiked around the country, stopping off at Berkeley to check out the anti-HUAC (House Un-American Activities Committee) student demonstrations going on there. In May 1960, a large group of students protested against HUAC's "Red-hunting." Berkeley was, according to Hayden, "the mecca of student activism." He met with a group of students who, according to historian David Farber, "meant to do something about what they saw going on around them." He also visited the headquarters of the National Student Association, not realizing it was a CIA-financed group whose magazine, *Encounter,* attempted to deter American youth from all things Communist.

Hayden returned to Michigan, where, he said, "I didn't get political. Things got political." In his senior year, Tom edited the university newspaper, the *Michigan Daily.* It was about then that he and a group of other students founded SDS, which at the time was a "tiny, liberal campus group with no clear agenda or political orientation."

In October 1960, primarily in his role as a student journalist, Hayden went to Atlanta to check out the Student Nonviolent Coordinating Committee (SNCC). It was, of course, at the height of the Kennedy-Nixon presidential campaign, and rhetoric both left and right was flying with every speech. After he left Atlanta, Hayden stopped off with SNCC members in Fayette County, Tennessee, where sharecroppers were demonstrating for voting rights.

He graduated from Michigan, then went back down South as SDS field secretary. In Mississippi he was beaten up; in Georgia he was jailed; but he kept at it, all the time sending reports back to SDS headquarters telling about Southern blacks' battles for justice. It was, he said, a "creative, revolutionary period."

On July 12, 1962, fifty-nine SDS delegates met at a United Auto Workers camp near Port Huron, Michigan. A handful were older trade-union activists and Socialist Party leaders, but most were students or recent graduates from New York, Michigan, Ohio, Pennsylvania, Georgia, and Texas. Some were already veterans of civil rights work in the South. Together, they hammered out what author James Miller* calls "one of the pivotal documents in postwar American history," the sixty-three-page "Port Huron Statement." Twenty-two-year-old Tom Hayden wrote the working draft and much of the final product of the SDS manifesto that served as the credo of America's New Left in the sixties.

We are the people of this generation, bred in at least modest comfort, housed now in universities, looking uncomfortably to the world we inherit.

When we were kids the United States was the wealthiest and strongest country in the world . . . Many of us began maturing in complacency. . . .

---

* In 1965, as an eighteen-year-old college freshman from Claremont, California, James Miller joined the SDS, marched against the Vietnam War, knelt in peace vigils, protested against military recruitment on campus, and occupied his college administration building. Later, however, Miller received his Ph.D. from Brandeis University, became a music critic for *Newsweek* magazine, and taught government at the University of Texas at Austin.

The Generation Gap

We seek the establishment of a democracy of individual participation, governed by two central aims: that the individual share in those social decisions determining the quality and direction of his life; that society be organized to encourage independence in men and provide the media for their common participation.

In a participatory democracy, the political life would be based in several root principles: that decision-making of basic social consequence be carried on by public groupings; that politics be seen positively, as the art of collectively creating an acceptable pattern of social relations; that politics has the function of bringing people out of isolation and into community . . .

"Participatory democracy" was perhaps the manifesto's most enduring concept, even though the SDS never clearly defined it. The idea did, however, as writer Paul Galloway says, address the "need for citizens to take part in the decisions that affected their lives." Actually, there may have been better sound than substance in the phrase; "participatory democracy" had a ring, a resonance, and it meant different things to different people. SDS member Al Haber says it was a "model, another way of organizing society . . . a charge to action." Another SDS member, Sharon Jeffrey, calls it "a source of inspiration and vision and meaning; it was an idea that I could commit myself to from the depths of my soul." And Tom Hayden, who wrote the words, says that participatory democracy mainly meant *action*. SDS members had behind them the fifties, "the so-called decade of apathy," and were "emerging from apathy."

Looking at photographs of the SDS founders as they were in the early sixties, you're struck by how very straight they seem: no long hair, no beards, no used military uniforms for clothing. A group photo taken at the SDS national council meeting in September 1963 shows them standing there, the guys in chinos and Madras plaid shirts, looking very much like the folk singers the Kingston Trio. Only one girl (and in '63 she would have been a "girl") was in pants; the others were in rather frumpy dresses.

Two members of the group—Tom Hayden and Rennie Davis— later became part of the "Chicago 8" charged with inciting the riots

197

that erupted during the 1968 Democratic National Convention in Chicago. At the time, it was the "Trial of the Century." It more or less got under way on September 24, 1969. The "Chicago 8" quickly became the "Chicago 7." When Black Panther Bobby Seale couldn't get the lawyer of his choice, he loudly disrupted the proceedings. At first, he was bound and gagged in the courtroom; then he was severed from the other seven for a later trial, which never occurred.

In the Port Huron Statement, the SDS claimed the Cold War was "symbolized by the presence of the Bomb." But as the sixties continued, concern over nuclear weapons was replaced by a more passionate concern over the Vietnam War. On April 17, 1965, the SDS sponsored the first anti-Vietnam march on Washington. About fifteen thousand people, most of them students, picketed the White House over America's participation in the Vietnam War.

By then, SDS had chapters on sixty-three campuses around the country, and the Washington demonstration prompted a number of colleges and universities to take a hard look at U.S. policy in Vietnam. A month later, a fifteen-and-a-half hour televised "teach-in" was broadcast to more than a hundred colleges via a radio hookup.

On January 5, 1967, Lady Bird Johnson wrote that "a miasma of trouble hangs over everything." It is "unbearably hard," she supposed, "to fight a limited war."

Confusion and opposition to the war continued to grow. By March, some two dozen "We Won't Go" groups existed on college campuses, with members pledging to refuse military service in Vietnam. The American Friends Service Committee (AFSC) and other pacifist groups attracted thousands of draft-age men. Many blacks rejected induction orders, saying, as SNCC leader Stokely Carmichael did, that the draft was "white people sending black people to make war on yellow people in order to defend the land they stole from red people."

Some induction-age men destroyed their draft cards. The SDS National Council encouraged draft resistance, and as its vice president Carl Davidson, remembered, "We sat down and purposely read all the laws around the draft so that we could violate every single one of them." They wanted, Davidson said, to "come up with a program that was *totally* illegal." Members of the Cornell University We Won't Go group began planning a national draft-card-burning event, and set April 15 as the day. "We have argued and demonstrated" to stop the Vietnam War, they said. "We have not succeeded. Murderers do not respond to reason." Powerful resistance was required: "radical, illegal, unpleasant, sustained."

On April 4, 1967, for the first time Martin Luther King directly attacked the Johnson Administration's actions in Vietnam. In a speech at New York's Riverside Church, he claimed that a disproportionate number of blacks were dying in the war—"to guarantee liberties in southeast Asia which they had not found in southwest Georgia and East Harlem." The American government, King claimed, was "the greatest purveyor of violence in the world today." He urged young men of all races to declare themselves conscientious objectors.* It was King's harshest criticism of the war, and it didn't go over too well with some influential liberals and some other civil rights activists. The NAACP said that merging antiwar and antisegregation efforts worked against both.

The day after King's speech, White House advisor John Roche sent an EYES ONLY memo to President Johnson:

> Yesterday's speech by Nobel Laureate Martin Luther King was quite an item. To me it indicates that King—in desperate search of a constituency—has thrown in with the Commies.
>
> As you know, the civil rights movement is shot—disorganized and broke. King, who is inordinately ambitious and quite stupid (a bad combination), is thus looking back to a promising future.
>
> The Communist-oriented "peace" types have played him (and his driving wife) like trout. They have—in effect—guaranteed him ideological valet service. There will always be a crowd to applaud, money to keep up his standard of living, etc. . . .

* See chapter on Vietnam for percentages of black and white casualties in the war.

In short, King is destroying his reputation as a "Negro leader" for a mess of "Charlie's'" pottage. He is painting himself into a corner with a bunch of losers.

Contributions to King's SCLC dropped sharply, but still, on April 15, he joined upward of two hundred thousand antiwar protesters at a rally in the Sheep Meadow in New York City's Central Park. It was a cold, gray day, and off and on it rained. But that didn't stop the rally and didn't even cut down on the numbers. The crowd was almost a cross-section of America: long-haired jeans-wearing hippies; middle-aged suit-wearing businessmen; housewives in little frock dresses. Nuns and priests in robes, college professors in gowns and mortarboards. Medal-decorated war veterans wearing blue hats marked "Veterans for Peace." Native Americans in tribal attire. Antinuclear activists and entire families. Many were protesting for the first time. For others, protest had almost become a way of life. Dr. Linus Pauling was there, as were singer Harry Belafonte, writer Norman Mailer, and television's "Man from U.N.C.L.E.," Robert Vaughn. However, not a single member of the United States Congress showed up for the Central Park rally.

In one corner of Sheep Meadow, a group of about sixty young men got ready to burn their draft cards—not the five hundred or so the rally organizers had hoped for, but perhaps enough to make a point. A chain of supporters ringed the youths to keep onlookers and reporters and police away. Those inside the ring passed their draft cards to someone who held an empty coffee can. The flick of a cigarette lighter, and the cards were burning to cries of "Resist! Resist!" A burly young man wearing an army uniform and a green beret on his blond head pushed into the middle of the crowd: army reservist Gary Rader. To the crowd's surprise, Rader pulled out his own draft card and set it on fire.

To no one's surprise, members of the New York Police Red Squad and FBI agents swarmed around the area. Two plainclothes officers pushed to the center of the crowd, and one, reaching into the coffee can, pulled out a scorched piece of paper. The crowd closed in on the agent with the paper, but the other man ran off. Probably as planned, the one with the paper yelled to the crowd, "Go get him!"

They did, and as the crowd moved away, the agent tucked the charred piece of paper into his pocket and sauntered off, "a smile on his face," a witness said.

Shortly after noon, the crowd began inching out of Central Park. At the head of the march were Martin Luther King, Dr. Benjamin Spock, Stokely Carmichael, and Harry Belafonte. Some blacks carried signs that read, "No Vietnamese Ever Called Me Nigger," as boxer Muhammad Ali had said when he refused to be drafted. Other signs proclaimed, "Hell, No, We Won't Go." Or "War Is Not Healthy for Children and Other Living Things." A child next to Dr. Spock carried a sign that read, "Children Are Not Born to Burn—Stop the War Now!" Some chanted, "Ho, Ho, Ho Chi Minh! The NLF* is gonna win!" While others sang out in cadence, "One, two, three, four. We don't want your fucking war!" "Hey, hey, LBJ. How many kids did you kill today?"

When they reached the United Nations building, an organizer asked New York Police Department official Sanford Garelik to move some police barriers to provide more room for the larger-than-expected crowd. Garelik was agitated and snapped back, "Look, you made your point! There's a lot of people against this war. Why don't you just go home?" Across the street, a group of counterdemonstrators recited the Pledge of Allegiance. Finally, about five at night, the rain-drenched crowd began to trickle away.

Across the country, in San Francisco, it was also raining. And as in New York, antiwar demonstrators protested—more than sixty thousand of them, including members of the Santa Clara County Labor Council. Thousands of trade union members were in the San Francisco demonstration, a sign that the peace movement was growing.

The New York rally's organizers—they called it the "Spring Mobilization" or "Mobe" (the National Mobilization Committee to End the War)—said it was "successful beyond all expectations." No longer could the Johnson Administration regard peace activists as a small

---

* The National Liberation Front. That is, the political apparatus of the Viet Cong.

minority of crazies. Actually, the administration didn't think they were "crazies." As Secretary of State Dean Rusk commented on NBC's *Meet the Press* the day after the rally, "I have no doubt at all that the Communist apparatus is very busy indeed in these operations all over the world and in our own country." Did he have any hard evidence to support his charge? With a slight grin Rusk replied, "I am giving you my responsible personal view that the Communist apparatus is working very hard on it." And from White House press secretary George Christian, word that the FBI was keeping a close watch on "antiwar activity."

On October 15, 1966, in Oakland, California, militants Bobby Seale and Huey Newton formed the Black Panther Party, with a manifesto calling for "power to determine the destiny of our black community." The emphasis, they said, would be on "organizing black defense groups" to end "police brutality." Taking the panther symbol from a Lowndes County, Alabama, political organization, the group wore black jackets and berets. They were in turns menacing and romantic, feared by whites and fanatically idolized by blacks.

The Panthers recruited members from Oakland's ghetto and questioned the procedures of police—"pigs in uniforms," as they call them—with law books. The Black Panthers soon attracted attention from a white population quickly growing more and more afraid of what might be happening with desegregation.

In what the *Los Angeles Times* referred to as "one of the most amazing incidents in legislative history," some twenty to thirty armed members of the Black Panthers stormed into the California State Assembly in Sacramento, to protest a pending arms-control bill, a ban against carrying loaded firearms within city limits. The Panthers claimed that such a law would keep black people powerless. Bobby Seale read Mandate Number One: As "the aggression of the racist American government escalates in Vietnam, the police agencies of America escalate the repression of black people throughout the ghettos." The time had come, Seale read, "for black people to arm themselves against this terror before it is too late." Panther protest or not, the bill passed, and on July 28, California governor Ronald Reagan signed it into law.

Almost as soon as the panthers were organized, police around the nation went after them; they particularly didn't like the Panthers' cry, "Off the pigs!" Within three years of their formation, the Panthers were involved in eight gun battles around the country, in which three police officers and five Panthers were killed. Four of those incidents were in Chicago; of these one is still talked about.

Early on the morning of December 4, 1969, eight policemen from the Cook County, Illinois, state's attorney's office crept up to the front door of 2337 West Monroe, a two-flat on Chicago's West Side. Another six officers were out back. The state's attorney—that is, the county prosecutor—claimed that the building was the stronghold of the Illinois Black Panther Party.

It was about 4:45 A.M. when Sgt. Daniel Groth knocked on the front door. No answer, so Groth knocked again, this time with his gun. The next seven minutes, filled with gunfire, make up one of the most disputed incidents of the sixties. Police concentrated most of their fire on the bedroom where an informant had told them Illinois Black Panther party leader Fred Hampton was sleeping. After the shooting stopped, Hampton was found dead along with another Panther, Mark Clark.

The police claimed the raid and the deaths of Hampton and Clark were justified. The Panthers claimed the raid itself had been only a pretext for killing Fred Hampton. In fact, they called it murder. A *Chicago Tribune* photograph taken after the raid, from inside Hampton's room, purported to show bullet holes in a doorjamb, bullets that had come *from inside* the room. In fact they weren't bullet holes but *nail heads*. Federal authorities finally admitted that only one shot had been fired by the Panthers, while police had fired at least eighty-two and maybe ninety-nine shots.

By 1969, blacks realized that, with the election of Richard Nixon and the Republicans, the federal government no longer could be counted on to come to their rescue. And by the end of the year it looked as if the Black Panther Party wasn't going to be around long. Fred Hampton was dead, as was Bobby Hutton. Huey P. Newton was in prison, Bobby Seale was charged with inciting a riot, Eldridge

Cleaver was in exile, David Hilliard was charged with threatening President Nixon, and nobody knew—or at least nobody was saying—where H. Rap Brown was.

Student Nonviolent Coordinating Committee chairman Stokely Carmichael was sent to jail in Canton, Mississippi, in 1966, for leading a peaceful civil rights march. After being released, he stood before a crowd of three thousand angry blacks and declared:

> This is the twenty-seventh time I have been arrested, and I ain't going to jail no more! The only way we gonna stop them white men from whuppin' us is to take over. We been saying freedom for years—and we ain't got nothin'. What we gonna start saying now is "Black Power!"

The crowd took up the chant and roared back: "Black power! Black power! Black power!"

H. Rap Brown followed Stokely Carmichael in 1967, as chairman of the Student Nonviolent Coordinating Committee, when Carmichael chose not to stand for reelection. Brown said that "John Brown was the only white man I could respect and he's dead." He proclaimed that "all tactics must be reconsidered" and replaced "Nonviolent" in SNCC's name with "National." When a group of whites shot up black homes in Prattville, Alabama, Brown announced, "We will no longer sit back and let black people be killed. . . . We are calling on full retaliation."

H. Rap Brown's perhaps too ambitious program and his own legal problems led to SNCC's becoming virtually defunct. He joined the Panthers, where he became justice minister, and in 1967, he was charged with inciting a riot in Cambridge, Maryland. It was there that he told a crowd of about four hundred blacks:

> It's time for Cambridge to explode, baby. Black folks built America, and if America don't come around, we're going to burn America down. . . . Burn this town down. When you tear

down the white man, brother, you are hitting him in the money. . . . Don't love him to death, shoot him to death.

After the rally, blacks and whites exchanged gunfire. No one was killed but a white police officer was shot in the neck, face, and hand. And Brown was wounded in the forehead by a shotgun pellet. The next morning, a school and two blocks of the city went up in flames. Brown told a Washington news conference that

Black people have been looting. I say there should be more shooting than looting. . . . The white man is your enemy. You got to destroy your enemy. . . . I say you better get a gun. Violence is necessary; it is as American as cherry pie.

H. Rap Brown later served prison time for a gun battle with New York City police, and during his term, he converted to Islam. He changed his name to Jamil Abdullah Al-Amin. Following his release from prison in 1976, Al-Amin moved to Atlanta, where he became a leader in the city's Muslim community. Friends there described him as a humble and respectable man who was working to clean up drugs and prostitution in the low-income neighborhood.

A man claimed that Al-Amin shot him, and the former SNCC and Black Panther leader was charged with aggravated assault, carrying a concealed weapon, and possessing an unlicensed firearm. Charges were dropped when the man recanted his story and said that authorities had pressured him into making the claim.

Then, in March 2000, Al-Amin allegedly shot two Fulton County, Georgia, deputy sheriffs, Ricky Kinchen and Aldranon English, as they tried to arrest him on charges of receiving stolen property, impersonating a police officer, and not having proof of insurance. Kinchen died but English recovered from multiple gunshot wounds to his thigh, arm, and right side. Officer English, his superiors said, identified the man who shot him as Al-Amin. And Al-Amin went into hiding. He was fifty-six years old, getting a bit long in the tooth for a militant or anyone else to be hiding out and constantly on the move. Four days later, federal marshals located Al-Amin in Whitehall,

Alabama, about 160 miles southwest of Atlanta. He was captured in a nearby woods and taken back to Atlanta to face murder charges.

Saturday, October 21, 1967, was the peak of "Stop the Draft Week," and an estimated 50,000 to 150,000 antiwar protestors assembled in front of the Lincoln Memorial in Washington. They watched a performance by the Bread and Puppet Theater; heard a short Peter, Paul and Mary concert; then listened as Phil Ochs sang "Days of Decision." Then it was time to move out. David Dellinger, one of the SDS founders, announce that the march would be the end of peaceful protest. "This is the beginning of a new stage in the American peace movement," he said, "in which the cutting edge becomes active resistance." The main demonstration broke up, but several thousand protestors headed across the Potomac River to the Pentagon.

This time, the government was ready; they'd ringed the Pentagon with military police. A few dozen of the more militant demonstrators attacked the circle of MPs, but the troops pushed and beat them back, arresting a few of them. Several hundred others began a sitdown in the Pentagon parking lot, and the Diggers—the same Diggers who'd helped out in other demonstrations in San Francisco and elsewhere—started bringing in food. And not surprisingly, a joint or two got passed around. The demonstrators sipped wine and the atmosphere was festive; people laughed and sang and several—this becomes one of the most famous scenes of the sixties' antiwar movement—put flowers in the troops' rifle barrels. Flower power.

As evening came on, people built campfires. Some sat in the lotus position and hummed "Ommmm." Some others sang "Silent Night."

Around midnight, paratroopers from the 82d Airborne Division replaced the MPs in the line around the Pentagon. Federal marshals were with the paratroopers and they got orders to attack. They pushed through the soldiers and cracked heads and bashed skulls. "Nonresisting girls," a witness claimed, were "kicked and clubbed by U.S. marshals old enough to be their fathers." Another witness said that the demonstrators "sang, The Star Spangled Banner and other songs, but the troops at this point were nonmen, the appeals were futile." Some one thousand demonstrators were arrested, but only two actually went to trial; and they were acquitted.

In the first week of August 1968, the Republican Party held its presidential nominating convention in Miami, and things went pretty much as planned. Oh, there was still a "We want Rocky!" cry now and then—a group of young Sarah Lawrence and Wellesley girls wearing miniskirts posed with New York governor Nelson Rockefeller. The "Rocky Girls," as they were known, radiated with golden tans acquired on tennis courts, beside swimming pools. Not to be outdone, the "Nixonettes" marched in. They weren't college girls, they were off-duty airline stewardesses and dancers in from New Orleans, but, hey! They wore miniskirts and blue jackets and those hot new go-go boots.

The Reverend Billy Graham offered a prayer. The delegates listened to a recorded message from former president Dwight Eisenhower welcoming everybody. Actor John Wayne inspired the delegates by reading, "Why I Am Proud to Be an American," then he promoted his new movie, *The Green Berets.*

That's about as exciting as it got at the Republican convention, historian Teddy White wrote. "Tedium," he said, "gripped the convention from the clack of the opening gavel." It may have been the most boring national party convention ever. Delegates dozed by swimming pools in the Miami sun, read newspapers while speakers droned on and on and on, some slept and woke up knowing they hadn't missed anything. Again quoting Teddy White: "Boredom lay on the convention like a mattress." As Richard Nixon himself wrote about the convention voting, "There were no surprises left."

There never was any doubt that Richard Nixon would win the nomination—he'd won every primary. No real threat from liberal Rockefeller or conservative Ronald Reagan. George Romney had stuck his foot in his mouth, then shot it off. "Nixon's the one," as the campaign posters proclaimed. And on the first ballot too.

The most exciting moment at the convention was the announcement of Nixon's running mate. Nixon and his friend John Mitchell had decided that question two weeks earlier: It was to be Spiro T. Agnew, governor of Maryland. When Nixon told a waiting press corps about his decision, "absolute shock and surprise greeted my announcement."

All that was left was for Nixon to read his awe-inspiring acceptance speech:

> My Fellow Americans: When the strongest nation in the world can be tied up for four years in a war in Vietnam with no end in sight, when the richest nation in the world can't manage its own economy, when the nation with the greatest tradition of the rule of law is plagued by unprecedented lawlessness . . . and when the President of the United States cannot travel abroad or to any major city at home without fear of a hostile demonstration—then it's time for new leadership for the United States of America.

Then, referring to himself in the third person Richard Nixon added:

> I see [a] child tonight. He hears a train go by at night and he dreams of faraway places where he'd like to go. It seems like an impossible dream. But he is helped on his journey through life. A father who had to go to work before he finished the sixth grade, sacrificed everything he had so that his sons could go to college. A gentle Quaker mother, with a passionate concern for peace, quietly wept when he went to war but she understood why he had to go. A great teacher, a remarkable football coach, an inspirational minister, encouraged him on his way. A courageous wife and loyal children stood by him in victory and also defeat. And in his chosen profession of politics, first there were scores, then hundreds, then thousands, and finally millions who worked for his success. And tonight he stands before you—nominated for President of the United States.

"On the whole, the convention came off very well," Nixon later wrote.

The delegates left Miami, sunburned, rested, and contented. At home, they turned on their television sets and watched the disorganized Democrats at their disorganized convention in a very disorganized Chicago and reminded themselves of Napoleon's adage: "Never interfere with the enemy when he is in the process of destroying himself." Another Napoleonic saying was that "From the sublime to the ridiculous is but a step."

With Lyndon Johnson out of the race, and Bobby Kennedy murdered, the campaign for the Democratic presidential nomination was down to Vice President Hubert Humphrey and Senator Eugene McCarthy. That wasn't much of a choice, some radicals believed.

The murder of Bobby Kennedy ended the last chance of antiwar groups. Eugene McCarthy stayed in until the last, but after his loss to Kennedy in California it was obvious that he couldn't win. Some Kennedy campaigners tried to push Senator George McGovern as an antiwar candidate, but McGovern didn't excite much enthusiasm that late in the game. Not that he excited much in 1972 when he finally won the nomination.

Tensions across the country were already at near-hysterical levels by the time delegates to the 1968 Democratic National Convention arrived in Chicago. Destruction was still evident from the rioting that had broken out on the South and West Sides after Martin Luther King was murdered. Robert Kennedy's last public words had been "On to Chicago."

Security at the city's International Amphitheatre was so heavy that the convention site looked like "a veritable stockade." Mayor Richard J. Daley, a major influence in the Democratic Party, said he wouldn't allow any attempt to disrupt the convention, which was exactly what radicals Abbie Hoffman and Jerry Rubin and others were vowing to do. It didn't help much when Chicago police announced reports that demonstrators were planning to spike the city's water supply with LSD. The governor ordered National Guard troops to protect the water supply. Another rumor had it that members of Chicago's largest street gang—they've gone through several names, but at the time they were called the Blackstone Rangers—would assassinate the presidential candidates, Mayor Daley, and several others. Hoping to make certain this didn't happen, Daley and the police "convinced" the Rangers' leaders to get out of town during convention week.

Hundreds of delegates jammed into Chicago's lakefront hotels, and thousands of demonstrators were living on the lakefront itself: Lincoln Park, Grant Park, and Hyde Park. Lincoln Park, on the city's North Side, had once been a graveyard; under its soil lay the bones of thousands of Confederate troops who had died at the Civil War's Camp Douglas prisoner-of-war facility on the South Side. In 2001, it's the location of one of the last big-city free zoos, and home to a growing population of Yuppies. In 1968, it became a temporary home for Yippies.

The Yippie movement originated as a joke, a combination of the hippie ethos and New Left activism, in late 1967 at Abbie and Anita Hoffman's apartment on St. Mark's Place in New York City. Jerry Rubin, who'd been a project director for the October Pentagon demonstration, was there with his girlfriend, Nancy Kurshan. As was Paul Krassner, editor and publisher of the radical magazine *Realist*. They were sipping a little pre–New Year's champagne and toking on a little—make that "a lot" of—grass. In the heart of New York's Lower East Side, the home of the city's hippie community, these five friends sat around planning what to do at the '68 Democratic convention. "There we were," Abbie Hoffman remembered,

> all stoned, rolling around the floor. . . . Yippie! . . . And so, YIPPIE was born, the Youth International Party. What about if we create a myth, program it into the media, you know . . . when that myth goes in, it's always connected to Chicago August 25 . . . come and do your thing, excitement, bullshit, everything, anything . . . commitment, engagement, Democrats, pigs, the whole thing. All you do is change the H in Hippie to a Y for Yippie, and you got it.

It was a joke grown out of dope. Historian Theodore H. White took them seriously, apparently not knowing where hippie left off and yippie began:

> The crazies sprout everywhere in today's world, but in America one of their covering titles is "Yippies." . . . The Yippies are a giant put-on, a visual pun, a strolling farce of lost and forlorn

people seeking identity who wear beads, or stovepipe hats, or Australian bandoliers, or walk barefoot carrying their belongings on their back or sleep in the open rain. They are sad people, and when one examines the seasonal clusters where they come to roost, in Cambridge or San Francisco or New York, tears come to the eyes at their diseases (usually venereal), their health (decayed from malnutrition and drugs) and the disturbances, rarely dangerous, of their minds. . . . The crazies—who are not stupid, only crazy—have learned the power of the mimeograph machine to rouse press attention, to entice television coverage to their happenings.

Chicago police were told that they'd be putting in twelve-hour days. They were told about the threats. They were told that policemen, dressed to appear like television cameramen and reporters, would be documenting demonstrators and any disorders to use in any court cases that come about. And they were taught how to use gas masks, because they likely would have to use tear gas—Mace and Federal Streamer were the brands—and all officers were equipped with aerosol cans of the chemicals. Police General Order 68-13 said that the sprays were to be used only when physical force was necessary.

A few days before the convention opened, the president of the Chicago Patrolmen's Association told a news conference that the police department would no longer play the old game of looking the other way during a tense confrontation with protestors. "We feel," he said, "that the insane tactics shown by some groups are getting out of hand. We want the public to know this and to back the policeman in the fight."

Leaders of the Mobe and Yippie movements tried to get permits to allow demonstrators to sleep in city parks at night, but the city refused. Movement leaders went to court, and the court turned them down. Many demonstrators decided to do it anyway, and many realized that they'd get hurt. Curfew was 11:00 P.M. Each night, police moved in to clear them out, sometimes using those new aerosol cans of tear gas the officers had been issued.

On August 22, a few blocks from Lincoln Park, police stopped two long-haired teenagers for curfew violations. Seventeen-year-old Dean

Johnson, a runaway from South Dakota, pulled a gun. Police said that he tried to fire the handgun, but it misfired. They pulled their guns and they didn't misfire. Three shots and Johnson was dead.

Abbie Hoffman and Keith Lampe of the underground newspaper *Seed* decided to hold a funeral service for Johnson. It was the first protest and the convention was still two days away. They handed out flyers in the Lincoln Park–Old Town neighborhood. They contacted Tom Neuman of New York's Lower East Side SDS chapter—the anarchist bunch called "Up Against the Wall Motherfuckers," later changed to simply "Motherfuckers" or the sanitized version, "Up Against the Wall." Many members of the group were already in town for the convention.

At the funeral service, Neuman told a small group—police were on hand to watch and listen—that Dean Johnson "died of pig poisoning . . . and the story [that Johnson pulled a gun] was probably written at one central office downtown." The nation was "suffering from pig poisoning and media poisoning."

By now, the Yippies were more or less organized. In Lincoln Park they'd set up a "communications center" consisting of a couple of folding tables, and were distributing mimeographed flyers, including an eighteen-point program for Yippies, a Yip map, and a program. They put out a request for "chicks who can type (and spell), cats who have wheels and want to do a digger trip to feed the masses." They handed out lists of the hotels where convention delegates were staying. And they passed around maps of the International Amphitheatre upon which they scrawled, "Break in Break in Break in . . . Security precautions taken by Convention bigwigs are a farce." And they held self-defense lessons: karate, snake dancing, and other crowd-protection formations.

So: The demonstrators were getting ready. The police were getting ready. Now the National Guard was getting ready. Approximately fifty-six hundred guardsmen mobilized at armories around the city, and they, too, practiced their civil-disturbance procedures. They were armed with M1 rifles, carbines, shotguns, and—like the Chicago police—tear gas and gas masks. They had at the ready twenty-five jeeps with concertina-wire-cage fronts to be used to move crowds around.

Several hundred FBI agents were in town, spying on the protestors, aiding the Secret Service, and working with convention security. The Army Security Agency (ASA) was there also, military teams using sophisticated electronic surveillance of the demonstrators and of Senator McCarthy's campaign workers, and listening to make certain nobody communicated demonstration plans by radio. Some ASA agents went undercover in Chicago's ghettos, others in the downtown Loop, and some tried to infiltrate demonstrators in the parks.

By the time the convention got under way, there were approximately a thousand federal agents in Chicago. By midweek, according to an ASA estimate, one out of every six demonstrators was an undercover government agent.

Other protest groups were in town by now, and they set up centers in Hyde Park on the South Side, on the near West Side, and in the Loop. Approximately twenty-five centers were operating with groups as varied as the Radical Organizing Committee, Resistance (draft resisters), Vets for Peace, Concerned Clergy and Laity, Committee of Returned Volunteers (ex-Peace Corp members), the New University Conference, a medical contingent, a contingent of high school students, and several women's peace groups. Some women's groups rented buses, but apparently suburban women were interested in peace at home—their own home—and few made the trip.

All types were there: hippies, housewives, veterans, students, and workers; slum dwellers and suburbanites; middle-class activists. Peace buttons and Viet Cong flags. Old and young—"McCarthy kids," as a group of his campaign workers were known because they were below the voting age of twenty-one.

Rumors continued: The Yippies had been growing marijuana in vacant lots in Chicago, getting ready for a giant smoke-in. Or, they'd developed portable music equipment that allowed them to fight cops and dance at the same time. There was a rumor that Yippie men had been exercising, getting in shape, so that they could seduce all of the female Humphrey delegates and that female Yippies would pose as hookers and then kidnap male Humphrey delegates. Probably the most interesting rumor was that the Mobe was organizing a thousand women who would take part in a march, and somewhere along the line they'd shed their bras in a "Bare Breasts for Peace Brigade" parade. And of course the news media was growing in number, in part, no doubt, because they'd also heard about the Bare Breasts for Peace Brigade, which, by the way, never happened.

On Sunday morning, the Mobe held its first organized event, a "Meet the Delegates" march, targeting the three main Loop hotels where convention delegates were staying, including the Conrad Hilton on South Michigan Avenue, across the street from Grant Park. By three o'clock about three hundred demonstrators were slowly marching in a circle in Grant Park. Ten members of the Rapid Transit Guerrilla Communications group wore skull masks and papier mâché masks of Lyndon Johnson and Hubert Humphrey. About seventy-five police officers stood across the street, guarding the hotel.

Up in Lincoln Park, the Mobe rounded up about five hundred people. Some wore Yippie! buttons. Others wore McCarthy pins. Some wore both. Some waved red banners and Viet Cong flags. As they headed toward the Loop, they were joined by dozens of reporters, several city corporation counsels, and a large contingent of Chicago policemen. Once in the Loop, they chanted, "Hey, hey, LBJ, how many kids did you kill today?" their chants echoing among the tall buildings. The police sent additional men to the scene, two busloads.

The five hundred from Lincoln Park eventually joined the three hundred from Grant Park. And that was just about it for Sunday's march. No arrests to speak of. Not much more than chanting and a brief address by Rennie Davis, telling the demonstrators that the march was a success, the crowd broke up. Reporters and TV crews were a bit disappointed. Not much there for the ten o'clock news, eleven o'clock if you're on the East Coast. West Coast and Mountain Time, take care of yourself.

Back to Lincoln Park, where the Yippies had planned a music festival. Bob Fass was there from New York's WBAI radio station, introducing the MC5, best known for their hard-rock song "Kick Out the Jams, Motherfucker." They were loud and the crowd danced and yelled. Very few could see the MC5, because police refused to let the

Yippies use their flatbed truck as a stage for the musicians. A stage, the police believed, would give the Yippies an opportunity "to incite the crowd."

The band continued playing, stage or not, and those on the periphery of the crowd pushed toward the center to see them, and that just added to the growing tension. By five o'clock the demonstrators had been joined by several thousand more people, most of them Chicago locals out to see "What's happenin', baby."

Suddenly, the power went out and the band's guitars and microphones no longer worked. Abbie Hoffman decided to have the flatbed truck driven into the park anyway, hoping to be able to convince police that using the truck would actually cut down on the tension instead of increasing it. Forget it. The police stuck to their orders and refused to let the truck move in. The crowd jeered.

The cops arrested the loudest protestors, and that made the crowd even angrier than they'd been, and they screamed obscenities: "Pigs eat shit! Pigs eat shit!" Several policemen used their nightsticks to beat back the crowd, and some officers shouted their own obscenities: "Get the fuck out of town. Go back where you came from, fags."

More shouting, more clubbing, more arrests. A small group sat down and began singing "My country, 'tis of thee . . ." A few people threw bottles at the cops and the cops smashed Yippie Stew Albert in the back of the head. The police took their prisoners and slowly backed away, forming a skirmish line.

Police commander Robert Lynsky called for reinforcements and asked Corporation counsel Richard Elrod if he could close the park early. Elrod said no. At six o'clock, another shift of policemen moved into the park. They'd been warned there likely would be trouble, so they came ready to kick butt and take numbers—wearing helmets, goggles, and gloves.

The crowd numbered at least five thousand, and Abbie Hoffman announced that the music festival was over, stopped by the police. With no music to listen and dance to, with the music festival over, most of the five thousand didn't know what to do: go home, go away, or go for broke and attack the cops? Beat poet Allen Ginsberg was in town and he tried to calm down the crowd with a chant, "Ommmm." It didn't work, but that didn't stop Ginsberg, who kept om-mmming away for the next seven hours.

A Gallup poll released just before the Democratic convention showed that fifty-three percent of American adults believed that sending troops to Vietnam had been a mistake. Two years earlier, only twenty-five percent had thought so.

Nighttime, and people gathered in small groups around the park, lighting bonfires and sharing marijuana. Every now and then the cops rushed in, pushed the protestors around, and stamped out the bonfires. The groups momentarily scattered. Some people turned over trash barrels and began banging on them like drums. Several hundred SDS organizers spread around the park, trying to talk the demonstrators into taking to the streets to confront the cops. Abbie Hoffman disagreed. Stay in the park past the curfew, he said, and when the police came to clear them out they would fight.

Meanwhile, police had an idea of their own: They formed a skirmish line around the park rest rooms. Maybe if the demonstrations couldn't go to relieve themselves they'd simply go, leave the park, go home, and all would be right with Richard Daley's world. The demonstrators, of course, realized what was happening and several hundred surrounded the police skirmish line, shouting obscenities. A few threw stones, and for a moment or two, the cops stood and took it. Then suddenly they charged the crowd, smashing and clubbing everybody they could reach. By then, most of the cops had removed their nameplates, so as not to let the demonstrators and news media know who was banging heads.

When the protestors retreated, the police went back to guarding the rest rooms. The demonstrators gathered again, and again the police charged and clubbed and smashed. Once more the protesters retreated and once more the cops returned to their rest-room patrol. It happened several times and became something like the child's game king-of-the-hill.

Just as the crowd of demonstrators cultivated rumors about what would happen next, police in the staging area—on standby in case they were needed—circulated their own rumors: Demonstrators had ambushed a group of cops near the park's ball diamonds, one rumor had it. About seven thousand people were surrounding the squad, another report claimed. When they went to check out the rumors, instead of finding a scene of bloodied men in blue, they discovered no sign of trouble at all. Oh, a group of girls came up and counted the number of police officers, almost—another rumor!—as if they were checking to see if they would outnumber the cops for another attack. And all around them, police were taunted: "Pigs eat shit! Pigs eat shit!"

Police did a bit of counting themselves, although by then it was dark and impossible to be certain how many of which side were there, doing what. The cops estimated that there were from six to seven thousand demonstrators in Lincoln Park. Or maybe it was only one thousand. The demonstrators' guesstimate put it at about a thousand of the pigs with another thousand national guardsmen hidden around the park periphery. Actually, there were fewer than two hundred uniformed police in the park. No sign of guardsmen.

There were almost as many reporters and cameramen as there were police officers. They swarmed through the park. Occasionally, there'd be a flash from a still camera. Now and then television lights illuminated part of the park and part of the crowd of demonstrators, who weren't doing much at that juncture beyond arguing about what they should do. When a reporter asked police lieutenant Raymond Skawski how he and his men would clear the park, Skawski said, "[By] whatever means are necessary. I'll have enough people. They are outnumbered and outmaneuvered. This isn't New York, this is Chicago."

Meanwhile, back at the Amphitheatre, the convention droned on. It was obvious that Humphrey would be the Democratic nominee. The droning stopped, however, when delegates began debating the Vietnam War. Momentarily, tempers flared.

Black Northern delegates sneered at white Southern delegates and called them racists. A fistfight erupted among delegates from Georgia. When CBS reporter Dan Rather tried to interview some of the delegates, a cop slugged him, security guards roughed him up, and they all hustled him out the door, on camera, live before America and the world. Seeing his fellow reporter attacked, anchor Walter Cronkite intoned, "I think we've got a bunch of thugs here, if I may be permitted to say so."*

The delegates finally voted on a proposed peace plank for the Democratic platform, written in part by former Bobby Kennedy aide, now Eugene McCarthy supporter, Richard Goodwin. McCarthy, George McGovern, and the youngest Kennedy brother—the only one left—Senator Edward "Ted" Kennedy, had all approved the plank. Even agents for Vice President Humphrey accepted the proposed plank, until someone in the White House called and ordered Humphrey to reject any statement that hinted that Lyndon Johnson had been wrong about Vietnam. When it came to a vote, the Humphrey-Johnson forces won, 1,567 to 1,041, and the peace plank lost. Antiwar protestors heard about it, and that set the stage for confrontation.

Mayor Daley had refused to give demonstrators a parade permit, but as expected, about ten thousand people gathered in Grant Park, ready to march to the Amphitheatre. And as expected, they were met by city and state police and national guardsmen. All day long, the protestors made speeches, and all day they listened to speeches. The time had come to act.

A group of young men rushed to a flagpole, pulled down the American flag, and ran up a red T-shirt. Police scurried to the scene with clubs swinging, but at least one of the men was a police undercover agent; so the cops weren't too sure who was who and whom they should bust. People scattered, and as twilight approached the demonstrators regathered in Grant Park.

Across the street, in the lobby of the Hilton Hotel, some convention delegates who'd been staying there got ready to leave, to go back to the Amphitheatre for the evening's vote on Humphrey or . . . Humphrey.

The demonstrators were also heading for the Amphitheatre. The authorities were ready and so were television crews. In 1968, television wasn't capable of running up a microwave mast or aiming a satel-

---

* The following night, Mayor Daley appeared with Cronkite in an interview, and Walter was apologetic.

lite dish and beaming a signal back to the station. In 1968, it all took time and permission for crews to lay cables, raise antennas, and get everything in line.

Richard Daley had refused permission to set up equipment that would let the crews send back live pictures, so cameramen filmed and taped the events, couriers* rushed the tapes to local stations, and delayed by as much as an hour and a half, but unedited, the whole world watched.

TV lights glowed, cameras rolled, marchers marched, and police and guardsmen attacked. Police clubbed the demonstrators and people screamed, bled, ran down the streets and into hotel lobbies. In the Hilton lobby, some delegates who'd tried to leave were driven back, handkerchiefs to their noses, because tear gas is an equal-opportunity experience. The Hilton's air-conditioning system sucked in the tear gas and sent it throughout the hotel, including room 2525A, Hubert Humphrey's suite. The tear gas came from national guardsmen, whose officer admitted ordering his men to fire because "the safety of my own men was threatened."

More cops arrived in patrol wagons, jumped out, and joined in the melee. In the glare of bright television lights, the tear gas gave Michigan Avenue a ghostly appearance. From his suite on the twenty-fifth floor, Humphrey looked down on the riot going on in front of the hotel. He saw the police beating the demonstrators, could see and smell the National Guard's tear gas, but he couldn't hear the crowd below shouting, "The whole world is watching! The whole world is watching!" As indeed it was.

The police and National Guard had blocked off Grant Park and Michigan Avenue with patrol cars and jeeps. Not only couldn't the demonstrators march to the Amphitheatre, they couldn't get away ei-

---

* For years it was standard: Chicago TV stations employed off-duty policemen to act as couriers, speeding—by motorcycle in the early days—film and tape back from the scene of a crime or convention in time for the news. Following the 1968 Democratic convention, many officers refused to work for some stations and networks—particularly NBC—saying that they didn't like the way the police were portrayed. Today, the courier system has virtually been replaced by microwave equipment.

ther. Authorities claimed all they wanted was to disperse the demonstrators, instead they had pinned them in. Some protestors tried to surrender by putting their hands on their heads, but as they were marched toward vans to be arrested, police beat and kicked them.

Somehow, a group called the Poor People's Campaign had secured a parade permit and this small contingent of blacks—incongruous in the middle of the night's events—marched down Michigan Avenue, complete with mule-drawn wagons. They got caught in the middle of the crowd, and the mules quickly grew restive. Both the antiwar demonstrators and the police realized it wasn't the damn animals' fault they were caught up in all of this. They let the Poor People's Campaign roll on through their lines, then they closed ranks and returned to fighting: cops against demonstrators.

"Hey, hey, go away. Hey, hey, go away." "Get the fuck out of here, fags!" "Peace now! Peace now! Peace now!" Neither the police nor the demonstrators would go away, and there certainly was no peace on Chicago's Michigan Avenue.

What had been an encampment in Grant Park became a battleground, and the unarmed protestors were losing badly. Chicago mayor Daley had unleashed his cops—the White House knew this but didn't interfere—and the police attacked and attacked and attacked. They clubbed people to the ground, then clubbed them again while they were on the ground. They dragged people across the well-worn Grant Park grass, and even as they threw them into patrol wagons,* they beat them again with billy clubs. Historian Teddy White called it "prodding recalcitrants who refuse to enter [patrol wagons] quietly." White stood in a room in the Blackstone Hotel, overlooking the Michigan Avenue riot, but apparently, he was watching another crowd somewhere else. *Prodding* is not the word most other witnesses to the event would have used. The late Robert Kennedy's aide Frank Mankiewicz said that the streets of Chicago were "flowing with blood."

---

* Chicago and many other cities formerly called their wagons "paddy wagons," a derogatory term reflecting the belief that "Paddies"—that is, the Irish—often were transported in them. However, in the 1990s, the preferred term in Chicago became *Squadrol,* at least in the media. To the general public, they remain "paddy wagons."

"The whole world is watching. The whole world is watching." But the presence of television cameras and reporters did nothing to restrain police brutality. In fact, the police attacked some reporters. NBC *Today* show anchor Hugh Downs commented from Chicago, "Some of us here have begun to feel that we are targets. Wearing a reporter's badge in Chicago this week is like being a Jew under Hitler." NBC news anchor Chet Huntley added, "Chicago police are going out of their way to injure newsmen, and prevent them from filming or gathering information on what's going on. The news profession in this city is now under assault by the Chicago police."

Minor riots broke out elsewhere in Chicago, not just in the area around the Hilton Hotel. Up and down Wabash Avenue, directly west of Michigan Avenue, from Fourteenth Street to Jackson and in several other downtown locations, demonstrators gathered, police squads arrived—remember, one in every six demonstrators was an undercover agent who could and did keep authorities advised about where the protestors were—and they beat, arrested, and loaded protestors into wagons.

From his fourth-floor hotel room, Senator McGovern looked down at the riot. "Do you see what those sons of bitches are doing to those kids down there?" he asked a crowd of visitors standing with him. At Eugene McCarthy's fifteenth-floor suite in the Hilton, the candidate saw the riot and said, "Good God, what's happening down there?" All week, McCarthy persistently tried to dissuade members of "McCarthy's Kids" from demonstrating. Now he said, "If I go down, I claim them. And they're not mine; I don't want any confusion here." The next day he let his suite be used as a clinic for injured protestors.* In all, 1,001 demonstrators were injured in the Michigan Avenue riots, and 101 had to be hospitalized. One hundred ninety-two policemen were injured, and forty-nine of them were hospitalized.

---

* At 5:00 the next morning police claimed that someone had been throwing things out the windows of McCarthy's suite. Officers rushed the hotel and attacked those in the room.

• • •

"Like millions of other Americans watching television that night," Richard Nixon wrote several years later, "I did not want to believe my eyes. It seems as if the Democrats' convention was confirming every indictment of their leadership that I have made in my campaign speeches." He added that "Television magnified the agony of Chicago into a national debacle."

Word of the riot got back to the convention at the Amphitheatre. Portable TV sets showed the delegates what had been going on up on Michigan Avenue. One problem that Richard Daley hadn't foreseen was that, in denying television news permission to cover the demonstrators live, he was forcing stations and networks to keep re-running old scenes. Each time old scenes were shown, the delegates, who couldn't hear the commentary, thought that another battle had broken out.

Senator Abraham Ribicoff interrupted his speech nominating Senator George McGovern to denounce the "gestapo tactics" of Chicago police. Mayor Richard J. Daley, with his son, future mayor Richard M. Daley, sitting beside him, cursed and shouted down Ribicoff's charge. Television cameras zoomed in on the elder Daley, his face purple with rage. "Da Mayor," or "Hizzoner," as he was known in Chicago, had packed the Amphitheatre with hundreds of his patronage workers, and they joined their boss in booing and jeering and shaking their fists at Ribicoff.

Finally, at 11:19 P.M. the convention got around to the reason the delegates (and the demonstrators) had come to Chicago. They nominated Hubert Humphrey for president. Surprise.

In September, a Gallup poll showed that fifty-six percent of the American people approved of the way Chicago police handled the demonstration. Only thirty-one percent disapproved. A later investigation described police response as "unrestrained and indiscriminate due, at least in part, to the belief that the mayor would condone their actions." Soon-to-be Illinois governor Daniel Walker called it a "police riot." When busloads of police reinforcements arrived on the Lake Shore Drive side of Grant Park, police filed out and lined up.

The Generation Gap

They jogged in place, raised their arms, and chanted, "Kill, kill, kill!" It was Mayor Richard J. Daley who said, "The policeman isn't there to create disorder. The policeman is there to preserve disorder."

According to Richard Nixon in 1969, there was a "silent majority."

If a vocal minority prevails over reason and the will of the majority, this nation has no future as a free society [and] so tonight—you, the great silent majority of my fellow Americans—I ask for your support.

As time and the war went on, many in the silent majority began to speak out against the fighting.

CHAPTER NINE

The Americanization of Richard Nixon: "I'm Not a Crook"*

Our nation stands at a fork in the political road. In one direction lies a land of slander and scare; the land of sly innuendo, the poison pen, the anonymous phone call and hustling, pushing, shoving; the land of smash and grab and anything to win. This is Nixonland. But I say to you that it is not America.
Adlai Stevenson, 1956

When the President does it, that means that it is not illegal.
Richard Nixon, interview with David Frost, May 19, 1977

Former president Harry Truman was not a Richard Nixon fan. Not by a long shot. In 1960, when Eisenhower's vice president ran for the top job himself, Truman commented, "I would never call Nixon a son of a bitch, because he claims to be a self-made man." The outspoken Truman also said that Richard Nixon "never told the truth in his life." Nixon may even have agreed with Truman. "If you can't lie," he once said, "you'll never go anywhere."

In 1969, President Nixon stopped off in Independence, Missouri, where Truman had retired. As a gift to the Truman Library, Nixon (or at least the National Archives) was donating Truman's old White House piano. Harry was eighty-four at the time and in declining health, but he met Nixon in the library, and the two even shook hands. Then Richard Nixon sat down at the piano—like Truman, he enjoyed playing the instrument, and also like Truman, he wasn't all that good. "I play everything in the key of G by ear," he said. Nixon played "The Missouri Waltz." He didn't realize that, despite his association with the tune, Harry Truman disliked it and once referred to the piece as "obnoxious." Didn't matter much. By then, Truman

---

* President Richard M. Nixon, news conference, November 11, 1973.

was hard of hearing, and after Nixon finished playing, Harry turned to his wife, Bess, and asked, "What was that?"

After his cat's-whisker-thin loss to John Kennedy in 1960, Nixon retired to California, but it was a short-lived retirement. On November 7, 1962, he ran for governor of California. And lost. He was so upset by the defeat that he asked his aide Herb Klein to go down to the hotel lobby and read his concession speech to members of the news media. While Nixon watched the announcement on television, reporters called for the candidate to talk to them personally. "Screw them," Nixon said, "I'm not doing it." Finally, he relented, but you can't say it was graceful concession. "You won't have Nixon to kick around anymore," the defeated candidate said, "because, gentlemen, this is my last press conference."

After losing his bids for the presidency and the California governor's office, Nixon published his book *Six Crises*, claiming that writing it had been a maturing experience.* Problem was, Nixon didn't write the book. The real author, except for the final chapter on the 1960 campaign, was Alvin Moscow. But then, it's likely that John Kennedy also didn't write his Pulitzer-prize-winning book *Profiles in Courage* either.

Richard Nixon almost lived up to his own theory: "In the United States, those who seek the presidency never win it." He explained that "circumstances rather than a man's ambition determine the result. If he is the right man for the right time, he will be chosen."

In 1968, eight years after losing the presidency and six years after losing the California gubernatorial race, Richard Nixon jumped back into the thick of politics. This time he won. He was, according to columnist Walter Lippman, a "new Nixon, a maturer and mellower man who is no longer clawing his way to the top." To which Nixon replied:

---

* Needless to say, losing the 1960 presidential election was one of Nixon's Six Crises.

> There certainly is a new Nixon. I realize, too, that as a man gets older he learns something. If I haven't learned something I am not worth anything.

Almost from the moment Richard Nixon won the presidency, he had to defend himself from his opponents. The day he was inaugurated, he almost had to defend himself physically. Despite heavy security precautions, some three hundred to four hundred protestors hurled rocks and bottles at President Nixon's limousine after he'd been sworn in at the capitol. "For the first few blocks," Nixon wrote, "the cheering crowds were friendly." Around Twelfth Street, protest signs began to appear, with a double line of police "struggling to keep the crowd back."

> Suddenly a barrage of sticks, stones, beer cans, and what looked like firecrackers began sailing through the air toward us. Some of them hit the side of the car and fell into the street. I could hear the protesters' shrill chant: "Ho, Ho, Ho Chi Minh, the NLF is going to win." A Viet Cong flag was lifted and there was a brief scuffle as some in the crowd tried to tear it down.

It was one of the largest protests ever at an inauguration and an inauguration whose crowds along the parade route were smaller than in years past. In 1965, an estimated 1.2 million people lined the inaugural route to get a look at Lyndon B. Johnson. In 1969, the number who lined up to see Richard Nixon was put at only 250,000.

Not just at the inauguration either. Antiwar protests outside the White House during the Nixon years occurred so often and were so loud that special counsel Charles Colson remembered:

> It was like living in a bunker. . . . I mean, you'd look out on the streets and you'd see thousands of people protesting. You literally were afraid for your life. There are times when I can remember saying, "I can't believe this is the United States of America, a free country," and here we are in the White House with barricades up and buses around the White House and tear gas going off and thousands—hundreds of thousands—of protestors out on the streets and troops sitting there.

The Americanization of Richard Nixon

President Nixon blamed it on university "faculty leaders and professional agitators and the pampered kids on campus." How bad was it? "Sometimes it was so loud you couldn't even go to sleep at night," he said.

First Lady Pat Nixon remembered her husband's sleepless nights:

Nobody could sleep with Dick. He wakes up during the night, switches on the light, speaks into his tape recorder or takes notes—it's impossible.

On March 28, 1969, Nixon's mentor, former president Dwight Eisenhower, died of congestive heart failure at the age of seventy-eight. In his memoirs, *RN*, Nixon says that "perhaps the best description I can give of Dwight Eisenhower is that he had a warm smile and icy blue eyes."

Before leaving the White House in 1961, Ike had already suffered three heart attacks. His fourth came in 1968 while the former president was in California. Flown back to Walter Reed Army Medical Center in Washington, D.C., Ike suffered his fifth heart attack while there. Less than two months later, he had a sixth, and the next day, August 16, 1968, he suffered his seventh attack.

Eisenhower graduated from West Point in 1915 and rose through the army ranks to commanding general of the European Theater in World War II. After the war, he was appointed president of Columbia University, then went into semiretirement. Nominated by the Republican Party in 1952, he became America's thirty-fourth president. In contrast to the Roosevelt and Truman years—marked with brawls between the White House and Congress—Eisenhower wanted peace, both world peace and peace at home. To that end, as historian Rita Lang Kleinfelder puts it, "the general turned into a caretaker."

The year that Ike died, U.S. combat fatalities in the Vietnam War topped the number of Americans killed in the Korean War: 33,629 in Korea and (by 1969) 33,641 in Vietnam. April 30, 1969, saw American forces in Vietnam at their peak numbers: 543,482.

One month after taking office, Richard Nixon—who'd barely lost the 1960 popular vote but who'd been badly defeated by JFK in the electoral college vote—called for a constitutional amendment to change the electoral college system. He didn't want to do away with the system, but recommended abolition of individual electors and proposed allocating electoral votes within each state on a basis proportional to the popular vote, and reducing from fifty percent to forty percent the electoral-vote plurality required to choose a president. Under the Nixon plan, if a candidate received the recommended forty percent of the vote, the two leading candidates would face each other in a runoff election. And the runoff would be based on popular vote, not on an election in the House of Representatives as mandated by the Constitution.

The proposal never made it into the Constitution. If it had, things in the twenty-first century might be different. In the 2000 election, Democrat Al Gore won the popular vote, but Republican George W. Bush—after more than a month of wrangling over contested votes in Florida—won the electoral count. If Richard Nixon's proposed amendment had made it into the Constitution, in 2001, Al Gore, not George W. Bush, would have taken the oath of office.

Truly, Richard Nixon had a way with words. Once, as vice president, he was attending a Republican fund-raising dinner in Chicago. In his address, Nixon warned against "the temptation to stand pat on what we have done." The story, in a newspaper's first edition, carried a headline "Can't Stand Pat, Says Nixon." For the second edition, the headline read, "Can't Stand Still."

When he was speaking to the U.S. Junior Chamber of Commerce in Detroit in June 1966, the president talked about his travels in South America, where—as later happened in Washington at his inauguration—protestors had lined the way. "I got stoned in Caracas," he said, adding, "I'll tell you one thing; it's a lot different from getting stoned at a Jaycee convention."

Dwight Eisenhower, who was not noted for his eloquent speaking, would have understood. Back in 1954, when the Republic of China threatened to occupy a pair of islands off Taiwan, White House press secretary James Hagerty told Ike, "Mr. President, some of the people in the State Department say that the Formosa Strait situation is so delicate that no matter what question you get on it, you shouldn't say anything at all."

"Don't worry, Jim," Ike said. "If that question comes up, I'll just confuse them."

As for Richard Nixon, during his appearance before a large crowd one day, a little girl—all innocence and worried by something she'd apparently heard on television—waved to the president and shouted, "How is Smokey the Bear?"

Nixon couldn't quite make out what the child had said and asked an aide, who whispered, "Smokey the Bear. Washington National Zoo."

With that, the president walked over to the little girl, took her hand, and said, "How do you do, Miss Bear?"

In 1960, Republican Richard M. Nixon lost to Democrat John F. Kennedy by 118,574 votes. Eight years later, 73,186,819 American citizens went to the polls to vote for a new president. Nixon beat Hubert H. Humphrey by 510,314 votes, with three million *fewer* votes than he'd received when he ran against Kennedy. Nixon got 43.4 percent of the vote, while Humphrey received 42.72 percent and Wallace counted 13.53 percent.

The big difference was that in 1960, Nixon received only 219 electoral college votes, 84 fewer than Kennedy. In 1968 he received 301 electoral votes, 110 more than Humphrey.

Kennedy won the 1960 election thanks in no small part to Chicago major Richard J. Daley, who allegedly unearthed thousands of long-dead voters to swing Illinois and its electoral college delegation to the Democrats. Some of Nixon's aides suggested that he challenge the Chicago vote, but he declined, saying that such a move would tear the country apart.

Although the Chicago Democratic Party may have fudged things a bit, it's also likely that Republicans in downstate Illinois did the same for their man. Richard Nixon knew this, and that's why he decided not to ask for a recount.

CHAPTER TEN

CUBA:
Island Paradise?

History will absolve me. *

> Fidel Castro, at his trial for a raid on the
> Moncada barracks, October 16, 1953

There was an Old Man with a beard,
Who said: "It is just as I feared!—
Two Owls and a Hen,
Four Larks and a Wren,
Have all built their nests in my beard.

> Edward Lear, Book of Nonsense (1846)

Just ninety miles from Miami, Florida, lies the Caribbean paradise of Cuba, which isn't now, and hasn't been for the past three decades, a paradise for anybody but an aging bearded dictator. Generations of Americans sailed and flew to Cuba to play in the Caribbean sands and gamble in the Havana casinos.

Of course much more than swimming and gambling went on in Cuba. Fidel Castro Rus had ousted Gen. Fulgencio Batista, who himself had ousted President Carlos Prío Socarrás. Castro became dictator for life, or as he called himself for the first six weeks, "prime minister"; in 1976 he took the title "president." Friction between the United States and Cuba grew when Castro's government began expropriating American-owned properties.

Earlier, President Dwight Eisenhower had given his backing to a CIA-sponsored coup in Guatemala, with the CIA training a hundred Guatemalan exiles and mercenaries at camps in Opa-locka, Florida, and Honduras. The coup worked, and President Jacobo Arbenz, who headed the most democratic government Guatemala had ever had, was tossed out. If the CIA could do it in Guatemala, Ike and Secre-

---

* La historia me absolverá.

tary of State John Foster Dulles thought, why not in Cuba? Fidel Castro certainly was a lot more radical than Arbenz had been.

On March 16, 1960, CIA chief Allen Dulles (John Foster's brother) laid on Ike's desk a "Program of Covert Action Against the Castro Regime." Its purpose was to "bring about the replacement of the Castro regime with one more devoted to the true interests of the Cuban people and more acceptable to the U.S.," done in such a manner "as to avoid any appearance of U.S. intervention." Just as they had done in the Guatemala coup, the Central Intelligence Agency would arm and train anti-Castro exiles known as the Cuban Liberation Corps—they were called *la Brigada*, the brigade, or Brigade 2506. They'd be trained in, of all places, Guatemala, which now had a government entirely to Washington's liking.

The CIA, the proposal said, had already prepared "an adequate paramilitary force outside of Cuba." To give voice to anti-Castro sentiment, America would support a radio station on Swan Island between Cuba and Mexico, to be "supplemented by broadcasting from U.S. commercial facilities paid for by private Cuban groups."

Not that an American-backed invasion would be a surprise. Castro had predicted it, constantly predicted it. Everyone talked about it and waited for it. In September 1959, Fidel began calling the United States "a vulture . . . feeding on humanity." The following February, Cuba signed an agreement to buy oil from the Soviet Union and made further agreements with other Communist governments.

Cuba was, as Washington officials continually reminded us, "only ninety miles from our shores, only eight minutes [by air] from our coast." By mid-1960, Castro had seized nearly all U.S.-owned property in Cuba, and the United States had broken diplomatic relations with the revolutionary government in Havana. Castro wasn't just sitting around smoking long cigars; he was also daring "the Yanquis" to invade. Well, we did.

Shortly after the November 1960 election, the U.S. State Department briefed John Kennedy in general terms about the CIA's plan. Shortly before he left office in 1961, President Eisenhower severed all U.S. ties with Fidel Castro's Cuba. On January 19, in a largely pro forma meeting—one president telling his successor what's going on in the world—Ike and JFK met and Eisenhower made reference to the small force of Cubans being trained by the CIA in Guatemala. Eisenhower recommended that Kennedy go ahead with the plan.

Under the plan, the twelve thousand armed members of the brigade being trained in Guatemala would land at an area of Cuba called the Bay of Pigs, a point of land whose name should immediately have rung alarm bells in Kennedy's PR office. The brigade would be aided by twenty-five hundred CIA agents on the island itself who would blow up bridges and knock out radio stations and in general raise hell once the force of exiles touched Cuban soil. The people of Cuba would stage a popular uprising, Castro would be out on his hairy ear, and all would be right with the Western Hemisphere. In the meantime, the radio station on Swan Island would pump out anti-Castro propaganda.

What Ike didn't tell Jack in their January meeting, and what even today isn't totally clear, was whether the American Mafia was also backing the brigade. After all, when Castro took control of Cuba, he'd booted out the Mafia-owned nightclubs and gambling dens. A Senate investigation later revealed that the CIA had talked with Mafia hitmen Sam Giancana,* known as the Godfather of Chicago, and John Rosselli about assassinating Fidel Castro.** One fanciful plan was to paint poison on the steering wheel of Castro's jeep—he still drove himself around town—with the idea that by touching the steering wheel Fidel would absorb enough poison to die. Or maybe doctor one of his famous cigars with a chemical that would cause his beard to fall out. How about, somehow, getting him to ingest an LSD-like substance just prior to one of his planned radio broadcasts, causing him "to become disoriented in the midst of his harangue."

---

* Giancana was sleeping with Judith Campbell, a long-time and still-active bed partner of John F. Kennedy. Sam once boasted to Judith, "Listen, honey, if it wasn't for me your boyfriend wouldn't even be in the White House."
** Both Giancana and Rosselli were murdered mob-style, Giancana in his Chicago-area home before he could testify before a Senate Intelligence Committee. Rosselli's decomposing body was found floating in an oil drum off Florida. Rumors persist that both men possessed information connecting the Mafia and the CIA with the 1963 assassination of John Kennedy.

Plans to use the Mafia are reminiscent of "dirty tricks" sometimes carried out by both Republicans and Democrats during the Kennedy-Nixon campaigns. One of the most famous dirty tricks of the 1960 campaign was played on Nixon by Kennedy's people in the midst of a whistlestop tour. Richard Nixon was standing on the rear train platform addressing the crowd when someone dressed as a rail conductor signaled the engineer to start the train off. The engineer did, the train left the station, and candidate Nixon was left speaking as the crowd began fading into the distance.

Cuba, the CIA planners realized too late, was not Guatemala. In fact, on April 10, 1961, Kennedy aide and speech writer Arthur Schlesinger Jr. told the new president why invading Cuba wouldn't work. "The operational planning for the Cuban project," Schlesinger wrote, "seems much farther advanced than the political, diplomatic and economic planning which properly should accompany it." He added that

> a great many people simply do not at this moment see that Cuba presents so grave and compelling a threat to our national security as to justify a course of action which much of the world will interpret as calculated aggression against a small nation in defiance of both treaty obligations and of the international standards we have repeatedly asserted against the Communist world.

The Soviet Union would use such an invasion to "bolster the Marxist interpretation of history." Whether that would also mean military retaliation, Sehlesinger wouldn't venture to say. He believed that it would cause nations around the world to provide funds for Cuba's defense and predicted that "the people who have been crowding [London's] Trafalgar Square to protest [nuclear weapons] will be crowding it again to shout for Castro and denounce the U.S. as the last stronghold of imperialism."

"What about the Senate Foreign Relations Committee?" Schlesinger asked, "What about the House Foreign Affairs Committee?" So far, Congress hadn't been told. "Someone should begin to think what they should be told."

When the CIA first presented its plan to him back in 1960, Dwight Eisenhower had backed it strongly. Now, Jack Kennedy gave the CIA his guarded and halfhearted approval. He didn't want to appear soft on Communism and the intelligence community convinced him that the invasion would succeed.

Seven days after Schlesinger's memorandum, on April 17, some fourteen hundred Cuban refugees invaded their homeland at the Bay of Pigs. Unlike the CIA-backed coup in Guatemala, this time the U.S. government withheld air support. The CIA's hoped-for support within Cuba also failed to materialize, and Castro's forces overwhelmed the poorly prepared and poorly backed expatriates. During the ill-fated three-day battle, more than two hundred invaders died, with about twelve hundred others being captured.

The CIA may have fooled Eisenhower into believing the Bay of Pigs invasion would work. Kennedy fooled himself. An after-the-fact, 150-page report by the U.S. inspector general's office outlined the problems.

Several things had gone wrong: The CIA hadn't checked with "the best operating talent available" on whether the whole thing was feasible. After finally realizing the project was in trouble, the agency hadn't advised JFK that the operation might not succeed. And, perhaps even before incoming President Kennedy had learned about the invasion, the higher-ups in Fidel Castro's regime in Havana already knew about it. This last is particularly strange: The invadee (Castro) had known about the Bay of Pigs before the invader (Kennedy) had.

According to the inspector general's office, the Bay of Pigs operation was "too large to be handled by the agency alone," yet how could the United States have expected a force as small as fourteen hundred soldiers to beat a vastly superior, well-trained, and motivated army on its own territory?

Several times in January 1961, Kennedy Administration officials met with the Joint Chiefs of Staff to talk over the planned invasion. Plainly, the JCS didn't believe it would work. Kennedy's new secretary of defense, Robert McNamara, was skeptical. JFK himself was leery of the proposal—after all, it could draw the United States into war with the Soviet Union.

Secretary of State Dean Rusk wanted to delay the action and try to get support from other OAS (Organization of American States) nations. The CIA argued that it couldn't delay the invasion, couldn't hold fourteen hundred supposedly trained men in the jungles of Guatemala and not expect word to leak out. Of course, the word was already out. And of course no plan is perfect.

The Bay of Pigs location, incidentally, was chosen because there's an airstrip nearby that could accommodate B-26 bombers that would be flown by émigré pilots from airfields in Nicaragua and also provide a place where air support, hopefully coming from within Cuba, could land. That is, Cuban Air Force pilots defecting from Castro could land their craft near the invasion site. In the event, none did. Morever, the Bay of Pigs was so swampy and mosquito ridden as to have been inaccessible to any other Cuban who might have wanted to defect.

On March 16 John Kennedy gave the go-ahead to a revised Bay of Pigs invasion plan—code-name Zapata—reserving the right to call it off up to twenty-four hours prior to the scheduled landing. Two weeks later, he set a tentative invasion date of April 10, later rescheduling it for the seventeenth.

On the fifteenth, B-26 bombers, bearing the markings of the Cuban Air Force and piloted by Cuban émigré pilots, launched preliminary strikes against airfields in Cuba. They only partially succeeded and probably did more harm than good by alerting the Cuban military that the Cuban Expeditionary Force (CEF) was on its way. On the sixteenth, President Kennedy decided that bomber missions set for April 17 would have to be postponed until the airfield at the Bay of Pigs was secured by the invaders. Consequently a planned second air strike against Cuban bases was never flown. When the actual invasion started, the Cuban army still had the air power to cripple the émigré forces, meaning the Cuban brigade was in trouble right from the beginning. When the B-26 bombers finally showed up over the Bay of Pigs beaches, the Cuban Air Force's fleet of T-33 jet trainers had an easy time of it, knocking the bombers out of the air.

The White House had rejected plans to send a couple of navy destroyers into the area to support the landing; they were to be kept, at a minimum, twenty miles off shore. Which meant that the CEF transports were easy prey for the Cuban Air Force. By 10:17 on the morning of the invasion, two CEF ships had been sunk, and a third was under heavy attack. Soon, two more vessels were under attack, and one of them was on fire. Sinking of the ships meant that much of the necessary supplies and ammunition for the Cuban brigade were gone.

Meanwhile, back on the beach, the brigade was crying for air cover, for ammunition, and for other supplies to fight off mounting pressure from Castro's forces that included tanks and jets. By now it was obvious that the planned action to disrupt services within Cuba, blowing up bridges and communications facilities, hadn't happened; the Cuban people were standing by Fidel.

On April 18, a message that came from the CEF beachhead said that they had "no ammo left for tanks and very little left for troops." Then: "Red Beach wiped out. Request air strikes immediately." And finally: "Please don't desert us. Am out of tank and bazooka ammo. Tanks will hit me at dawn. I will not be evacuated. Will fight to the end if we have to." On the nineteenth: "Out of ammunition. Men fighting in water. If no help given Blue Beach lost."

In the aftermath, President Kennedy asked retired army chief of staff Gen. Maxwell D. Taylor to head a committee to investigate the failure of the Bay of Pigs operation. His report blamed everybody.

- President Eisenhower should have canceled the operation long before it got under way; if not, change it into an amphibious operation wholly controlled by the Department of Defense.

- When the idea of the invasion was presented to President Kennedy, those in charge of the operation "did not always present their case with sufficient force and clarity" to allow the new administration to understand "the consequences."

- President Kennedy and his senior officials were "greatly influenced by the understanding that the landing force could pass to guerrilla status" if the CEF couldn't hold the beachhead. That is, if they were losing, they could just fade into the nearby bush and jungle.

- The Joint Chiefs of Staff didn't do an adequate job in assessing the military feasibility of the operation, and, despite reservations, they gave the impression that they approved Operation Zapata.
- Finally, it was a mistake trying to run the operation from Washington, rather than entrusting responsibility to a commander closer to the point of combat.*

The Central Intelligence Agency also conducted a study into the disaster, and perhaps strangely enough, the agency blamed itself, a fact that outraged most agency people. Only twenty copies of the CIA's own report were produced, and within months all but one was destroyed. That one 150-page copy of the report sat locked away for more than thirty years, finally being released in 1998 in response to a Freedom of Information Act request.

While many survivors (and many other Cubans in exile in the United States) blamed John Kennedy for failing to approve air strikes to back up the seaborne rebels, the CIA report blamed the CIA. Agency leaders had "failed to advise the president, at an appropriate time, that success had become dubious and to recommend that the operation therefore be canceled."

Mainly, the Bay of Pigs debacle was due to the CIA's ignorance and incompetence and its arrogance toward the Cuban exiles it trained and equipped. "The fundamental cause of the disaster was the agency's failure to give the project, notwithstanding its importance and immense potentiality for damage to the United States, the top-flight handling which it required." They screwed up such seemingly simple things as language; few of the CIA personnel training the émigrés spoke Spanish and those who did "treated the Cubans like dirt."

Operation Zapata was neither a true covert operation nor a conventional invasion. It depended on a revolt that never occurred, inadequate air cover, and interagency coordination that failed. That just about sums it up. Within days of the disaster, the Kennedy Ad-

---

* This last was also an argument heard during the Vietnam War, that Washington macromanaged the fighting from the White House war room.

ministration began changing its foreign policy and rethinking its trust in the CIA. "How could I have been so stupid?" JFK asked his advisers. In public, President Kennedy took full responsibility for the fiasco. In private, he blamed CIA head Allen Dulles for not properly informing him in advance of the real chances of success or failure. Soon after the Bay of Pigs, Dulles resigned. As for the president, two weeks after the failed attempt, Kennedy's standing in the public opinion polls went up to an unprecedented eighty-three percent favorable rating.

The upshot from America's standpoint was that President Kennedy took a new approach in his effort to undermine Castro's control of Cuba and to prevent the spread of the Cuban revolution to Latin America. He instituted and strengthened a trade embargo on the island that basically stands today.

The upshot from Cuba's standpoint was that it enabled Premier Castro to convince Soviet premier Nikita Khrushchev that he should openly support Cuba with military aid and missiles. That would bring about the next near-disaster in the island paradise of Cuba, when we and the Soviets almost blew ourselves to hell.

Greenbrier is a five-star resort in the rolling hills of West Virginia, about four hours' drive from Washington, D.C. It began operations in the eighteenth century, when water from its sulphur springs became fashionable as a "curative" for just about any ailment wealthy tourists of the time could imagine. The Old White Hotel, as it was called then, was where President Woodrow Wilson honeymooned with the second Mrs. Wilson.

During World War II, ten days after the attack on Pearl Harbor, the U.S. State Department began shipping in hundreds of Germans—mainly diplomats and their families—who were left in America after fighting broke out. By the end of March 1942, more than eight-hundred prisoner-of-war "guests" were housed at the resort at the expense of the American government.

Fewer than twenty years after the POWs departed the Greenbrier, the U.S. government once again imposed on the resort for the use of the facilities—not to house POWs this time, but to house the president and vice president of the United States, the cabinet, the U.S.

Supreme Court, and members of Congress. All in case of a nuclear war. Beneath the Greenbrier's white walls and gently rolling golf course, the federal government built a 112,000-square-foot concrete bunker. As well as living quarters, the bunker had heat, air conditioning, food, and water enough to last at least a month. About once a month the food would be recycled, so to speak, with new rations brought in and the month-old meals fed to Greenbrier employees, who thought it strange that, once a month, they'd get better than normal foods.

The bunker had offices for everyone involved, as well as living quarters for them and their families. It was built because the Soviet Union had set up missiles in Cuba, only eight minutes from America.

This secret last-ditch hideout for the American government remained—more or less—secret until 1992, when the *Washington Post* broke the story. No longer a secret, today you can visit the bunker. Tours run through it twice a week.

In September 1962, the Soviet cargo ship *Omsk* docked in Havana, and that night its cargo of medium-range missiles was unloaded. A week later, another shipment arrived carrying longer-range missiles.

On October 14, an American U-2 spy plane flew over the island as part of the CIA's regular surveillance of Cuba. On the sixteenth, President Kennedy telephoned his brother Bobby, the attorney general, and asked him to come to the White House. Based on photos taken from the U-2, the intelligence community was convinced that Russia was placing missiles and maybe even some atomic weapons in Cuba. Launch sites were being prepared and missiles and warheads were on the way. If, as some complained, America's scheme to invade Cuba at the Bay of Pigs had been a crackbrained idea, then the Soviet Union's plan to install nuclear missiles ninety miles away from Florida was dangerous almost beyond comprehension.

In the White House Cabinet Room, the CIA made a formal presentation. Photographs taken by U-2 pilots were shown, and experts, Bobby Kennedy wrote, "arrived with their charts and their pointers and told us that if we looked carefully, we could see there was a surface-to-surface missile base being constructed in a field near San

Cristobal, Cuba." There also was evidence that the Soviets were building a submarine base not too far away.

The Bay of Pigs incident had humiliated the young president. Leaving aside the danger posed by a missile base damn close to Miami Beach, allowing them to remain there would ruin Kennedy and his fellow Democrats. It was, after all, election time, and Republicans were "viewing with alarm" reports that Democrats weren't doing enough to protect America. Senator Homer E. Capehart of Indiana, among others, momentarily forgetting the Bay of Pigs debacle, suggested that the United States should take military action against Cuba.

Several weeks earlier, Bobby Kennedy had met with Soviet ambassador Anatoly Dobrynin who had told the attorney general not to worry about the amount of military equipment Russia was shipping to Cuba. Dobrynin said that according to Soviet chairman Khrushchev there would be no ground-to-ground missiles or other offensive weapons placed in Cuba. The military buildup, Dobrynin claimed, wasn't very significant. Would Khrushchev do anything to disrupt U.S.-Soviet relations? Of course not. Nikita liked Jack, Dobrynin said; he wouldn't do anything to embarrass him.

Unknown to President Kennedy, Khrushchev had bragged to Fidel Castro that putting missiles in Cuba was something that not even Joseph Stalin would have dared. Khrushchev's colleague Anastas Mikoyan told a secret briefing of Soviet diplomats in Washington that putting missiles in Cuba would bring about a "definite shift in the power relationship between the socialist and the capitalist worlds." Which, if true, certainly would embarrass Nikita's friend Jack.

So, on the morning of October 16, President Kennedy had enough proof to take Fidel Castro and Nikita Khrushchev to court, so to speak. Dean Acheson and Vice President Lyndon Johnson wanted to launch airstrikes against Cuba and knock out the missile sites before things got too far along and then invade Cuba and kick Castro's butt. On the other hand, Adlai Stevenson, Kennedy's man at the United Nations, suggested trading with Russia: You remove your missiles from Cuba and we'll remove our missiles from Turkey. In truth, our fifteen Jupiter missiles in Turkey were obsolete and we'd get rid of them soon anyway. We'd give up the naval base at Guantanamo Bay, Adlai suggested, and the Russians would make Cuba a demilitarized zone.

Some, a small minority, Bobby Kennedy claimed, suggested that since America's strategic weapons position was so strong, we should ignore the whole thing. Jack Kennedy rejected that idea from the start. Khrushchev had lied to him about the missiles; Dobrynin had lied to Bobby about the missiles. JFK wasn't about to believe the Soviets, not now. The consensus seemed to be that the United States should hit Cuba hard and hit them fast, without warning.

To study the problem, the president set up an informal body of advisers later called the Executive Committee of the National Security Council: ExComm. Mainly, it was made up of Kennedy loyalists such as Vice President Johnson, Secretary Rusk, Attorney General Bobby Kennedy, Gen. Maxwell Taylor, Ted Sorensen, George Ball, and McGeorge Bundy. Former secretary of state Dean Acheson was part of ExComm, but he quit in disgust when Bobby Kennedy basically repeated what he'd written to Jack: "My brother is not going to be the Tojo"—Japan's leader at the time of Pearl Harbor— "of the 1960's."

The Joint Chiefs of Staff virtually had pushed for just that, a Pearl Harbor–type first-strike surprise attack on Cuba. The idea that seemed to hit strongest, however, was a quarantine of Cuba; set up a blockade and seal off the island. If that didn't work, then send in the bombers and, if necessary, ground troops to invade the island. Only, this time there'd be no Bay of Pigs affair.

When Wednesday's U-2 snapshots came back in, they showed that work on the original, football-field-size-missile site was progressing. And several other sites were also being prepared. The sites could be ready to go within a week. Thursday's photographs were even more chilling; the missiles going into Cuba had about half the current ICBM (Intercontinental ballistic missile) capacity of the entire Soviet Union. Just a bit more than Khrushchev and Dobrynin had claimed. From the way the sites were being built, the experts could even tell the likely targets in America. Within a few minutes of their being fired, "eighty million Americans would be dead," Bobby Kennedy remembered.

Air force chief of staff Gen. Curtis LeMay, who'd commanded bomber forces in both England and the Pacific in World War II, wanted to attack immediately; it was essential, he believed. The president asked LeMay what the general thought Russia's response would be, and General LeMay assured him that there would be none. Now, Kennedy didn't believe that. The Soviets can't "let these things go by without doing something"; they couldn't permit the United States "to take out their missiles, kill a lot of Russians, and then do nothing. If they don't take action in Cuba, they certainly will in Berlin."

ExComm continued meeting throughout the week, weighing the proposed quarantine and blockade against an invasion and a sneak air attack. By the twenty-second, JFK had made the decision to go ahead with the blockade. That afternoon, he called congressional leaders to the White House and outlined the situation and his plan. The congressmen didn't like it. They didn't want a blockade; they wanted an immediate invasion of Castro's island paradise. Teach that cigar-smoking, long-haired, SOB a lesson he'd never forget. President Kennedy said he was going ahead with the quarantine.

At six that night, Kennedy received Soviet ambassador Dobrynin, told him that we knew about the missiles, and ordered them removed; he told the ambassador what America was going to do, and when Dobrynin left the White House, the ambassador looked badly shaken.

At seven that night, President Kennedy went on national television and told the country what was happening and what to expect. It scared hell out of us:

> The path we have chosen for the present is full of hazards, as all paths are, but it is one most consistent with our character and courage as a nation and our commitments around the world. The cost of freedom is always high, but Americans have always paid it. And one path we shall never choose, and that is the path of surrender or submission.

The navy organized a fleet of 180 vessels and the army and marines assembled a quarter of a million troops. Just in case.

TV newsmen drew maps that featured sweeping arcs purporting to show just where in America Cuba's missiles would hit, and where they would hit was just about every large city except Seattle, Washington, which was too far away. With that, schoolchildren everywhere, except Seattle, began practicing the same exercise their older brothers and sisters had practiced back in the fifties: duck and cover. Hide under your desk, which, as everyone knew, would offer more than enough protection from an atomic bomb.

In Cuba, workmen continued construction of the missile sites and Soviet-bloc ships continued to steam toward Cuba. The U.S. Joint Chiefs of Staff, with a we-know-what's-really- going-to-happen-when-the-blockade-fails attitude, gave the president an estimate of expected casualties in the event the United States invaded Cuba to remove the missile sites. It wasn't pretty. Cuba had a 270,000-man army just waiting for an invasion, and the Soviets had stationed 40,000 troops on the island to augment those forces. We could expect upward of 25,000 American dead and wounded if we invaded the island. And by the time American forces got to the missiles, they might not even be there; the Cuban-Soviet teams likely would already have launched them, which meant they'd already have hit American cities, which meant as soon as they were in the air and seen for what they were we'd launch a counterattack on both Cuba and the Soviet Union, which meant the Soviet Union and its Warsaw Pact puppets would launch a counter-counterattack on America and Western Europe, which meant we might all end up under a radioactive cloud from which no school desk could protect us.

This time it wasn't a practice session. The Pentagon placed all American missile crews on maximum alert. They loaded all strategic bombers with nuclear bombs. The planes were almost constantly in the air. As soon as one landed, another took off: some 800 B-47s, 550 B-52s, and 70 B-58s. Nuclear warheads were activated on 100 Atlas, 50 Titan, and 12 Minuteman missiles and on all American carriers, submarines, and overseas bases. All commands were at Defcon-2, the highest state of readiness short of war itself.

On the twenty-third, at the United Nations, U.S. ambassador Adlai Stevenson publicly confronted Soviet Ambassador V. A. Zorin in a dramatic televised meeting of the Security Council. It was a dramatic and, for America, a thrilling confrontation: One of the nation's brightest minds openly challenging the Russians with photographic proof as a hole card. Zorin denied the Soviets were doing anything wrong, and besides, the United States had no proof:

> Stevenson: Well, let me say something to you, Mr. Ambassador, we do have the evidence. We have it, and it is clear and incontrovertible. . . .
>
> I remind you that the other day you did not deny the existence of these weapons. But today, again, if I heard you correctly, you now say that they do not exist, or that we haven't proved they exist.
>
> All right, sir, let me ask you one simple question. Do you, Ambassador Zorin, deny that the U.S.S.R. has placed and is placing medium- and intermediate-range missiles and sites in Cuba? Yes or no? Don't wait for the translation, yes or no?
>
> Zorin: I am not in an American courtroom, sir, and therefore I do not wish to answer a question that is put to me in the fashion in which a prosecutor puts questions. In due course, sir, you will have your answer.
>
> Stevenson: You are in the courtroom of world opinion right now, and you can answer yes or no. You have denied that they exist, and I want to know whether I have understood you correctly.
>
> Zorin: Continue with your statement. You will have your answer in due course.
>
> Stevenson: I am prepared to wait for my answer until hell freezes over, if that's your decision. And I am also prepared to present the evidence in this room.

With that Stevenson unveiled the photographs taken of the Soviet missiles and sites. The effect was devastating. Stevenson knew it, Zorin knew it, and the whole world knew it. The Russian bear had been caught with his hand in the nuclear cookie jar.

Presented with evidence that Russia had been lying about not putting missiles in Cuba, both NATO and the Organization of American States approved the Kennedy Administration's plan to blockade

Cuba. Their endorsement gave the quarantine legitimacy; the Western Hemisphere and, in fact, the Western World stood together against Russia.

Friday, October 26, was a day of good news and bad news, or as Secretary of State Dean Rusk said, "We're eyeball to eyeball, and I think the other fellow just blinked." Soviet chairman Khrushchev sent President Kennedy two letters. The first letter—a rambling, very long and very emotional letter apparently written by Nikita himself—took a soft line that Russia would remove its missiles in return for assurances that America would not invade Cuba. The second—seemingly written by a Kremlin committee—took a harder line and demanded the United States remove its missiles from Turkey in return for the Soviets taking their missiles out of Cuba.

As soon as the soft-line letter arrived, ExComm members were optimistic. The hard-line letter was formal and more demanding. Hope turned to despair.

In between the letters word came from long-time ABC radio and television reporter John Scali. The Soviet embassy had approached him with a proposal that the Soviet Union would remove its missiles under United Nations supervision if the United States would lift the blockade and pledge not to invade Cuba. Basically, it was the same proposal Khrushchev had made in his first letter.

Kennedy had ordered the CIA to increase the twice-a-day U-2 flights over Cuba to one every two hours, but one of those flights had run into trouble. A Cuban surface-to-air missile (SAM) had shot down the reconnaissance plane, and pilot Maj. Rudolph Anderson Jr. of South Carolina was killed. Kennedy earlier had warned that if the Cubans or Russians shot down one of our planes he'd order our bombers to attack Cuba. He thought better of it and took no overt action in reprisal.

While Kennedy and Khrushchev exchanged messages of threats and counterthreats, Defense Secretary Robert McNamara assembled an invasion force in Florida, the Caribbean, and in southern bases and ports that rivaled task forces organized during World War II. They hoped that, unlike the Normandy landing, this one would be a secret: All America knew it and the Soviet Union knew it. One television comic said that if we sent any more troops to Florida the state would tip over into the ocean and we wouldn't have to worry about Cuban missiles hitting Miami.

ExComm, meanwhile, debated what to do with Chairman Khrushchev's two somewhat conflicting letters. Attorney General Bobby Kennedy came up with what, at the time, seemed too simple a solution, but which we now realize was a brilliant idea: answer the first letter and pretend the second one had never arrived. That's what they did. And, for the moment at least, we all lived happily every after.

Well, not all of us. In Havana, Fidel Castro was furious. Khrushchev hadn't consulted him and Fidel nearly blew his fatigue-hatted top when he learned that Nikita was taking back his missiles. According to Che Guevara, who was with Castro when Fidel learned about the settlement, Castro cursed, he kicked the wall, and he smashed a mirror.

Not everybody in America agreed with the settlement either. Air force general Curtis LeMay, who had wanted to bomb hell out of Cuba, pounded on the table and told Kennedy, "It's the greatest defeat in our history, Mr. President."

Even former secretary of state Acheson thought we hadn't gone far enough. "So long as we had the thumbscrew on Khrushchev, we should have given it another turn every day."

All in all, though, the peaceful resolution of the Cuban Missile Crisis seemed to prove the wisdom of what was called "flexible response": We didn't have to launch nuclear missiles at the first sign of crisis. And getting us out of what undoubtedly was a dangerous situation gave John Kennedy stature in the international community that the Bay of Pigs fiasco had damaged.

At home, it not only gave him stature, it gave him popularity. Immediately after the Cuban Missile Crisis, the American people rallied around Jack Kennedy just as they had after the Bay of Pigs. They gave him an astronomical eighty-two-percent approval rating. It amazed even the president, who said, "My God, it's as bad as Eisenhower. The worse I do, the more popular I get."

For Nikita Khrushchev, the Cuban Missile Crisis marked the beginning of the end. He'd believed his intelligence experts, who had told him the Soviets could erect the missile sites in total secrecy; even though, after the 1960 U-2 incident, they should have realized America's reconnaissance capabilities likely would discover the construction. Khrushchev listened to his advisors, who'd told him that even if the Americans learned what was going on in Cuba, although they might protest nuclear missiles on our doorsteps, they "wouldn't act." Nikita listened to his military advisors, and in the end, he paid for listening to bad advice, paid with his job.

As for Dean Rusk's "eyeball-to-eyeball" comment, Soviet foreign minister Andrei Gromyko had an answer, which lost a lot in the translation: "I am looking forward to talking with you balls to balls."

In December 1962, after things had settled down from the missile crisis, the Kennedy Administration secured the release of the 1,113 Cubans whom the abortive Bay of Pigs operation had left in Cuba. Eventually, Cuba would release a total of 9,703 people—the Bay of Pigs prisoners, some Americans who had been living on the island, and about 1,500 Cuban-born U.S. citizens. It cost us about $53 million in medical supplies and food.

CHAPTER ELEVEN

Music, Music, Music:
All That Rock

I can't understand all the fuss over Elvis. I think I have a better voice than he does.
Gladys Presley, Elvis's mother

"I Want to Hold Your Hand"
Song title, John Lennon and Paul McCartney, 1963

About 4:30 one hot summer's afternoon, fifteen-year-old Paul Mc-Cartney heard a group called the Quarrymen* at a garden party at St. Peter's Parish church in Woolton, a suburb of Liverpool, England. It was July 6, 1957,** and the singer-guitarist of the group was six-teen-year-old John Lennon. At the time he was just a bit inebriated, thanks to several beers. The Quarrymen swung into the Del Vikings' "Come Go with Me." Later that day, McCartney joined the group in playing Eddie Cochran's "Twenty Flight Rock." This amazed John Lennon. He was "as good as me." Two weeks afterward Paul joined the band. Later, John and Paul left the Quarrymen to form their own group, Johnny and the Moondogs. Later in the year, Paul's friend and schoolmate George Harrison—he was known as "Little George"—began tagging along on the Moondogs' bookings and oc-casionally filled in on guitar. Soon, the Moondogs renamed them-selves the Silver Beatles. According to Lennon, he had a vision, a strange man rising out of a "flaming table," saying, "You are the Bea-

---

* Named after the Quarry Bank Grammar School.
** Various sources gave a different date for the church garden fete. It may have been in 1955 or in 1956.

tles, with an A." Another version is that the name was a play on Buddy Holly's group the Crickets.

Later they changed the name to simply the "Beatles." The rest, as they say in all the bad movies, is history. When they played their first gig at Liverpool's Casbah, they met their first drummer, Pete Best. It would be August 1962 when John, Paul, and George asked Best to leave, and Ringo Starr* made his debut, replacing Best on drums.

English groups and their groupies were so fiercely loyal that when Best was forced out and Ringo brought in, Best's fans almost rioted, and Beatles manager Brian Epstein** feared for his life.

At the time, John was twenty-two, Paul was twenty, and George was nineteen. Ringo was twenty-three.

In 1963, the Beatles made it to the top of England's *Mersey Beat* poll with "Please Please Me," their first number-one hit. They had four more hits in England that year. Late in the year, America's Capitol Records, which to this point had been only mildly interested in the Beatles, released "I Want to Hold Your Hand," and it was an overnight success, which needless to say made the company sit up and listen. Record company officials weren't the only ones.

"We have a new group who may be visiting America soon," a young Cambridge University don wrote to a friend at the University of California at Berkeley, where he'd just spent a year teaching. The group was worshiped in London, he wrote, "as I think no other entertainer ever has been (I mean that—it's fantastic!). Called The Beatles 4 Kids from Liverpool, rough, cheeky, swingy, very much wartime kids, and full of gutsy energy." It was January 3, 1964, and he was right in his prediction that they'd be coming to America.

In America, rock music changed forever in 1964. On February 7, the Beatles arrived in New York to begin their U.S. tour. An estimated three to five thousand—some say it was closer to ten thousand—screaming young girls were waiting at JFK airport for them. Even the Beatles hadn't expected anything that big.

---

* Ringo had been with the group Rory Storme and the Hurricanes.
** Epstein died in 1967 of an apparent overdose of sleeping pills.

Two days later, they made their American television debut* on *The Ed Sullivan Show,* performing "All My Loving" and "She Loves You" and "I Want to Hold Your Hand." After their *Sullivan Show* appearances, the Beatles rode a wave of chart-busting successes: three number-one songs in rapid succession. On the ninth, they also taped another *Sullivan Show* performance that would be aired later in the month to even more screaming and acclaim, if that was possible. On the eleventh, their Washington, D.C., concert drew seven thousand shouting, shrieking, and screaming fans. In Cleveland, they were so popular that the city's police chief stopped the group's concert, claiming the audience's emotional frenzy posed a health risk. By April, they owned the hit list: Two months after first landing on America's shores, and thanks to four U.S. record companies manufacturing their records, the Beatles singles ranked one through five in sales. In July came their film *A Hard Day's Night.*

Audiences, mainly teenage girls, were thrilled. "Beatlemania" had arrived, and by 1968 they had sold more than $154 million in records.

They were so famous that Beatle John Lennon observed, "We're more popular than Jesus now. I don't know which will go first—rock 'n' roll or Christianity." The comment, it can be said, raised hell.

English groups such as the Beatles, the Rolling Stones, and the Kinks spearheaded what came to be called the "British invasion" of America. Their music was fresh and infectious, and it gave new life to the rebellious side of rock 'n' roll.

The sixties were the Beatles' decade—it began with them and they grew up in it—but not far behind them were the Rolling Stones. The original group of Mick Jagger, Keith Richards, and Brian Jones first got together at a pub called the Bricklayers Arms in late 1961. They shared a taste for rock 'n' roll, rhythm and blues, and almost all things raunchy. During a court hearing about having a nude girl present in his home at a "drug party," Keith Richards said that "We are not old men. We are not concerned with your petty morals which are illegitimate."

---

* Jack Parr had shown film clips of the Beatles on January 3, and they had also been covered by network news.

The Stones, particularly Richards, were fans of fifties rock star Chuck Berry and covered several of his hits, but they remained something of a cult group until the summer of 1965, when their "Satisfaction" was released. It remains a rock classic.

The Stones' raunchiness remained, however, and in 1967, American DJs, rather than play the then-risqué "Let's Spend the Night Together," turned to the record's flip side, and "Ruby Tuesday" became a number-one hit, which proves that sometimes you can't lose for trying.

Even as the Beatles were working their way through U.S. Customs at JFK Airport in February 1964, American boys began combing their fifties-era pompadours into bangs and shaking out their ducktails. Looking back nearly forty years later, the Beatles, their music, and even their longish hair weren't nearly as upsetting as at the time, an uptight society would have us believe. After all, we'd survived Elvis with his sideburns and swivel hips.

Hair. With the growth of hair, it seems, a revolution in the making almost became a revolution in reality. As had Frank Sinatra before them, the Beatles attracted young girls—teeny-boppers they would later be called.* Young boys believed young girls were attracted to the Beatles' long hair, "the guys with the cancerous crew cuts," a disc jockey once called the group. Whether girls really liked the Beatles for their hair didn't matter; boys thought they did, and many boys let their own hair hang down.

For a generation that had grown up with close-cropped locks, this was a major rebellion in itself. And if we could rebel in how long we let our hair grow, we could rebel in other ways, not the least of which was in the form of facial hair. It is not overreaching to say that the Beatles' long hair led the way in the changes in our politics, our attitudes, art, music, the downfall of a president, and even to the loss of a war. All of that, of course, led directly to the way we are today.

---

* As had Sinatra's publicity agents before them, the Beatles' handlers paid some young girls to attend the group's concerts and scream to high heaven whenever the four singer-musicians appeared, sang, breathed, or did anything.

Back in 1960, three friends from Detroit's Brewster Housing Project formed a trio, calling themselves the Primettes—they were supposed to enhance an all-male group known as the Primes—and cut their first record for Motown, "I Want a Guy." The record didn't amount to much and Motown's Berry Gordy insisted that the group change its name. So Diana Ross, Mary Wilson, and Florence Ballard became the Supremes.

Early in 1964, the Supremes recorded a tune rejected by another Motown group, the Marvelettes, and it was big. "Where Did Our Love Go" hit the charts while the Supremes were touring with Dick Clark's Caravan of Stars. By the end of the summer, "Where Did Our Love Go" was number one on the charts and the Supremes were headlining the Caravan of Stars.

The Supremes were the quintessential Motown combination: molded into gaminelike purveyors of soul, wide eyed and breathy. Motown's team of Eddie Holland, Norman Whitfield, and Lamont Dozier transformed, shaped, and taught the Supremes (and almost all of the label's acts) how to dress, walk, talk, and sing.

So molded, the Supremes turned out a series of group hits: "Baby Love," "Stop! In the Name of Love," and "You Keep Me Hanging On."

Along with the Supremes, Motown scored successes with Gladys Knight and the Pips ("I Heard It Through the Grapevine"), Jimmy Ruffin ("What Becomes of the Broken Hearted"), and a group of brothers out of Gary, Indiana, the Jackson Five. For the most part Motown leaned toward singles. And obedience to the Holland-Whitfield-Dozier molding. Motown owner Berry Gordy aimed his artists and groups in the direction of nightclubs and acceptable "family" entertainment.

Robert Allen Zimmerman was born in the small mining town of Hibbing, Minnesota. In high school, he formed a group he called the Golden Chords and tried to imitate Little Richard and Buddy Holly, because, of course, they were among the top performers of the time. He entered the University of Minnesota but dropped out after a year in order to have more time performing at local coffeehouses.

That's just about the time he began replacing his own background with myth. He was, a friend said later, "someone who was continually inventing himself." At different times he claimed to be an orphan from Oklahoma, an itinerant carnival worker, a bass player with Bobby Vee, or Bobby Vee himself. He also changed his name to Bob Dylan, in honor of poet Dylan Thomas.

His new persona in tow, Dylan was singing in Denver's Gilded Garter between bump-and-grind strippers. He found a model in the wandering dustbowl singer Woody Guthrie—"my last idol," Bob Dylan called him, adding, "My future idols will be myself." He hitchhiked to New York in search of Guthrie, who was by then dying of Huntington's disease, and hung around the Greenwich Village folk scene.

His early songs were much in the Woody Guthrie vein: "Talking Bear Mountain," "Picnic Massacre Blues" (from a newspaper item), and "Talking John Birch Paranoid Blues." He took some old folk tunes and gave them more modern lyrics and a more modern sound. He wrote "Blowin' in the Wind," which became a big hit in 1963 when the group Peter, Paul and Mary covered the tune, selling more than 300,000 copies in the first two weeks. The song became the anthem of the protest movement, and Bob Dylan became its hero. When asked, "Which side of the war are you on?" he answered, "Which side can you be on."

Folk singer Joan Baez was already an established protest singer, and she did a lot to boost Dylan during his early career, promoting his songs and sharing concert bills. Together, they became the king and queen of folk music. When Dylan "defected" to rock music, it shattered both Dylan's image and his romance with Baez, which may explain why, although it was held down the road from his place near Woodstock, Bob Dylan didn't show up at Woodstock.

Officially designated the "Woodstock Music and Art Fair: An Aquarian Exposition," Woodstock didn't take place at Woodstock, New York. Originally, it was to have been held at Wallkill, New York, but weeks before the festival was to have taken place the town council enacted an ordinance preventing it from occurring. Then it was moved to Woodstock, scheduled for August 15–16, 1969. Officials at Woodstock refused permission for the event, so festival backers moved it fifty-five miles away to dairy farmer Max Yasgur's thirty-seven-acre alfalfa field near Bethel, paying him fifty thousand dollars.

They'd expected about 50,000 people over the three days of the event, but some 450,000 people—mostly white, mostly young, mostly middle class—crowded the farm. For the next three days the crowd—in numbers larger, for example, than Charlotte, North Carolina (441,297), and only a bit smaller than Cleveland (498,246)—shuffled through incessant rain. The alfalfa field quickly became a quagmire inhabited by uninhibited counterculture elements and would-be denizens of the counterculture. "Everyone swam nude in the [farm's] lake," a journalist wrote. "Balling [that is, having sex] was easier than getting breakfast, and the 'pigs' [the police] just smiled and passed out the oats." When local police didn't try to stop crowd members from doing just about anything they wanted to do, the participants established their own culture with their own rules, rituals, costumes, and standards of behavior. The counterculture blossomed. As singer Janis Joplin said, "We used to think of ourselves as little clumps of weirdos, but now we're a whole new minority."

Inadequate food, water, and toilet facilities, mounds of garbage, drugs virtually there for the taking, nudity, and nonstop sex, that's what Woodstock was made of. That and music by such performers as Santana, Jefferson Airplane, Ravi Shankar, Jimi Hendrix, Joan Baez, Arlo Guthrie, and the Grateful Dead. Blood, Sweat and Tears; Crosby, Stills, Nash & Young; Sly and the Family Stone. Sha-Na-Na, Johnny Winter, Canned Heat, Joe Crocker, Country Joe McDonald and the Fish, the Who, and many more. There were, however, many other performers who weren't there, not least the Beatles, the Rolling Stones, Bob Dylan, Simon and Garfunkel, the Doors, Stevie Wonder, and Led Zeppelin.

At one point, there'd been a twenty-mile-long traffic jam along Highway 17B as people tried to get in; a traffic jam without road rage. It was the worst traffic jam in New York's history, but seldom did stalled motorists resort to honking their car horns. Instead, they took out their guitars and tambourines and played and sang. They shared food and drink and drugs.

When their cars and vans could no longer move along the roads, they abandoned them. The crowds pushed up against the fences until the fences gave way, and then pushed on in. Most of those who attended the festival didn't pay the original six-dollars-per-day[*] price, or any other price for that matter. Ticket takers eventually gave up the effort, which may explain why some uncut tickets to the three-day event today go as memorabilia for as much as a thousand dollars each.

Despite all of this, the audience seemed to have a good weekend, and there was very little trouble. There were some instances of drug overdose. Police reports claim that three festivalgoers died, but almost as an offset two babies were born during the weekend.

Arthur Vassmer, a shopkeeper in Bethel who lived through Woodstock, said that he learned one thing from the three-day festival:

> If you ever hear of anybody that ever has a Woodstock or festival like that, remember one thing you want to buy: peanut butter and jelly. That's the first thing I run out of. I should have put fifty cases of peanut butter and fifty cases of jelly. I found out later that peanut butter is very good for you.

Today, thousands claim Woodstock gave them a "totally different outlook on life." It was "three days of peace and music," a "total experience," "a happening," days and nights of "heady music and of sometimes headier marijuana."

Once inside Max Yasgur's field, the crowd pitched tents and tepees and settled in for the duration. For as far as the eye could see, there was nothing but young people "walking, lying down, drinking, eating, reading, singing." They slept in the open and made love in the open. They waded and swam in the marshes. Some of them even tried to milk Yasgur's cows. "We were exhilarated," a member of the audience known as the "Woodstock Nation" remembered.

---

* That was six dollars for advance tickets. Later, the price changed to seven dollars per day and, finally, to eight dollars for the final group of tickets printed.

By the end of the sixties, rock 'n' roll's upbeat tunes had given way to the harder-edged, more political music now called simply "rock." From the hoarse folk-rock ballads of Bob Dylan to the acid-tinged fantasies of Jimi Hendrix and the Grateful Dead, songwriters and singers expressed the turbulence of the times.

By the seventies, rock had spun off into the heavy metal music of Iron Maiden and Def Leppard, the defiant lyrics of punk bands the Clash and the Ramones. Yet, James Taylor and Billy Joel crooned to stadiums filled with swooning fans.

The fifties rhythm-and-blues shows with B. B. King and Bo Diddley changed in the eighties and grew into Broadway-like concerts with props, lights, costumes, dance, and smoke machines. A glittering one-gloved Michael Jackson did the moonwalk; Madonna, in a metal-bra, starred in slick, sex-based productions.

Where have all the Buddy Hollys gone? When did Little Richard and his "Tutti Frutti" turn sour? Sheer talent and sheer manic energy.

CHAPTER TWELVE

Sixties Women:
Beyond the Pill

Join the union, girls, and together say, "Equal Pay for Equal Work."
Susan Brownell Anthony, The Revolution, March 18, 1869

No girl child born today should responsibly be brought up to be a housewife. Too much has been made of defining human personality and destiny in terms of the sex organ. After all, we share the human brain.
Betty Friedan, 1968

On January 9, 1965, American men went into mourning. The pretty girl we'd grown up with had developed (in more ways than one) into a beautiful young woman, and that talented and intelligent young lady had just gotten married: Annette Funicello.

When she was just thirteen years old, she'd joined cartoonist, theme-park entrepreneur, and television producer Walt Disney's TV series, *The Mickey Mouse Club*. Annette hardly needed, and on the show didn't use, her last name. Undoubtedly, she helped the show to become a success, and undoubtedly, the show boosted her to stardom. At one point, she was receiving more than a thousand letters a week, mainly from young boys who were in love with her and young girls who wanted to emulate her.

After her *Mickey Mouse Club* debut, Annette recorded the first of her seventeen albums and her first single hit, "Tall Paul." In addition to the TV show, Annette made several movies for Disney, including *Babes in Toyland* in 1961. And then came a string of non-Disney features—the beach party series, everything from *Beach Party* to *Muscle Beach Party* to *How to Stuff a Wild Bikini*. Interestingly enough, Annette herself didn't wear a bikini during her movies. Even though he had nothing to do with the films, Walt Disney asked her not to wear something so revealing, and Annette decided to do the movies

in swimsuits that certainly showed off her grown-up Mousketeer figure but weren't as skimpy as the ones others in the cast wore.

There was, however, trouble in Annette's better-than-reality Hollywood life. During her less-than-award-winning, but mainly successful, movie career Annette Funicello began to feel symptoms of
what eventually was diagnosed as multiple sclerosis. Still, she continued working. By 1987, Annette was mainly doing TV commercials.
It was, she says, her peanut-butter-makin'-mom career period.

Annette's multiple sclerosis continued its inexorable downward
course until, whenever she'd be seen in public, she was either in a
wheelchair or in a motorized cart. But the spirit that Walt Disney had
first seen in Annette forty-five years earlier continued to burn
brightly.

In 1890, the U.S. census department listed 124 women engineers
and surveyors. It also listed 217 women company executives, 1,143
women clergy, 60 blacksmiths, 24 cabinetmakers, and one woman
wheelwright. By 1907, according to Lydia Kingsmill Commander in
The American Idea, the number included "946 commercial travelers,
261 wholesale merchants, 1,271 officials of banks, 100 lumber-
men"—notice that she doesn't go into "lumberwomen," "lumber-
persons," or "lumberjills," since there was no such thing as political
correctness at the time—"113 woodchoopers, 84 civil engineers and
surveyors"—that's down from the 1890 figure—"1,932 stock raisers,
143 marble cutters, 595 butchers . . . 10 wheelwrights, 8 steam boil-
ermakers, 2 roofers and slaters, 1 well-borer, and a licensed pilot on
the Mississippi." While the list might seem long, you have to realize
that this is just about it. Women could also be schoolteachers or
nurses. A few were physicians.

More than half of America's workforce today is made up of
women; however, the number of occupations they hold down is still
limited. Seventy-five percent of all employed women work in some
twenty occupations, eighty percent of whose workers are women.
Which may or may not include wheelwrights.

With a grant from Planned Parenthood, Drs. Gregory Pincus,
John Rock, and M. C. Chang began work on an oral contraceptive.
Five years later they began large-scale field tests in Puerto Rico and
Haiti, and on May 9, 1960, the Food and Drug Administration

(FDA) approved Enovid 10, the Pill, as an oral contraceptive.* They cost fifty-five cents each.

On November 17, 1965, after reviewing 175 cases, the FDA said that it could find no evidence that birth-control pills cause blood clotting. Later, however, the FDA asked birth-control-pill manufacturers to add a printed warning to the package, telling users of possible health risks. Meanwhile, evidence continued to mount that oral contraceptives increased the danger of blood clots. And in 1970, ten years after the FDA first said the Pill was safe to use, the agency issued a warning to more than 350,000 physicians about the risks associated with birth-control pills.

Warning or not, within two years of its introduction, 1.2 million American women were on the Pill; within five years the number was up to 5 million, and by 1973, about 10 million women were using oral contraceptives. Today about 10.4 million American women are on the Pill.

It's estimated that more than a third of all American women in their early twenties take oral contraceptives. At least 45 million American women have used the Pill at some point—seventy-four percent of all women. That's about eighty-two percent of all American women now alive who've ever had sex.

The Planned Parenthood Federation of America, which after all had funded the original work on the Pill, remains firmly in favor of it. "Birth control in general," says association president Gloria Feldt, "and the pill in particular, is the most profound advance in social justice and gender equality ever in history." She adds that "When a woman can control her own fertility, she . . . can determine the course of the rest of her life."

Others agree and say that if it weren't for the Pill, the women's liberation movement itself likely would have faltered.** The Pill be-

---

* Earlier, Enovid 10 had been prescribed for "female disorders."
** There's the story, true as it turns out, that in the seventies, a group of Scots were holding a festival in Chicago, and early in the morning of festival day a group of kilt-wearing men were walking through the Grant Park. A Scotsmen unwittingly wakened a homeless man who had not yet recovered from a night of cheap wine. The man roused himself, saw the kilted Scotsmen, and muttered aloud, "Damned women's libbers."

came the "holy grail" of sixties feminists. For one thing, it allowed women to complete their education before having children; I'll finish med school (or law school or whatever) and then have children, was the thought for many women. By 1970, the number of women entering medical and law schools began to climb, and for the first time, women made up ten percent of first-year law students; by 1980, that was up to thirty-eight percent. With a fairly reliable method of birth control, women also began marrying later.

The Pill, however, carried with it several problems, not the least of which was the possible danger to the user's health. In 1968, Pope Paul issued an encyclical upholding the Catholic Church's prohibition against artificial contraception, which is not to say many Catholics didn't use (or don't use today) some form of "artificial birth control." In fact, at the time of the pope's anti-birth-control encyclical, a majority papal commission report recommended birth-control methods be left to the consciences of married couples. A Gallup poll at the time showed that fifty-four percent of American Catholics opposed the encyclical, while just twenty-eight percent approved.

Widespread use of the Pill brought about some not-so-widespread instances of promiscuity, which helped increase the number of people contracting STDs, sexually transmitted diseases. The Pill not only increased sexual activity, it probably increased the number of partners, for both men and women. In other words, the Pill fired the first round in the sexual revolution. Both women and men developed a more open attitude toward sex. They could enjoy sexual relationships in a far different and, as it turned out, more open manner. It changed the nature of male-female relationships, making them more equal.

One thought that pushed the Pill's acceptance was that it allowed women to control their own bodies, no longer having to rely on men for contraception. But why, some women now ask, should *they* be the ones who have to worry about taking a pill every morning, or using a diaphragm or a cervical cap, or whatever? Why shouldn't *men* have to take a pill? A quick answer: Who's going to trust a guy you just met at a singles bar who says, Sure, I'm on the Pill.

Today, the Pill is the most popular form of contraception in America. The second most popular: surgery. Health officials don't consider condoms a form of birth control, but rather a method of trying to control sexually transmitted diseases.

A hundred years ago the concept of sexual politics would have been unthinkable, and today the idea of a "sexual revolution" may even appear laughable, the stuff of comics and late night TV. But just as the sixties were a time of antiwar protests they were also a time of rallies against sexual discrimination. In the same year that Enovid 10 first went on the market, the courts ruled that D. H. Lawrence's novel *Lady Chatterley's Lover* could be sold in America.

Meanwhile, some Marxist psychiatrists blamed the problem of sexual repression of the masses on their old enemy capitalism. Capitalism, Herbert Marcuse and William Reich argued, demanded self-restraint and compulsive work, both of which were antithetical to liberated and spontaneous sexual expression. The bourgeoisie had forged an identity around the confinement of sexuality "within the private domain of the heterosexual family." The permissive "swinging sixties" became a metaphor for contemporary social conflict.

What just as likely really happened was that people had grown tired of the old sexual repression. The Pill was readily available. In the 1960s the relations between men and women shifted. What once had been considered pornography entered mass media, and sexuality became both political and open.

It had been coming for a long time. A famous case in Puritan colonial Massachusetts involved a wife who admitted in court that she'd taken a lover. She justified her behavior by saying that her husband spent so much time hunting and fishing that he'd neglected his conjugal duties. The court sentenced both her and her lover to time in the public stocks. Ordered to occupy the stocks right beside them was the woman's husband, who, the court ruled, had clearly driven her to it.

With more free time and more places outside the home in which to spend that free time, the sexual revolution took off. Enclosed cars—and a lot more of us had cars in the 1960s than at any previous point in our history—gave us a "home away from home" in which to indulge in and enjoy sex. In earlier days, reproductive and productive activity took place in the same setting: the home.

Generally, the only time you had your own home was after you got married.

Often in the 1950s the so-called "natural response" by good girls was, to use a much later phrase, "just say no." However, even then things were changing. During the fifties, for example, all but two states dropped their bans on contraceptive information or devices. Abortion in America remained illegal until 1973, when the U.S. Supreme Court ruled in *Roe v. Wade* that unrestricted first-trimester abortion was a constitutional right in the United States. Which is not to say abortions weren't being performed before then. More than a quarter million illegal abortions were performed each year during the fifties and sixties, causing forty percent of all maternal deaths.

Truly, as singer Bob Dylan put it in 1964, "The times they are a-changin'." In the fifties, good girls "just said no." In the sixties, the Pill brought on the sexual revolution, which brought on a perceived need for legal abortion, which wouldn't be available for several more years. At the same time, many men no longer believed they had to participate in contraception, men who had grown accustomed to the freedom of sex and unaccustomed to using old-fashion "rubbers"—again, these weren't your father's overshoes—which brought a resurgence of sexually transmitted diseases, which showed up in Vietnam when VD blossomed. Penicillin, which came into wide use in World War II, might not take care of VD or STD. But as a favorite sixties character used to say, "What, me worry?"

Sex, in any position, in any form, was good; denial was bad. And the sexual revolution spread, from youthful flower children to middle-class and working-class America. "Free love" was in town and ready to play. "Wife swapping" became a suburban diversion, and both men and women, who until then had been resigned to sexual disappointment, went looking for exotic adventures and sexual fulfillment outside marriage. Divorce rates soared. The federal courts, citing free speech as outlined in the First Amendment, allowed pornography. No longer did young boys have to turn to the pages of *National Geographic* magazine to see bare breasts; we could buy—perhaps we had to buy it under the counter, but still we bought them—magazines with wall-to-wall boobs, butts, and articles about the good life. The Hollywood movie industry got in on the revolution and gave "mature" audiences films filled with what once had been "obscene" language and, of course, nudity. In 1968, Hollywood adopted a rating system that included "R" (restricted) for obscenity and bare breasts and "X" for downright explicit sex acts.

Marilyn Monroe, who knew a thing or two about the subject, said that "When I started modeling, [having sex] was like part of the job. All the girls did it." As she put it, "It wasn't any big dramatic tragedy. Nobody ever got cancer from sex."

In 1963, housewife and freelance magazine writer Betty Friedan wrote an article for *McCall's* magazine, based on answers she'd received from a questionnaire to her fellow Smith College alumni, class of 1942. The questionnaire had raised more questions than it answered. Education hadn't prepared the women for the roles in life they seemingly were expected to play—keep a good house for their husbands, raise bright and healthy children, breast-feed the youngest while dusting and mopping. But was it the education that was inappropriate, or women's roles that were wrong?

The male publisher of *McCall's*, Friedan remembered years later, believed that her interpretation of the questionnaire answers was wrong. Despite some underground efforts by female editors at the magazine, *McCall's* rejected the article. *Ladies' Home Journal* bought it, but when Friedan saw how the magazine's editors had rewritten and changed what she'd been trying to say, she took back the article. She tried it with a third women's magazine, *Redbook*, but the editor there said that "Betty has gone off her rocker." Friedan's article, the editor said, "threatened the very foundations of the women's magazine world—the feminine mystique." Friedan believed that "I and every other woman I knew had been living a lie, and all the doctors who treated us and the experts who studied us were perpetuating that lie." Women's lives, she believed, "were built around that lie."

That's when Betty Friedan expanded her ideas into a book, a bestselling book, as it turned out, *The Feminine Mystique*. In it, she protested sexual inequality, referring to it as "A Problem That Had No Name."

If women were really people—no more, no less—then all the things that kept them from being full people in our society would have to be changed. And women, once they broke through the feminine mystique and took themselves seriously as people, would see their place on a false pedestal, even their glorification as sex objects, for the putdown it was.

Meanwhile, magazine articles continued to tell American men "How to Manage a Woman." Television sitcoms gave us a father who knew best, and the elections in the fifties gave us a father figure in the White House. In a way, we gave ourselves Ozzie Nelson, a bemused father who apparently never held a job that entailed his going beyond the family's driveway.

Twenty-one-year-old singer Connie Francis had two of the top "popular" songs in 1960: "My Heart Has a Mind of Its Own" and "Everybody's Somebody's Fool."* Later that year she made her movie debut in the teen hit *Where the Boys Are*. Which gave her yet another hit, the title song.

Other newcomers in the movie included leggy Paula Prentiss, blond Dolores Hart (her character fell for a strangely non-sun-tanned George Hamilton IV), and gangly Jim Hutton. The plot was simple: Four Midwest college girls (yes, it's politically correct in 1960 to call them "girls," just as it was politically correct to call female college students "coeds," which today isn't advisable) drove down to Fort Lauderdale, Florida, for spring break. Thousands of college students, they'd been told, would crowd the beach and there would be lots of beer and good times. It would be a relatively peaceful and proper vacation.

So, these four girls were driving down to Florida when they picked up hitchhiking Jim Hutton, which of course would never happen in the twenty-first century to motorists who are afraid to pick up anybody, hitchhikers who are afraid to be picked up, and it's difficult stopping for anyone when you're zooming along an in-

---

* Connie Francis had been around since 1958, and in 1959 had the hit song "My Happiness."

terstate highway. Not to mention the illegality of it all in many states these days.

So, these four girls rented a by-the-week motel room, which was much larger and cleaner than you can get for the equivalent price today. Not to mention that, by the end of the movie, the population of the room had increased about fourfold.

The second day there, the girls sat around the motel swimming pool talking about their lives. The beach was nearby, but even in 1960 it was crowded. Twenty thousand boys and girls would be there! they exclaimed. Too crowded to see the sun, much less get the requisite and politically correct suntan.

Already, the girls had been propositioned by college boys who, much as they do today, considered it their social obligation to bed any and all young ladies they could.

However: This was 1960, and "good girls" didn't do that sort of thing. Well, maybe, but one of the four actually "did it," which of course was part of the plot, girls trying too hard to satisfy their own desire to be popular by satisfying the boys' lust.

Long and leggy Paula Prentiss had been propositioned by tall and gangly Jim Hutton, but of course, she'd turned him down. Oh, she approved of sex, but it had to occur *after* marriage. In fact, she wanted to be a "baby machine," she said, with infants popping out early and often.

And as the sun slowly sets over lovely Fort Lauderdale, we leave *Where the Boys Are.* It is, perhaps, a morality play of the early sixties. By the end of the decade, not only did college-age boys and girls become "men and women," not only did spring break madness move on to Myrtle Beach and Padre Island, not only did such rites of spring become known for wild times, wild people, and even wilder drugs, but the whole morality issue changed. It's doubtful today that any group of young ladies sit around a pool or anywhere else proclaiming that "Good girls don't do it." Certainly you're not likely to find anyone who admits she wants to be a "baby machine."

In the fifties, as one veteran of the decade put it, "The only thing that mattered was if you could get a date with a football player." Then things changed. The sexual revolution happened. Young people began refusing merely to accept the values of their elders. Where mom and dad had necked (and sometimes "gone all the way") in the back-seat of a car, somewhere in the sixties unmarried couples began living together. Openly.

Somewhere in the 1960s, young people heard talk about what newspaper columnist Abigail van Buren referred to as "brotherhood and equality and justice," and they wanted to "live what they have been taught." As the counterculture phrase had it, they wanted to do their own thing.

The feminist movement was more than just sex in the sixties, and it was far from a total success. The decade brought changes in politics, war, health, racial relations, and education, but it didn't bring about equality between the sexes. For instance, in 1960, Michigan State University officials expelled a female student because she'd been raped—she had, officials claimed, "asked for it." Two years later, a Stanford University couple both drank hard at a fraternity party, then both passed out on the frat-house lawn; he was suspended from school for a quarter; she was suspended for two quarters, twice as long, because she had "left herself defenseless in the presence of a male."

On March 9, 1960, Hollywood released the movie *Can-Can*, and although it was neither a financial nor a critical success it did get world attention in a special way. During the filming of the movie, Soviet premier Nikita Khrushchev was touring the United States, and he visited the *Can-Can* set. Things were going well as dancers Shirley MacLaine and Juliet Prowse rehearsed the leg-kicking, skirt-lifting, pulse-raising, riotous title-song dance. Nikita seemed to have a smile on his face, which wasn't surprising given the nature of the dance and the attributes of Prowse and MacLaine.

"Immoral!" Nikita declared. It seems he thought their legs had kicked too high and their skirts had been lifted too far. Entirely too riotous for the Kremlin, no doubt. One wonders, however, if Mrs. Khrushchev hadn't been along, what would have happened to Nikita's pulse?

Just as blacks tried to tear down the hierarchy and privilege of race in the sixties, so did women. However, in many ways women weren't as successful in getting equality. African American women, for example, often sided more with African American men than they did with women of any race; many felt they had to secure their freedom as a people before they could worry about getting freedom as a sex.

For others, the "New Feminism" was the most significant movement of the sixties. At the beginning of the decade, so-called "traditional" feminism consisted of Donna Reed in high heels and pearls pushing a vacuum cleaner around an already perfect home while husband Alex Stone (he was a pediatrician) was off somewhere making money for Donna and all the little Stones.

The sixties began fewer than twenty years after the Great Depression ended, and many women remembered the insecurities of that time. They had, at the least, read about global war, looked around at them at the growing financial affluence, and said, What the hell am I doing?

More and more women in the 1960s began to examine their lives, but as singer Peggy Lee asked, "Is that all there is?" In 1961, as much to placate leading Democratic women as anything else, President Kennedy created a Commission on the Status of Women and appointed former first lady Eleanor Roosevelt to chair it. Mrs. Roosevelt was one of the leading feminists of her time. The commission's report demanded an end to job and legal discrimination against women, and feminists cheered. The Roosevelt report also acknowledged "the fundamental responsibility" of women to remain "mothers and housewives," which didn't sit too well with the New Feminists.

But along comes Betty Friedan and her *Feminine Mystique* in 1963 and the formation of NOW, the National Organization for Women, in 1966. NOW members dedicated themselves to changing "the false image of women now prevalent in the mass media, and in the texts, ceremonies, laws, and practices of our major social institutions." By the end of the year, NOW counted three hundred charter members—Friedan was its first president—and by the end of the decade, that number was up to eight thousand.

With the possible, only possible, exceptions of the civil rights and antiwar movements, nothing has so fundamentally altered American life as has the women's rights movement. It has changed the way America works, lives, loves, and plays. It has changed marriage and family life, the way we make babies—well, *if or when* we make babies—the way we educate ourselves and our children, and even the way we govern ourselves. There remains a wide gap in salaries, a wide gap (called the corporate glass ceiling by some) in the heights to which men and women can rise in business, and a wide gap in government. The White House, U.S. Supreme Court, and Congress basically remain largely male, middle aged, white, and wealthy. Other nations, from Great Britain to India to Israel, have elected women as leaders of their government. About the closest America came was in 1984 when Democrat Walter Mondale chose Geraldine Ferraro as his vice-presidential running mate. The Mondale-Ferraro ticket, however, lost by almost 17 million votes to Ronald Reagan and George Bush.

NOW was a liberal reform organization when it began in the mid-sixties—founder Betty Friedan said that "this is not a bedroom war. This is a political movement"—but by the end of the decade more radical groups emerged, led by younger women. Liberation for their sex, rather than reform of the nation's laws, became the core of their demands. And in 1970, Kate Millett brought out her best-selling *Sexual Politics*, arguing that sexuality is deeply political, and warned that conventional sexual relationships of the time failed to recognize the rights of women.

Women may or may not have helped their cause in 1968 when they held "braless" days in several American cities. A group of feminists protested the Miss America pageant by throwing bras, girdles, hair curlers, and copies of *Cosmopolitan* magazine into a "Freedom Trash Can." That brought about stories that the protestors "burned their bras." They didn't, but from then on the public mistakenly identified the women's liberation movement as "bra burners."

Diana Dwan Poole didn't do much bra burning in 1969. Born in the small town of Benton Harbor, Michigan, she was an army nurse with the 67th Evacuation Hospital at Qui Nhon in Vietnam. It shocked the hell out of her, as it would have shocked the hell out of just about anyone. "I was head nurse in casualty receiving and triage," she remembered, "and that was bad." They had "casualties right off the field, still in uniforms, handing me their boots saying, M'am, my foot is in there, could you sew it back on, and it was, and we did, we sewed it back on." Diana "remembered them all, believe me." This one soldier

said Promise me I'm not going to die. I never lied to them. If they were going to die, I told them, because, if you're going to die, and all, you don't need somebody lying to you. . . .

See, I was twenty-three, and they were like nineteen, so they were my brother's age, my real brother's age. They were all my brothers. . . .

I saw a lot of them die, and none of them were easy, but believe me, they are in a better place than I am right now. . . .

Often, she remembered, in Vietnam "We had red alert sirens going and I'd dive underneath my bed and slag out my flak jacket, put it on, and head to the hospital because if there was a red alert we were going to get patients."

Like many men who served in Vietnam, Diana had a hard time adjusting to life back in America. And men who'd served there caused a lot of her problems; it was, they believed, a "man's war." Long after the war, she was wearing one of her old uniform shirts when she was stopped by a man. "What are you doing wearing that shirt?" he asked. "You didn't earn it." She told him to look at the label: "One Each OD, Women's Size Small, and I don't think it would fit you. I earned it all right." So the man said, "Well, there weren't any women over there." And Diana answered, "You're right, we were little girls, we weren't women."

Nineteen sixty-eight may easily be designated one of the weirdest in history. Okay, if not weird, how about portentous—that is, "as exciting wonder and awe."

A forty-year-old "singer" who said, "I really believe I'm nineteen," appeared on television and called himself "Tiny Tim," his long fuzzy hair down to his shoulders and wearing what we'd later designate as a "nerdy" outfit, including orange socks and a plaid shirt. He played a left-handed ukelele and sang "Tip-toe Through the Tulips with Me" in a falsetto voice, because, he claimed, God inspired him to do it that way. He quickly became a cult hero, and his album sold 150,000 copies in the first fifteen weeks. The following year Tiny Tim and a seventeen-year-old woman he called "Miss Vicky" were married before some 48 million television viewers on *The Tonight Show*. Tim and Miss Vicky divorced five years later.

In 1968, John Lennon and Yoko Ono recorded an album together, then posed nude for the cover. The album was banned.

Sales exploded for the classic book *I Ching* or the *Book of Changes*, about Oriental theology, religion, sorcery, witchcraft, Zen, and magic. Its most popular edition, a scholarly version out of Princeton University Press, went from selling about a thousand books a year to fifty thousand. Obviously, buyers thought it outlined something more than just fun and games.

The off-Broadway musical *Hair* billed itself as "the first tribal-love-rock musical." *Hair* had its origins in New York's hip East Village, which, as the song says, was "what's happening." The show opened on April 29, 1968, and first ran for 1,742 performances, thanks to a favorable review by *New York Times* critic Clive Barnes, who called it "the frankest show in town . . . the first Broadway musical in some time to have the authentic voice of today rather than the day before yesterday." Opening with the cast dispersed throughout the theater—in balconies, on ramps, climbing the catwalks, in the orchestra, and a few even on stage—*Hair* shocked some people with its songs called "Sodomy," "Colored Spade," and "The Bed"—and surprised others with "Aquarius"—the 5th Dimension turned it and "Let the Sunshine In" into major hits the following year—and the title song, "Hair."

Rock ballrooms were the big thing in 1968, including the Fillmore in San Francisco, Fillmore East in New York, Boston Tea Party in Boston, and Kinetic Playground in Chicago. By the end of the century—gone, all gone.

In 1968, for the first time, a woman (Ruth Eisemann-Schier) appeared on the FBI's Ten Most Wanted list.

In 1968, Valerie Solanis, a bit player in Andy Warhol's movies, used a .32-caliber revolver to shoot the man who's been called the father of pop art, hitting Warhol twice in the stomach. Andy lived. Back in 1961, an art dealer had advised Warhol to paint what was important to him. Because the artist ate a can of soup every day, he stenciled rows of Campbell's soup cans. It was one of his most successful works.

He later did silk screens of paper money, Coke bottles, Elvis Presley, and Marilyn Monroe. In 1963, his paintings were featured at New York's Guggenheim Museum, and the *New York Times* asked, "What is it?" Warhol surrounded himself with the so-called "beautiful people" and, in the catalog of his 1968 exhibition in Stockholm, predicted that "in the future, everyone will be famous for fifteen minutes."

Warhol was lying in a hospital bed, recovering from five hours of surgery after being shot by Valerie Solanis, when he heard about Robert Kennedy's death. More or less heard. A television was going somewhere, he remembered, he heard "the words "Kennedy" and "assassin" and "shot" over and over again. He didn't understand that it was Robert Kennedy—"I just thought that maybe after you die, they rerun things for you, like President Kennedy's assassination."

As for Valerie Solanis, who gained her fifteen minutes by trying to kill Warhol, Andy said he remembered her talking "constantly about the complete elimination of the male sex," that the result would be an "out-of-sight, groovy, all-female world." She was the founder of SCUM (Society for Cutting Up Men).

In 1968, Greek multimillionaire Aristotle Onassis proposed to former first lady Jackie Kennedy. She'd once said that "I can't really marry a dentist from New Jersey." As John Kennedy's widow, she received $175,000 a year from his family, a $10,000 annual government pension, and protection by the Secret Service. She'd lose all of that if she married Onassis, so on her behalf Teddy Kennedy went to Athens to negotiate a prenuptial settlement. The agreement came to something like, $3 million up front in cash and the annual interest on a $1 million trust for each of her two children until they reached twenty-one.

Onassis asked Lynn Alpha Smith, his secretary, if she thought $3 million was too much. "Hell, no," Smith replied. "You can buy a supertanker on that, but then you have to pay fuel, maintenance, insurance, and a lot of extras." So the deal was okayed, and from then on Onassis's office staff referred to Jackie as "Supertanker." As in "It's Supertanker on the phone."

• In 1968, the American Medical Association (AMA) formulated a new standard of death: "brain death."

• In 1968, Simon and Garfunkel won a Grammy award for "Mrs. Robinson," theme song of the movie *The Graduate.*
• In 1968, a Florida heiress left $450,000 to 150 stray dogs.
• And in 1968, U.S. troop strength in Vietnam reached 540,000, and the Vietnam War became the longest war in U.S. history.

In 1964, a young singer named Cherilyn Sarkisian began her musical career. Using the name Bonnie Jo Mason she recorded the little-heard and easily forgotten songs "Ringo, I Love You" and "Beatle Blues." When they didn't do much for her career, Bonnie teamed up with a short singer/songwriter and they called themselves "Caesar and Cleo," the act's name an attempt to capitalize on the uproar over Liz Taylor and Richard Burton's *Cleopatra* film. Well, Caesar and Cleo didn't make it, or at least the name didn't. Bonnie, however, for a long while kept the Cleopatra-style bangs and let her hair hang down.

In 1965, the duo came up with a hit, "I Got You, Babe," just about the time Caesar and Cleo changed their names to Sonny and Cher. For Cher, at least, as their 1967 song said, "The beat goes on."

On February 19, 1962, a seventy-nine-year-old Greek-born researcher named George Papanicolaou died. Back in 1928, when Papanicolaou was only forty-five, he'd discovered a test for uterine cancer. It didn't gain clinical acceptance until 1943, when information about the test was written up in a medical journal. Since then, scientists claim that it's saved thousands of lives. The test is the pap smear, and who knows how many more might have been saved if it had been available earlier.

As for Papanicolaou, most medical students even today don't recognize his name. The study of medicine is a technical education, no matter that physicians sometimes speak of it as the "art of medicine." Unlike other, more liberal arts fields, it doesn't inculate knowledge for the sake of knowledge. Physicians and nurses learn what a pap smear is, but they don't learn and don't care who George Papanicolaou was. After all, all he did was invent the damn test.

Meanwhile, a second, more insidious, process was at work. Over the years, much of the research in medicine was done by men, for men, and tested on men. White men, at that. Forget the fact that George's smear test is used in diagnosing a woman's disease. Just get on with it. All of this began changing in the 1960s, but the acceptance of women in medical research had a long, long way to go.

Back in the 1940s, scientist Percy LeBaron Spencer, of the Raytheon Company, discovered the microwave oven. What Spencer actually discovered was that microwave signals had melted a chocolate bar he had in his pocket. In 1947, at the thirty-second National Hotel Exposition, Raytheon introduced the microwave oven based on Spencer's candy-bar accident. Raytheon planned to rent the ovens to catering services at five dollars a day. Others, about the size of a refrigerator, were to be sold for use on trains and ocean liners. The cost: $3,000.

In 1967, the Amana Company introduced the first home microwave oven. It was about the size of a room air conditioner and cost $475. Leftovers would never be the same. Not to be beaten, and to assure that we didn't just "zap" leftovers, to promote its own line of microwave ovens the Litton Company brought out Stouffer's line of frozen foods. That way we could toss away our previously cooked food and start out fresh with previously cooked food. Truly, we've come a long way.

After all, the sixties was when a great flood of "labor-saving devices" began arriving to free housewives of their daily toil.

To understand how it all worked, you have to remember that in the 1960s most scientists—like most medical researchers—were men. So while they were saving housewives a bit of labor, they were saving husbands' labor as well. Take two items that came to popularity in the sixties: dishwashers and garbage disposal units. Up until then it was seen as a husband's job to dry the dishes that his wife had washed. Dishwashers, of course, were also dish *dryers*, so hubby got out of the job. However, no matter what manufacturers claim, even today you have to prewash dishes before putting them into the dishwasher, so the woman's work truly continued.

Another of the husband's jobs was to take out the garbage. Disposal units reduce that task. So who really benefited from the new technology?

We think of the sixties as a time of liberation for women, and to an extent they were. But women had (and still have) a long way to go, in some cases just to get back where they were. For instance, in 1955 thirty-eight percent of American women worked outside the home. Their work, however, remained the "traditional" jobs for women: schoolteachers, secretaries, and nurses. Relatively more women earned college degrees in the thirties than they did in the fifties. In 1930 two out of five bachelor's and master's degrees were awarded to women, and one out of seven doctorates. By 1962 the figures had dropped to one in three and one in ten. In 1879, thirty-eight percent of all college and university teachers were women, but by 1959 they accounted for only twenty percent.

The fifties' image of a woman was young and frivolous and almost childlike. She was fluffy and feminine and passive. She was content in a world of bedroom and kitchen, of sex and babies and home. The sixties began to change all that. A cigarette commercial said, "You've come a long way, baby," but truly you've a long way to go.

In 1965, a study indicated that the average stay-at-home housewife worked about fifty hours a week—half on child care and half on housekeeping. Trouble is, that's about the same amount of work that housewives put in back in 1912. The big difference between 1912 and 1965 wasn't in how *much* work a housewife did but in *who* did the work. In 1912, even moderately affluent middle-class housewives had at least one servant to help her do the laundry and get dinner on the table. In the 1960s, thanks to those "labor-saving devices," the servants were gone and she did most of the work herself. With, of course, the help of her new microwave oven.

Husbands help around the home. But not much. A 1983 study showed that, on average, husbands whose wives worked outside the home contributed ten minutes more a day to housework than husbands whose wives stay at home. Glad we got our priorities straight.

In 2000, a United Nations report cited 80 million unwanted pregnancies and 20 million unsafe abortions. It also reported on millions of beatings and rapes and infanticides and "honor" killings of women. Discrimination and violence against women "remain firmly rooted in cultures around the world." "Passed down from one generation to the next," the report said, "ideas about 'real men' and 'a woman's place' are instilled at an early age and are difficult to change."

Only fifty-three percent of births in developing countries are attended by professionals, which translates into the "neglect of 52.4 million women annually." About 50 million abortions are performed annually, of which about 20 million are unsafe and result in the deaths of 78,000 women and the suffering of millions more.

At least 60 million young girls, mostly in Asia, are listed as "missing" as a result of infanticide and neglect: "As many as 5,000 women and girls are murdered each year in so-called 'honor' killings by members of their own families."

Come a long way? Well, maybe not.

CHAPTER THIRTEEN

High Ole Times:
"Blowing in the Wind"

If you're going to San Francisco, be sure to wear some flowers in your hair.
John Phillips, song lyric

You will see something new.
Two things. And I call them
Thing One and Thing Two.
Dr. Seuss (Theodor Seuss Geisel), *The Cat in the Hat* (1957)

An old formula had it that: "Beats + LSD = Counterculture." The Beats, or the Beat Generation, surfaced shortly after World War II in New York's Greenwich Village and San Francisco's Barbary Coast. In the fearful 1950s, Beat poets, musicians, painters, and philosophers somehow survived, but they were repressed. A thin layer of Beatness pervaded our lives, our dress, our sometimes youthful and casual pursuit of pleasure. And then we grew up. We had birth control, we had rock 'n' roll music, we had the Beatles and long hair, we had "acid dreams," and sexual liberation. We had us a grand ole time in the sixties.

It was midnight on a cold early spring night, and the Dutchess County, New York, assistant district attorney pushed through the front door of an upstate mansion near Millbrook. Backing him up was the county sheriff and all of the deputies they could lay their hands on. They were raiding the place, hoping to confiscate drugs and arrest anyone using drugs or doing anything else illegal.

The Millbrook mansion was about two hours north of New York City, owned by twin brothers Tommy and Billy Hitchcock and their sister Peggy. The Hitchcocks were grandchildren of the founder of

Gulf Oil and the niece and nephews of financier Andrew Mellon. They had lots of money and they spent it. The Millbrook mansion, though it badly needed renovation, consisted of several thousand acres of land, half a dozen houses, along with several other buildings and sixty-four rooms complete with gargantuan fireplace, parquet floors, Persian carpets, crystal chandeliers, and gingerbread ornamentation.

At one point, as many as twenty-five to thirty people lived there and had formed a commune. Included in the group were several academics and university graduate students, as well as a group living in one of the buildings known as "the ashram." Some commune residents took to wearing clothing made of buckskin or rainbow-colored, tie-dyed material. They went barefoot, tossed away undergarments long before going braless became the "in" thing, let their hair grow long (often weaving flowers into their long locks), rang bells, and chanted mantras. They called themselves "Wildflower," "Bear," "Mountain Girl," and "Cowboy." They chanted "Free Love!" and lived up to the chant. As one critic put it:

> Fleeting glimpses were reported of persons strolling the grounds nude. To fears of drug-induced dementia were added pot-induced pregnancy. The word was that . . . the panties were dropping as fast as the acid.

With the raid on the Hitchcock-Millbrook commune, "Acid Wars," the establishment's attempt to rid the country of LSD, was under way.

The assistant Dutchess County prosecutor who raided Millbrook hoping to close down the commune? He went on to later fame and glory in the Richard Nixon Watergate scandal as one of the leak-fixing "plumbers": G. Gordon Liddy, the "G-Man," as he likes to be called. The man Liddy tried to send to jail, the man who began the Millbrook commune, was former Harvard University adjunct professor Timothy Leary.

What Dutchess County authorities hoped would be the bust to end all busts took place in March 1966, with winter still holding on to the Millbrook area. It was cold, and G. Gordon Liddy was shivering "in a concealing clump of brush some thirty yards from the front of the building, waiting." Leary's headquarters at Millbrook, Liddy wrote,

was the equivalent of a hotel. Informants advised [the prosecutor's office] that people, often couples, would arrive, sometimes to stay the weekend. They would be assigned a room for storage of their effects and to which they could retire after participating in the various group activities . . . lectures by Leary, community ingestion of marijuana and hashish, and distribution of the "sacrament" of LSD by Leary's then girlfriend (later wife) Rosemary, who was referred to as "the Blessed Mother."

Meanwhile, events in the mansion dictated when the raid on Millbrook would take place. The sheriff and assistant prosecutors waited until the individual "guests" retired for the night. Usually, that was about 11:00 P.M., but this night, Leary had "gathered his guests into a large living room." The room was dark save "for the random flashing of colored lights." Aha! the forces of law thought: "They're lookin' at movies." Probably porno scumbag movies. The sheriff assigned a deputy—there was "some competition for the assignment"—to get into binocular range and check out what was going on inside.

But the scout returned, disgusted. "It ain't no dirty movie," G. Gordon Liddy quoted the deputy as reporting. "Them hippies" were watching a waterfall!

"It goes on and on and nothing ever happens but the water. I kept watching, you know? I figured there'd be, you know, broads jumpin' in and out or something."

"No broads?" the deputy was asked.

"Nothing! Nothing but water. Them people are crazy!"

Liddy and the sheriff rushed the mansion, "a thundering herd of deputies right behind us." As they ran up the steep interior stairs, coming down to meet them was Tim Leary with Rosemary at his side. "Rosemary," Liddy observed, "was wearing a diaphanous gown. Leary was wearing a Hathaway shirt. Period." Since the stairs were steep, the raiders had to crane their necks upward. Liddy's first view of the good doctor was "revealing."

Upstairs, doors to the various rooms popped open along the hallway as the deputies raced "to their assigned floors, halls, and rooms." Men and women in various stages of undress looked out at the onrushing lawmen, some calling, "Oink, oink!" and "Fascist pigs!" to "the deputies' heavy-booted deployment." Others grabbed guitars and joined in the fun, according to the G-man, "by improvising on the spot some surprisingly good folk songs in keeping with the spirit of the occasion."

"Oh, they're busting Doctor Leary
Cause the evening, it was dreary
And the fuzz had nothin' better else to do.
We got sheriffs out the ass
Cause they're looking for our grass
And they hope to find a ton of acid too!"

In Leary and Rosemary's room, Rosemary clutched a small, ornate brass urn, crying out, "Don't you dare touch that! . . . That's my sacrament!" Inside the urn the deputies found "a dried, ground vegetable matter that was unmistakably a good grade of marijuana." Down in the "waterfall room," the lights were still low, and Liddy and Sheriff Charlie Borchers smelled something awful, like something dead. Borchers used the toe of his shoe to poke at a dark mass on the floor: "Christ, Liddy . . . they've even got a dead dog in here."

Not exactly; the pooch wasn't dead, just stoned on a contact high. Groaning and rolling over, he lurched out of the room.

Throughout the mansion, deputies pushed through closed doorways and, in one instance, caught a nude couple in mid-missionary position, the man "at his apogee," Liddy wrote. "Freeze!" the deputy shouted, his massive .357 Magnum revolver aimed, in approved two-handed pistol-course position, at the startled couple. Pausing, the man looked at the deputy and his weapon and said, "You're kidding."

Assistant District Attorney Al Rosenblatt accidentally knocked a heavy framed picture off the wall. As the picture fell it struck a man sitting cross-legged directly underneath it, his back against the wall. The picture hit him on the nose, sending copious amounts of blood flying into the air. "They've shed blood!" Liddy quoted a young lady as crying, "Human blood!" Others added to the charge. "Violence!" "Police brutality!"

Meanwhile, outside, a carload of college-age men pulled into the Millbrook mansion driveway. Inside were three Princeton University students who'd earlier attended a dance at the nearby then-exclusive but since-defunct Bennett Junior College, whose student body consisted of some of the neighborhood's very rich sons and daughters. So, outside Millbrook, were three happy if drunken college students, one of them the son of a steel-company president. Inside, uniformed deputies were trying to name, tag, and book Leary's "guests." One Princetonian struggled drunkenly out of the car; the second set off a string of firecrackers—whap, whap, bam—and the third shouted: "Party! Party! Party!" About then, they spotted the deputies, and one of the guys decided "Ish a costume party. Lookit alla cowboys!" Obviously, word hadn't gotten out that the party at Millbrook was over.

Inside, the mansion's formerly genial host, Tim Leary, was still wearing nothing but his Hathaway shirt. This didn't please Dutchess County district attorney John Heilman, who by then had arrived to witness the bust of the century. Seeing the half-naked Leary upset Heilman. "Pants!" someone yelled. "The district attorney wants pants on this man!" and a deputy handed Leary a pair of trousers. The former Harvard don struggled unsuccessfully to put them on. "I told you," Leary said, "these belong to my son."

"Guests," deputies, DAs, and assistant DAs, not to mention three drunk and disappointed Princetonians, all milled around Millbrook. By then, the mansion was as loud and boisterous as neighbors had complained it had been all along. To get some quiet and talk, Liddy and Leary went off to another room. At the time, law enforcement officers weren't required to inform suspects of their rights, but according to G. Gordon Liddy, he "had advised the sheriff's officers" to do just that as a matter of course. Liddy, after all, was a former FBI agent and wanted to keep everything on the up and up.

So Liddy interviewed Leary and asked him if he was aware of his right to have an attorney present. Yes, Liddy quoted Leary as saying,

I intend to contact an attorney, probably the Civil Liberties Union, just as soon as you people clear out of here, if you ever do. In the meantime, I'm hoping you'll understand if I say nothing to you in response to your questions.

Liddy stood and got ready to leave the room. "Sit down, sit down," Leary said. "It isn't often these days I get a chance to talk to a civil Philistine." And the talk began a strange on-again, off-again relationship between LSD guru Dr. Timothy Leary and "civil Philistine" G. Gordon Liddy. Two decades after Liddy tried to prosecute Leary, the two went on a cross-country lecture tour together.

After the raid, authorities set up roadblocks around Millbrook and for a year thoroughly searched everyone and every vehicle that came around. Finally, in 1967, after a year of internal pressure and outside conflict, the owners of the Hitchcock commune at Millbrook closed down the scene. The high old times moved elsewhere.

After his Millbrook arrest, Tim Leary did, as he'd said he might, get the ACLU to defend him. During a hearing before county judge (and former district attorney) Raymond Baratta, ACLU attorney Noel Tepper called as witnesses several Hindu priests who testified that the drugs—and there hadn't been a lot, at that—seized in the Millbrook raid had "religious significance." Moot point. As the hearing continued, the U.S. Supreme Court handed down its *Miranda v. Arizona* decision, declaring police must inform suspects of their rights to remain silent and to have an attorney before questioning. *Miranda* also required the offer of free legal counsel, and that was something none of the officers (including former FBI agent G. Gordon Liddy) had done. With that, everyone pulled in at the Millbrook bust was, as Liddy said, "off the hook. . . . Off Leary went to other pursuits. And so did I."

If all had gone according to plan, Timothy Leary might have wound up in the ranks of the military, perhaps even leading men into battle in Vietnam. During the late thirties, he'd enrolled as a cadet at the U.S. Military Academy at West Point, but early on he had a run-in with the army establishment. Leary had a drinking problem and agreed to drop out of the academy if the school dropped all charges of alcohol abuse.

Born to a dentist and a schoolteacher in 1920 in Springfield, Massachusetts, Leary took a Ph.D. in clinical psychology at the University of California at Berkeley. Later he joined the Harvard Center for Research in Personality. Lecturing in Philadelphia, Leary said that since his "illumination" after eating seven "sacred mushrooms" three years earlier, "I have devoted most of my energies to try to understand the revelatory potentialities of the human nervous system and to make these insights available to others." He added:

> Remember that God (however you define the Higher Power) produced that wonderful molecule, that extraordinarily powerful organic substance we call LSD, just as surely as "He" created the rose, or the sun, or the complex cluster of molecules you insist on calling "your self."

In August 1960, Leary began a research program based on an earlier visit to Mexico in which he'd been introduced to "magic mushrooms." The mushrooms produced a psilocybin—that is, the hallucinogenic—effect. He was joined by another professor, Richard Alpert (later known as Ram Dass of the Lama Foundation commune in northern New Mexico), and soon others—both faculty and students—enlisted in the research. Two years later, Harvard fired Alpert from his tenured-track position when he became involved in a gay romantic relationship.

They fired Leary, not because of any romantic relationship, gay or straight, but because of his magic-mushroom research. That, and something stronger. In 1963, Michael Hollingshead, a British philosophy student who'd heard about his work, contacted Leary and introduced him to a new drug that had been synthesized by Dr. Albert Hoffman of Switzerland. Like mushrooms, this new drug was hallucinogenic but was much more potent: lysergic acid diethylamide, also known as LSD or, simply, "acid."

In fighting his firing by Harvard, Leary published an article entitled "The Fifth Freedom: The Right to Get High." "Make no mistake," he wrote,

The effect of consciousness-expanding drugs will be to transform our concept of human nature, human potentialities, [and] existence. The game is about to be changed, ladies and gentlemen. Man is about to make use of that fabulous electrical network he carries around in his skull. . . . The verbal dam is collapsing. Head for the hills, or prepare your intellectual craft to flow with the current.

Timothy Leary became something of the North American "LSD philosopher," a "guru," in the idiom of the day. He claimed that "Your only hope is dope," and preached that not only were LSD and other psychedelic drugs enjoyable, but the revelations they induced were positively beneficial.

Leary and Alpert, along with their graduate student Ralph Metzner and several others, formed IFIF, the International Foundation for Internal Freedom. It didn't take long for IFIF to attract several thousand dues-paying members. They began what they called "colonies for transcendental living" at two old houses in Newton, Massachusetts, hippie communes before hippie communes became the in thing.

Timothy Leary later founded the "League for Spiritual Discovery," claiming that "It will be an LSD country in fifteen years." Leary based his league on the sacramental use of hallucinogenic drugs and predicted that, soon, the "Supreme Court will be smoking marijuana." "It becomes," he claimed, "necessary for us to go out of our minds in order to use our heads."

At the time, producing and using LSD were legal and many individuals took the drug in a rather casual manner: poet Allen Ginsberg, for instance, musician Charlie Mingus, and writer Ken Kesey. It was Kesey, with his 1962 best-selling book *One Flew Over the Cuckoo's Nest*, who became something of a poster child of the sixties. *Cuckoo's Nest* grew to be a favorite in communes and college dorms, something of an acid head's bible.

After Harvard fired Leary, he traveled around the country promoting LSD as a spiritual cure-all and offering the mantra "Turn on, tune in, drop out." But in 1966, LSD and its psychedelic relatives were banned by federal and state laws. When Leary and his daughter tried crossing the U.S. border from Mexico, authorities arrested them on charges of possessing marijuana.

In 1959, Ken Kesey and his wife, Faye, were living in Palo Alto, California, in a group of cheap little houses known as Perry Lane. Among the residents were writer Larry McMurtry, Leary's former Harvard colleague Richard Alpert, and a wild-haired kid named Jerry Garcia, a musician. Author Tom Wolfe described the scene at Perry Lane:

> All sorts of people began hanging around Perry Lane. Quite an . . . *underground* sensation it was, in Hip California. Kesey, Cassady, Larry McMurtry . . . Ed McLanahan and Bob Stone, [all there] because they had heard about it, like the local beats—the term was still used . . . The Lane's fabled Venison Chili, a Kesey dish made of venison stew laced with LSD, which you could consume and then go sprawl on the mattress in the fork of a great oak in the middle of the Lane at night and play pinball with the light show in the sky. . . .

While attending a graduate writing program at Stanford University—he'd won a Woodrow Wilson fellowship—Kesey had become acquainted with LSD. With a twenty-dollar inducement he'd volunteered to be a subject in a Veterans Administration hospital controlled experiment with psychoactive drugs. "They gave me this pill," he said, "or shot me up with this something that they didn't tell me what it was, then for eight hours they watched me: recorded my blood, my breathing." Kesey got a job in the hospital, "so I could take these drugs from the ward. I ended up finding out that the key I was given opened the doctor's office." The hospital gave Kesey a basis for his novel (*Cuckoo's Nest* takes place in a mental hospital with a hell-raiser named McMurphy leading a group of merry patients, including a giant Native American called "Chief," in a rebellion against their sadistic keeper, Big Nurse) and LSD gave Kesey a meaning in life. Ken Kesey became a true acid believer.

In July 1963, a developer bought most of the property along Perry Lane, and that sent Kesey looking for someplace else to live. Using money that was rolling in from *One Flew Over the Cuckoo's Nest*,* he bought a small house in rural La Honda, California, and a number of the old Perry Lane crowd (including Jerry Garcia) showed up on his doorstep and camped in the nearby woods, creating an impromptu commune. LSD was still legal and at La Honda it was plentiful among the Kesey-centered group that came to be known as the Merry Pranksters.

Carolyn Adams met Jerry Garcia at La Honda and later married the Grateful Dead leader. "Six boards nailed together with a tarp over the top," she remembered of their first home "—that was the bedroom." There was "a tree house, and some old outbuildings that were converted into sleep areas, and then there were vehicles as living arrangements."

A bit later [writer] Hunter Thompson introduced Kesey to the Hell's Angels [motorcycle gang], who with the help of LSD fit into the scene far better than anyone could have imagined. [Poet] Allen Ginsberg, who was present at the first encounter of Angels and Pranksters, observed "the blast of loudspeakers . . . a little weed in the bathroom . . . one muscular smooth skin man dancing for hours . . . and four police cars parked outside the gate."

In 1964, Kesey and the Pranksters drove across country in their psychedelic-painted, Day-Glo-Colored 1938 International Harvester bus bearing the sign "Caution: Weird Load." In place of the bus's original designation sign, the Pranksters inscribed the word *Further*.

---

* The money is still rolling in. In the spring of 2001, Chicago's Steppenwolf Theatre opened a production of *Cuckoo's Nest* on Broadway.

For much of the trip, Neal Cassady drove the bus; he was the original wheelman from Jack Kerouac's *On the Road*.*

Kesey and company careened down the highway, dropping acid, smoking marijuana, popping pills, reading comic books, and advocating the psychedelic experience. Heading into a town, Kesey would wear a pink kilt, pink socks, patent-leather shoes, and swath his head in an American flag. Sitting atop the bus, he'd play the flute, a true counterculture Pied Piper.

During the trip (pun intended), the Merry Pranksters rolled into the commune at Millbrook, New York, which by then was sort of the East Coast version of La Honda. The two group leaders almost got together: Ken Kesey (full-tilt raucous) and Timothy Leary (more subdued and mystic). However, Leary was down with the flu and either coming down from or going up on an intense LSD trip. "I didn't know history was being made," Leary said later, "a meeting of the acid tribes. I was preoccupied with other things." So Ken and the Pranksters got back on the bus and drove off.

Kesey later claimed that he'd intended to make a movie out of the cross-country bus trip, calling it *The Intrepid Traveler and His Merry Band of Pranksters Look for a Kool Place*. It never got off the ground, in part because of technical problems. Kesey used a bus-powered tape recorder to go along with silent film of what was going on during the trip. Problem was that, whenever the bus sped up or slowed down, the recorder changed speeds. Kesey and a Hollywood film editor working with him were never able to synch the sound with silent film that the Pranksters had shot. Kesey gave up.

Several years—and another generation—later the project moved closer to completion. Simon Babbs, the son of Kesey's longtime friend and fellow Prankster Ken Babbs, and Kesey's son Zane, transferred the film and audiotape to a digital editing machine, and with the help of modern computer software, they put together *Kool Place*. Modern science catching up with the bus headed "Further."

---

* Cassady died along a Mexican railroad track in 1968, a year before his road buddy Kerouac.

Beginning in 1966, the Merry Pranksters began holding a series of public LSD parties, calling them "Trips Festivals." The Pranksters even had their own "house band," the Grateful Dead.

Acid, Kesey and the Merry Pranksters claimed, was a means of exploring one's inner world and reinventing the one outside. In the 1966 San Francisco Trips Festival, a multimedia combination of rock, light shows, and acid droppings, a crowd of twenty-four hundred drank LSD-laced punch from a baby's bathtub. "Can you pass the acid test?" Ken Kesey asked.

Faced with several arrest warrants, Kesey became a fugitive in both the United States and Mexico but finally was caught and convicted. He was sent to a work farm for five months. When he got out, in late 1967, Kesey moved to Oregon, where he and his family settled on his brother's farm outside Springfield. Some of the Merry Pranksters migrated to Springfield, and Kesey's farm became the next commune, with as many as sixty people living there.

It all began to get to Kesey, however—five or six years in communes, the psychedelic bus tour, and the Trips Festivals. For a while, he turned against the commune scene and began calling the experience the "Communal Lie."

During Woodstock, singer/guitarist B. B. King took to a young man named Hugh Romney and began calling him "Wavy Gravy." The name's stuck ever since. Hugh (or Wavy) was a member of a western state commune known as the Hog Farm that was founded in 1965. Romney was an actor and comedian in New York, but in the late 1950s he moved to California where he hung out with Ken Kesey and the Merry Pranksters. Romney taught improvisation at Columbia Pictures and entertained children, some of them technically brain dead. He and a group of friends had been offered use of a farmhouse and thirty-odd acres of land in Sunland, California, "on a mountain overlooking the San Fernando Valley." In return, commune members would tend the property owners' herd of hogs. As a commune, the "Hog Farm" was born, and it became something of a counterculture legend. They had an array of geodesic domes, tents, and shacks, where members lived. They often carried slop for the hogs in containers on their backs, walking along dirt roads that frequently were impassable by motor vehicles. They lived on brown rice and discarded overripe produce from restaurants in the area, kept a community stash of clothing, and indulged in play and psychedelics.

Their reputation grew so wide that they attracted crowds of would-be Hog Farmers. Including one young man who brought along several girlfriends: Charles Manson. This was long before Manson and his "girls" went on a rampage in 1969, killing actress Sharon Tate and six others. The Hog Farmers thought something weird was going on with Charlie, so they kicked the killer-to-be and his friends off the ranch.

Still, some of the Hog Farm's neighbors didn't like the idea of all these hippies "living in sin" and fornicating in public, or so some claimed. Neighbors especially didn't like the growing crowds that flocked to the farm on weekends. Neighbors even blocked access to roads and the Hog Farmers had to clear an old Forest Service road to get to and from the commune.

By 1967, the Hog Farmers had acquired some old buses, and wanderlust hit the group. They began taking trips (pun intended again) to rock concerts, where they did as much entertaining as the scheduled entertainers themselves did. By 1969, their reputation was so strong that backers of the Woodstock Festival asked the Hog Farm to run a free kitchen for concertgoers. They not only gave away free food, but free medical attention, taking care of drug-related freak-outs. That's when B. B. King crowned Hugh Romney as "Wavy Gravy."

By the time the festival was over, and the Hog Farmers had made their way back west—they had a twelve-acre ranch in Llano, New Mexico—their reputation had preceded them. "Hundreds and hundreds of people," Wavy Gravy said, "had loaded their stuff up and hopped into cars" and shown up in New Mexico to join the party at the Hog Farm. They'd line up at dinnertime to be fed. Soon, however, Wavy Gravy and the Hog Farmers realized that their own reputation was doing them in; they just couldn't handle the crowds. So back into their buses. They attended another festival—this one in Texas—where they again tried to feed the crowds and give medical attention to those in need.

The New Mexico Hog Farm still exists, with some largely independent branches in California. As for Hugh "Wavy Gravy" Romney, he moved to Berkeley, where he continued doing charitable work and poking fun at the political process, all the while entertaining the people and clowning around for children. He even had a flavor of ice cream named after him, as did Jerry Garcia of the Grateful Dead.*

It's not only a way of thinking that sets the counterculture apart, it's money, or rather the lack of it. For instance, in the thirties New York City's Greenwich Village was the East Coast center of counterculture (or whatever you want to call it), with bohemians and beats, artists and jazz musicians, holding forth. In the nineteenth century, San Francisco's Barbary Coast drew madams and cardsharks to bordellos and gin mills.

But then both sections—"the" places to live for those who wanted to appear hip**—became gentrified and old warehouses and old whorehouses gave way to loft-living, art galleries, and boutiques. The counterculture simply couldn't afford the cost of living in what was now the high-rent district. They moved on to cheaper and more run-down locations, to where their sometimes unusual lifestyles didn't seem out of place: the East Village in New York and the Haight-Ashbury area in San Francisco. To some noncounterculture individuals these enclaves were homes to hard drugs, heavy crime, and Godless anarchy. To those in the lifestyle they were joyous centers of peace and love and expanded consciousness.

By 1966, the Haight-Ashbury district had become the epicenter of counterculture, with flower children arriving by the thousands, looking for a hassle-free place to live cheaply, love freely, and openly

---

* Both flavors were with Ben and Jerry's— "Wavy Gravy" and "Cherry Garcia." The once laid-back company later joined the list of firms bought out by multinational conglomerates, and it's unknown if Wavy Gravy and Cherry Garcia flavors (or, for that matter, the company itself) will be around long.
** The word *hippie* didn't make its appearance until the spring of 1967; although, there certainly were hip people long before then. In 1967—the "Summer of Love"—the crusading magazine *Ramparts* ran an article entitled "The Social History of the Hippies."

buy acid and other drugs. Now and then they'd search for values they couldn't find at home or anywhere else. So many drugs flowed around Haight-Ashbury, the corner became known as "Hashbury," as in hashish. The corner became the bastion of American resistance to just about everything except resistance.

Music groups such as the Grateful Dead (with lead singer Jerry Garcia), Jefferson Airplane (with Grace Slick), and Big Brother and the Holding Company (with Janis Joplin) took to the Haight and went on to change the nation's style of music from the rock/pop form of carefully choreographed and slicked-back fifties and early sixties look and sound into something deliberately at odds with "mainstream" plastic society.

Take Grace Slick. Grace Wing (as she was called before her 1961 marriage to the boy next door, Jerry Slick) was born in the so-called heartland city of Chicago in 1939. When she was twenty-seven years old, Grace replaced lead singer Singe Anderson with the Jefferson Airplane, and the group took off. Her voice and hypnotic dark-eyed good looks pushed the band to stardom. On January 4, 1967—a date declared favorable by an astrologer—the Airplane soared at a "Gathering of the Tribes" at Golden Gate Park. It was known as the "Human Be-In." As author Chris Strodder put it, "Grace Slick is admirably unapologetic about affairs with A: most drugs known to man; and B: most men known to drugs." She has survived, however, to, at this writing, the ripe old age of sixty-two.

Not so lucky was Janis Joplin. Born in Port Arthur, Texas, in 1943, she was known for years as "Pearl." Joplin's growly, in-your-face, whiskey-husky voice was nearly perfect for the type of blues performed by Big Brother and the Holding Company. Fellow singer and friend Judy Collins claims that Joplin "shouted her story and spilled it out into the world with an abandon that had genius in it." Ethel Merman, a singer from another generation, added that Janis "has problems [but] being heard ain't one of 'em." Like Ethel herself, Merman said, Joplin "gives an audience their money's worth." Janis Joplin was tied romantically, or at least sexually, with such celebrities as Eric Clapton, Jimi Hendrix, Kris Kristofferson, and even talkshow host Dick Cavett—she claimed Cavett's was the only TV talk show worth appearing on and she did, about twice a year. Not to mention football great Joe Namath and various and assorted members of her band.

Singer David Crosby tells of the time Janis Joplin first met Jim Morrison, who may or may not have been the love of her life. Janis, you can't sing blues worth a damn, Morrison told her, which of course didn't make Joplin too happy and she stormed out of the room and grabbed a bottle of Jim Beam bourbon. Not to drink, mind you. Instead, she "took the bottle back into the room with Morrison, where she broke it on his forehead." True love never did run smooth.

Janis Joplin and Grace Slick and Jimi Hendrix all performed at Woodstock in 1969, though not on the same day. Hendrix, in fact, was the highest-paid act at Woodstock: $36,000 for two sets. The Who, for instance, played for $12,500.

When Hendrix died of a drug overdose on September 18, 1970, Janis reportedly said, "Dammit! He beat me to it!" But not for long. Three weeks later, on October 3, Janis also died of a drug overdose.

The Grateful Dead played at Woodstock, but lead singer Jerry Garcia didn't like it. Woodstock was "a bummer,"

> . . . terrible to play at . . . like playing at nighttime in the dark; and we were looking out, in the dark, to see what we knew to be [at least] four hundred thousand people. But you couldn't see anybody. You could only see little fires and stuff out there on the hillside, and these incredible bright supertrooper spotlights shining in your eyes. The stage was all wet, there were electric shocks from our instruments. People freaking out here and there and crowding on the stage. People beyond the amplifiers were hollering that the stage was about to collapse. . . . It was like an incredible huge people show. . . . The thing was that it was all all right. . . . There wasn't any hassle there. There wasn't anybody scoffing at it or anything like that. . . . It was like I knew I was at a place where history was being made.

The way of life of the sixties cultural revolution emcompassed sex and dope and rock 'n' roll and communes. Jerry Garcia, perhaps more than most others, was part of it all. The Grateful Dead was the archetypal commune band.

Known earlier as the Warlocks, the Dead derived its name from an *Oxford English Dictionary* notation on the burial of Egyptian pharaohs. Jerry Garcia had taught himself to play guitar at age fifteen by slowing down his record player to 15 rpm, in order to learn the solos on Harry Smith's six-LP album *Anthology of American Folk Music.* The founder of the jug-band Warlocks/Grateful Dead developed a fascination with folk, blues, and bluegrass.

The Grateful Dead's early years were spent at the heart of the Haight-Ashbury district, in a rambling old Victorian mansion at 710 Ashbury Street. Garcia and the Dead joined the Merry Pranksters' weird scene in about 1964 and three years later became part of the Olompali Ranch commune north of San Francisco, California, on 690 acres.

The Olompali Ranch—think of it as the Grateful Dead's "rural retreat"—lasted from 1967–69 and consisted of the extremes of communal experience: It was wealthy and then it was poor; it was both secular and spiritual; it knew great joys and great tragedies.

The ranch began when Don McCoy rented the property's main house and asked a group of about twenty-five of his friends to move in. McCoy had a "substantial" inheritance and he and his brother had done well operating a heliport; they also owned and rented out houseboats in Sausalito. Money was no problem.

As more of McCoy's friends joined the commune outside Novato, they came to be known as the "Chosen Family." A member who called herself "Sheila USA" said that "God chose us to be family with each other, and also, we chose each other for family." Don McCoy paid all of the commune's bills and bought his friends motorcycles, horses, light show equipment, and even gave one member 7,000 to pay off some old debts.

Jerry Garcia's wife and fellow communer Carolyn Adams Garcia, however, says that everybody kicked in fifteen bucks a week to keep Olompali Ranch going. "It was per person," she says, "I don't care if it was you and your girlfriend and you never eat, you have to pay the fifteen bucks,

Because there's toilet paper, there's electricity, and I was the collector and cook. We had a hilarious time. It was like a made up family. I just remember how warm and comforting and nurturing and pleasant the times were that we had there.

Back at the corner of Haight and Ashbury, the Psychedelic Shop became the unofficial meeting place for hippies and the source of beads, bells, incense, feathers, records, and books about drugs. The Diggers, an anarchistic street-theater group, dispensed such necessities as clothing, medical care, food, and "surplus energy" at their Free Store.

In the fall of 1966, the Diggers combined avant-garde street-theater with radical politics. To help feed Hashbury denizens, they practiced "garbage yoga," that is, they took society's leftovers and distributed free food to the needy in Golden Gate Park. Actually, most of the food wasn't "garbage"; Digger women usually charmed vendors and restaurant owners into giving them leftovers. A lot of food came from area farmers' markets at the close of the business day. Digger Judy Berg recalled that they had a credo: "Do your own thing"—no restraints, no rules—and "Everything is free." Sympathetic physicians began offering free medical care in the district, and the service soon developed into the Haight-Ashbury Free Medical Clinic.

It's uncertain how many communes operated during the movement's peak years from 1960 to 1975. After all, getting away from it all (including governments) was one of the ideas. Some groups lasted only a matter of days. Some still exist today. Not all communes were formed by hippies; indeed, hippie communes probably were a minority of such organizations, albeit a sometimes vocal minority.

As for the Haight-Ashbury district, well, the days of the hippies are all but gone now. At the corner itself, there is that quintessential Yuppie hangout, a Ben and Jerry's ice cream parlor. Probably a Starbucks coffeeshop too.

Eventually, many hippies and freaks realized that drugs offered diminishing returns. For some the drugs was the ultimate downer: Jim Morrison, Janis Joplin, Jimi Hendrix, Al Wilson of Canned Heat, Brian Jones of the Rolling Stones, Keith Moon of The Who, and Pigpen of the Grateful Dead. "Every junkie," Neil Young of Crosby, Stills, Nash, and Young warned, "is like a setting sun."

• • •

In 1960, foreign car manufacturers had four percent of the American new car market. A decade later, the number was up to seventeen percent. One reason was that American cars were no longer as well made as foreign models. In a seven-year period, 1966–73, U.S. automakers had to recall 30 million American cars because of serious defects. While American car quality went down, assembly-line workers' pay went up until they were earning far more than the median national wage for manufacturing work.

Prices weren't the only thing up. The U.S. crime rate in 1960 was up an astounding ninety-eight percent over 1950.

CHAPTER FOURTEEN

The Final Frontier:
One Small Step

Extremism in the defense of liberty is no vice; moderation in the pursuit of justice in no virtue.

Barry Goldwater, Republican presidential nominee, 1964

I'm the only president you've got.

President Lyndon Baines Johnson, 1964

In order to keep out the Texas heat, the Houston Sports Association built what some called the "Eighth Wonder of the Modern World": the Houston Astrodome, the first domed all-weather stadium. It cost $30 million and was the world's largest air-conditioned room—45,000 plus seats. No worries about the weather, because conditions in the Astrodome would be perfect for sports.

It had at least 4,596 faults. That is, 4,596 transparent plastic panels in the dome. And that certainly was a problem. You get an outfielder looking up at the dome and it was pretty tough to see a high pop fly with the light streaming in. Not to mention the effect of the gray steel girders that formed the panels. Fly balls just seemed to disappear in the glaring light. In an early game between the Houston Astros and the Baltimore Orioles, players made a combined total of six errors, at least half of which were directly due to the dome's crazy-quilt background.

Fans, engineers, ballplayers, and baseball executives offered more than a thousand suggestions on what to do. One of them was to use orange baseballs and give the players special sunglasses. That one didn't get very far.

Finally, they painted the dome's panels, all 4,596 of them, a dark gray to shut out the sun and to match the girders. Which, of course, caused another problem. Originally, with all that sunlight coming in, they'd planted regular grass. With the panels painted over, and with sunlight blocked out, the grass died. So make that 4,597 problems.

Dome owners called in the Monsanto Company to get rid of the real grass and to cover the interior with green plastic grass: Astroturf.

On October 1, 1958, the National Aeronautics and Space Administration (NASA) was organized, officially starting America's race into space. We almost lost. Actually, we did lose at first, but in time we caught up.

Almost three months after the Soviet Union sent its first *Sputnik* into orbit, the United States finally put a satellite into space: *Explorer I*, launched on January 31, 1958.

When the Soviets sent *Luna II* to the moon, it became man's first contact with the moon. Instead of making a soft landing as it had been designed to do, *Luna II* made an undignified crash on the surface. Still, the Russians got there. "We have beaten you to the moon," Nikita Khrushchev said in Des Moines, Iowa, that fall, during a tour of the United States, "but you have beaten us in sausage making."

On the second anniversary of *Sputnik*, the Soviets launched *Luna III*, the first satellite to orbit the moon. By the end of the month, Moscow newspapers had released photographs taken of the far side of the moon.

As the fifties ended, NASA introduced the seven pilots chosen to be America's first astronauts: Scott Carpenter, Gordon Cooper, John Glenn, Gus Grissom, Wally Shirra, Alan Shepard, and Deke Slayton. The United States and the Soviet Union were in a race to get into space, but the Russians were still winning.

On March 12, 1961, Soviet cosmonaut Yuri Gagarin became the first man in space. Three weeks later, on April 5, Alan Shepard became America's first astronaut in space. It was only a twenty-minute suborbital flight, so we remained, as Bozo the Clown would say, "almost winners" in the space race. We didn't have a rocket powerful enough to put a human in orbit. For the rest of the year, the Russians continued to literally fly circles around us, sending cosmonaut Gherman Titov on seventeen orbits around the Earth.

Then, on February 20, 1962, an Atlas rocket blasted astronaut John H. Glenn Jr. into space, and America took a long step toward catching up. Encased in a bulky pressurized suit, strapped into a seat, and crammed into his tiny *Friendship 7* Mercury spacecraft, Glenn put his life at risk. He orbited the earth three times, traveling at 17,500 miles per hour, about 160 miles above earth. Glenn saw four earth sunsets, and during his first "night," Perth, Australia, set up a beacon for him; they turned on all of the city's lights to show Glenn the way and their support.

When the capsule's autopilot function failed, Glenn took over and piloted it manually. He was in his second orbit when Mission Control received a signal from the craft indicating that the heat shield, designed to prevent the capsule from burning up during reentry, was loose. Mission Control wasn't sure what had happened and whether the capsule's life-saving heat shield would hold during reentry into the atmosphere. Glenn struggled to maintain control of the spacecraft, watching as huge chunks flew past the window.

Normally, the space capsule's retropack package would be jettisoned after the rockets were fired to slow it for reentry. In this case, however, Mission Control ordered Glenn to retain the retropack to hold the heat shield in place. After four hours, fifty-five minutes, and three orbits of the Earth, John Glenn manually fired the retrorockets and safely returned to Earth. The heat shield held, and the only injuries he suffered were scraped knuckles as he exited the capsule after a safe splashdown.

The successful completion of Glenn's mission did much to restore American prestige worldwide. Six days after his successful flight, Washington celebrated John Glenn Day, and on March 1, an estimated four million New Yorkers turned out to give him a ticker-tape parade. Glenn appeared before a House committee and predicted that the Soviet Union would lead the space race for some time, but he believed America would be first to reach the moon. There would be risks involved in the manned space program. "There will be failures. There will be sacrifices."

On October 29, 1998, the seventy-seven-year-old space pioneer (and later U.S. senator and presidential candidate) returned to space aboard NASA's STS-95 shuttle as a member of a seven-person crew—

seven, the same number as made up the entire Mercury astronaut program. "Person," because this time there were women in the American space program. Glenn's part in the mission, purportedly, was to study the parallels between space flight and the aging process. Or it could have been NASA's (and America's) way of saying thank-you to John Glenn.

His first trip into space had lasted less than five hours. The second time around, he was up almost nine days. Unlike the first trip into space in 1962, when Glenn and the shuttle touched down in 1998, he got sick to his stomach and threw up. Well, you can't get everything right every time.

On January 26, 1967, it began snowing in the Midwest. It stopped snowing on January 27. The storm dumped twenty-three inches of snow on Chicago and virtually closed the city down. Elsewhere, other cities got even more snow. Lansing, Michigan, got twenty-five inches of snow in twenty-four hours, and if that isn't a record it should be.

The same day as the big Midwestern snow, astronauts Gus Grissom, Ed White, and Roger Chaffee climbed into the *Apollo I* spacecraft at Cape Canaveral for a test run. Their real mission was scheduled for three weeks later. As they'd be for the real mission, the astronauts were strapped in their seats, the cabin was pressurized, and they were breathing pure oxygen. Suddenly, one of the three—probably Chaffee—cried, "I smell fire!" Then, "Fire aboard the spacecraft." In seconds the hundred-percent oxygen atmosphere burst into flames. A TV camera trained on the hatch window caught a flurry of activity inside the craft, then a flash of white-hot flame. Grissom, White, and Chaffee didn't have a chance. They died in less than a minute. It took close to six minutes to open the hatch. Chaffee was still strapped to his seat. Grissom and White lay in a tangle of arms and legs, melted nylon and electrical insulation.

"If we die," Gus Grissom had once said, "we want people to accept it. The conquest of space is worth the risk of life."

The public couldn't accept it, and neither could NASA. The agency set up a special review board, which—in language that all "special review boards" seem to use—attributed the tragedy to "some minor malfunction or failure of equipment or wire insulation." There were "many deficiencies in design and engineering, manufacture, and quality control," and "113 significant engineering orders" had not been carried out during the spacecraft's construction. NASA never did determine exactly how the fire started, but it got down to two things: the hundred-percent oxygen atmosphere—where a simple spark can cause an explosion—and inadequate escape facilities. Since it had only been a test, with no fuel in the rocket tanks, there wasn't even a firefighting crew standing by. As for that hundred-percent oxygen system, NASA officials early on knew the danger, but they didn't do anything about it, because any redesign might have caused a delay and we might have lost the race to the moon.

The *Apollo 1* deaths did what NASA had tried to avoid—set back the moon project—but once things were running again, they ran smoothly. NASA changed procedures and tested and retested the immensely complex spacecraft. It switched to a sixty-forty atmosphere mix of oxygen and nitrogen. And it began making spacesuits out of nonflammable glass fabric.

On October 11, 1968, twenty-one months after the deaths of Grissom, White, and Chaffee, *Apollo 7* became the first manned flight after the disaster. All systems were go as astronauts Wally Schirra, Donn Eisele, and Walt Cunningham lifted off on an eleven-day mission to qualify the craft for flight to the moon. With that, the pace to reach the moon quickened.

At 7:51 A.M. on December 21, 1968, a thirty-five-story-tall Saturn 5 rocket blasted *Apollo 8* into space from the Cape Kennedy Space Center in Florida, with astronauts Frank Borman, Jim Lovell, and William Anders aboard. They flew in the so-called "barbecue mode"; *Apollo 8* slowly revolved—one revolution per hour—to bask evenly in the sun. In the sunlight, the temperature was 250 degrees. In the shade, it was a minus 250.

Borman and ground controllers worked to position the spacecraft. Frank fired the rocket engine for exactly 2.4 seconds to make a slight course correction. The three men in their tiny spacecraft were nearly seventy thousand miles away from earth, traveling at fifty-eight hundred miles an hour toward the moon.

Borman, meanwhile, was feeling "poorly," as the saying went. At lift-off he'd become slightly nauseated and uneasy. In fact, all three astronauts had, but Lovell and Anders got over it. Borman didn't and whatever was ailing him got worse. Mission Control knew nothing about it, because the *Apollo 8* crew elected not to say anything that might hint of anything wrong.

Lovell was the mission navigator and he took sightings on stars, the earth, and the moon. *Apollo 8*, he told ground controllers, was on an almost perfect course.

Borman was supposed to sleep, but he couldn't. With Mission Control's permission, he took a Seconal tablet, a short-acting sleeping pill. When he woke up he felt even worse than before he'd gone to sleep. He vomited and had diarrhea. The crew still hadn't reported his illness.

Apollo 8 was a hundred thousand miles from earth, traveling at fifty-five hundred miles an hour, when the crew finally decided to tell ground control about Frank's illness. But they didn't want the public, millions of people around the world, to know about the problem, so they decided to tell ground controllers through a "tape dump." Large quantities of data, and in this case information about Borman's illness, can be "dumped" to the ground in only a few seconds.

When controllers heard about the illness, they contacted Dr. Charles Berry, the astronauts' physician. In a private conversation not released to the public for four hours, Dr. Berry talked with the *Apollo 8* crew, checking Borman's symptoms:

> Berry: Did you have a sore throat?
> Borman: The roof of my mouth was sore. Roger.
> Berry: And as we understand it at the moment, Frank, neither Bill nor Jim have anything at the present time except some nausea. Is that right?
> Borman: No. None of us are nauseated now. We are all fine now.

At 100,000 miles from his patient, it wasn't exactly a house call, but Dr. Berry made the diagnosis: Frank Borman had the flu—the first case of "flu in space." Berry prescribed Lomotil to prevent motion sickness and Marezine to ease Frank's diarrhea and stomach cramps. *Apollo 8* made no further illness report.

The Final Frontier

At 3:06 P.M. on December 23, the crew gave the world a Christmas present from space: spectacular pictures showing how earth looks from two hundred thousand miles away. The pictures were in black and white, but Jim Lovell said that the earth was brown and the water was blue.

Within minutes of the picture show, the spacecraft came under the influence of the moon's gravity and *Apollo 8*'s speed increased. Sixty-nine hours after takeoff Borman, Lovell, and Anders were about to become the first men to leave Earth's gravitational field.

After a few hours sleep, the crew made a slight course correction. Mission Control gave them permission to go into lunar orbit, the first Earth men to do so. But at the moment the spacecraft was offering its backside to the moon in preparation for orbit insertion, and the three astronauts couldn't see much.

> *Apollo 8:* As a matter of interest, we have yet to see the moon.
> Capcon: Roger, *Apollo 8*, Houston. What else are you seeing?
> *Apollo 8:* Nothing. It's like being on the inside of a submarine.

The spacecraft was racing with the moon, sixty-nine miles above the lunar surface. In moments it would be out of communication with earth as it moved to the far side of the moon where, direct point-to-point radio contact would be lost. "Thanks a lot, troops," Lovell reported. "We'll see you on the other side." Borman, Lovell, and Anders were about to become the first humans to see first hand what others had seen before only by satellite pictures.

Radio contact was lost for fifteen minutes, and when it resumed—and after everyone reported how grateful they were to be back in communications—ground control asked the obvious question:

> Capcon: *Apollo 8,* Houston. What does the ole moon look like from sixty [nautical] miles?
> *Apollo 8:* Okay, Houston. The moon is essentially gray, no color. . . .

So, after traveling more than a quarter of a million miles, the astronauts looked at the moon in living black and white.

Apollo 8: "Looks like plaster of Paris or sort of a grayish deep sand. We can see quite a bit of detail, the Sea of Fertility doesn't stand out as well here as it does back on earth. There's not as much contrast between that and the surrounding craters. The craters are all rounded off. There's quite a few of 'em, some of them are newer. Many of them look like—especially the round ones—look like they were hit by meteorites. . . ."

On their second and ninth orbits of the moon, the crew pointed their onboard television camera at the cratered, pitted lunar service. It was Christmas Eve, and the crew read from the Bible: "In the beginning, God created the heaven and the Earth. And the earth was without form, and void, and darkness was upon the face of the deep. . . ."

The Bible reading, with all three astronauts taking part, drew both intense joy and intense dissent. Acting NASA administrator Dr. Thomas O. Paine called it "the triumph of the squares—the guys with computers and slide-rules who read the Bible on Christmas Eve." Atheist Madalyn Murray O'Hair, the woman who got prayer removed from public schools, said, "I think the astronauts were not only ill advised but that it was a tragic situation . . . that they should read portions of the Genesis Bible which is accepted by a very minor number of persons in the total world."

Frank Borman apparently felt much better following his case of space flu; of course, his raised spirits might be due to the miniature bottle of brandy the crew had smuggled on board. "And from the crew of *Apollo 8,*" Frank said, "we pause with good night, good luck, a Merry Christmas, and God bless all of you—all of you on the good earth," which apparently took in Madalyn Murray O'Hair, whether she liked it or not.

At 1:10 A.M. on Christmas Day, the crew of *Apollo 8* began the long trip back to earth. Jim Lovell radioed back, "Please be informed there is a Santa Claus."

Almost four years earlier, on February 17, 1965, NASA had launched the unmanned *Ranger 8* mission from Cape Canaveral.

Three days later it had landed on the moon. It would be four years more before man equaled that trip. Big difference, of course. Not only was *Apollo 11 manned,* it came back. The Associated Press radio wire relayed almost minute-by-minute reports:

AP71HB
U R G E N T
(Cape Kennedy)—All continues to go well with the Apollo eleven countdown. The huge Saturn Five rocket is scheduled to blast the moon astronauts aloft at 9:32 a.m. (EDT)
ED823ACD July 16

Astronauts Neil Armstrong and Edwin "Buzz" Aldrin were about to follow the Ranger 8 probe's lead and land on the moon.

AP75HB
U R G E N T
(Cape Kennedy)—All conditions are go for the historic launching of Apollo eleven.
ED828ACD July 16

Earlier, the crew of *Apollo 10* had done everything *except* touch down on the lunar surface. Now, while astronaut John Young orbited sixty-nine miles above the moon in the command module (nicknamed "Charlie Brown"), Gene Cernan and Tom Stafford took their lander (nicknamed "Snoopy") down to within 47,500 feet of the surface. "We're right there! We're right over it!" Cernan exclaimed to Mission Control, "I'm telling you, we are low! We're close, babe! This is it!"

Only it wasn't, at least not for Stafford, Young, Cernan, "Charlie Brown," and "Snoopy." And not with the crews of *Apollo's 8* and *9.* The crew of *Apollo 10* had to come back without actually landing on the surface. That, of course, was what they were supposed to do and they did. But can you imagine the frustration they must have felt? They got up there and that was great, but to be so close and not have it in the cards—or at least not in NASA's plans—for them to land!

AP79HB
B U L L E T I N
Apollo launched.
                                                    ED832ACD July 16

AP81HB
B U L L E T I N
(Cape Kennedy)—Apollo eleven is in orbit.
                                                    ED845ACD July 16

AP82HB
U R G E N T
Apollo (tops)
(Cape Kennedy)—Man set off for the Moon today as America's Apollo-eleven astronauts took off from Cape Kennedy right on schedule at 9:32 a.m. (EDT)

The launch—witnessed by (m) millions the world over—was successful from the very beginning. . . .
                                                    ED855ACD July 16

In the heat of the assassination of President John F. Kennedy, America changed the name of the centuries-old Cape Canaveral to "Cape Kennedy." Ten years later the cape itself resumed the name Canaveral, with the rocket facility being called the "Kennedy Space Center."

The flight from Earth to the moon took three days and was uneventful, if flying from the Earth to the moon could ever be "uneventful." For the landing, Armstrong and Aldrin moved into the lunar module *Eagle*, leaving Michael Collins in the command module *Columbia*.

Eagle descended to about three hundred feet above the moon's surface. And second by second, Armstrong acted like the pilot he was, taking command, because the site originally chosen to land in the Sea of Tranquility wasn't suitable, too many boulders would make setting down there too dangerous—"a football field-sized crater,"

Armstrong said later, "with a large number of big boulders and rocks for about one or two crater diameters around us."

Aldrin: Lights on. Down two and a half. Forward. Forward. Good. Forty feet. Down two and a half. Picking up some dust. Thirty feet, two and a half down. Faint shadow. Four forward, four forward, drifting to the right a little. Six [static] . . . down a half.
Capcom (Deke Slayton): Thirty seconds.

The lunar module (LM) was about to run out of rocket fuel. If that happened, Armstrong wouldn't be able to control the landing. He said later that he'd given the LM only a fifty-fifty chance of landing safely.

Aldrin: [static] . . . forward. Drifting right . . . [static] . . . Contact light.Okay, engine stop, ACA out of detent.
Armstrong: Got it.
Aldrin: Mode controls, both auto, descent engine command override, off. Engine arm, off. Four thirteen is in.

Armstrong and Aldrin made it with less than twenty seconds of descent fuel left.

Armstrong: Houston. Tranquility Base here. The *Eagle* has landed.
Capcom: Roger, Tranquility. We copy you on the ground. You've got a bunch of guys about to turn blue. We're breathing again.Thanks a lot.

It was one of the most dramatic, heart-stopping, exciting moments in history. And the whole world watched. What could be more exciting?
Well, there was a moonwalk or two. After a sleepless night—like children waiting for Santa Claus on Christmas morning, Aldrin and Armstrong couldn't stop thinking about what was ahead—Mission

Control gave them permission to go for a stroll outside. Neil Armstrong opened the door of the craft. Reaching the second step of the ladder, he pulled a D-ring and deployed a TV camera. It was 10:56:20 P.M. (EDT).

> Houston (Bruce McCandless): Okay, Neil, we can see you coming down the ladder now.
> Armstrong: Okay, I just checked—getting back up to that first step, Buzz, [the LM footpad]'s not even collapsed to far, but its adequate to get back up. . . . It takes a pretty good little jump. I'm at the foot of the ladder.

He gave a second-by-second account, just in case something went wrong: The TV picture gave out or he just simply sank over his head in moon dust.

> Armstrong: The LM footpads are only depressed in the surface about one or two inches. Although the surface appears to be very, very fine grained, fine. . . . I'm going to step off the LM now. . . .

And then he was there, and what he said—man's first words uttered on the Moon—were heard above static and cheers and tears: "That's one small step for man, one giant leap for mankind."

He had intended to say "for *a* man," and maybe he did, but there was static or maybe the voice-activated microphone cut out or whatever. It didn't matter. Man was on the moon.

Nineteen minutes later, it became "men on the moon." Buzz Aldrin followed Neil onto the lunar surface. The two astronauts bounced around and went into tourist mode, taking pictures of each other, of the lunar surface, of a plaque reading, HERE MEN FROM THE PLANET EARTH FIRST SET FOOT UPON THE MOON JULY 1969 A.D. WE CAME IN PEACE FOR ALL MANKIND.

They erected a three-by-five-foot flag, a metallic flag, because without wind, it wouldn't stand upright. For the next two and a half hours Aldrin and Armstrong evaluated their equipment and their clothing and took more photographs. They collected about forty-eight pounds of moon rocks and soil. They set up scientific experiments—an aluminum sheet to trap solar-wind particles, and laser reflectors—for astronomers back on Earth to study. Then it was time to leave.

In many parts of the country, the moon landing and walk took place in the middle of the night. A lot of people watched until the wee small hours of the morning, which meant they were in no shape to go to work the next day. In many parts of the country, in cities that normally were so busy that you'd be up to your armpits in fellow workers, nothing happened. Nothing. Everybody stayed home to catch up on their sleep. You could, as someone said, roll a bowling ball down Main Street and not hit anybody. In fact, a TV reporter in Detroit put it just that way. He wanted to dramatize it by actually rolling a bowling ball down Woodward Avenue, but he couldn't find a bowling alley open to borrow a ball.

Twenty-one hours and thirty-six minutes after the *Eagle* landed at Tranquility Base, Armstrong and Aldrin lifted off from the moon's surface to rendezvous with Collins, jettison the LM, and aim *Columbia* back for Earth, back home. The flight from the moon to the Earth was uneventful, if flying from the moon to the Earth could ever be "uneventful." They were ten seconds behind schedule when Columbia splashed down in the Pacific off Hawaii. And did Armstrong, Aldrin, and Collins get to go to Honolulu or someplace nice? Of course not. It was, after all, a government operation. They were kept in quarantine until August 10, just in case they'd brought back any space bugs with them.

Nine years after President Kennedy said that "This nation should commit itself to achieving the goal, before this decade is out, of landing a man on the moon and returning him safely to earth," America did just that. A year less than the decade he'd forecast.

But was it "one giant leap for mankind" or one giant waste of money? Each moon trip cost around half a billion dollars. Vice President Spiro Agnew used the moon landing to try to promote a race to Mars. NASA argued for human settlements on the moon. Either would be vastly expensive. Walter Cronkite of CBS News, always a big space fan, said that going to the moon put the hippies and other dissidents in their place.

What we really did was to demonstrate a giant amount of ingenuity and courage. Think of all of those millions of parts and wires and fuel working together precisely; that's ingenious. And courage? As one astronaut said, "You're sitting in the ship, on top of the rocket, waiting to be launched into space, and you can't help remembering that it was all built by the lowest bidder."

Following *Apollo 11*, four more moonshots took place, for a total of ten men walking on the lunar surface—leaving footprints, equipment, maybe even chewing gum wrappers and empty film boxes. Even a golf ball astronaut Alan Shepard smuggled on board; he made what undoubtedly is the longest chip shot in golf history. A scientific experiment, he said, to show how far a golf ball would go in one-fifth earth gravity and no crosswind.

Luckily, he didn't shank it.

CHAPTER FIFTEEN

This Old House:
Childhood's End

In the future everybody will be world famous for fifteen minutes.
Andy Warhol, Catalog of his photo exhibition in Stockholm, 1968

"Is That All There Is?"
Peggy Lee, song title, 1969, lyrics by Jerry Lieber

On September 8, 1961, the American Medical Association (AMA) reported that a study of three thousand men showed a clear statistical link between heart disease and smoking; subjects who smoked more than forty cigarettes a day suffered twice as much heart disease as light smokers or nonsmokers. It had been at least 354 years—since the founding of Jamestown, Virginia, in 1607—that Americans had been smoking tobacco—in cigarettes, cigars, and pipes—chewing tobacco, and dipping snuff.

We believed early advertising claim that "more doctors recommended" certain brands of cigarettes and that there wasn't "a cough in a carload." We even smoked one brand "for a treat instead of a treatment." But it wasn't until 1966 that the manufacturers were required to print warnings from the U.S. Surgeon General on cigarette packages: "Caution: Cigarette smoke may be hazardous to your health." Meanwhile, the argument continued between smokers and nonsmokers.

In the 1960s America's homicide rate was 4.7 per 100,000 population. The suicide rate was higher, 10.6 per 100,000, and it cut across all segments of American society.

Marilyn Monroe may have been one of those suicides. Film star, celebrity, and arguably one of the most beautiful and sexy women of her time, she died, on August 5, 1962. She was found dead in her Hollywood home, due to a combination of sleeping pills and alcohol. Possibly an overdose, possibly murder, possibly suicide.

"I seem to be a whole superstructure with no foundation," she once said. "I'm working on the foundation." She'd been born Norma Jean Baker on June 1, 1926, in Los Angeles of "uncertain parentage," meaning it's uncertain whether her mother and father were married, or who her father was. It is certain that Norma Jean's mother was sufficiently disturbed mentally that she had to be institutionalized. By the time Norma Jean was a teenager, she'd been shipped from orphanage to orphanage and foster home, been beaten, neglected, and raped. When she was sixteen, she married merchant seaman James Dougherty. It was 1942, and when Dougherty went to sea Norma Jean went to work as a painter at an aircraft plant in Bakersfield, California. It was there that her life began to change. An attractive brunette, she became one of the thousands of World War II's "Rosie the Riveters."

A *Yank* magazine photographer took Norma Jean's picture, and after it was published, other area photographers offered her some small modeling jobs. By the time she was twenty, she'd divorced her husband, changed her hair color, turned her back on her past, and taken her new name of Marilyn Monroe.

Two years later, Marilyn was in the movie *All About Eve*, but hers was only a bit part. She had a more impressive role in *The Asphalt Jungle*, an old-fashioned crime movie. Originally, she wasn't to have been given a credit in *Jungle*, but when screening audiences saw her they responded so enthusiastically—she was sexy, defenseless, and spoke with a little-girl voice—that studio executives reluctantly included her name.

She was *Life* magazine's April 7, 1952, covergirl, and inside, the article said that her taste in music was "distinctly highbrow, running to composers like Hungarian modernist Béla Bartók." But it was neither the *Life* cover nor the story inside that set off a nationwide buzz about Marilyn Monroe. Rather, it was her picture as Miss February in a Western Lithograph Company calendar that did it. The photo showed Marilyn languishing on a red velvet background. Nude.

An anonymous caller had tried to extort ten thousand dollars from 20th Century Fox, where Marilyn's career was showing signs of progress: Pay me, the caller said, or I'll tell everybody about Marilyn's naked calendar pose. The studio refused to pay but pressured Marilyn into denying that she was, indeed, the nude blonde on the calendar. But she decided to make a clean breast of it, as it were: "Sure, I posed." She'd been hungry when she agreed to pose for the calendar and needed the pay for food. Later, when asked if she'd had anything on during the photographic shoot, Marilyn replied, "Yes, the radio." The public rallied behind her and thousands of copies of the Tom Kelley photograph showed up in college dorms, men's barbershops, and locked bathrooms. And in would-be publisher Hugh Hefner's new magazine, *Playboy*. For five hundred dollars Hefner bought the rights to the photo. Glorious skin on a red draped background, a staple in her navel. It made a success out of Hefner's *Playboy* magazine and a star out of Marilyn Monroe.

In a scene in the movie *Love Happy* with Groucho Marx, Marilyn, who was cast as a dumb blonde, walked up to the private detective played by Groucho and said, "Some men are following me." Groucho answered, "I can't imagine why."

Obviously he *could* imagine; off camera he told Marilyn, "You have the prettiest ass in the business."

In 1954, Marilyn Monroe married baseball legend Joe DiMaggio, and they went to Japan for their honeymoon. DiMaggio was doing a celebrity tour, but military officials approached Marilyn and asked her to entertain troops still serving in Korea. The crowd-shy Joe declined to go along with her, and Marilyn stood before some hundred thousand troops gathered in an outdoor amphitheater to hear her perform. Later, when she rejoined DiMaggio in Tokyo, she told him, "Joe, you've never heard such cheering." And the man who was more than just a little familiar with crowds answered, "Yes I have."

During the filming of a now-famous scene in *The Seven Year Itch*, Marilyn stood over a subway grating in New York City as the air blew her skirt high above her almost perfect legs, high above her panties. The scene was shot on location at 2:00 A.M. "Higher, higher," the early-morning crowd of onlookers screamed, while Joe DiMaggio stood stone faced and silent. Above all, it seemed, he valued *his* dignity, what the public would think of *him*, and he watched his wife expose herself in public for money, financial exploitation. The still picture became a billboard and a best-selling pinup, but DiMaggio wanted Marilyn to play the scene only for him.

Later that morning, Marilyn and Joe had a bitter fight. The following day he flew back to California. Alone. And the marriage was over. They remained close friends, and later she told her maid that DiMaggio had been the love of her life. When she died she had a poster-size picture of Joe DiMaggio in her closet.

Her fans wanted Marilyn to remain a pouting sex goddess, but she wanted to be taken seriously as an actress. She headed for New York to study at the Actors Studio under drama coach Lee Strasberg she even lived with Strasberg and his family. While studying at the studio, Marilyn met and married playwright Arthur Miller. But just as her first two marriages failed to last long, neither did her third.

Miller wrote the movie *The Misfits* for Marilyn, but by the time it was filmed she'd become increasingly difficult to work with: chronically late on the set and just as chronically dependent on alcohol and sleeping pills. She spent time in a psychiatric clinic and was plagued by insomnia and a lack of self-confidence. Before *The Misfits* opened, she and Miller divorced.

In 1962, she started work on a new film, *Something's Got to Give*. In May, she left the set and flew from Hollywood to New York City's Madison Square Garden, where she appeared in a cream-white, skintight, beaded sequin dress she had to be sewn into. In probably the most famous rendition of the song ever, she sang "Happy Birthday, Mr. President" to John F. Kennedy. The audience howled.

Marilyn had been so late on the set so often that 20th Century Fox began a breach-of-contract suit against her. Marilyn never completed *Something's Got to Give*, and only a few brief clips and a handful of still photographs remained from the filming. At the time, she was, if anything, even more beautiful than ever, the sex kitten replaced by a lovely and sophisticated and nude young woman, swimming alone in a pool.

JFK's birthday bash was one of Marilyn Monroe's final public appearances and fueled rumors that she and Kennedy were having a torrid affair. Not only Jack Kennedy and she but brother Bobby as well, as if the brothers had passed Marilyn between them. Maybe even to brother Ted. Then came rumors of attempts to keep Marilyn quiet to protect Jack and Bobby's reputations.

She was abused early and often, both physically and mentally. Exploited, maneuvered, and manipulated. Marilyn said the film industry "should behave to its stars like a mother whose child has just run out in front of a car. But instead of clasping the child to them, they start punishing the child."

At her funeral, her friend and drama coach Lee Strasberg delivered a tribute to Marilyn Monroe. She had become a legend, he said. "For the entire world she became a symbol of the eternal female." Norman Mailer wrote:

> So we think of Marilyn who was every man's love affair with America, Marilyn Monroe who was blonde and beautiful and had a sweet little rinky-dink of a voice and all the cleanliness of all the clean American backyards. She was our angel, the sweet angel of sex, and the sugar of sex came up from her like a resonance of sound in the clearest grain of a violin.

From singer-songwriter Elton John came the simple "Goodbye, Norma Jean."

Marilyn's last movie line was "How do you find your way back in the dark?"

"Just head for the big star straight on," she's told. "The highway's under it, and it'll take us right home."

The last line for Marilyn, the last line of the Arthur Miller–written movie *The Misfits*, and the last movie line for her costar, Clark Gable. Just days after he finished *The Misfits*, Gable died.

Film critics never considered Gable a great actor, but to the public he was the King long before Elvis Presley took the crown. For much of his thirty-year career in movies, Gable was a top box-office star. He won an Oscar and shocked moviegoers in *It Happened One Night*—bare chested, not an undershirt in sight. If Clark Gable can get by without an undershirt, many young men believed, why can't I? And the sale of undershirts plummeted. But he was best known for playing Rhett Butler to Vivien Leigh's* Scarlett O'Hara in *Gone With the Wind*.

---

* Vivien Leigh died on July 7, 1967, three years after Gable.

In 1942, with World War II under way, Gable's blond and beautiful wife, Carole Lombard, went east on a bond-selling drive, then rushed back to California to be with Clark. To get home quicker, she chartered a private plane. It crashed and Lombard died.

With Lombard's death, Clark Gable retired from films and joined the army air force as a private. He was soon commissioned (serial number: 0-565390) and put in charge of making training films in England. To film aerial operations, he sometimes flew on B-17 bombing missions, a fact that didn't escape Germany's air marshal Hermann Goering, who put a bounty on the movie star's head: five thousand dollars to any Luftwaffe pilot who shot down Gable.

No one ever collected the bounty, and Clark Gable made it safely back home, where he was awarded the Distinguished Flying Cross and the Air Medal. By then, Gable was a major, and the war was almost over. The officer handling Gable's discharge? Another actor-turned-soldier, Capt. Ronald Reagan.

During the filming of *The Misfits* the fifty-nine-year-old Gable performed many of his own stunts, and insiders believe this physical strain brought on the heart attack that killed him. That and the emotional strain of waiting around in the desert heat for his unreliable costar. Clark Gable died on November 16, 1960.

The 1960s were the peak period for Bond, James Bond. In 1962, for a salary of $16,500, thirty-two-year-old Sean Connery starred as the title character in the first Bond film, *Dr. No.* By 1966, Connery's salary had risen to $750,000, which by almost anybody's standards was a good pay hike.

James Bond was the fictional spy created by a real spy, Ian Fleming, and sometimes the deeds of the literary spy mocked those of the human one. During World War II, Fleming served as an aide to the chief of British Naval Intelligence, taking the code name 17F, not nearly as cool as Bond's 007. The fictional character almost entered print under a different name: "James Gunn." Fleming changed it to James Bond, the name of the real-life author of one of Fleming's favorite books: *Birds of the West Indies.* Fleming's James Bond, of course, also went in for birds, although of a different variety. Ian Fleming died on August 12, 1964. Bond movies and Bond books continue today in something of a cinematic and literary afterlife.

That same year, two other well-known authors passed on to that great editorial room in the sky. Terence Hanbury White had written novels about Britain's King Arthur. In 1958, they were combined, condensed, and changed for a Broadway musical, *Camelot.* T. H. White was fifty-seven when he died.

Grace Metalious was a lot younger when she died in 1964, only thirty-nine. A somewhat blousy and unkempt woman who lived the typical life of so-called "trailer trash," she catapulted to fame in 1956 with her novel *Peyton Place.* For the times, it was a sexy, sensational book, and became a less sexy, less sensational movie by the same name. Television took it up and the sex and sensationalism shrank even more. Metalious died of chronic liver disease.

"Beat" writer Jack Kerouac was born in Lowell, Massachusetts, and went to Columbia University on a football scholarship before dropping out. He once described literature as "the tale that's told for no other reason but companionship." His first novel, *The Town and the City,* didn't do much, and it was *On the Road,* coming seven years later, that made him famous and epitomized the Beat philosophy. Jack Kerouac died in 1969. Or as his friend and fellow Beat writer, Allen Ginsberg put it: "He drank himself to death. Which is only another way of living, of handling the pain and foolishness that it's all a dream, a great baffling silly emptiness, after all."

In 1965, years of heavy smoking caught up with jazz pianist and singer Nat "King" Cole; he was one month shy of his forty-sixth birthday. Earlier, he'd led his own trio to success but went solo and, in 1948, began a career that included such hits as "Nature Boy," "Mona Lisa," "Unforgettable," and "Ramblin' Rose."

Nat Cole became the first African American performer to cross the Las Vegas color line when he signed a two-year contract with the Sands Hotel. The contract even guaranteed him full access to the hotel's facilities, which certainly hadn't been the case when Cole toured nightclubs in the South. Once, in Birmingham, Alabama, he was given police "protection," because the White Citizens' Council had been campaigning against "decadent" Negro music. It was an all-white audience, and police didn't do much to protect him. Six men leapt over the footlights and attacked Cole. Later, the audience

315

gave him a standing ovation, but Cole had to cancel the concert to be checked out by a doctor.

In 1956, Nat "King" Cole had a fifteen-minute-long television series on NBC, the first prime-time network series headlining a major African American performer. Despite the popularity of his records, *The Nat King Cole Show* initially had poor ratings, and that scared off some sponsors. Other sponsors refused to risk the wrath of Southern viewers. Many other performers, however, hoped the show would last, and both black and white artists appeared with him for next to nothing. Less than a year after it began, NBC pulled the show off the air.

Nat "King" Cole's smooth voice greatly influenced many other singers, including Sam Cooke and Otis Redding. Even rock 'n' roll star Chuck Berry believed that "if I had only one artist to listen to through eternity, it would be Nat Cole." On February 15, 1965, Nat Cole died of lung cancer.

On February 19, 1970, a California court convicted former Harvard University professor-turned-high-priest-of-the-drug-culture Timothy Leary of holding two marijuana cigarettes and sentenced him to ten years in prison. They sent Leary to the California Men's Colony at San Luis Obispo. But he didn't stay locked up long.

With the help of the radical group "Weatherman" (later, the Weather Underground*), Leary planned an escape, and on September 13, he moved hand over hand along a cable suspended over the prison fence, then slid down to freedom. He crawled to a ditch, where he waited until a car came along and stopped at a prearranged spot. A woman, who may have been political activist Bernardine Dohrn, jumped out of the car and Leary jumped in. As the car headed north, the woman helped Leary dye his hair, change clothes, and gave him a set of false identification papers. They changed cars at a rest stop, and Leary left his prison clothing behind to be picked

---

* The June 1969 Students for a Democratic Society manifesto began with a line from a Bob Dylan song: "You don't need a weatherman to know which way the wind blows."

up by occupants of another car and deposited at another rest stop a hundred miles south of San Luis Obispo, an effort to fool police into believing Tim was headed for Mexico. Instead, the LSD guru headed north, first to a safe house in North Oakland, and then to a ranch farther north. Three days later, using yet another set of false papers, Tim Leary was in a Black Panther compound in Algeria.

"They [Weather] are not in hiding," Leary wrote, "but are invisible." They were "in every tribe, commune, dormitory, farmhouse, barracks, and town house where kids are making love, smoking dope, preparing for the future." Finally, someone—it's not certain who—betrayed Timothy Leary in 1973. He was recaptured and returned to prison, where he spent the next three years. After his release, he worked with a group called SMILE (Space Migration, Increased Intelligence, Life Extension). And in 1982, he teamed up with his old nemesis from the days of the Millbrook commune, G. Gordon Liddy. Together they worked a sort of vaudeville-debate circuit.

By 1996, Leary was suffering from terminal prostate cancer. He was, as one critic put it, "just another artifact from the psychedelic era," like lava lamps, tie-dyed t-shirts, and love beads. To ease his final days, he sucked on balloons filed with nitrous-oxide, laughing gas, passed to him by his personal assistant, who called herself "Trudy Truelove."

His home in Benedict Canyon high above Beverly Hills was decorated in "early fraternity house," a slate-gray pool table held up by construction girders, overstuffed sofas, and comic-book art. On the dining-room wall hung a psychedelic poster from an old Don Knotts movie.

By the spring of 1996, Tim Leary was dying, and looking forward" to it. He told CNN television correspondent Anne McDermott that "I've lived a wonderful life with wonderful friends, and I want my friends to join me in a great going-away party." They did. In his final days, old friends went to visit Tim Leary, almost as if they were on a pilgrimage: filmmaker Oliver Stone, John Lennon's widow Yoko Ono, actress Winona Ryder, former Mama Michelle Phillips, former Los Angeles Dodgers catcher Johnny Roseboro, Susan Sarandon, and Tim Robbins. And Ram Dass, known to Leary in their Harvard University days as Richard Alpert.

Leary once said that he'd take a "suicide cocktail" rather than continue to suffer. It wasn't needed; on May 31, 1996, he died quietly in his sleep. The man whose name remains frozen in time as the drug guru of the sixties once said that he wanted to continue his frozen existence; he'd asked that his body be frozen in a cryogenics lab for future resurrection. In a last-minute change of mind, however, Leary asked that his body be cremated and the ashes rocketed into outerspace along with that of *Star Trek* originator Gene Roddenberry.

Tim Leary's last words were "Why not?"

At last report, the 1938 International Harvester bus Ken Kesey and his band of Merry Pranksters took on a nationwide LSD-fueled trip in 1964 still exists. Though long retired from active duty, its Day-Glo colors are quietly fading away as it sits at Kesey's ranch near Pleasant Hill, Oregon. The trip was immortalized in author Tom Wolfe's book *The Electric Kool-Aid Acid Test.* Ken Kesey is alive, well, and still kicking up a psychedelic fuss.

On May 1, 1960, while flying an American U-2 spy plane over the Soviet Union, Francis Gary Powers was shot down. On August 1, 1977, as he was piloting a traffic helicopter for Los Angeles station KNBC-TV, Gary Powers's craft ran out of fuel and crashed. Powers died and was buried in Arlington National Cemetery.

In 1969, the little girl who led us down a yellow brick road died. Judy Garland had been a child performer and, as a teenager, an MGM studio bit player when ten-year-old Shirley Temple turned down the role of Dorothy in *The Wizard of Oz.* At age sixteen, Judy wasn't the child author L. Frank Baum had envisioned when he wrote the book. Strapped in to hide her budding breasts, Judy swept away movie audiences the way the fictional tornado swept Dorothy and her little dog Toto out of Kansas.

Following *Oz*, Garland went on to star in dozens of other films, including the Andy Hardy series with Mickey Rooney and musicals *Meet Me in St. Louis** and *Easter Parade.* MGM fired her in 1950, but four years later she made a memorable comeback as an aspiring ac-

---

* Directed by her second husband, Vincente Minnelli, the father of Judy's daughter Liza.

tress in *A Star Is Born*, receiving an Oscar nomination. In 1960 Judy Garland became something of a cult figure with her successes at New York's Carnegie Hall and London's Palladium. Her network television show often saw her sit at the stage's edge, singing of that land over the rainbow.

But there were potholes in her yellow brick road. For years, Judy Garland had virtually lived on pills to get her going in the morning (and in an effort to keep her weight down) and pills to get to sleep at night. She grew more and more unreliable, arriving late for some performances, even missing others. Her mental and physical health deteriorated. She went through drugs, booze, suicide attempts—at least two, including slashing her wrist and cutting her neck—and five marriages. And on June 22, 1969, Judy Garland's rainbow faded forever. Her latest husband found her dead, locked in their apartment bathroom. The medical examiner ruled accidental barbiturate poisoning as the cause of death; she had shot up with an unusually strong potion of heroin on top of alcohol. She was only forty-seven years old.

Three days before Judy Garland died, another long-time movie actor passed away: Leo Gorcey. In 1938, when he was twenty-one years old but small for his age, Gorcey appeared as Spit in the first Dead End Kids movie. Wearing a beanie or tweed cap, Spit was the on-screen leader of a gang of not-so-tough teenagers on New York's pre-World War II sidewalks. After four years and at least half a dozen movies, Gorcey quit the Dead End Kids series and helped form the funnier, if even less realistic, Bowery Boys movie gang. Leo Gorcey was forty-five.

Boris Karloff, the original monster in the movie *Frankenstein* and a three-role actor in the classic *The Mummy*, also died in 1962. Bela Lugosi* had portrayed Dracula a year before *Frankenstein* and been offered the role of the monster. He turned it down. Karloff picked it up, and he rode it to fame and typecasting.

---

* Bela Lugosi died in mid-1956, forgotten by all but a few of Hollywood's big names. According to his wishes, Lugosi was buried in his Dracula cape.

Another typecast actor who died in 1969 was Gabby Hayes, the gray-bearded, grumbling, but trusted western movie sidekick of Hopalong Cassidy, Roy Rogers, Gene Autry, and John Wayne. Hayes, who wasn't western at all—he'd been born in New York City—appeared in some two hundred cowboy movies and countless TV programs. For a while Gabby Hayes had his own afternoon television show (sponsored by Puffed Wheat and Puffed Rice: "They're shot from guns!") during which he introduced B movies for the under-twelve set. Noted for his tall tales, Hayes frequently ended his yarns with the phrase "That's my story, and I'm stuck with it."

In the late fifties, a U.S. House of Representatives subcommittee held hearings about television quiz shows and radio "payola." Producers of some TV quiz shows had given contestants the answers to their questions. Some radio disc jockeys were accused of taking payola—that is, bribes—to play certain records.

The payola investigation had focused on Dick Clark and Alan Freed. At the time, half of the records Clark played on his show *American Bandstand* were handled by his own outside company, and that was a conflict of interest. ABC television, which aired Clark's show, gave him an option: Choose *Bandstand* or his business. He chose the TV show and divested himself of all outside music interests before being called to testify.

On May 19, 1960, a grand jury indicted disc jockey Alan Freed and four other New York deejays on charges that they'd accepted payola. In the end, none of the four were packed off to prison; however, the federal government's investigation into payola charges ruined the careers of dozens of people. Alan Freed once claimed he had never accepted payola but said he'd taken "consulting fees." Later, he admitted to a New York newspaper columnist that he'd accepted payola but that it shouldn't be regarded as a crime. He plead guilty to charges of commercial bribery (thirty thousand dollars in bribes from five record companies) and received a three hundred dollar fine and six months probation. The Internal Revenue Service got in on the act, claiming that Freed had failed to report fifty-seven thousand dollars in income from 1957 to 1959. In November 1960, Alan Freed's bosses fired him.

This Old House

Freed had been the father of rock 'n' roll. "Anyone," he claimed, "who says rock 'n' roll is a passing fad or a flash in the pan has rocks in his head, dad!" Freed was never able to salvage his career after the payola scandal and would die broke and broken hearted. On New Year's Day 1965, while cooking dinner for his family and friends, Alan Freed doubled over in pain. He was bleeding from a gastrointestinal ulcer— "a lot of blood everywhere," his son Lance remembered, "and he was very, very frightened." They took Freed to a nearby hospital, where a doctor told family members that Alan had only a ten percent chance of making it through the night. He died twenty days later, on January 20, 1965. A coroner's report listed the cause of death as liver failure. He was forty-two years old.

Back in 1965, when 525 black civil rights protestors crossed the Edmund Pettus Bridge in Selma, Alabama, they were greeted by the boots and batons of state and local police officers and sheriff's deputies. The protestors had just begun a march to the state capital in Montgomery to push for voting rights. Among the marchers was Marg McNamara, Secretary of Defense Robert McNamara's oldest child. The secretary didn't know Marg had been on the march until after it was over.

Police used tear gas, whips, and nightsticks on the marchers, and seventeen demonstrators had to be hospitalized. More than sixty others required emergency treatment.

On the last day of the 1965 Selma march, three members of the Ku Klux Klan forced off the road a car driven by white Detroit housewife and mother of five Viola Gregg Liuzzo. Then, they shot and killed her. Liuzzo's passenger, Leroy Moton, who was black, survived by pretending to be dead.

Moton recalled that seconds before the shooting Mrs. Liuzzo had said, "I was just thinkin' of this song—'Before I'll be a slave, I'll be buried in my grave.'" Morton leaned over to turn on the radio and at that moment, as Viola Liuzzo spoke the word *grave*, she was shot. Moton was injured by flying glass, but the blood from that glass, and his pretending to be dead, saved his life.

The next day, President Johnson announced on television the arrest of four Ku Klux Klansmen in connection with Mrs. Liuzzo's murder. How had the FBI solved the Liuzzo case in twenty-four hours? Simple—one of the Klansmen in the car was a paid FBI informant.

The remaining three Klansmen were arrested and tried twice by state courts. Each trial ended in a hung jury. In December 1965, a federal court found them guilty of conspiracy to deny a citizen of her constitutional rights and gave them ten-year sentences.

In September 2000, citizens of the now mostly black town of Selma, Alabama, once again marched across the Edmund Pettus Bridge, this time to celebrate the election of a new mayor. James Perkins, an African American, had defeated long-time mayor Joseph Smitherman, a white. Smitherman had been mayor during the original Selma march and was—some say he remained so—a defender of segregation. He claimed that he lost the election in 2000 because "They brought in all these celebrities to energize the voters." Others said that the community had undergone three decades of struggle and wanted a change.

CHAPTER SIXTEEN

A Sixties Hangover:
The Seventies

What a waste it is to lose one's mind or not to have a mind is very wasteful.
Vice President J. Danforth "Dan" Quayle, address to the
United Negro College Fund, May 1989

The trial of the Chicago 7, which came out of the Democratic National Convention in 1968—Yippies against police—finally ended on February 18, 1970, with the jury deciding that five of the seven had indeed incited riots but had not conspired to do so. Two others were acquitted of all charges. Federal Judge Julius Hoffman, whom defendant Abbie Hoffman irritated by calling him "Julie," sentenced all seven, plus two of their lawyers, to contempt-of-court jail sentences. Eventually, all charges were either dismissed by higher courts or dropped by the government. All that was left of the '68 convention and riots, whether Yippie- or police-caused, was a bad taste in the mouth about Chicago that lasted long into America's next generation. It would be thirty years before the Democrats would stage another national convention in Chicago.

Some of the defining moments of the sixties came in the seventies.

On Thursday, April 30, 1970, President Richard Nixon announced that he was sending American troops to Cambodia, an obvious escalation of the Vietnam War after he'd earlier promised to end the conflict. "If," Nixon said, when the chips are down, the world's most powerful nation . . . acts like a pitiful, helpless giant, the forces of totalitarianism and anarchy will threaten free nations and free institutions throughout the world.

Some congressmen didn't agree and saw Nixon's actions as a constitutional crisis. The president was sending American troops into yet another combat situation without congressional approval. But, as Nixon would say later about another event, "when the President does it, that means that it is not illegal."

For ten years, Cambodian chief of state Prince Sihanouk had kept his country out of war by allowing the North Vietnamese to use his eastern provinces for transport, storage, and sanctuary. But in March 1970, while Sihanouk was in Moscow, General Lon Nol seized power and immediately appealed to the United States for aid in preventing a communist takeover. On April 25—five days *before* his announcement—Richard Nixon began shipping small arms to Cambodia, and on April 29, he sent in twelve thousand U.S. and eight thousand South Vietnamese troops.

In an April 30 television address to the nation, Nixon told Americans that the "incursion"—he refused to call it an invasion—would take only six to eight weeks, and in that time American forces were to drive the communists out of Cambodia. He claimed that this would insure a military success in Vietnam.

The Cambodian invasion itself didn't amount to much as far as the Vietnam War was concerned. Spies in the Saigon government had informed Ho Chi Minh about the planning long before it was executed, and by the time American forces arrived in Cambodia, North Vietnamese troops were long gone. U.S. troops captured a few enemy supplies and then returned to Vietnam.

The U.S. invasion/incursion of Cambodia meant more in America than it did in Vietnam. Within minutes of the president's announcement, antiwar activists took to the streets in New York and Philadelphia. Nixon referred to the demonstrators as "bums," while American soldiers in Vietnam were the "greatest."

Two terms frequently used in the sixties were *establishment* and *outside agitator.* According to the establishment, nearly everyone who protested, demonstrated, or objected to whatever was happening during the era was an outside agitator.

Massive numbers of protesting students gathered on college and university campuses around the country. Kent State University was one of them.

The city of Kent was at the time, and remains now, not much more than a sleepy village in north-central Ohio, about ten miles from Akron, thirty miles from Cleveland.

On Friday, May 1, 1970, the city of Kent was being its usual sleepy self, but soon its sleep was to be disturbed. Antiwar sentiment was running high because of President Nixon's Cambodia actions. A crowd of about five hundred students gathered on the university commons in response to a group of graduate history students calling themselves WHORE, World Historians Opposed to Racism and Exploitation. The Commons sits in the middle of campus, a large grassy area that's not only a convenient meeting ground for students moving between dormitories and classes, but an area traditionally used for rallies and demonstrations. So, answering the WHORE call, so to speak, students cheered and booed and spoke out against the Cambodian incursion in particular and the Vietnam War in general.

They claimed that as a consequence of Nixon's actions the U.S. Constitution had become a lifeless document, murdered by the president. And to symbolize this "murder," they burned a copy of the Constitution. Several students volunteered to burn their draft cards and a few veterans even offered up their military discharge papers. Then the rally broke up,

The weather was warm—the first warm night of spring—and the thought of flowing beer sent the crowd moving away from the university and toward downtown Kent. Friday usually was a night of student socializing along North Water Street, whose bars and rock music were well known throughout the area. As the demonstrators moved downtown, a few threw rocks and bottles at the rare police car driving by. They tossed bottles through a couple of storefront windows and built bonfires at street corners. Shortly after 11:00 P.M. students formed a human chain in the middle of the street and began a snake dance. The atmosphere was lighthearted, if a bit frenetic. By this time, Kent police chief Roy Thompson had called out all twenty-one members of his department as well as officers from Portage County and surrounding communities. Officers in riot gear stopped the crowd at the intersection of Main and Water Streets and fired tear gas shells to disperse the demonstrators.

Kent mayor Leroy Satrom had been in Aurora, Ohio, attending a Law Day celebration and then getting into a poker game. When he returned to Kent shortly after midnight, he found a chaotic scene: Broken glass littered the street, the remains of bonfires smoldered, several police cars were damaged, and his law enforcement officers were decked out in riot gear. While in Aurora, he'd heard rumors of a plan by the radical Weathermen to burn down the army ROTC building.* After meeting with Chief Thompson, Mayor Satrom declared a local state of emergency, then telephoned Ohio governor James Rhodes. "SDS students [have] taken over a portion of Kent," he told the governor, and asked Rhodes to call out the National Guard. The governor agreed that things were looking bad and sent a single guard officer, Lt. Charles J. Barnette, to look over the scene.

Mayor Satrom also ordered all bars closed and the sale of liquor stopped, but that only made things worse. Hundreds of tavern customers poured out into the streets. Police fired tear gas at them and herded bar customers back toward the university campus. They stopped near the intersection of East Main and Lincoln Streets, and, while standing on campus property, challenged the city police "to violate the campus sanctuary." Kent city police waited for Kent University authorities to help out, but that help never came. University police chief Donald L. Schwartzmiller felt that his men were needed to guard campus property and not to stand alongside city officers. By 2:30 Saturday morning, the town was quiet. Later that day a few students even volunteered to help store owners clean up the mess created the night before.

---

* There is no evidence that the Weathermen were in town or on campus at the time.

Mayor Satrom and other city officials met with the National Guard representative to wrangle over the situation. At about 5:00 P.M., Satrom again asked Governor Rhodes to send in the Guard.

Rumors grew: Radical Weathermen were going to burn down the whole university, the local army recruiting office, and the local post office. The *Akron (Ohio) Beacon Journal* headlined a report, "Weathermen Observed on Campus and Positively Identified," and "Evidence of Weapons on Campus." Again, the report was unsubstantiated, but university officials obtained a court injunction prohibiting any damage to campus buildings and distributed a leaflet outlining the order.

That night, a crowd of around a thousand students and local residents surrounded the wooden ROTC barracks, and about an hour later someone set the building on fire. A high school student later confessed the arson to the FBI, but he was never indicted or charged.

Campus police hadn't been there to stop the arson. The crowd had arrived around 8:00 P.M., but the campus cops didn't show up until 9:15. The building burned to the ground, detonating live ammunition stored inside the building. Firemen, who'd arrived nearly two and a half hours too late, claimed protestors punctured and cut open fire hoses.

Campus police chief Schwartzmiller reportedly called on Kent city police to help but was told that all city police officers were busy protecting the downtown area. Schwartzmiller got the impression that city police were "getting even" with him for not sending campus police to aid city officers in the Friday-night fights.

Around 10:00 that night, National Guard troops arrived in town, Company H, 107th Armored Cavalry (Troop G), and Company A, 145th Infantry Regiment. They cleared the campus, forced the protestors into school dormitories, then patrolled the campus. National Guardsmen claimed that on several occasions townspeople came up to them and said of the students, "Kill those SOBs if they cause any more trouble" and "Get tough with them!"

By Sunday morning, nearly a thousand Ohio National Guardsmen occupied the campus, and it looked more like a war zone than a sleepy university. The day was warm and sunny when Governor Rhodes helicoptered in from Cleveland, where he'd been campaigning. He held a news conference and announced that the protestors were "worse than the [Nazi] brownshirts [of Germany] and the communist element . . . the worst type that we harbor in America." He said he would seek a court order declaring a state of emergency—that is, martial law. He actually never did, but his mentioning a court order led both Kent University and city officials to believe he'd put the campus under martial law with the Guard in control.

At Rhodes's news conference, Ohio National Guard adjutant general Sylvester Del Corso proclaimed that "We will apply whatever degree of force is necessary to provide protection for the lives of our citizens and their property." Governor Rhodes denied that his statements about brownshirts and Communists had been "inflammatory"; however, in speaking to members of the National Guard, he said:

> You men are up against the scum of America, but be careful. They are vicious, organized, and dangerous. Your job is to protect the citizens of Kent and Portage County, where no one will be safe if we fail, and remember, your commanding officer has said we can stop them with gunfire if necessary.

In effect, with that statement, Rhodes changed the Guard's mission from one of protecting lives and property "to that of breaking up any assembly on campus, peaceful or otherwise."

Meanwhile, a deluge of sightseers had arrived in the city. While thousands of students protested, at least another thousand onlookers and observers ringed the demonstration. Ringing *them* were the thousand guardsmen armed with M1 rifles and carrying masks to use if tear gas were fired. A hundred or so guardsmen stood between the protestors and the burned-out hulk of the ROTC building.

Around dusk Sunday, a crowd gathered near the Victory Bell—ordinarily rung after athletic victories—on the student commons behind Taylor Hall, about fifty yards north of a small shelter called "the Pagoda." An official read the crowd the Ohio Riot Act.* When the protestors didn't disperse, guardsmen fired tear gas into the crowd.

---

* Generally, unless a riot act is read, officially there is no riot, no matter what happens. Basically, riot acts order crowds to disperse by a certain time; if they do not, they are subject to arrest.

Demonstrators moved away from the Victory Bell and gathered in downtown Kent, where they blocked traffic. At 11:00 P.M., an official once more read them the riot act. Demonstrators threw rocks and shouted obscenities, and National Guardsmen fired more tear gas. National Guard troops also used a bayonet charge to clear demonstrators from the area. Several people were injured—"several guardsmen from rocks, and two or more people bayoneted by guardsmen," wrote Kent State professor James Best.

Classes resumed on Monday, with the charred remains of the ROTC barracks bearing testimony to what had happened over the weekend. A rally was planned for noon at the Victory Bell. Originally it had been scheduled to protest the Cambodian invasion, but now the focus changed to protest the presence of the National Guard on campus. Meanwhile, Guard commander, Gen. Robert Canterbury, had his own ideas. If the students gathered to protest, his men would disperse any assembly. "It would be highly dangerous," Canterbury warned, "to hold the rally." When told that despite its having been declared illegal people were still coming to the rally, General Canterbury said that "These students are going to have to find out what law and order is all about."

Kent State policeman Harold Rice rode in a National Guard jeep, accompanied by a driver and two riflemen, using a bullhorn to order students to disperse. The university had declared demonstration banned in the belief that Governor Rhodes had declared martial law. Protestors threw rocks and bottles at the jeep and the police and guardsman retreated.

By 11:45 A.M., ninety-nine National Guardsmen were facing a crowd they estimated at upward of forty-five hundred, gathered on the commons.* Some of the crowd wanted to protest; others—perhaps as many as three thousand—could best be described as spectators or "cheerleaders," and were there merely to see what was going on. The demonstrators chanted, "Pigs off campus," and "One, two, three, four; we don't want your fucking war." Some threw rocks

* In a later survey, seventy percent of Kent State University students said they believed that less than two thousand students were on the commons at the time of the incident.

and stones at guardsmen. General Canterbury ordered his troops to lock and load their rifles, to be ready to fire if necessary.

Under Ohio state law, the guardsmen could, and did, carry live ammunition. Unfortunately, Kent State students seem not to have been aware of this. Certainly, they believed the guardsmen wouldn't fire on them.

General Canterbury ordered the guardsmen to drive the protestors off with tear gas, but the gas had little effect, thanks in part to a stiff cross-wind and in part to the Guard's poor aim that sent more of the gas among the spectators than among the protestors. With tear gas having so little effect, about seventy-five guardsmen—men of Companies A and C and Troop G—moved forward, their rifles loaded, safeties on, and bayonets fixed. Each man wore a gas mask. Most carried M1 rifles and some had .45 caliber pistols as sidearms. Some carried shotguns loaded with birdshot and buckshot, considered nonlethal except at close range. They forced the crowd backward toward a fenced-in athletic field. "I could not believe it," said a reporter of the scene.

Company A was on the right flank, Company C was on the left, and Troop G was in the center. General Canterbury wasn't in uniform, but wore a business suit instead as he marched behind his men.

Many in the crowd tossed rocks and bottles at the troops and shouted, "Shoot! Shoot!" Guardsmen fired more tear gas into the crowd, but because of the fence, the protestors couldn't disperse even if they'd wanted to. A skirmish line of guardsmen marched toward the crowd, and as the crowd separated in front of them, the guardsmen continued on. The crowd closed ranks behind the troops, effectively blocking the Guard's passage. The crowd threw more rocks at the guardsmen and the guardsmen fired more tear gas at them. Demonstrators hurled Guard-fired tear gas canisters back toward the guardsmen, and guardsmen traded rocks and bottles with the crowd.

Suddenly, guardsmen realized that, like the demonstrators they'd surrounded earlier, they were now trapped. Canterbury ordered them to retrace their steps to the top of an area known as Blanket Hill, back down to the commons, and across to the ROTC building. That led the crowd to believe that the Guard was retreating, that the protestors had won the day, so the protestors began marching lockstep with the guardsmen, all the while cursing and mocking them. Most of the protestors were sixty to seventy yards behind the Guard.

"All of a sudden," Kent State senior Bill Reymond remembered, "everything just blew up." It was 12:24 P.M. when a group of twenty-eight guardsmen suddenly opened fire. According to the sound film shot at the time, within thirteen seconds they fired sixty-seven shots,* some into the air, some into the crowd. Fifty-five shots came from rifles, two came from .45 caliber pistols, and one was from a shotgun.

Four students lay dying and nine others were wounded.

John Paul Filo, a Kent State photography major, snapped a picture of a young girl kneeling over one of the wounded, Jeffrey Miller, calling for help. His photo of Mary Ann Vecchio appeared on the front pages of newspapers and magazines around the world and galvanized American college and university students.**

In just a matter of seconds, *Time* magazine reported, the usually placid Kent State campus was converted "into a bloodstained symbol of the rising student rebellion against the Nixon Administration and the war in Southeast Asia."

Student Mary Hagan witnessed the shooting and said that after the incident she heard students calling to National Guardsmen for help but that the guardsmen refused. Another student called a campus telephone operator to ask for ambulances to aid the wounded but claimed the operator said that she didn't "want anything to do with it."

The shots and tear gas had dispersed most of the crowd, but about three hundred regathered on a nearby slope. This time, faculty members convinced them to disperse.

Over the public address system, a school official announced, "By order of President [Robert] White, the university is closed. Students

---

* Some sources give this as sixty-one shots.
** Mary Ann Vecchio wasn't a college student herself. Only fourteen years old at the time, Vecchio was a runaway who wasn't necessarily there at Kent State as an antiwar demonstrator, but had been simply looking for a place to crash and spend the night. She was calling for help, she said later, because she felt she could do nothing else.

should pack their things and leave the campus as quickly as possible." Classwork for the remainder of the semester would have to be completed at home; it would be the summer session before campus activities resumed.

General Del Corso claimed that guardsmen had been forced to open fire on their attackers, that "The guard expended its entire supply of tear gas and when it did, the mob started to move forward to encircle the guardsmen." The killing and wounding of students was regrettable but unavoidable, he said. After all, a sniper had fired the first shot.*

Guard commander Gen. Robert Canterbury said that "In view of the extreme danger to the troops, they were justified in firing." In Washington, President Nixon issued a statement, in effect blaming the students for getting themselves killed. "This should remind us all once again that when dissent turns to violence it invites tragedy."

On May 14, 1970, police in Jackson, Mississippi, killed a Jackson State student and a high school senior during a demonstration. Five days later, Hosea Williams, vice president of the SCLC, led ten thousand marchers from Perry, Georgia, to Atlanta to protest the deaths in Ohio and Mississippi. Called the "March Against Repression," it was one of the largest gatherings in the South in five years. However, it failed to reignite the civil rights movement.

About a month after the Kent State shooting, the rock group Crosby, Stills, Nash & Young gave an outdoor concert in Cleveland. They sang "Ohio" and the crowd rose to its feet and cried and applauded. They heard the drum of death, they sang—four dead in Ohio.

On May 9, 1970, a crowd estimated at from sixty to one hundred thousand peaceful demonstrators gathered in Washington, D.C., at the Lincoln Memorial to protest the Cambodian invasion/incursion. President Nixon surprised them by making a predawn visit to talk

---

* An FBI report later said that there had been no sniper. Rather, light had reflected off the lens of a camera.

about the problem. "I know that probably most of you think I'm an SOB," he told the demonstrators, "but I want you to know I understand just how you feel."

Elsewhere around the country, frustration became rage and rage erupted into violence. Students attacked ROTC buildings at more than thirty universities, not just at schools such as Berkeley in California where protest was usual, but in Alabama, Michigan, New Mexico, Nebraska, Virginia, and South Carolina. In the weeks after the Kent State shootings, students at 350 universities went on strike, and protests closed down about 500 campuses, many (like Kent State) for the remainder of the semester. So many schools, so many demonstrations, that the wire services began doing news reports on campuses that did *not* have protests.

It had become a "them-versus-us" issue. Conservatives lined up behind Nixon.

Twenty thousand demonstrators in St. Louis marched in support of the president. Prowar students at Brigham Young University in Utah held a rally calling for law and order. And in New York City, an estimated one hundred thousand construction workers and longshoremen—they were among laboring groups who backed President Nixon and the war and who were collectively labeled "hardhats"— gathered to support the White House Vietnam policy. When antiwar students showed up, the workmen attacked them, injuring seventy students. As an observer noted, "They went through those demonstrators like Sherman went through Atlanta."

Several hundred federal employees marched in favor of Nixon's address, carrying a banner attacking what they called, "Federal Bums Against the War." But more than two hundred State Department officers and workers resigned to protest the Cambodian action.

On June 13, 1971, the *New York Times* ran excerpts of a massive secret government study called *History of the Unites States Decision-Making Process on Vietnam Policy: 1954–1968*. To the public it became known simply as "the Pentagon Papers" and consisted of seven thousand pages chronicling U.S. actions concerning Vietnam.

Increasingly, as the Vietnam War dragged on, Secretary of State Robert McNamara had become disillusioned, and he had commis-

WHAT THEY DIDN'T TEACH YOU ABOUT THE 60S

sioned the study. It was written secretly by about three dozen Pentagon Defense Department aides at his instruction. One of the aides was Daniel Ellsberg, a forty-year-old Harvard-trained economist, a former Marine officer, and a Massachusetts Institute of Technology fellow employed by the RAND Corporation. Just as the Papers themselves had been written secretly, Ellsberg secretly copied them and turned them over to *New York Times* reporter Neil Sheehan in 1971.

From 1962 to '64, Neil Sheehan was a United Press International correspondent and the *New York Times's* Saigon Bureau chief. Early on he exposed problems with the U.S. effort in Vietnam and the corruption of President Ngo Dinh Diem's regime. In 1968, Sheehan broke the story of the Joint Chiefs of Staff's request for more troops following the Tet Offensive.

On May 6, 1971, Ellsberg wrote about the Vietnam War:

> We are willing to violate traffic laws to try to end the war; the government is willing to violate the Constitution to keep the war going. The demonstrators are determined to act nonviolently. . . . But the U.S. government, and city and state governments, are willing to . . . visit the official violence that is commonplace to Vietnamese upon wives, sons, grandmothers, in American cities. In this effort, city police use clubs and boots on humans in the mob frenzy with which soldiers in Vietnam [use] rifles and grenades, artillery and napalm, on helpless civilians.

Ellsberg became one of America's most renowned peace activists, and at the prompting of fellow activist Marcus Raskin, he gave *Times* reporter Sheehan a copy of the Pentagon Papers. Ellsberg admitted that what he'd really wanted was a splashy Senate hearing, complete with TV lights and reporters scribbling away. He'd even considered flying over Washington in a helicopter and dropping the papers, a sort of activist rain. When he couldn't get senators interested in the papers (and realized that the helicopter idea wasn't very practical), Ellsberg passed them on to Sheehan and the *Times*. On June 13, the papers hit the newsstands.

The Pentagon Papers took in presidential administrations up to, and including, Lyndon Johnson's. They did not include the Richard

Nixon Administration, but when the Nixon White House learned that the study was about to be made public, it fought publication, claiming such action would harm U.S. defense and diplomatic interests. The *Times* took the matter to the U.S. Supreme Court. Its lawyers argued the papers' historical value and the high court agreed. By a vote of six to three, the U.S. Supreme Court upheld the newspaper's Constitutional right to print the papers, and the *Times* went back to publishing them.

When the Nixon Administration couldn't stop the newspaper, it went after the man who had leaked the papers. The Administration organized a secret "special investigative unit" known as the "Plumbers" to investigate, and if possible discredit, Daniel Ellsberg. They went so far as to break into Ellsberg's psychiatrist's office looking for damaging personal information. Among the Plumbers was one G. Gordon Liddy, who says of the events, "I had my marching orders." On June 17, 1972, the Plumbers broke into the Watergate Hotel offices of the Democratic National Committee. Did the Nixon Administration have anything to do with that? His White House press secretary said he wouldn't comment "on a third-rate burglary attempt." Nixon himself answered that

> I can categorically say that no one on the present White House staff, no one in this administration, presently employed, was involved in this very bizarre incident.

On December 21, 1970, singer Elvis Presley visited President Richard Nixon in the White House Oval Office, and it's difficult to say who was more thrilled. Photographers snapped away at the conservatively dressed president and the flamboyantly outfitted Presley. Nixon showed Presley around the office, and Elvis showed the president some of his law-enforcement paraphernalia he'd brought along.

In a memorandum outlining the meeting, Nixon aide Egil "Bud" Krough wrote that "Presley indicated that he had been playing Las Vegas and the president indicated that he was aware of how difficult it is to perform in Las Vegas." Elvis also "indicated that he thought the Beatles had been a real force for anti-American spirit . . . that the Beatles came to this country, made their money, and then returned to England where they promoted an anti-American theme." The president "nodded in agreement," Krough added.

Indicating "in a very emotional manner" that he was "on your side," Presley repeatedly told the president that he "wanted to be helpful, that he wanted to restore some respect for the flag which was being lost." What he wanted was to be a special drug investigator and carry a U.S. marshal's badge. He felt, Egil Krough wrote his boss, that "he could be helpful to [the president] in his drug drive."

As the meeting ended, "in a surprising, spontaneous gesture [Elvis Presley] put his left arm around the president and hugged him." Nixon gave Elvis a special marshal's badge.

The 1960s were over and with them went many of the civil rights protests. Both the times and the people were a-changin'. Protests were aimed at ending the Vietnam War, but it would take five years and the fall of a president before the antiwar protests and the war itself came to an end.

In July 1974, the U.S. House Judiciary Committee voted to recommend impeachment of President Richard Nixon for obstructing an investigation of the Watergate break-in and for the misuse of the FBI and the IRS. On August 8, Nixon announced, "I shall resign the presidency effective at noon tomorrow." He became the first U.S. president to resign the office. Congressman Gerald Ford, who'd been appointed vice president when Spiro Agnew* resigned under charges that he'd taken bribes while governor of Maryland, became president.

On April 14, 1975, U.S. aircraft ended the evacuation of military families from Vietnam. On the twenty-ninth, President Ford ordered the final thousand Americans, and about fifty-five hundred South Vietnamese who'd aided and sometimes fought side by side with American troops, evacuated to offshore ships. About nineteen hours after the airlift began, the final American helicopter flew out of Saigon.

---

* It was Agnew who once said, "[Those] phony intellectuals . . . don't understand what we mean by hard work and patriotism. . . . If you've seen one ghetto area, you've seen them all."

A Sixties Hangover

On April 30, a North Vietnamese tank crashed through the gates of the presidential palace in Saigon, and a single soldier ran forward to raise the flag of the Provisional Revolutionary Government. However, television cameras missed the action, so the sequence was repeated for them.

After thirty years, the struggle both to prevent and create a unified Vietnam was over. From 1950 to 1975, the United States granted $15.2 billion in aid and spent $141 billion on the war itself. In that time, more than 58,000 American lives were lost.

In June 1972, a young girl named Kim Phuc had just left a Buddhist pagoda in the village of Trang Bang and was running along the road when she and her family were hit by napalm dropped by a South Vietnamese fighter plane. The ARVN pilot claimed that he saw people running toward the South Vietnamese troops' positions. He claimed that he saw the civilians carrying weapons and in a split-second decision, diverted from his target to dive and attack the group.

Two of Kim's cousins died from the napalm. She stripped off her burning clothing and ran screaming down the road. Journalists and photographers saw her coming. A film cameraman caught her as she came running toward him. A photographer snapped a series of still photos. It had been only one sortie, one single bombing run, but that was enough. The film and photos of her didn't exactly stop the war—by the time of the napalm incident, almost all U.S. ground forces had been brought home from Vietnam—but it became an icon for the peace movement. It embarrassed the American government and was extremely damaging to the government in South Vietnam. Communist North Vietnam used the picture as a propaganda tool.

In April 1979, a group of Vietnam veterans, led by former infantry corporal Jan Scruggs, formed the nonprofit Vietnam Veterans Memorial Fund to provide a "tangible symbol of recognition" of those who died in Vietnam. A young and virtually unknown architect, Maya Ying Lin,* created the Wall, as it's informally known. The

---

* On May 1, 1981, a panel of eight artists and designers unanimously accepted the design submitted by twenty-one-year-old Maya Ying Lin of Athens, Ohio. At the time, she was still a student at Yale University. Her design won over 1,420 other entries.

Vietnam Memorial is 246.75 feet long, made of Indian black granite, cut and fabricated in Vermont, and sits on the mall in Washington, D.C., its wings pointing to the Washington Monument and the Lincoln Memorial.

It is a stark, simple memorial and perhaps that's what makes it so moving to the more than forty million visitors to the Wall each year. That and the names of more than fifty-eight thousand men and women killed or missing in action, their names grit-blasted into the granite. The names are clean and crisp, not like the way the men and women died.

More than a dozen names on the Wall represent men who are neither missing nor dead. Originally listed as killed in action, they survived only to discover that they'd been listed as dead and their names had been blasted into the Wall. Their names cannot be removed, because they're etched forever into the granite.

Epilogue

To be perfectly honest about it, I think I was caught up a little with the intrigue of it.
Judith Campbell Exner, on her relationship
with President John F. Kennedy

"Where Have All the Flowers Gone?"

Pete Seeger, song title 1961

We lost our innocence in the sixties. We didn't believe in the man in the moon, we put a man *on* the moon.

Many who fought in Vietnam and many who remained at home never understood why America was there. In 1945 we welcomed home millions of soldiers, sailors, airmen, and marines. In the 1960s we spat upon them, protested against them, shunned, ignored, and reviled them. Yet it was not the American people who failed in Vietnam. It was American policy.

The Vietnam War often pitted children against parents. It brought down one president and made another so desperate in his effort to remain in office that he had to resign in order to avoid an impeachment trial.

The 8,752,000 men (and about 11,000 women) who served in Vietnam were, generally, the baby boomers and the children of baby boomers whose families had the weakest hold on America's postwar prosperity; about eighty percent of American enlisted men in Vietnam came from working-class and poor families. On average they came out of small towns and off farms. The sons of America's richest who lived in well-to-do suburbs did not fight. They sought and usually received exemptions and deferments from the draft; instead of going off to war, they went off to college, first undergraduate, then graduate, then sometimes postgraduate school. Some went farther, to Canada or England.

Because of Vietnam a generation of Americans grew to question everything. And it's only by questioning that we learn. All too late we learned that the price of a military victory in Vietnam was higher than American interests could justify.

The 1990s saw a phenomenon whereby young American adults (often known as Yuppies—young urban professionals*) would pile into their sport utility vehicles (SUVs), drive miles out into the countryside, and then trudge through—depending on where they lived—snow, mud, sleet, rain, or even sunshine. The object: cut down a Christmas tree to decorate the family condominium or suburban home. Not for them the practice that had been commonplace since the 1800s, simply going to a neighborhood lot and buying a precut, already shedding tree. Getting back to nature, this phenomenon was.

In the 1960s there was another custom, and, it too, was widespread: aluminum Christmas trees with rotating electric-light-color wheels that changed from red to blue to yellow to green. (Easy assembly, no tools required! Simply fit the branches into slots on a center pole!) Unlike natural trees, these silver-colored devices were perfectly symmetrical, cone-shaped articles. (Noncorrosive aluminum foil! Thick, full branches strong enough to hold the sturdiest ornaments! Comes with a metal stand!) Cheap too.

As the new century began, and the number of Christmas-tree-cutting Yuppies increased, aluminum trees made a small comeback. The second time around, however, they weren't quite so cheap. A seven-and-a-half-foot tree could cost you four hundred dollars. But, then, if you'd kept the one you bought back in the sixties, you wouldn't have to buy a new one.

Music in the sixties was downright frenetic: "Hair," "Eve of Destruction," and "Journey to the Center of the Mind." Teenagers then (as do many grown-up teenagers now) listened and saw the Beatles

---

* It's uncertain where the word "Yuppie" originated, but consensus is that it came into use about 1982.

Epilogue

as a basic part of their life's experience. Perhaps without their (or even our) realizing it, the Beatles changed our lives. To many, the Beatles and their music and their hair were a form of protest.

For many in America, the 1960s were magical times—times for coming of age and times for coming apart. Much has changed since the sixties—much in America, the world, and in us.

We like to visit the sixties, at least visit words and pictures and memories of the time. In the sixties, America grew up.

Some 1960s-era communes lasted weeks, while others lasted years, and some still exist today in the twenty-first century. Possibly one thing that closed down some of them was that, simply put, life in a commune was more difficult than their founders had imagined. A member of The Farm commune remembered "having soybeans for breakfast, lunch, and dinner, and nothing else." At the time, she lived in a house in Summertown, Tennessee, with fifty or so other people. It had no running water, no flush toilet, and no electricity. At first, many of those who lived on The Farm thought living under such conditions was exciting. But then they began having babies. And having kids, this ex-communer said, "made you more sensitive to the lack of necessities."

So as time went on hippies became parents, and their outlook— not to say the world itself—changed. In the 1990s, some members of The Farm developed a commune they call Rocinante, after Don Quixote's horse.

Rocinante is decidedly different, sort of an elder commune. It's a retirement home for aging hippies.

Once we were hip. Now, we think about hip replacements.

Bibliography

Unpublished Sources and Primary Material

ABC-TV News, "Cops shot trying to arrest ex-Panther, one dies," March 17, 2000.

Agnew, Spiro. Speech at a Republican fund-raiser in New Orleans, La., October 19, 1969.

Angajanian, Rowena. B.A. thesis, Middlesex Polytechnic Institute, May 1988.

CBS-TV report, November 25, 1959.

CNN-TV report, October 27, 1995.

Donahue, Joe. Operations Officer, Global Landmine Survey, Vietnam Veterans of America Foundation. Personal correspondence, August 20, 1999.

Foreign Relations Series Volume Summary, Vol. X, Cuba, 1961–1962.

Interview, "Dateline NBC," NBC-TV, March 9, 2000.

Johnson, Lyndon. Speaking at Akron, Ohio University, October 21, 1964.

Krough, Egil "Bud" Krough. Memo "Meeting with Elvis Presley," December 21, 1970, National Archives.

Miller, Arthur. *The Misfits* (motion picture), 1961.

Nixon, Richard. Speech, November 2, 1969.

———. Televised speech, April 30, 1970.

———. Televised interview with David Frost, May 19, 1977.

Oswald, Marguerite. Testimony before the Warren Commission.

"Our People," WTTW-TV, Chicago, July 25, 1968.

Schlesinger, Arthur Jr. Correspondence with President John F. Kennedy, April 10, 1961.

Smith, H. N. Papers, Box 6F6, Bancroft Library, University of California at Berkeley.

Smith, Howard K. ABC-TV, May 17, 1961.

Tilmon, Jim. Telephone interview, February 12, 2001.

Warren Commission exhibit #391.

Bibliography

Warren Commission exhibit #1399.
Warren Commission exhibit #2240, 2.

Books

Adler, Bill. *The Johnson Humor.* New York: Simon' and Schuster, 1976.
———. *The Washington Wit.* New York: Macmillan, 1967.
Ali, Aariq, and Susan Watkins. *1968: Marching in the Streets.* London: Bloomsbury Publishing, 1998; reprinted by The Free Press, 1998.
Ammer, Christine. *Fighting Words.* 2d ed. New York: NTC/ Contemporary Books, 2000.
Anderson, Jack. *Jack and Jackie.* New York: William Morrow, 1996.
Anderson, Terry. *The Movement and the Sixties: Protest in America from Greensboro to Wounded Knee.* New York: Oxford, 1995; reprinted 1996.
Anson, Robert Sam. *McGovern.* New York: Holt, Rinehart and Winston, 1972.
Aron, Paul. *Unsolved Mysteries of American History.* New York: Wiley, 1997.
Atkinson, Rick. *The Long Gray Line: The American Journey of West Point's Class of 1966.* Boston: Houghton Mifflin, 1989; reprinted by Owl Books, 1999.
Baldwin, James. *The Fire Next Time.* New York: Dial Press, 1963.
Bernstein, Irving. *Promises Kept: John F. Kennedy's New Frontier.* New York: Oxford, 1991.
Beschloss, Michael. *The Crisis Years: Kennedy and Khrushchev, 1960–1963.* HarperCollins, 1991.
Bly, Robert. *Iron John: A Book About Men.* New York: Addison Wesley, 1990.
Boller, Paul, F., Jr. *Congressional Anecdotes.* New York: Oxford, 1991.
———. *Presidential Anecdotes.* New York: Oxford, 1981.
———. *Presidential Campaigns.* New York: Oxford, 1984; revised and updated, 1996.
Bottorne, Edgar. *The Balance of Terror: A Guide to the Arms Race.* Boston: Beacon Press, 1972.
Bradford, Sarah. *America's Queen: The Life of Jackie Kennedy Onassis.* New York: Viking, 2000.

Bradley, Becky, and Susan Goodwin. *American Cultural History: 1960–1969.* Kenwood, Texas: Kenwood College, 2000.

Brailler, Jess, and Sally Chabert. *Presidential Wit and Wisdom.* New York: Penguin Books, 1996.

Branch, Taylor. *Pillar of Fire: America in the King Years, 1963–1965.* New York: Simon and Schuster, 1998; reprinted by Touchstone, 1999.

Brash, Sarah, and Loretta Britten, eds. *Our American Century: Turbulent Years, The 60s.* Alexandria, Va: Time-Life Books, 1998.

Burrows, Terry, ed. *Visual History of the Twentieth Century.* London: Carlton, 1999.

Caputo, Philip. *A Rumor of War.* New York: Holt, Rinehart and Winston, 1977; reprinted by Ballantine Books, 1978.

Chafe, William H. "Mississippi Burning," in *Past Imperfect: History According to the Movies.* Mark C. Carnes, ed. New York: Henry Holt, 1995.

Chubet, Carolyn, ed. *America A to Z: People, Places, Customs and Culture.* Pleasantville, N.Y.: Reader's Digest, 1997.

Coffey, Michael. *Military Blunders.* New York: Hyperion, 1999; originally published as *Days of Infamy.*

Colbert, David, ed. *Eyewitness to America: 500 Years of America in the Words of Those Who Saw It Happen.* New York: Random House, 1997.

Dalton, David, and Lenny Kaye. *Rock 100: The Greatest Stars of Rock's Golden Age.* New York: Cooper Square Press, 1977; revised 1999.

Davidson, Lt. Gen. Phillip B., USA (Ret.). *Vietnam at War: The History, 1946–1975.* Novato, Calif.: Presidio Press, 1988.

Davis, John H. *Mafia Kingfish: Carlos Marcello and the Assassination of John F. Kennedy.* New York: McGraw-Hill, 1988; reprinted by Signet Books, 1989.

Davis, Kenneth C. *Don't Know Much About History.* New York: Crown, 1990.

Davis, Peter. *The Truth About Kent State.* New York: Farrar, Straus and Giroux, 1973.

Davis, Townsend. *Weary Feet, Rested Souls: A Guided History of the Civil Rights Movement.* New York: W. W. Norton, 1998.

D'Emilio, John, and Estelle Freeman. *Intimate Matters: A History of Sexuality in America.* New York: Harper & Row, 1988.

Bibliography

Dickerson, Nancy. *Among Those Present: A Reporter's View of Twenty-Five Years in Washington.* New York: Random House, 1976.

Dictionary of American History. New York: Scribner's Sons, 1976.

Duffy, P., and Vincent L. Ricci. *The Assassination of John F. Kennedy: A Complete Book of Facts.* New York: Thunder's Mouth Press, 1992.

Dunnigan, James F., and Albert A. Nofi. *Dirty Little Secrets: Military Information You're Not Supposed to Know.* New York: Quill/Morrow, 1990.

———. *Dirty Little Secrets of the Vietnam War.* New York: Thomas Dune Books/St. Martin's Press, 1999.

Epstein, Edward Jay. *News from Nowhere: Television and the News.* New York: Random House, 1973; reprinted by Dee Books, 2000.

Fall, Bernard. *Last Reflections on a War.* New York: Schoken, 1964; second printing, 1972.

Farber, David. *The Age of Great Dreams: America in the 1960s.* New York: Hill and Wang, 1994; reprinted by HarperCollins, Canada, 1998.

———. *Chicago '68.* Chicago: University of Chicago Press, 1988; reprinted 1994.

Flexner, Stuart, and Doris Flexner. *The Pessimist's Guide to History.* New York: Avon, 1992.

Friedan, Betty. *The Feminine Mystique.* New York: W. W. Norton, 1963; 10th anniversary ed., 1973.

Fursenko, Alexandr, and Timothy Naftali. *One Hell of a Gamble: Khrushchev, Castro, and Kennedy, 1958–1964.* New York: W. W. Norton, 1997.

Galloway, Paul. "A Radical Recalls 'the Rage,'" in *The Chicago Tribune,* July 7, 1987.

Gentry, Curt. *J. Edgar Hoover: The Man and the Secrets.* New York: W. W. Norton, 1991; reprinted by Plume Books, 1992.

Gettleman, Marvin E., ed. *Vietnam: History, Documents, and Opinions on a Major World Crisis.* New York: Fawcett Crest, 1965.

Ginsberg, Allen. *Collected Poems: 1946–1980.* New York: Harper & Row, 1984.

Goldberg, M. Hirsh. *The Blunder Book.* New York: Quill/Morrow, 1984.

Goldstein, Richard, ed. *Mine Eyes Have Seen: A First-Person History of the Events That Shaped America.* New York: Touchstone Books, 1997.

Goodwin, Doris Kearns. *No Ordinary Time: Franklin and Eleanor Roosevelt, The Home Front in World War II.* New York: Simon and Schuster, 1994.

Goodwin, Richard. *Remembering America: A Voice from the Sixties.* Boston: Little, Brown & Company, 1988; reprinted by Harper & Row, 1988, 1989.

Gordon, Lois, and Alan Gordon. *American Chronicle: Six Decades in American Life, 1920–1980.* New York: Atheneum, 1987.

Graham, Hugh Davis. *The Civil Rights Era.* New York: Oxford, 1990.

Grant, Ed, and Mike Kill. *I Was There: What Really Went On at Kent State.* Lima, Ohio: C. S. S. Publishing, 1974.

Green, Jerry. *Super Bowl Chronicles: A Sportswriter Reflects on the First 30 Years of America's Game.* 2d ed. Indianapolis, Ind.: Masters Press, 1995.

Guthman, Edwin O., and Jeffrey Shulman, eds. *Robert Kennedy in His Own Words.* New York: Bantam, 1988.

Halberstam, David. *The Best and the Brightest.* New York: Random House, 1972.

———. *The Fifties.* New York: Random House, 1993.

Hendin, Herbert, and Ann Pollinger Haas. *Wounds of War: The Psychological Aftermath of Combat in Vietnam.* New York: Basic Books, 1984.

Herring, George C. *America's Longest War: The United States and Vietnam, 1950–1975.* New York: McGraw-Hill, 1979; 3d ed., 1996.

Hersh, Seymour M. *The Dark Side of Camelot.* Boston: Little, Brown and Company, 1997; reprinted by Back Bay, 1998.

Heymann, C. David. *A Woman Named Jackie.* New York: Lyle Stuart, 1989.

Hillstrom, Kevin, Laurie Hillstrom, and Roger Matuz. *The Handy Sports Answer Book.* Detroit: Visible Ink, 1998.

Howard, Gerald, ed. *The Sixties.* New York: Washington Square Press, 1982.

Hunt, John Gabriel, ed. *Inaugural Addresses of the Presidents.* New York: Random House, 1995.

Hunt, Michael. *Lyndon Johnson's War: America's Cold War Crusade in Vietnam, 1945–1968.* New York: Hill and Wang, 1996.

Jackson, Blair. *Garcia: An American Life.* New York: Penguin, 1999.

Bibliography

Jackson, Kenneth. *Crabgrass Frontier: The Suburbanization of the United States.* New York: Oxford, 1985.

Jacobs, Ron. *The Way the Wind Blew: A History of the Weather Underground.* London: Verso, 1997.

Jamison, Andrew, and Ron Eyerman. *Seeds of the Sixties.* Los Angeles: University of California Press, 1994; reprinted 1995.

Jensen-Stevenson, Monika, and William Stevenson. *Kiss the Boys Goodbye: How the United States Betrayed Its Own POWs in Vietnam.* New York: Penguin Books, 1990; reprinted by Plume Books, 1991.

Johnson, Claudia Alta Taylor (Lady Bird). *A White House Diary.* New York: Holt, Rinehart and Winston, 1970.

Johnson, Paul. *Modern Times: The World From the Twenties to the Eighties.* New York: Harper & Row, 1985; first published in England as *A History of the Modern World: From 1917 to the 1980s,* 1983.

Joseph, Peter, ed. *Good Times: An Oral History of America in the Nineteen Sixties.* New York: Charterhouse Books, 1973; reprinted by Morrow, 1974.

The Justice Department's Summary of the FBI Report ("The Justice Department Summary") in *The Congressional Record.* Washington, D.C.: Congressional Printing Office, January 15, 1973.

Kadane, Kathy, and Alfred Rascon. "A Case of Forgotten Valor," in *Vietnam,* October 2000.

Kaiser, Charles. *1968 in America.* New York: Weidenfeld & Nicholson, 1988.

Kaiser, Robert Blair. *RFK Must Die! A History of the Robert Kennedy Assassination and Its Aftermath.* New York: Dutton, 1970.

Kelly, Walt. *Pogo,* syndicated, 1970.

Kennedy, John F. "The War in Indochina," in *John F. Kennedy: A Compilation of Statements and Speeches Made During His Service in the United States Senate and House of Representatives.* Washington, D.C.: Legislative Reference Service (nd).

Kennedy, Robert F. *Thirteen Days: A Memoir of the Cuban Missile Crisis.* New York: McCall, 1968; reprinted by W. W. Norton, 1969.

Kleinfelder, Rita Lang. *When We Were Young: A Baby-Boomer Yearbook.* New York: Prentice Hall, 1993.

Leary, Timothy, with Richard Alpert. "The Fifth Freedom: The Right to Get High," in *Harvard Review*, 1 (4) (Summer 1963).

Leepson, Marc, ed. *Webster's New World Dictionary of the Vietnam War*. New York: Simon & Schuster Macmillan, 1999.

Lewis, David L. *King: A Critical Biography*. Urbana, Ill.: University of Illinois Press, 1970; reprinted as *King: A Biography*.

Lewis, Jerry M., and Thomas R. Hensley. "The May 4 Shootings at Kent State University: The Search for Historical Accuracy,"in *Ohio Council for the Social Studies Review*, Vol. 34, number 1 (Summer 1998).

Liddy, G. Gordon. *Will: The Autobiography of G. Gordon Liddy*. New York: St. Martin's Press, 1997; reprinted 1998.

Luttwak, Edward, and Stuart L. Koehl. *The Dictionary of Modern War: A Guide to the Ideas, Institutions and Weapons of the Modern Military Power Vocabulary*. New York: Random House, 1991.

Macedo, Stephen, ed. *Reassessing the Sixties: Debating the Political and Cultural Legacy*. New York: W. W. Norton, 1997.

Mahoney, Richard D. *Sons & Brothers: The Days of Jack and Bobby Kennedy*. New York: Arcade, 1999.

Manchester, William. *The Death of a President*. London: Michael Joseph, 1967.

Marwick, Arthur. *The Sixties*. Oxford, U.K.: Oxford University Press, 1998.

Matthews, Christopher. *Kennedy & Nixon: The Rivalry That Shaped Postwar America*. New York: Touchstone, 1996.

May 4 Site and Memorial brochure, Kent State University Relations and Marketing, nd, np.

McCombs, Don, and Fred L. Worth. *World War II: 4,139 Strange and Fascinating Facts*. New York: Wings, 1983.

McNeil, Alex. *Total Television*. 4th ed. New York: Penguin Books, 1980.

Miller, James. *Democracy Is in the Streets: From Port Huron to the Siege of Chicago*. New York: Simon and Schuster, 1997.

Miller, Timothy. *The 60s Communes: Hippies and Beyond*. Syracuse, N.Y.: Syracuse University Press, 1999.

Millett, Alan R., and Peter Mislowski. *For the Common Defense: A Military History of the United States of America*. New York: The Free Press, 1994.

Bibliography

Moore, Lt. Gen. Harold G., and Joseph L. Galloway. *We Were Soldiers Once . . . and Young: Ia Drang, The Battle That Changed the War in Vietnam.* New York: Random House, 1992.

Morrison, Joan, and Robert K. Morrison. *From Camelot to Kent State: The Sixties Experience in the Words of Those Who Lived It.* New York: The New York Times Books, 1987.

Mueller, Mike. *Motor City Muscle.* Oceola, Wisc.: MBI Publishing, 1997.

Nelson, Walter Henry. *Small Wonder: The Amazing Story of the Volkswagen Beetle.* Boston: Little, Brown & Co., 1965; reprinted 1970.

Newman, John. *JFK and Vietnam: Deception, Intrigue, and the Struggle for Power.* New York: Warner, 1992.

Nixon, Richard. *RN: The Memoirs of Richard Nixon.* New York: Grossett & Dunlap, 1978.

O'Neill, William O. *Coming Apart: An Informal History of America in the 1960s.* New York: The New York Times Books, 1971.

Parmet, Herbert S. *Jack: The Struggles of John F. Kennedy.* New York: The Dial Press, 1980.

Patterson, James T. *America in the Twentieth Century: A History.* New York: Harcourt Brace Janovich, 1976.

Plunkett-Powell, Karen. *Remembering Woolworth's: A Nostalgic History of the World's Most Famous Five-and-Dime.* New York: St. Martin's, 1990.

Posner, Gerald. *Case Closed: Lee Harvey Oswald and the Assassination of JFK.* New York: Random House, 1993.

Prados, John. *The Hidden History of the Vietnam War.* Chicago: Ivan Dee, 1995; reprinted, 1998.

Reeves, Richard. *President Kennedy: Profile of Power.* New York: Touchstone, 1994.

Report of the National Advisory Commission of Civil Disorders. New York: 1968.

Roberts, Chambert. "The Day We Didn't Go to War," in *Reporter,* September 14, 1954.

Rust, William. *Kennedy in Vietnam: American Vietnam Policy 1960–63.* New York: Scribner's Sons, 1985; reprinted by DaCapo, 1987.

Safire, William. *Before the Fall.* Garden City, New York: Doubleday, 1975.

Schlesinger, Arthur M., Jr. *Robert Kennedy and His Times.* Boston: Houghton Mifflin, 1978.

———. *A Thousand Days: John F. Kennedy in the White House.* Boston: Houghton Mifflin, 1965.

Schlesinger, Arthur M., Jr., ed. *The Almanac of American History.* New York: Brompton Books, 1993.

Scott, Walter. "Walter Scott's Personality Parade," in *Parade,* July 9, 2000.

Scranton, Chairman William. *Report of the President's Commission on Campus Unrest.* Washington, D.C.: U.S. Government Printing Office, 1970.

Shenkman, Richard. *I Love Paul Revere, Whether He Rode or Not.* New York: Harper Perennial, 1991.

Shesol, Jeff. *Mutual Contempt.* New York: W. W. Norton, 1997.

Sitkoff, Harvard. *The Struggle for Black Equity: 1954–1980.* New York: Hill and Wang, 1981.

Smith, Page. *Daughters of the Promised Land: Women in American History.* Boston: Little, Brown & Company, 1970.

Smith, R. Harris. *OSS: The Secret History of America's First Central Intelligence Agency.* New York: Delta, 1974.

Smith, Wes. *The Pied Pipers of Rock 'n' Roll: Radio Dejays of the 50s and 60s.* Marietta, Ga.: Longstreet Press, 1989.

Spector, Ronald H. *Advice and Support: The Early Years of the U.S. Army in Vietnam, 1941–1960.* New York: The Free Press, 1985; originally published as *The United States Army in Vietnam,* 1983.

Stebben, Gregg, and Jim Morris. *White House Confidential: The Little Book of Weird Presidential History.* Nashville, Tenn.: Cumberland House, 1998.

Steinman, Ron. *Women in Vietnam: The Oral History.* New York: TV Books, 2000.

Stephens, Autumn. *Wild Women of the White House.* Berkeley, Calif.: Conari Press, 1997.

Stevenson, Jay, and Matthew Budman. *The Complete Idiot's Guide to American Heroes.* New York: Alpha Books, 1999.

Strodder, Chris. *Swingin' Chicks of the '60s.* San Rafael, Calif.: Cedco Publishing, 2000.

Sullivan, William C. *The Bureau: My Thirty Years in Hoover's FBI.* New York: W. W. Norton, 1979.

Bibliography

Swanson, Stevenson, ed. *Chicago Days: 150 Defining Moments in the Life of a Great City.* Wheaton, Ill.: Catigny First Division Foundation, 1997.

Taylor, Tim. *The Book of Presidents.* New York: Arno Press, 1972.

Teaford, Jon C. *The Twentieth-Century American City.* Baltimore: Johns Hopkins, 1973.

Teoidori, Massimo, ed. *The New Left: A Documentary History.* New York: Bobbs-Merrill, 1969.

Tolkien, John Ronald Reul. *The Hobbit; or There and Back Again.* London: Furth, 1937.

Tran Van Don. *Our Endless War: Inside Vietnam.* San Rafael, Calif.: Presidio Press, 1978.

Videl, Gore. "Eleanor Roosevelt,"in *New York Review of Books,* November 18, 1971.

Walker, Martin. *The Cold War: A History.* London: Walker and Walker, 1993; reprinted by Henry Holt, 1995.

Warhol, Andy, and Pat Hackett. *POPism, The Warhol '60s.* New York: Harcourt Brace Janovich, 1980.

Wells, Tom. *The War Within: America's Battle Over Vietnam.* Los Angeles: University of California Press, 1994; reprinted by Owl Books, 1996.

Westmoreland, Gen. William. *A Soldier Reports.* Garden City, N.Y.: Doubleday, 1976; reprinted by DaCapo, 1980; second reprint, 1989.

Whitcomb, John, and Claire Whitcomb. *Great American Anecdotes.* New York: Quill/Morrow, 1993.

———. *Oh, Say Can You See: Unexpected Anecdotes About American History.* New York: Quill/Morrow, 1987.

White, Theodore. *The Making of the President 1964: A Narrative History of American Politics in Action.* New York: Antheneum, 1965; reprinted by Signet Books, 1966.

———. *The Making of the President 1968: A Narrative of American Politics in Action.* New York: Atheneum, 1969.

Williams, Juan. *Eyes on the Prize: America's Civil Rights Years, 1954–1965.* New York: Viking, 1987.

Wolfe, Tom. *The Electric Kool-Aid Acid Test.* New York: Farrar Straus and Giroux, 1958.

World Almanac and Book of Facts: 1999. Mahwah, N.J.: World Almanac Books, 1999.

Why Watts Exploded: How the Ghetto Fought Back. Los Angeles: Socialist Workers Party, 1965.

Wright, Mike. *What They Didn't Teach You About World War II.* Novato, Calif.: Presidio Press, 1998; reprinted 2000.

Zinn, Howard. *The Twentieth Century: A People's History.* New York: Harper Perennial, 1980; revised and updated, 1998.

Newspapers and Wire Service Reports

Akron Beacon Journal, May 24, 1970.

Associated Press, February 8, 1968.

Associated Press, May 4, 1970.

Associated Press, February 24, 1998.

The Chicago Daily News, August 23, 1968.

The Chicago Tribune, May 24, 2000; July 3, 2000; August 10, 2000; September 21, 2000; January 14, 2001; January 26, 2001.

The Detroit News, January 7, 1969.

The London Evening Standard, March 4, 1966.

The *Los Angeles Times,* August 15, 1965.

The *New York Times,* October 21, 1962; July 7, 1964; April 5, 1967; July 28, 1967; April 30, 1968; August 25, 1968; December 2, 1968.

Selma, Alabama Times-Journal, July 5, 1964.

The Sunday Oregonian, July 17, 1988.

Magazines

The Economist, September 16, 2000.

Esquire, December 1976.

Life, August 29, 1969.

Newsweek, October 28, 1962; June 12, 1967; September 1, 1969; January 11, 1988; August 13, 2000.

Ramparts, March 1967.

Time, January 3, 1964; April 29, 1966.

Vietnam, February 2000.

VFW, April 1997.

Women's History, Summer 1996.

Index

Index

Index

Index